Lady Morgan (Sydney)

Lady Morgan's Memoirs Autobiography, Diaries and Correspondence

Lady Morgan (Sydney)

Lady Morgan's Memoirs Autobiography, Diaries and Correspondence

ISBN/EAN: 9783742808738

Manufactured in Europe, USA, Canada, Australia, Japa

Cover: Foto ©Andreas Hilbeck / pixelio.de

Manufactured and distributed by brebook publishing software (www.brebook.com)

Lady Morgan (Sydney)

Lady Morgan's Memoirs Autobiography, Diaries and Correspondence

CONTENTS.

	Page
CHAPTER I.—First Year of Married Life	1
CHAPTER II.—Death of Mr. Owenson	19
CHAPTER III.—Kildare Street	25
CHAPTER IV.—First Visit to France—1815-1816	39
CHAPTER V.—Publication of France—1817	65
CHAPTER VI.—Out of England into France—1818	78
CHAPTER VII.—Sojourn in Italy—1819	89
CHAPTER VIII.—Letters and Gossip	104
CHAPTER IX.—Still in Italy—1820	128
CHAPTER X.—The Book on Italy	143
CHAPTER XI.—Life and Times of Salvator Rosa	152
CHAPTER XII.—Writing the Life and Times of Salvator Rosa—1823	159
CHAPTER XIII.—Connexion with the New Monthly—1824	187
CHAPTER XIV.—Lord Byron and Lady Caroline Lamb	198
CHAPTER XV.—The Year 1825	214
CHAPTER XVI.—The Year 1826	224
CHAPTER XVII.—The O'Briens and O'Flaherties—1827	233
CHAPTER XVIII.—Letters and Diaries—1829	271

CONTENTS.

	Page
CHAPTER XIX.—The Second Work on France—1830	227
CHAPTER XX.—Last Years in Dublin—1831	319
CHAPTER XXI.—A Flying Visit to England—1832	335
CHAPTER XXII.—Dramatic Scenes and Sketches—1833	353
CHAPTER XXIII.—The Béguine—1834	380
CHAPTER XXIV.—Cheltenham and London—1835	396
CHAPTER XXV.—Last Return to Kildare Street—1836	411
CHAPTER XXVI.—Farewell to Ireland—1837	418
CHAPTER XXVII.—Settlement in London—1838	431
CHAPTER XXVIII.—Albert Gate—1838	438
CHAPTER XXIX.—London Life—1839	447
CHAPTER XXX.—Albert Gate Conceded—1842	469
CHAPTER XXXI.—Death of Sir Charles Morgan—1843	478
CHAPTER XXXII.—First Years of Widowhood	484
CHAPTER XXXIII.—Retired from Work	491
CHAPTER XXXIV.—The Leaves Falling	500
CHAPTER XXXV.—Lady Morgan and Cardinal Wiseman	506
CHAPTER XXXVI.—Death of Moore	517
CHAPTER XXXVII.—Fall of the Leaves	524
CHAPTER XXXVIII.—Passing Away	537
CHAPTER XXXIX.—The End	544
CHAPTER XL.—Conclusion	549

LADY MORGAN'S MEMOIR.

CHAPTER I.

FIRST YEAR OF MARRIED LIFE.

HAVING with difficulty won his wife, Sir Charles Morgan had to encounter the greater difficulty of making their married life answer the ardent promises and protestations with which he had invoked it. His was a more than ordinary hazardous choice. His wife, accustomed to unlimited flattery, general admiration and entire independence of action, to say nothing of the deference with which she was treated by every member of her own family circle, was very imperfectly prepared for the subordination and restraint of marriage. Her strong will and great determination of character had hitherto been virtues; henceforth, they bade fair to become inconveniences in her domestic life, whilst her entire control over her own resources withdrew from her husband that power of the purse, which, in governments and in private life, is the most effective instrument of control. It required a rare mellowness of character and a remarkable combination of qualities to extract quiet domestic happiness from such perilous materials. Sir Charles had been a very ardent lover, but the probabilities seemed many, that he would be a disenchanted husband. The result, however, proved that there is no infallible judgment except that which is formed after the event! The marriage proved in all respects a remarkably happy one. Sir Charles was a man of a sweet and noble nature, generous, highminded, entirely free from all meanness or littleness, tender-hearted and affectionate, with a vehement and passionate temper, excessively jealous of his wife's affection, but not in the least jealous of her genius and success. He was the most enthusiastic of her admirers, the most devout believer in her powers of mind, acquirements and genius; but he was also a man of great firmness of character, strength of mind, and integrity of principle. There was nothing weak about his love for her; indeed, he was greatly her superior in solidity of character and soundness of judgment. He was rather indolent, had no ambition, and as little vanity or self-love as a man could have,—and be mortal. He had every quality in private life to ensure a woman's respect; being upright, truthful, straightforward, reserved, and reticent. His very faults, and most of all, his sharp temper, gave him an advantage over his wife. Lady Morgan held him in unbounded respect, and at the bottom was rather afraid of him; he had the qualities which rule a woman, and which all women love to find in a man. She could depend upon him for guidance and control, and that to a woman is more even than affection. He was not a man of genius, but he was a great deal wiser than his wife. Nevertheless, her strong individuality asserted itself; she had much influence with him, and whenever there was a conflict of inclination between them, she always got her own way. She loved society,—distractions,—to be in constant movement,—to see everything—to hear everything—to have incessant change of scene. Possessed of an unfailing flow of spirits, and constitutionally cheerful; she had an extremely good temper which, however, did not hinder her from being sometimes wilful and provoking. The result was, that their opposite qualities, working upon each other, and controlled by mutual good sense, produced the most agreeable effect. If she did not change his nature, she modified his tastes and his habits, so that they never went anywhere without each other, and as she could not live, except in society, he went into it with her; she could always succeed in getting him to do whatever she wished, or to go wherever she liked, though not without some grumbling and occasional protest. He kept her steady, and she kept him from stagnating into indolent repose.

The first year was very stormy, not without seasons of fine weather, but not "set fair." Afterwards, the domestic atmosphere cleared, their mutual qualities adjusted themselves, and, like the people in the winding up of a fairy tale, "they lived happily ever after." The works she wrote after her marriage take a different rank to those she wrote previously, and bear the impress of her constant intercourse with her husband's sterling and highly cultivated mind. It has fallen to the lot of very few distinguished women to be so happily mated.

Miss Owenson did not come to her husband portionless; she had saved about five thousand pounds, the proceeds of her writings; this sum was settled upon herself, and it was stipulated in the marriage settlement that she was to have the sole and independent control over her own earnings, whilst the reversion of Sir Charles Morgan's fortune was settled upon the daughter of his first marriage.

The following letters to Mrs. Lefanu, give an account of her early married life at Baron's Court.

Lady Morgan to Mrs. Lefanu.

BARON'S COURT,
February, 1812.

You, who have followed me through the four acts of my comedy, seem to cut me dead at the fifth, and leave me to the enjoyment of my own catastrophe without sympathy or participation; not a single couplet to celebrate the *grand event*, not even one line of prose to say " I wish you joy." It is quite clear, that like all heroines, I no longer interest when I gain a husband.

Since you will not even ask me how I am, I will volunteer the information of my being as happy as being " loved up to my bent " (aye, and almost beyond it) can make me, and, indeed, so much is it true, "the same to-day, to-morrow, and for ever," that I can give you no other notice of my existence than that miraculous one of a man being desperately in love with his own wife, and she " nothing loath."

Though living in a palace, we have all the comfort and independence of home; besides bed-rooms and dressing-rooms, Morgan's study has been fitted up with all the luxury of a *joli boudoir* by Lady Abercorn (who neither spared her taste nor purse on the occasion). It is stored with books, music, and everything that can contribute to our use and amusement. Here "the world forgotten, and by the world forgot," we live all day, and do not join the family till dinner time, and as *chacun a son goût* is the order here, when we are weary of argand lamps and a gallery a hundred feet long in the evening—we retire to our own snuggery, where, very often, some of the others come to drink coffee with us. As to me, I am *every inch a wife*, and so ends that brilliant thing that was GLORVINA.

N.B.—I intend to write a book to explode the vulgar idea of matrimony being the tomb of love. Matrimony is the real thing and all before but "leather and prunella."

This chapter I dedicate to Bess. Sir Charles desires me to assure you of his highest consideration: an enthusiast in *everything*, he is a *zealot* as to talent, and one of your old letters has roused all his fanaticism in your favour; he longs as much to know you as I do to see you, *et c'est beaucoup dire!* for that, I fear, for a long time there is no chance.

Lady Morgan to Mrs. Lefanu.

BARON'S COURT.

I have just learned from Olivia that you are ill; it is quite too *bad* that you, who are so much to so many, should be so often laid up, while those who are nothing to nobody, are going about with health and spirits sufficient to bore and annoy all their acquaintances; but so it is in this best of all possible worlds! My little billet crossed your kind and delightful letter, which I have not answered just because I had nothing to say worth the trouble of poring your poor eyes over my illegible scribble; and next, because I keep writing to you in store, as children do their *bonne bouche*,—the best thing for the last.

A *chance* (studiously sought for) threw it in my way to speak of dear Tom to the Chancellor. He is himself a good old Christian, upon the good old plan, and the little sketch I gave of Tom as a primitive minister of a primitive religion, as one whose vocation seemed to have "come from above," and yet as one "more skilled to raise the wretched than to rise," seemed to please him. Shortly after, he asked me if he had not married a daughter of Dr. Dobbins!

I merely mention this to you, because the Chancellor has the disposal of the patronage of the Archbishop of Dublin, and that he is to be entirely guided by the fitness of persons to fill their stations, and not by interest or influence. He is a most excellent churchman, and not at all a man to *rebuter* any application made to him on just grounds. "On this hint" you may act.

Colonel Gore is your "*slave and blackamoor.*" The day he arrived here, in the midst of a dinner, silent and solemn as the dulness of *bon ton* could make it, he cried out, "Lady Morgan, I am under more obligations to your friend than to all the world besides." "What friend?" "Why Mrs. Lefanu to be sure; she taught my Phillip to read Milton," &c., &c.

I long to hear from you; by this I hope you have seen my dear Olivia; she is England mad, would *we were all* settled there. Here or there, *partout où vous êtes, et partout où je suis*, I must always be among the number of those who respect you most and love you dearest.

God bless you ever,
S. MORGAN.

PS.—Poor, dear, excellent Bess is, I suppose, as usual, your nurse and companion. She is, indeed, the inestimable daughter of an inimitable mother, and in my opinion, her whole life has been active, useful, and of practical excellence. She is one of the sinners who devote themselves to the "nothingness of good works."

The tone of the following letter is very much softened and subdued from the "saucy Arethusa" style of former times.

It will be seen that all the kindness and luxury

with which she was surrounded did not prevent Lady Morgan from wishing to have an independent home of her own.

Lady Morgan to Lady Stanley.

BARON'S COURT, NEWTOWN-STEWART,
April 28, 1812.

I never answer your dear, kind, welcome, and clever letters at the moment I wish to answer them (which is the moment they are read) both for your sake and my own, because I wish to delay the moment of *bore* to you, and to keep in view a pleasure for myself. To hold intercourse with you of whatever description, has always been to me a positive enjoyment since the first moment I saw you, and that was not the least happy moment of my life. I was then full of the spirits which create hope in the mind. I was beckoned on by a thousand bright illusions, and it was a delicious event to meet half way in my career such a creature as yourself. In short, my dear friend, our physical capabilities for receiving pleasure wear out rapidly in proportion to their own intensity, and those who, like me, see life through the dazzling prism of imagination long before they are permitted to enter it, must, like me, find the original infinitely inferior to the fiction; still I have no reason to complain. I have associated myself to one who feels and thinks as I do, and this is, or ought to be, the first of human blessings; but *his* thoughts and feelings are still of a *higher* tone—they are not qualified by that light *vanity* which brings my character down to the general level of humanity. In *love* he is Sheridan's Falkland, and in his views of things there is a *mélange* of cynicism and sentiment that will never suffer him to be as happy as the inferior million that move about him. Marriage has taken nothing from the *romance* of his passion for me; and by bringing a sense of *property* with it, it has rendered him more exigent and nervous about me than before. All this is flattering and delightful, and yet I do not say with Richelieu, "C'est être bien à charge, que d'être trop aimé," yet, for his sake, I would be almost contented to be less loved, because I should see him more happy. He admires the picture I have drawn of you, and often says " Of all the persons you have mentioned to me, Lady Stanley is the only woman I wish to know."

You will laugh at this wife-like letter; but provided you do laugh, I am satisfied. Could you take a peep out of your secluded Eden at the vicissitudes and miseries of those who live in the world, you would hug yourself in your own "*home-felt certainty*" of peace, comfort, and competency. The worst of all human evils you never can have known—*poverty!* As Ninon says upon a gayer subject, "On peut s'en rapporter à moi." I am, however, for the present, living upon fifty thousand pounds a year, and shall do so for another year *if I choose;* but although our noble hosts are everything that is kind and charming, we prefer a *home of our own*, be it ever so tiny. Since I wrote to you, we have lost the beautiful Countess of Aberdeen, Lord Abercorn's favourite daughter. It was *a heavy blow*.

I am delighted your winter has been cheered by the society of your new son-in-law, and the amiable Emma. My dearest Olivia comes here in *June*, if her *health permits*, and after that I must settle in England and she in Ireland. I am at work again; but with the sole view of making some money to furnish a bit of a house in London, which, *coûte que coûte*, we *must* have. My book will be a *genuine* Irish romance of Elizabeth's day, founded on historic facts. I would not write another line, to add the fame of Sappho to my own little quota of reputation, did not necessity guide my worn out stump of a goose-quill. My imagination is exhausted, and those *hopes* and *views* which in the first era of life give such *spring* to mind, and such energy to thought, are all dead and gone. At present nothing would give me more pleasure than to meet you in London when we go there. We are daily expecting the arrival of Lord Aberdeen and his little daughters, and Lady Marian Hamilton, and shortly Lord and Lady Hamilton and their family, so we shall have a house full; but people are mistaken as to the pleasures of a large society in great houses—there is an *inevitability* about it that is a *dead bore*.

I long to hear how the dear little farm is going on, and all the improvements. Is the pig alive? is Poll as brilliant as ever, and Mrs. Jones wedded to her sentimental lover? And *you?* Do you walk about with the little black silk apron and feed the pets? Pray write to me, and soon—directly; this I ask in the honesty of earnest wishes. Sir Charles requests I will say something for him. What can I say, but that he is

prepared to like you as much as he has already learnt to admire you, and so I am, as ever,
                    Yours, affectionately,
                           SYDNEY OWENSON MORGAN.

The genuine Irish romance that was to furnish the little house of our own in London was the *O'Donnel.* Lady Morgan happily changed her plan. Instead of an historical novel of the days of Queen Bess, founded on facts, she wrote a delightful sketch of the Ireland she knew so well.

CHAPTER II.

DEATH OF MR. OWENSON.

THE first heavy sorrow of her life came upon Lady Morgan a few months after her marriage. Her father, whose health had long been breaking, died in the early spring. He lived to witness the happiness and prosperity of both his children, and he died at the house of Lady Clarke, surrounded by every care and kindness that affection could bestow. The following letters tell of Lady Morgan's grief. The natural position between a parent and child had, in their case, been reversed. Ever since her mother's death she had felt that it was for her to take care of her father, instead of her father taking care of her; but this did not interfere with her own romantic admiration for him, nor the affectionate respect with which she regarded him.

Lady Morgan to Sir A. Clarke.

May 23, 1812.

MY DEAREST CLARKE,

'Tis an excess of selfishness in me to write to you under my present feelings, as, except to detail my own

misery, I have little else to say. To express my sense
of your benevolence, of your affectionate attention to
our dear, dear father, I cannot. I have been saved nothing in not being with you; I have not only strongly
imagined every scene and moment of misery and sadness, but I have added to it all the horrors of suspense
and anxiety. I have lived on from post to post, always
hoping the best, fearing the worst, and not knowing
what part to take or how to act. Still I thought this
shock would prove like the last, though Morgan gave
me no encouragement; but I believed, as he knew not
the constitution the disease had to contend with, that
he might have been mistaken. In short, it appeared to
me impossible that my own dear father, who was my
child as well as my father, *could die*—nor I don't believe it yet! it is to me as if a curtain dropped before
life. I can look neither to the past nor to the future
without connecting everything with him, and the present is all, all him. The tie which existed between
us was not the common tie of father and child. He
was the object for which I laboured, and wrote, and
lived, and nothing can fill up to me the place he held
in my heart. My dearest Clarke, forgive me, but my
tears, the first I have freely shed, are falling faster
than I can write, and I scarcely know what I say.
God knows, I want not to add to your sadness. Every
body here is very good to me, and my dear husband
supports, comforts, and devotes himself to me; but he
could not know how endearing poor papa was, or how
much out of the ordinary run of fathers. You knew

him, and loved him, and were his child. I am very weak and ought not to write so.

They allow me to breakfast and dine in my own sitting-room, which is a great comfort, and I have not seen a creature since my misfortune, but Lady Abercorn, who is all affection and pity. They want me to drive to Derry, or somewhere, with Morgan; but where can I go that the image of my dead, dear papa, will not follow me? What trouble, what expence, what suffering and sadness *you* must have had? God bless you, for all; but goodness is of no avail. If my dearest, suffering Livy will not come to me, I will go to her, and this scene would be a change and a benefit to her.

My dearest Clarke, I remember buying or paying for a watch last summer, for poor, dear papa,—I wish you would wear it! I have just had a petition from a starving English actor and his family, travelling through here, that almost reconciled me to an event that put the object I loved beyond the reach of poverty or care. I am so altered in the course of three days you would not know me. Livy was such a blessing to the last to her poor father. Has Mrs. Doyle, the Lefanus, or any of her friendly friends been with her? Morgan, who is all tenderness, and goodness, and generosity, is bent on re-uniting me to Livy at any sacrifice. This business has fallen like a thunderbolt on me. I knew not what step to take. It is odd, that when Livy wrote word of papa's talking of going to the theatre, Morgan said it was the worst symptom that had appeared yet, and when I laughed at him, he said we all deceived ourselves. I have not courage to ask you any particulars. I know all that could be done was done. God bless you for it. My eyes are so inflamed Morgan won't allow me to write any more.

God bless and preserve you,

S. O. M.

PS. by Sir Charles.

PS.—Dear Livy, she is in no condition to write to you, and would only increase your sufferings, nor can I say more than that the sight of her wild and tearless eyes almost distracts me; however, you must both give only a short season to sorrow. I would not say to you do not lament, but bear in mind, my dearest Livy, that after all this is a most merciful dispensation of Providence, especially to the object of our lamentation. What is more now to the purpose, come down and see what a good husband I am, and what an affectionate brother you have; change of scene and of air will be of the greatest use to you, and if the most perfect sympathy have any consolation, you will find it in stopping with Syd. and your affectionate Morgy.

Lady Morgan to Mrs. Lefanu.

June 26th, 1812.

Your message to Sir Charles would have insured you an immediate answer to your letter, if there were no other inducement to write to you; and that you have not heard from me before arises from some mistake about being detained here or in Dublin; I have only this morning received it. Sir Charles desires me to say that, from all he hears and knows of you, he is become too much interested in your life not to feel anxious for its preservation and comfort, and that, as far as his knowledge and ability can contribute to either, they are devoted to your service. He says, however, that you have given too vague an account of your symptoms for him to form a correct judgment. He dare not risk an opinion without being more master of the subject. He wishes he was near you, and would be happy to do anything for you. He is very sensible of, and grateful for, the tenderness you express towards me, thus admitting him to the circle of your friends; and I believe you have had few more zealous candidates for the honour.

Everything that you say about Dublin is very seductive, but we really are in a pitiable state of hesitation at present. They have not the remotest idea that we can or will leave them as long as they remain in Ireland, and yet they talk of that being a year or two. If we (*what they would call*) desert them, we shall risk the loss of their friendship, which would indeed be a loss; but if we remain we lose time, and it is quite fit that Morgan should establish himself soon somewhere. Add to this that they, I believe, have a real affection for us; but we are dying to be in our own little shabby house, and are tired of solitary splendours, and of the eternal representation of high life, and you will then believe that we are rather in a

puzzle. Morgan, in the end, will be solely guided by
honour (leaving interest, and inclination, and even
happiness out of the question), which he strains to a
point of romantic refinement. We expect Lord and
Lady Hamilton (another invalid). I showed Lord
Aberdeen your critique on noble authors; he said,
"had you judged differently, he would have formed a
different judgment of you, from what he was inclined
to do." Arbuthnot, who is coming over as secretary,
I know intimately; but I am sick of the idea of place-
hunting or place-asking. I suppose, by this, you are
at your Sabine Farm, at Glasnevin: would I were with
you for a week! *Mais pour aller à Corinthe le désir ne
suffit pas;* but I should like to have you alone, that is,
in the midst of your own family, for if *you* don't pa-
tronize *my* Lords and Ladies Fiddle Faddle, I will vote
your Miss Macguffins, and the rest of your twopenny
Misses and Masters, and some few of your *good* Mistresses this, and worthy Misters t'others, *dead bores!*
I, at least, have something for my *pride*, but the
"*Damn nigger you get for your money*" is quite below
purchase! Native worth and native genius (like your
own) must always hold the ascendant in whatever
circle it is to be found, and if you find not these
amongst a certain class, you find something else with
people of rank; you get the next best thing, *education*,
which, with English people of fashion of the present
day, you never fail to find. The young people of this
family (including the son-in-law, Lord Aberdeen)
have more acquirements and accomplishments, more
literary and general *savoir* than (with the almost

single exception of your own family), all the youth of Dublin put together. The women not only speak French and Italian as well as English, but are good Latin scholars, and unquestionably the best musicians I know; and yet I never heard the Ladies Hamilton particularly distinguished for their education above other girls of fashion. I never mean to say that the *first class* of society have more genius or more happiness than any other, I only insist that they have the *next best things*, and as I find it easier to get at a countess or a marchioness than at a Mrs. Lefanu, *faute de mieux*, I put up with their ladyships, cutting dead the Miss Macguffins and the Mistresses O'Shaughnessey's, for whom (*de loin*) I have a great respect. The fact is, a dull worthy is not the less *dull* to me for being a worthy and not an earl! Lords or commons, a bore is a bore, and I think you will agree with me that a vulgar one is worse than a polished one, as an Irish diamond, though "a lustre-looking thing," is best after it has received a little working. You who are *a real* brilliant, I am sure I should always have discovered your "original brightness" in whatever setting I should have found it. I know your intrinsic value, and prize it at its worth; meantime, let me prefer the rose diamonds of my Lord and Lady Fiddle Faddle to the Kerry stones of the Miss Macguffins; one, at least, has a polished surface, the other retains the "laste taste in life" of the clay! I have not left myself room to say *Je vous aime de tout mon cœur*. Love to all, Joe included.

S. O. M.

Lady Morgan to Mrs. Lefanu.

BARON'S COURT,
June 7th, 1812.

MY DEAREST FRIEND,

"To each his suffering;" you have had your portion, and it would have been unfair and unjust to have written to you under the influence of my sadness, and have drawn from you an unavailing sympathy at the moment you have been so actively and beneficially engaged in soothing and comforting my dear Olivia, who feels your goodness in her "heart of hearts." You are a *true friend,*—I have always thought so,—I have always said so, and every year of our friendship has given me fresh reason to confirm my opinion. The dearest and strongest tie, which time, nature, habit, and acts of reciprocal affection can form, has been wrenched from my heart; I ought long since to have been, and yet was not, prepared for it. It was a dreadful break up to the feelings; it is so much of life broken off. A host of dearly remembered events, feelings, and associations, are necessarily gone with it. Were it possible I could ever again love anything so well, I can never again love anything so long. The best point of existence with me is over, and new ties and new affections must be light in their hold, and feeble in their influence, compared to those "which grew with the growth and strengthened with the years." My dear husband, Olivia, yourself, and one or two more objects are still left me, to whom I will cling. It is my intention to sacrifice for the rest of my life to the HEART, and to live in Ireland, if those I love cannot live with me in England, where interest and ambition equally call Morgan and myself; *he* has no *wish*, scarcely any *will*, but *mine*, and is ready to make *my* country *his*, "*my* people *his* people.". As yet, our views are very misty; Lord and Lady Abercorn are very desirous we should remain with them, as long as they stay in Ireland, at least if not after; but as that will probably be for a year or two, it would be *impossible*. We have not, however, said so.

We have lately added to our party,

"The travelled Thane, Athenian Aberdeen,"

As Lord Byron calls him. He is reckoned among the "rising young men" of England, and is one of the *virtuosi* who purchased a farm at Athens, where he resided for some time. He was the husband of Lord Abercorn's lately deceased and beautiful daughter. The meeting was very afflicting, and for some time threw a shadow over our circle.

What think you of the state of public affairs? our letters to-day, from England, say that the opposition still hold out, though offered six places out of twelve in the Cabinet, or seven out of fourteen. What a *bouleversement* in the state of things when stars and garters go a begging!! and commoner's misses refuse to become princesses!!* The Cabinet remains empty

* Alluding to the gossip of the day that the Duke of Clarence had been *refused* by Miss Tilney Long, the luckless "great heiress" of the period.

because no one thinks it worth their while to accept a place in it, and yet all this we have lived to see! If the opposition permit themselves in their condescension to be prevailed upon to govern an empire, your brother will find his own level, and you will have your *levers et couchers*, and we shall find with Louis the Fourteenth's courtiers that Cuff Street "est faite pour n'être comparée à rien" (which, by-the-bye, and with deference to Mr. Lefanu, is more true than of the Louvre) and that "il ne plait pas à Glasnevin." In the midst of all this political *tourbillon*, people still submit to be pleased and amused, and run after your comedy as they would have done in the prosperous and Augustan days of Queen Anne. Lady Abercorn tells me she has had great accounts of its success from all sides. As she knows your *bonne fortune* is mine, she indulges me with hearing of the good tidings. Livy says you think she could write a comedy; I think so too, she has an immense fund of true comedy in her own character, but writing is such a distinct thing from ourselves that no inference can be drawn from thence. Lord Byron, the author of delightful *Childe Harold* (which has more *force, fire,* and *thought* than anything I have read for an age) is cold, silent, and reserved in his manners,—pray read it if you have not. When I was in London, Lord G. Greville read me a poem of his own on the same subject as *Childe Harold*. The rival lords published their poems the same day; the one is cried up to the skies, the other, alas, is cried down to ——!

We expect Livy here, but she seems either unwilling or unable to leave home. We have no chance of going ourselves to Dublin till winter; by that time, every one that I have known and lived with (save yourself, the Atkinsons, and the Mason's) will have left it; indeed they are almost all gone already. It is astonishing the changes that have taken place in the little circle of my intimacy within a few years, either by death or departure to England. Among my literary friends, dear Psyche (Mrs. Tighe), Cooper, Walker, and Kirwin are no more!

Sir Charles's desire to know you increases daily. Shall we ever all meet again and all be happy together? At least write to me, and under all changes and circumstances, believe I love you tenderly and sincerely.

S. O. M.

There is no letter or memorandum to show the exact time when Sir Charles and Lady Morgan quitted the family of Lord Abercorn, to begin housekeeping for themselves, nor the immediate occasion that gave rise to it. The splendid slavery of her life was a position Lady Morgan found untenable, and it is probable that after her marriage she felt less inclined to tolerate the fine ladyism of the Marchioness than when she was in the position of a young lady. The separation took place, however, without any break in their friendly relations, though the intimacy gradually subsided. Lady Morgan was always anxious that Sir Charles should exert himself and not settle down into indolent comfort. For herself, activity and independence of mind and body were indispensable, and there is no doubt she exerted all her influence over Sir Charles

to induce him to give up his connection with the
Marquis, and took advantage of the first opportunity
to break away.

They went to stay with Sir Arthur and Lady Clarke,
until they found a house to suit them. Eventually
they found a house in Kildare Street—not large, but
pleasant, and with some pretensions to a handsome
appearance. Lady Morgan had the pleasure of fitting
up her library after the fashion she had imagined and
described in her *Novice of St. Dominic*, years ago,—the
story that was begun when she and her sister were
with their father in Kilkenny.

The prospects of Sir Charles and Lady Morgan
were tolerable, but not brilliant, as Sir Charles had
his practice entirely to establish. But this change
from a courtly to a city life was the best event that
had ever befallen him. The constant intercourse with
the brilliant, active mind of his wife, quickened his
faculties, and called out the capabilities which had lain
dormant or had fallen into disuse. He obtained the
appointment of physician to the Marshalsea, and succeeded, in a reasonably short time, in establishing a
tolerable practice.

A few years after his marriage, Sir Charles published
a work called *Outlines of the Physiology of Life*, setting
forth psychological opinions, boldly averred, and distinctly stated, instead of being put forward as hypo-
thesis or left to inference. It was not an age of philosophic tolerance. Science was expected to be strictly
orthodox in its theology. The work provoked a storm
of opposition and censure, both religious and secular;

the result was, that Sir Charles retired from general practice, though he retained his appointment to the Marshalsea. He devoted himself to literary labour, and joined with Lady Morgan in efforts to extend the knowledge of the condition of Ireland, to spread liberal opinions in politics, and to create a Public Conscience to which Irish wrongs and Irish difficulties might appeal. To these objects they both devoted themselves; especially they were staunch advocates of Catholic emancipation, when advocates were an abused minority, and their exertions were recognised when that much vexed and agitated question was at last set at rest. But this is anticipating Lady Morgan's story.

CHAPTER III.

KILDARE STREET.

ANOTHER letter from Dr. Jenner to Sir Charles; they did not often write to each other, but they knew that whilst they lived they each possessed a friend, and it is this consciousness of possession that makes us rich, not the act of "counting out our money," like the king in the nursery rhyme.

BERKELEY,
March 14, 1813.

MY DEAR FRIEND,

My epistolatory sins multiply upon me at such a rate, I am almost ashamed to face a correspondent of any description, and quite so to appear before you. Where are my congratulatory replies to your Dublin letter, announcing your marriage? Literally *in nubibus*. I say *literally*, for scores of them passed through my brain in forms so airy, that they flew aloft before I could catch one to fix upon paper. The sober truth is, procrastination, that thief of comfort as well as time, took an early possession of me, and it is in vain now to attempt an ejectment. Let me tell you one thing, by the way, that when they flew up, they carried with them my best wishes for you and yours.

I have not been in town since the summer of 1811, nor much at Cheltenham, preferring, whenever I am permitted, the enjoyment of my cottage, in this my native village. But don't think I spend my time in idleness. My pursuit has lately been, when uninterrupted by vaccination, the morbid changes in the structure of the livers of brutes, which has led me to some conclusions respecting the same changes in the human. 'Tis hard, methinks, that the poor animal that is content with what the meadows afford for his daily bill of fare, and whose cellar is the pond or the brook, should perish from the same diseases as the drunkard; but so it is. There are plants which, somehow or another, are capable of throwing the state of the liver into that sort of confusion which calls hydatids into existence. These do not continue long in their native state, but produce a great variety of tubera, cartilaginous, bony masses, &c. In other instances, the disease originates in the biliary ducts, which become astonishingly enlarged, and thickened in every part of the liver, and finally destroy it in various ways. This is the outline of my research. The hydatid I can call into existence in the rabbit in about a fortnight.

I most heartily wish well to the scheme you have in view, and shall use my best endeavours to promote it. I know but little of the locality of Dublin; but it is my intention to spend a good deal of the ensuing season at Cheltenham, where I shall probably see many Irish families of respectability; then, be assured, I shall think of you, and be enabled, I trust, to do something more than merely think. Don't let me redden your cheeks beyond the point to which nature has brought them, but I must conscientiously say, that if your merits meet with their reward, your *fingers' ends* will grow sore with professional exercise. Let me advise you to take up some scientific pursuit, which will admit of an exhibition—why not mineralogy? You are quite at home there. I have a medical friend who has long ranked as the first physician in one of the largest cities in these realms, and whose fossils were the *stepping stones* that led him into the wide fields of practice.

If you can bear to write to such a correspondent, pray let me hear from you ere long, and believe me, with every friendly wish to you and yours

Your much attached

EDWARD JENNER.

The next letter is from Lady Morgan to Lady Stanley. It gives a pleasant picture of herself in her new home (35, or as it is now numbered, 39, Kildare Street), and the skilful ease with which she took up her position as mistress of a house. Lady Morgan was very practical and prided herself upon her good housekeeping. She possessed a natural gift of being comfortable, and making her house so to herself and to all her friends.

Lady Morgan to Lady Stanley.

35, KILDARE STREET, DUBLIN,
Monday, May 17.

Vous voila aux abois ma chère dame!! You see I am not to be distanced; retreat as you will, I still pursue. When I am within a mile of you, you will not see me; when I write you will not answer; and still here I am at your feet, because *I will not be rebutée*, nor (throw me off as you may) will I ever give you up until I find something that resembles you, something to fill up the place you have so long occupied; the fact is, my dear Lady Stanley, it is pure selfishness that ties me to you. *I do not like* women, I cannot get on with them! and except the excessive tenderness which I have always felt for my sister be called friendship, you (and one or two more, *par parenthèse!*) are the only woman to whom I could ever *lier* myself for a week together. *Devancer son sexe* is as dangerous as *devancer son siècle*; it was no effort, no *willing* of mine that has given me a *little* the start of the major part of them; dear little souls! who, as Ninon says, "trouvent *commode* d'être jolie." The principle was *there; active* and *restless*, the spur was given, and *off I went,* happy in the result that my comparative superiority obtained me *one* such friend as yourself— that is, as you *were;* but I fear you now cut me dead.

We have at last got into a home of our own; we

found an old, dirty, dismantled house, and we have turned our *piggery* into a decent sort of hut enough; we have made it clean and comfortable, which is all our moderate circumstances will admit of, save *one little bit of a room*, which is a real bijou, and it is about *four inches by three*, and, therefore, one could afford to ornament it *a little*; it is fitted up in the *gothic*, and I have collected into it the best part of a very good cabinet of natural history of Sir Charles, eight or nine hundred volumes of choice books, in French, English, Italian, and German; some little miscellaneous curiosities, and a few scraps of old china, so that with muslin draperies, &c., &c., I have made no contemptible *set* out. *I was thinking, that may be Susette* could enrich my store in the old china way, if she has any refuse of that sort which you may have thrown her in with your cast-off wardrobe—a broken cup, a bottomless bowl, a spoutless teapot,—in a word, anything old and shattered, that is china, and of no value to you, will be of use and ornament to me, and Captain Skinner has promised to bring it over for me.

With respect to authorship, I fear it is over; I have been making chair-covers instead of periods; hanging curtains instead of raising systems, and cheapening pots and pans instead of selling sentiment and philosophy. Meantime, my husband is, as usual, deep in study, and if his *popularity* here may be deemed a favourable omen, will, I trust, soon be *deep in practice*. Well, always dear friend; any chance of a line in answer to my three pages of verbiage? Just make the effort of *taking up the pen*, and if you only write

"Glorvina, I am well, and love you still," I will be contented. Under all circumstances,

     Yours affectionately,
        S. MORGAN.

Sir Charles Morgan's step-mother had married, for her second husband, William Bingley, the animal biographer; here is a letter from him about his literary undertakings.

William Bingley to Sir Charles Morgan.

     CHRISTCHURCH, HANTS,
      June 30, 1813.

DEAR MORGAN,

You will think me, as you have no doubt long ago thought me, a very miserable correspondent; but the fact is, that of late my time has, in a most unusual manner, been occupied. The *History of Hampshire* has not merely been at sixes and sevens, but at sixteens and seventeens. A certain flowery-named gentleman, as I conceive, has by no means fulfilled his engagements with me, which I intend very shortly to prove. I mean to call for a full investigation into my whole conduct relating to it, which I hope the trustees will not refuse to enter into. Lord Malmesbury was with me some time on the subject about three weeks ago, and I firmly believe is my friend; at all events, I shall not let the matter rest until I have a full arrangement of the business. My evidence on the subject is indisputable; and I have a letter promising a compensation in case of a failure in obtaining the

requisite number of subscriptions. It is really too
bad that I should be a loser by a work which I was
positively invited, and, contrary to my own inclination, to undertake. If all at last goes on well, I hope
to complete it in the course of about a year and a-half.
This is no trifling concern to me, and has cost me
much anxiety. When things go on somewhat more
smoothly, I hope to become a better correspondent
than I hitherto have been.

You, I presume, are by this time comfortably settled
in your new residence, and, as I should conceive, find
domestic pleasures infinitely to be preferred to those
of pomp and bustle in a house not your own. This is
peculiarly the case with me. Since I have been in
Christchurch this time, I believe I have only dined
from home about four times, nor do I ever wish to be
from my own premises. Mrs. Bingley has been most
lamentably unwell ever since our arrival. She has
three times only been out of the house, nor do I at
present see any immediate prospect of her recovery.
It will indeed greatly rejoice me when she is again
able to go abroad.

When you next write you must inform me how
many patients you have got. I presume that your
knocker must, by this time, be almost worn out. I
am glad your packages arrived safely; but I must
confess, when I was putting your chattels together, I
did not conceive that I was doing it for a voyage to a
foreign country.

The new edition of the *Animal Biography* has been
published about three months; and Longman and Co.

have just written to request that I would prepare a new edition of the *Welsh Tour*. This is what I scarcely expected, as two or three years ago I had been informed that the copies were going off very slowly. It is my present intention to throw the work into a somewhat different form, and print it in one volume instead of two.

By the way, I have been employed, during the evenings, in preparing a little introductory work on Zoology, the first sheet of which is printed. This, at present, is unknown I believe to any except the bookseller and my family. The plan is nearly the same as that of *Animal Biography*, and it has been prepared chiefly for the purpose of affording a popular view of the Linnean system. I am very anxious for its success, although I have sold the copyright. It will be in one duodecimo volume, and it is my intention to follow it up with another on the subject of Botany and Mineralogy.

Mrs. Bingley unites with me in kindest remembrances to yourself and Lady Morgan.

I am, dear Morgan,
Most truly yours,
WILLIAM BINGLEY.

PS.—Little Susan and Tom are going on wonderfully well; their progress is more rapid than I could have conceived it possible, but their capacities are greater far than those of any children I have ever yet seen.

The next letter is from Emily Lady Cahir, Countess of Glengall; and relates to an enquiry Lady Morgan had made about a man whose adventures seemed to offer a type for the hero of the novel (*O'Donnel*), on which she was then engaged. Lady Cahir was herself the model for Lady Singleton, in the same story. One almost wonders that some of the fine ladies whom Lady Morgan produced in her works, etching them in aquafortis and colouring them to the life, did not assassinate her by way of return, especially as she invariably introduced a sketch of herself in one corner of all her pictures, taking up all the wisdom and common sense going, as well as being the most agreeable character in the story!

November 6, 1813.

My dear Lady Morgan,

You see that I do not lose a moment in obeying your orders, and be assured that you ought to give me some credit, as I am in general but a bad correspondent. Your inquiries as to whether you are to make Mr. Shee your hero, has amused me considerably. The *Evening Post* inserted a long list of lies upon his subject, at which I laughed heartily at the time. You certainly could not have applied to a better person than myself for information with respect to him, as I know his birth, parentage and adventures, perfectly. He is of a low family. One of his sisters was bound to a milliner, at Kilkenny, and used to bring ribbons, gauzes, &c., to the Miss Bensfords, when their father was Bishop of Ossory. Another of his sisters was married to a coachmaker. His brother was foreman to the said coachmaker, and is now elevated to the rank of gauger in the excise by Lord Cahir's interest. The hero was in the Irish brigade at St. Domingo; but as to his prodigies of valour, I never heard anything of them. He came to London starving. Lord Cahir fed him with money till he was rather tired of so doing, and offered to get him a commission in the army, which he declined, unless the Duke of York would give him a majority at once. Lord Cahir was induced to present a memorial to this effect, and the answer was, that it was then unheard of in the service, but that a cornetcy was at Lord Cahir's command. Shee declined it. He then married the daughter of a button maker, by whom he expected to get some cash. Being also disappointed in this, and fighting considerably with the lady and her buttons, he packed up his portmanteau and set off to France, where he entered the French service, and became aid-de-camp to General Clark, who is a distant relation of his. He has since been made a lieutenant-colonel of a regiment, and was mentioned in some of the French generals' despatches in Spain, as having eaten up the English army. By some extraordinary accident, however, Lord Wellington has "lived to fight another day;" and should the hero Shee be taken, which is by no means impossible, he will swing on Tyburn tree. Nothing, in my mind, can justify a man in fighting against his own country,—not even your seducing pen can make it palatable to my old English prejudices, particularly when he had a very reasonable sufficiency in this country; for I have forgotten to state that Lord Cahir gave him a farm near Cahir, out of which he at this moment receives a very handsome profit rent. Had he chosen to have gone into our service, Lord Cahir would have pushed him forward; as it is now fourteen years since he was offered a commission, he might have been as high in the English as he is now in the French service, without the stigma of being a traitor, and without the certainty of being hanged, if taken. Lord Cahir did push on another brother to the rank of major in our army, in which rank he died. So much for our hero. And now I have only to request you to burn this letter, as I have no inclination to be quoted in anything that concerns him.

Excuse me now, if from being over anxious for the fate of a work, which, coming from your pen, will, I am sure, have so much to recommend it, I venture an opinion. Do not mix anything of religious or political opinions in a work intended only to amuse,—it will lay you open to animadversion, and party may influence opinion.

Yours truly, E. Cahir.

This was very sage advice, but felt to be impossible by the Wild Irish Girl. An Irish story, without religion or politics!

During the whole of the first year of her residence in Kildare Street, Lady Morgan was busy upon *O'Donnel*, a national tale, for which it may be remembered she gathered the materials on her visit to Dublin, before her marriage. It was published by Colburn, early in 1814, and dedicated to the Duke of Devonshire. She received five hundred and fifty pounds for the copyright. The first edition consisted of two thousand copies, and a second edition was printed in February 1815. It is an immense improvement upon all her previous works, being written in a natural style, without the high-flown rhetoric or pedantic allusions which disfigured and overlaid her earlier stories. Her own words and opinions are embodied in the Duchess of Belmont,—a sort of feminine Puss in Boots, clever, witty, sensible, and worldly, with a sufficiently good heart to make the reader take an interest in her. In the beginning she appears as a neglected governess, in the family of Lady Singleton, who is the type of Lady Cahir, whose letter has just been quoted. She is admirably drawn. The governess, by some sleight of novel-writing, becomes Duchess of Belmont, the wife of an old peer, having declined to be his mistress. He dies (off the stage), and she re-appears on the scene as a rich and brilliant widow with a magnificent title. She is the same in all her qualities as when she was Miss O'Haggerty, the governess; but every word she utters in her new character is picked up like pearls and diamonds, and every caprice admired. Lady Morgan, delighted to pay any outstanding debts of insolence, slight or absurdity she might hold against the real great ladies whom she met with; and the transformation of Miss O'Haggerty, the governess, to the Duchess of Belmont, is very amusing and well managed. The hero is not a traitor, but a very charming Irish gentleman *pur sang*, whose fortunes had fallen below his merits, and the Duchess is his good angel, who incites him "to be not afraid to take his fortune up." After much romantic incident, in the course of which he narrowly escapes being hanged, he marries the Duchess, regains the estate of his ancestors, and all ends happily. In the first sketch of her novel, O'Donnel was actually hanged, and Lady Morgan wrote such a moving account of the execution, that it drew tears from her own eyes. An old friend to whom she read it, said, wiping her eyes, " Yes, my dear, it is very beautiful, but I will never open the book again, it makes me too miserable. Don't hang him." Lady Morgan profited by the advice, and every reader of the novel will rejoice that she changed his fate.

O'Donnel retains its freshness to the present day. Any one wishing to read a novel which shall produce that delightful feeling of dissipation which is supposed to make novel reading so dangerous (but which, alas, so few novels now-a-days succeed in inspiring), should read *O'Donnel*. The scope and design of the work are admirable. The Irish social questions of the day are very ably treated; and what was then more to the purpose, they were presented in an effective dramatic shape, so as to be intelligible to the most careless reader.

O'Donnel had a success exceeding that of *The Wild Irish Girl*. The *Quarterly* reviewed it as bitterly as it had reviewed *Ida of Athens*, being exceedingly indignant at the audacity of the social and political truths contained in it. The reader who remembers the incident of the white satin shoes will be amused at the ceremonious assurance of his high consideration with which Lord Hartington, now become Duke of Devonshire, acknowledges the dedication of *O'Donnel.*

The Duke of Devonshire to Lady Morgan.

DEVONSHIRE HOUSE,
February 17, 1814.

MY DEAR MADAM,

Your letter was sent after me into the country, which must be my apology for my apparent delay in answering it, and in assuring you how very much gratified I am by your kind remembrance and attention in dedicating your new work to me.

It will not, I hope, be long before I have the pleasure of reading it.

Believe me, my dear Madam,
 Your Ladyship's sincere and
  Obliged servant,
   DEVONSHIRE.

CHAPTER IV.

FIRST VISIT TO FRANCE—1815-1816.

In the year after the publication of *O'Donnel*, the continent being now open, Sir Charles and Lady Morgan went to Paris to see the country under the restored *régime*, and of course to write a book about it. They took with them letters of introduction, and they were admitted into Parisian society of every shade of politics. They saw all the most noted men of literature and science, and the women whose beauty, fashion, or talent for intrigue, had made them queens of society. As a picture of the feelings and passions which were struggling and seething underneath the restored *order*, her work on France is vivid and true. She paints the contradictions struggling to assert themselves—the ill-suppressed minority—the ignorant and limited prejudices of the Bourbon party; the oppressions, and triumphs, and disgusts, are all exhibited as in a kaleidescope;—for she went from Bourbon *soirées*, where the company were singing "Vive le roi quand même," to salons where the return of "*l'autre*" was still hoped for and expected. She formed a friendship with Madame Patterson Bonaparte, with Madame de Genlis, with Dénon the famous Egyptologist, and with Lafayette. Both she and Sir Charles were intimate with the Comte de Segur; the Abbé Gregoire; with the Comte de Tracy, the idéologiste; with Cuvier. The women who made society as brilliant as the hues of the feathers on a pigeon's breast, or the glancing of diamond dust, initiated her into the feminine coquetries and fascinations of toilettes, and took her to see the *trousseau* of the Duchesse de Berri. Lady Morgan was admired and *fêted*, and received all the intoxicating homage of a Parisian success. The notes and letters sent to her would be invaluable as models of graceful phraseology and precious as autographs, and must have been delightful to receive; but the mere printed transcript of these airy trifles would not interest the general reader. Very different, however, is the case with the correspondence of Madame de Genlis and Madame Patterson Bonaparte. These women belong to history; they lived with kings and princes, with philosophers and artists; there is about them the light of courts and palaces; a perpetual curiosity and romance.

Poor old Madame de Genlis! In her "grande" solitude one wonders if it were in her own "Palace of Truth;" but no,—if we recollect aright, *that* palace Madame de Genlis declared to be uninhabitable for mortals, and it was demolished to point the moral of the tale! One is glad to catch a glimpse of the mother of Pamela for the sake of the tales with which she delighted our youth. Pamela, as everybody knows, married Lord

Edward Fitzgerald, and Pamela's daughter was the charming Lady Guy Campbell, a great friend of Lady Morgan's, and still extant.

Madame de Genlis to Lady Morgan.

CONVENT OF THE CARMAELITES,
RUE DE VAUREGARD, PARIS,
June 8, 1816.

The name of the author of such charming works is as well known to Madame de Genlis as it ought to be; although she lives in a great solitude she will be charmed to know personally her, the sentiments of whose soul she already loves and adores. She will have the honour to let her know if her health and mode of life will permit her to pay a visit to Lady Morgan. As Madame de Genlis is living in a religious house, she cannot receive visitors in the evening. Any way, she will not be at liberty on Wednesday next, but would be very happy if Monday or Tuesday would be convenient to Lady Morgan. It seems to Madame de Genlis that Thursday is a very distant day. She entreats Lady Morgan to accept her thanks. It is Madame de Genlis who would have been the first to solicit the favour of seeing Lady Morgan, if she had known she was in Paris.

One of the most remarkable of the acquaintances made by Sir Charles and Lady Morgan during their visit to France was with Madame Jerome Bonaparte, the American wife of the Emperor's brother, whom he had abandoned in a cruel and dastardly way. The lady, however, was not of the *pâte* out of which victims and martyrs are made; she was a woman of high spirit, and held her difficult and painful position with a scornful courage, that excites a deep pity for the woman's nature so cruelly scathed and outraged. Her letters to her friend will be read with interest. They are clever, *mordants* and amusing; but the bitter sense of wrong cannot be concealed.

Madame Patterson Bonaparte to Lady Morgan.

Paris,
September 23, 1816.

My dear Lady Morgan,

You have not written me a line since your departure. I hope you have not forgotten me, as I admire and love you more than any one else. I have been to see Dénon and Madame D'Houchin; they are both your adorers, and express the greatest affliction at your departure. The most agreeable thing you could do for your friends would be to return as quickly as possible. The French admire you more than any one who has appeared here since the Battle of Waterloo in the form of an English woman. The Princess of Beauveau has been to see me, and is very kind *à mon égard* as well as very judicious in admiring and loving you. Countess Rumford saw me at our minister's, invited me to a *soirée*, and came to see me. I get on very well now, but my health has been very bad since I have lost the pleasure of your society. I suffered for two weeks more than I can express from the pain of my teeth. Mrs. Marton is still in the figurative style. Her imagination is as fertile as ever, and as I am matter of fact, I avoid her society as much as possible. A friend of hers told me you had treated her harshly; I replied, "Lady Morgan has too much sense to be imposed upon, and too much truth to encourage falsehood in others; and as she had her choice of society in Paris, it was unnecessary for her to pass over impertinence in any one. That the Marton might derive pleasure and instruction from your society; but that you could gain nothing from hers." I have not seen her since, so suppose her friend related my observations. Gerard goes on as usual and talks a great deal of you. I have been there once since your departure.

Dénon has promised me an engraving of you. The Esmenards say he has not done you justice.

Baron Humboldt was at Madame Rumford's the other night. I met Mrs. Popkins at a *soirée* at Mrs. Curzon's, where was Lady Oxford who has been twice to see me since. *Fashions* continue the same. Mrs. Popkins was afraid to look at me, for reasons which you know. Every one talks of the work which you are to publish, and great expectations are formed from it. I tell every one, that I do not know what will be in it; but that I suppose it will be worthy of you. They say you are devoid of all affectation or pedantry, and that you assume less in society than any one ever did who possessed so much reputation. In short, I can assure you with truth, that I never heard any one so eulogised as you are in Paris.

I meet Madame Suard every week at Madame Rochefaucauld's. She does not condescend to take great notice of me; I suppose because she thinks I could not understand her wit, which, by the way is rather *obsolete*. My friend Miss Clagston is coming from Cheltenham to enliven my solitude this winter; I am so often ill, and my spirits are so much affected by the state of my health, that the presence of some one who loves me would be a great source of comfort. My dear Lady Morgan, you must write me sometimes to let me know how you and Sir Charles are, and what you are doing. I shall do myself the pleasure of writing you *de temps en temps*, although I was afraid of writing to Miss Sweeney; my style not being *recherché* enough for such a *bel esprit* as she is. Adieu.

Believe me ever,
Most affectionately yours,
E. Patterson.

My best love to Sir Charles. Madame La Rochefaucauld desires to be remembered to you. We had a ball at Mrs. Gallatin's. I wish you had been there. I shall give you all the news.

Madame Patterson Bonaparte to Lady Morgan.

PARIS, No. 14, RUE CAUMARTEN,
November 28, 1816.

DEAR LADY MORGAN,

I have had the pleasure of receiving your agreeable letter of the 29th of October, and have executed all your commissions except that *auprès de* Madame de Genlis. I have been so unwell and occupied with moving my lodgings and receiving my friend Miss Clagston, that it has been quite impossible for me to visit the penitent at the Carmelites, however, I shall certainly go to her or write her, you may be assured. Your fairy prince, the dearest little prince in the world, has been enchanted at your recollection of him, and charges me to tell you everything that is true and agreeable for him. He means to go to Dublin in the spring, and intends writing to you—bientôt en attendant ce qui arrivera d'ici au printemps. La princesse m'a chargée de vous remercier de ce que vous avez ecrit à son égard et de la conserver dans votre souvenir. In fact, if I were to write all that your admirers and friends tell me, I should never put my pen down. Madame D'Houchin, the Gerards, &c., desire me to talk to you of them, and all think it quite absurd for you to leave Paris. I meet the Beauveaus at Madame Rumford's every week, when there is an assemblement of *gens d'esprit*, not that I mean to call myself one of them; however, people say

I am very good, and that is my passport to these re-unions. Madame Rochefaucauld sees company every Tuesday, when I meet Madame Suard, who is *tout autre chose que bonne.* Madame de Villette begs to be remembered to you, and always says, " pour cela, ma chere, Milady Morgan a beaucoup d'esprit et beaucoup de naturel." I have been asking after the *Novice of St. Dominic,* but it has not been seen by any of your friends, yet. The *Missionary* every one knows, *par cœur.* Your work on France is anxiously expected, and if it is what every one supposes it will be, as nothing mediocre can come from you, all those who love you will be highly gratified. Your " Muse of Fable" has gone from Paris to make mischief in some other place, and to torment her Jerry Sneak *comme à l'ordinaire.* They say she throws her shoes at his head, and tells him an old husband must bear every thing from a young wife, particularly such a beauty and wit as she is. Mrs. Marshall has another child; I told her she was a great favourite of yours, and that the " Muse of Fable" was unworthy her regard. Miss Clagston is at present staying with me, which renders my time more pleasant.

By the way, although I sent my love to Mr. North, I was very angry with him; he wrote me once after I saw him at Cheltenham, to which I very goodnaturedly replied, and he never gave himself the trouble to acknowledge the reception of my letter. Lady Falkener, a very bad person and a great *intrigante,* wanted to marry an old maiden sister to him, and fancied that he liked me better, in consequence of which she tormented me terribly. How is that delightful person, Miss Bessey S.? your *soi-disant* friend, who fancied that you preferred her society, and that Mr. North was in love with her. I cannot forget her ugly face and absurd pretensions, and never think of her without laughing immoderately.

Dear Lady Morgan, I have been very ill and very *triste, tout m'ennuie dans ce monde et je ne sais pas pourquoi,* unless it be the recollection of what I have suffered. I think the best thing for me to do is to return to my dear child in the spring; I love him so entirely, that perhaps seeing him may render my feelings less disagreeable. I hate the *séjour* of America, and the climate destroys the little health which has been left me; but any inconveniences are more supportable than being separated from one's children. How much more we love our children than our husbands—the latter are sometimes so selfish and cruel, and children cannot separate their mothers from their affection.

I have seen all the persons who interest you since the reception of your letter, except Monsieur Dénon; but Madame D'Houchin has seen what you have written, and will tell him everything. Adieu; write me sometimes, I entreat you, and believe me truly and affectionately

Yours, E. P.

PS.—I hope Sir Charles does not forget me, and beg him to accept my best wishes and recollections. I am going to Madame La Rochefoucauld's, with whom you are so great a favourite, this evening.

After her return from Paris to Kildare Street, and while engaged in preparing her work on France, Lady Morgan kept up a brief correspondence with many of the political personages whom she had met. She sent one of her books—most likely the *O'Donnel*—to Lafayette, who was then living a patriarchal life amid his children and grandchildren at his chateau La Grange. He had seen so much in his time from the first American war downwards, had been a courtier in the brilliant society of the old *régime*, a favourite with Marie Antoinette, whom he had helped in her whim to go to the *bal de l'Opera*, had been mixed up in so many great events, and he had rubbed against so many great men, that in the latter days, one would have expected him to be a master figure himself; wise both in old experience, and with the wisdom that comes after events; but he just missed being a great man. He was thoroughly honest and good, but not of a sufficiently large type to fill his space on the canvas.

M. Lafayette to Lady Morgan.

La Grange,
October 30, 1816.

Your letter of the 21st September, dear Miladi, has been received in our colony with a sentiment which could only be surpassed by the happiness of receiving yourself. I am equally proud and happy at your partiality for our towers and for their inhabitants, whose distant admiration for you has become tender and confiding. Your short sojourn here has left an impression upon us which makes us proud of corresponding with you, and we hope to receive another visit soon; and we comfort ourselves with the pleasant thought that you have made us a promise; already we are beginning to look about to see what would please you when you come.

We show less philosophy than you about the misfortune for which we were already very sorry before we knew how much worse it was. It is vexing to think that the work which fulfilled so perfectly the expectations of your friends, should have been for you alone the occasion of a disappointment. The copy you had the goodness to send to me has not come to hand. I expect it with great impatience.

I see that you have much amusement in retracing the articles of the last royal ordinance upon the physiognomics of your different friends. The party that you have left pretty well united, finds itself cut in two, like a polypus, and makes two distinct bodies, which make grimaces at each other, *en attendant*, the moment to eat each other up. The friends of Legitimacy, however, must not confound themselves by making part of a body of a different nature. Your acquaintances of the *salons* will be able to tell you that the ministerialists are the constitutionalists of '89; it is a calumny to impute to them that they would use force. The others do not share their moderation. It is with the impartiality of a true patriot that I ought to seek to render justice to all. There are, nevertheless, in the new chamber, some of my friends whom I cannot speak of with so much catholicity. It is not down in our country seats, it is in the *salons* that you will hear the reports of this civil war. M. de Chateaubriand is become the champion of Ultraism. Since the publication of his last work he has grown ten feet higher. I rather like to see the Ultras making a refuge for the ministers by putting forwards the liberal principles which we have been preaching to them in vain for the last thirty years. All these undulations alter nothing of the depths of things; let us try to turn everything to the profit of liberty. I am only speaking now of the underminings and *tracasseries* of the society of the *salons*. See! I am also doing a little in politics myself! You know that very few of our summer days have the inconvenience of heat, therefore I pity you for your walk; the rains are dreadful here; we are afraid we shall have great losses in our harvest. The bread is bad and dear—a franc for a four pound loaf. Our sheep suffer also from the damp herbage this year. Mine, however, about which you are good enough to inquire, have not suffered so much. You see that we here have also complaints to make, besides other misfortunes, the impression of which is too deep to be complained about. The two last years of war have taken away from our peasantry the provisions which would have enabled them to meet this year of dearth; but they have, in the course of the revolution made a provision of energy and good sense, which makes them stronger and more enlightened under the strokes of fortune than they would have been thirty years ago. We sympathise with all our heart with the misfortunes

of your brave compatriots, so worthy of a better fate.
We must hope that their neighbours will occupy themselves in finding out and developing the good qualities they possess.

My daughters, my grandchildren and all the generations here desire to offer you the expression of their gratitude and attachment, which sentiments animate all the inmates of La Grange. Believe me, my dear lady, I join with them in the renewal of the tender and respectful homage with which I am

Your devoted,
LAFAYETTE.

While the book on France was growing under Lady Morgan's hands, a very sharp battle was being fought for it between author and publisher. Mr. Henry Colburn, a young man whose fortunes were still to be made, had brought out *O'Donnel*, and had done very well with it; that story was already in a third edition, and Lady Morgan was pressing him very ardently for a further share in the profits of her success. For *France* he offered her seven hundred and fifty pounds. She thought the sum too little, insisting on, at least, a thousand pounds. In the fear of losing his bargain, Colburn raised his price, as will be seen. In the next letter, from the pen of this London bibliopole, occurs the first notice of the establishment of the *Literary Gazette*, which was to form a new era in literature; of course the "new epoch" to him meant another vehicle for announcing his own publications.

II. *Colburn to Lady Morgan.*

LONDON,
December 19, 1816.

DEAR MADAM,

I am just returned from the city, and have scarcely time to save the post, and say that I really considered the offer I made you handsome, and as liberal a one as in common prudence could be made under the particular circumstances. Without seeing the contents, which certainly promised well, I naturally expected the most interesting work on the subject that has appeared; but however excellent and *original*, you perhaps have no idea how great a disadvantage to the sale is the number of works on the same topic that has *already appeared*.

I should indeed be sorry that you should be compelled to arrange with any other bookseller, and whatever *apparent* advantage there may be in publishing with any other, I am very confident, on a proper *balancing*, of its *being in my favour*. No one bookseller, I am certain, takes the tenth part the pains I do in advertising, and in *other* respects I do not think any one will *in future*, cope with me, since, from January next, I shall have under my sole control *two journals*, viz., the *New Monthly*, which flourishes as well as possible in England, and my new forthcoming *weekly* literary journal, which is to be sent *free by the post* instantly all over the country like a *newspaper*, and to foreign parts. It is to be called *The Literary Gazette and Journal of the Belles-Lettres*. The publication will form a new epoch in literature; it will please and astonish the public by its novelty, and cut up the sale of my rival reviews and journalists by the *novelty* of its plan; the VALUE of its contents, and the *preferable mode of publication—thirteen* numbers for one of the Quarterly! but more of this anon, in my prospectus.

To conclude at once, though at a really great risk, I will consent to undertake to pay the one thousand pounds, and on my *honour* if it succeed better than expected, I will *consider myself accordingly your debtor*, BESIDES making up to you the other *fifty pounds* on *O'Donnel* that you may no longer regret the third edition.

That I may make arrangements accordingly, I will beg your ultimatum by return of post. I am obliged to conclude,

Being, dear madam,
Yours, very truly,
H. COLBURN.

Colburn's offer, as amended, was accepted, and the work went on, with some delays and hitches in its progress, the chief one of all being the illegibility of Lady Morgan's MS., which Colburn plaintively mentions more than once. There was also great delay in sending the proofs, as it is incidentally mentioned that the post only went three times a week. Colburn spared neither pains nor expense to make the work perfect, employing a careful scholar to read Lady Morgan's careless proofs, and to edit them.

Sir Charles Morgan contributed several chapters

to the work on France, embodying his observations on the state of medical science, political economy, and French jurisprudence, both as it existed in that day and as it had been at the period of the Revolution. These chapters are valuable, but somewhat too heavy for the slighter and brighter portions of Lady Morgan's own share of the work.

CHAPTER V.

PUBLICATION OF FRANCE—1817.

On the 17th of June, 1817, Colburn wrote to Lady Morgan announcing that *France* was published, and that she was finely off, meaning on the swelling tide of his boat puffs and preliminary paragraphs. The first edition was in two volumes, quarto; and Colburn expressed his firm assurance of being able to sell the whole of this first edition by the first of July.

The work on France made a great sensation It was so long since France had been open to the English, that it was fresh ground to that generation; indeed, it wore a new face to all the world; for the restored France of 1816 was a different world to what had been the France of the old *régime*, or the France of the Consulate and the Empire. Lady Morgan's work was seized upon with avidity by readers of all classes, and provoked criticism as diverse as there were shades of opinion about Legitimacy, Bourbonism, Liberalism, and the Orthodox anti-Jacobin Church and State true blue intolerant Toryism.

The clamour of abuse was enough to have appalled a very stout heart. The praise and admiration, though quite as hearty, came from a less influential party. Lady Morgan was so thoroughly sincere in her liberal opinions that she did not at all realise the horror and obloquy her opinions caused. She had also the support and countenance of her husband, whom she both loved and reverenced; this was a protection and shelter which defended her from the storm to which she was exposed. The party critics treated her opinions as synonymous with all that was irreligious, unwomanly and detestable.

The work itself, which provoked all this clamour, is extremely brilliant and clever; the sketches of manners, opinions and people, are bright, vivid, and touched in with a life and vigour that impresses the reader with their truthfulness. The sketches of the French peasantry are excellent and graphic; her own experiences amongst the Irish peasants gave her a practical insight into the general conditions of this class. The notices of French society, both Royalist and Bonapartean, are charming and sparkling. She had keen perceptions, and admirable powers of narrative; but in *France*, her wit, for the first time in her published works, touches on flippancy, and she allows herself to expatiate, with more complacency than good taste, on the compliments and attentions she received. A Parisian *succès de société* such as she had achieved, was enough to turn the head of any woman, and especially of an Irish woman.

It was a pardonable vanity; but it gave her enemies a handle against her. It was easy to make "a hit, a very palpable hit," at her careless self-revelations of vanity; but the adverse party were blind and clumsy in their abuse, and in their zeal outran all truth and discretion. A more moderate style of abuse would have done Lady Morgan more injury with her public, though it might have been less injurious to herself. She was fed on flattery and detraction; and she had to receive both, without any of the mitigating influences which usually interpose between the giver and the receiver. If she were coarsely abused, she was as coarsely flattered to her face; and those who in later life observed her, could trace the scars of these long bygone years. Her notoriety was beyond what any other woman has ever had to endure "who kept her fame." That this notoriety had a scathing and deteriorating influence, cannot be denied; but in the heat of so much party scandal no aspersion was ever cast upon her personal character and prudent conduct as a woman.

The *Quarterly* assailed Lady Morgan in an article which has become almost proverbial for its virulence and bitterness. That article was eminently unjust; it was far-fetched in its criticism and unfair in its conclusions.

Lady Morgan was rather proud than otherwise of the commotion it made; and she amply avenged herself by putting John Wilson Croker, who had the credit of writing it, into her next novel, *Florence Macarthy*,—the novel being at least as likely to live and circulate as the article.

The following *jeu d'esprit* from the pen of her sister,

Lady Clarke, is an amusing and not unfair version of this once famous and formidable article.

> The book we review is the work of a woman,
> A fact which we think will be guessed at by no man,
> Who notes the abuse which our virulent rage
> Shall discharge on its author in every page.
> And who is this woman—no *recent* offender,
> A Jacobin, Shanavest, Whiteboy defender.
> SHE who published "O'DONNEL," which (take but our word)
> Is a monstrous wild "tissue of ALL THAT'S ABSURD"—
> Indeed there's a something in all her romances,
> Which, to tell our opinion, does not hit our fancies.
> No, give us a novel, whose pages unfold
> The glories of that blessed era of old,
> When Princes legitimate trod on the people,
> And the Church was so *high* that it out-topped the steeple;
> No, give us some Methodist's maudling confusion,
> RELIGION in SEEMING, in FACT, PERSECUTION;
> Some strange Anti-Catholic orthodox whining,
> At this age of apostacy wildly repining!!
>
> This WOMAN!—we scarce could believe when we read.
> Retorts all the charges we heaped on HER head;
> And leads to rebellion young authors, by shewing,
> That calling *hard names* is by no means *reviewing*.
> She boasts that we've not spoilt her market in marriage,
> That vainly her morals and wit *we* disparage;
> But surely that man is the boldest in life,
> Who, in spite of our ravings, could take her for wife;
> And therefore we now set him down without mercy
> As the slave of enchantment, "THE VICTIM OF CIRCE."
>
> Now to come to the matter in hand—we advance
> 'Tis "AN IMPUDENT LIE," when she calls her book "FRANCE;"
> A title that would not be characteristic,
> Unless for a large Gazetteer or Statistic.
> For we hold that it is not allow'd in a work,
> To form our opinions by *Ex pede Herc*.
> She ought to have visited Lyons, Bordeaux,
> And peeped into Marseilles, and Strasburgh, and Meaux;

For though the design of the Congress miscarries,
And Jacobins kick against Louis—at Paris,
Though Freedom lies bleeding and chain'd *on the Seine*,
And the emigrants *there* mould the state upon Spain.
In the rest of the kingdom, for what she can tell,
The impudent jade, things may go mighty well.

Next comes her arrangement!—(when this we denounce
We must eke out our charge with a bit of a bounce;
And o'erlook the confusion which reigns in our head,
To charge it at once, on HER book in the stead)—
Of this book, my good readers, in vain you may hope
An account of its merits, its plan or its scope;
For the tale *she* relates does not chime with the view
Which *we* take of France in our *loyal review*.
And though we should rail till our paper were shrinking,
Alas! we should but *set the people a thinking*.
On the list of ERRATA 'twere better to seize,
For thence we may conjure what blunders we please.

These mixed with the few, which the best author makes,
In a work of such length, and *our own worse mistakes*;
With some equivocation, and some " *direct lies*,"
Of abuse will provide our accustom'd supplies;
Which largely diluted with loyalty rant,
With much hypocritical methodist cant,
Mis-quotations, mis-statements, distortions of phrase,
Will set the HALF-THINKERS (we judge) in amaze,
And this " WORK MOST AUDACIOUS," this " woman so mad,"
This compound of all that's presumptuous and bad—
(Tho' we should not succeed in repressing her book,
And the youth of our land on its pages still look,)
Will perceive, with her friends, midst the people of fashion,
That the *Quarterly* scribe's in a desperate passion.
Postscriptum—we'd near made a foolish omission,
And forgotten a slur on her Second Edition.
Though perhaps, after all, she may have the last word,
And reply to our " wholesome " remarks—by a Third—
And thus, like a sly and insidious joker,
The malice defeat of an *hireling* CROKER!!

Looking to the correspondence of Lady Morgan, we pick our pleasant way through heaps of the friendly and familiar letters which, in those days, softened the warfare in which she was engaged with her enemies, and particularly with the malignant countryman of her own who had once been her friend, and had possibly aspired to become her husband. We pass over many tempting notes—hearty, sympathetic, eloquent. Here, however, is something to arrest the eye from Alicia Lefanu, whose writings are ever welcome for her brother's sake and for her own.

Poor, graceful, gracious Mrs. Lefanu! ill in body, anxious in mind, and worried in addition with bad Memoirs of her brother, Richard Brinsley Sheridan!

Mrs. Lefanu to Lady Morgan.

Ash Wednesday,
February 19, 1817.

Many thanks, dear Lady Morgan, for your frequent and kind inquiries. I am very ill, and hopeless of being better. My great anxiety about Joseph made me forget and neglect myself until severe pain forced me to resort to medical aid. A severe cold, caught on Christmas day, and great uneasiness of mind, have put me in a state of continual suffering.

I wish I was able to write any satisfactory account of my brother. Watkins's history of him and my family is a tissue of falsehood. What satisfaction could it be to him to write the life of a man whom he evidently hates and basely calumniates? Of my family history he knows nothing: he must be a very impertinent fellow to take the liberties he has done with a family he could know nothing of.

But S. White did worse; for he fabricated letters from my mother, &c., that she could not have written. He was the natural son of an uncle of my mother, who left him five hundred pounds, with which, and my father's assistance, he set up a school; but he never was acknowledged as our relation,—we never were boarded with him or placed under his care, &c., &c.,—all lies.

My mother's sketch of a comedy, unfinished, was put into my brother Richard's hands by my father at Bath, when we were resident there; but my father never even hinted that he had made any use of it in *The Rivals*. Of my own knowledge I can say nothing, for I never read it.

I hope your labours will soon be over and amply rewarded. Much is expected from you; and I trust you will not disappoint expectation.

Believe me, affectionately yours,
ALICIA LEFANU.

I beg my kind compliments to Sir Charles.

Our next letters are from Madame Patterson Bonaparte. With her airy manner, her beauty and her wit, she would have made an excellent princess, American as she was. One wonders that Napoleon should have been blind to her capabilities—he, whose motto was, the "tools to him who can use them." Mr. Moore is, of course, Tom Moore, the poet.

There is no need to draw attention to the passage on "the loves of the Duke of Wellington." Madame Bonaparte speaks of such things with the gaiety and ease of a perfect Parisienne.

Madame Patterson Bonaparte to Lady Morgan.

PARIS, *May* 8, 1817.

MY DEAR LADY MORGAN,

Your kind letter by Mr. Moore reached me, and I have been prevented replying to it by a variety of circumstances. My health has become worse than it has been, and they now say it is a disease of the liver, added to debility of lungs. I know not what it is, but I am very tired of suffering, and must make a journey to procure present relief.

All your friends are well and anxious about you as ever. Madame Suard makes many inquiries of you and your work. I go once, *par semaine*, to Madame Rochefaucauld, where I find the same society you left. It is impossible to see Madame D'Houchin, as the hours generally appropriated to visits are spent by her in sleep. She dines at half-past nine. M. Dénon has been good enough to see me sometimes, which I attribute to the partiality with which you distinguished me. I know nothing more flattering than your regard, and am very grateful, I assure you.

Madame de Villette is to me what she has always

been,—a constant friend. She is equally faithful in her admiration and love of you; and never speaks of you but in the way every one who is not envious must do.

France is the country you should reside in, because you are so much admired and liked here. No Englishwoman has received the same attentions since you. I am dying to see your last *publication*. Public expectation is as high as possible; and if you had kept it a little longer, they would have purchased it at your own price. How happy you must be at filling the world with your name as you do! Madame de Staël and Madame de Genlis are forgotten; and if the love of fame be of any weight with you, your excursion to Paris was attended with brilliant success. I assure you, and you know I am sincere, that you are more spoken of than any other person of the present day. Mr. Moore seldom sees me,—I did not take with him at all. He called to show me the article of your letter which mentions the report of the Duke of Wellington's *loves*. I am not the Mrs. —— the great man gives as a successor to Grassini.

You would be surprised if you knew how great a fool she is, at the power she exercises over the Duke; but I believe that he has no taste *pour les femmes d'esprit;* which is, however, no reason for going into extremes, as in this case. He gave her an introduction to the Prince Regent, and to every one of consequence in London and Paris. She had, however, no success in France, where her not speaking the language of the country was a considerable advantage to

her, since it prevented her nonsense from being heard.
Do not tell what I have written to you of this affair,
since I should pass for malicious and unfriendly towards my compatriot and relation. She writes, too,
all the paragraphs you may have seen in the newspapers; and might revenge herself by saying some
spiteful things of me through that channel.

The Prince de Beauveau asks me after you, and
has, I believe written you. They are all going to
Spa for the summer.

Madame de Genlis has had the daughter of the
Duke of Orleans confided to her care for the purpose
of education. I have heard this piece of intelligence,
for the authenticity of which I cannot, however, vouch.

I know not a single syllable of the political news of
France or any other country, nor do I even read the
gazettes at present. My bad health and *ennui* more
than occupy me, and deprive me of all interest in life.

Mr. Moore writes you everything you desire to
know of your friends here. He goes often to Mrs.
Bradshaw's. Have you seen the voyage of Madame
Clairvoyante?

Adieu, my dear Lady Morgan. Do not forget me.
Write me sometimes, and believe me ever most affectionately attached to you.

How is Sir Charles? Pray give my love to him,
and ask him what I must do to get well.

I shall write you a long letter when I am better.
I am confined to the house at present.

Mrs. the "Muse of Fable," has come back after a tour
to the south of France. Did you know she was in

love with De C——e last summer, and that she attended his levees very regularly for the purpose of captivating him? I fancy, however, he scarcely knew she was in his *salon*, or dreamed of the ravage he made on her heart. His *attentions* did not flatter very much, it appears, by her falling in love with another person since. I seldom see her at present. Adieu once more.

Yours truly,
E. PATTERSON.

Madame Patterson Bonaparte to Lady Morgan.

PARIS,
August 11, 1817.

DEAR LADY MORGAN,

Sir Charles's letter of which you inquire through Mr. Warden, was received by me a long time ago. Since then I have the pleasure of writing you a long letter with all the news of Paris. Your work on France has appeared through a French translation, in which they have suppressed what they thought best, and have arranged what they chose to give the public in the way best suited to their own purposes. I read it cursorily, in English, as the person who lent it me could permit me to keep it only six hours. It appeared to me, like everything you write, full of genius and taste. Its truths cannot at this moment be admitted here, but in all other countries it will have complete success. The violent clamour of the editors of the Paris gazettes proves that it is too well written; were it an insignificant production they would say less about it. They are publishing it in America, where your fame has been as much extended as in Europe, and where your talents are as justly appreciated.

I have not seen Madame D'Houchin and M. Dénon for a long time. My health obliged me to spend some weeks in the country and Madame D'Houchin you know, wakes when other persons sleep, which renders it impossible to enjoy her society without paying the price of a night's repose, and this to me is very difficult since I have lost my health. Your old friend and admirer, M. Suard, is dead of old age. I met him two weeks previous, at a party, where he enjoyed himself as much as any of us. His widow gave a dinner the day week after, because she was afraid of being *triste*, she said. Since then she receives as usual, and takes promenades on the Boulevards, because "bon ami m'a dit qu'il fallait vivre." Her friends are encouraged to flatter themselves, that her great sensibility will not kill her; at the same time that it induces her to give them parties and attend their *réunions*. She grieves in the most agreeable way to all those who find her house convenient or her society desirable.

Madame de Villette is exactly as you left her. Mr. Warden and herself are my neighbours for the present; I shall bid them adieu in six weeks.

My desire to see my child is stronger than my taste for Paris. I really am of your opinion, the best thing a woman can do is to marry. It appears to me that even quarrels with one's husband are preferable to the *ennui* of a solitary existence. There are so many hours besides those appropriated to the world, that one does not know how to get rid of (at least one like me has, who have no useful occupation), that I have sometimes wished to marry from *ennui* and *tristesse*. You never felt *ennui* in any state, because, when absent from society, you cultivate talents which will immortalize you. I know no person so happy as yourself. Madame de Staël died regretting a life, which she had contrived to render very agreeable in every way. Her marriage with Mr. Rocca is thought very superfluous. The liberal system she pursued through life forbids us to attribute other motives to her last matrimonial experiment,—unless that of tranquillizing the conscience of her young lover may be added. All her most intimate friends were ignorant that a marriage existed, and unless her Will had substantiated the fact, would have treated her marriage ceremony as a calumny. Marrying a man twenty years younger than herself, without fortune or name, is a ridicule in France, *pire qu'un crime*. Her son, by him, is called one of her posthumous works. What think you of the *Manuscript of St. Helena* being attributed to her and Benjamin Constant? Is it possible to carry absurdity and the desire of rendering her inconsistent further? I have heard persons gravely assert that she wrote it.

Adieu, my dear Lady Morgan; do not forget me when I shall be at a greater distance from you. Your recollection accompanies me to the New World, where I wish I may meet any one half as agreeable. My son is like you; they write me he is *pétri d'esprit*, and promises to develope great talents. I believe *difficilement* that any good awaits me, because I am constantly disappointed and distressed. Do you think it easy to judge of the future capacity of a boy of twelve years? I fear he may not justify what his teachers now predict of him, and that after exciting my hopes he will become like the generality of people, *médiocre* and tiresome. I hope Sir Charles likes me always, and that my most *affectionate* regards will be accepted with as much pleasure as I offer them through you. How is the *bel esprit*, Bess Sweeney? She was a successful impostor with many persons in Cheltenham, where she passed herself for your friend, for a wit, and for the object of Mr. North's preference, all at the same time. She was a lofty pretender.

Yours, affectionately and sincerely,
E. P.

PS.—Write me addressed to my banker here. After my departure, Warden will send you my address, *dans l'autre monde*.

The next letter is from Lady Charleville. The letters of Madame Bonaparte and Lady Charleville are in as great a contrast as the writers in their personal appearance, characters and fortunes. Lady Charleville was large, stately, and imposing, with magnificent grey eyes, a courtly, formal manner, and a deeply-toned voice, which made her most trifling observations impressive—rendered all the more so by her habit of addressing every one as "Ma'am," or "Sir." Madame Bonaparte was fair, dodu, and piquant, with particularly beautiful arms. She had

been flattered and spoiled—the idol and queen of her
native city, Baltimore. She made a brilliant marriage
with the brother of the First Consul, then on the
point of becoming Emperor; but instead of sharing
the rising fortunes of her young husband, she had
been subject to the bitterest insult and outrage that
could be offered to a woman. Her marriage was
broken; her child made illegitimate; her prospects
in life killed; and she herself, stripped of her husband's protection when little more than a girl, flung
upon the world to sink or swim as she could. It is no
wonder that her letters bear the impress of a life run
to waste, and a heart turned to bitterness. Napoleon
trampled down many things in his march through life,
but the ravage made in the hearts and souls of those
whose interest stood in the way of his plans, was more
cruel and fatal in their effects than the mere loss of
life and limbs on his fields of battle.

Lady Charleville's letters, like those of Madame
Bonaparte, contain some of the news going about
society, but none of the scandal of the period; there
is an absence of the cruel keenness and bitter dissatis-
faction—one might almost call it jealousy—that mark
similar topics in the letters of Madame Bonaparte.
Lady Charleville's life had been that of an invalid,
and, in other respects, not free from the ills that
every one born of woman is heir to in this world.
When she was a young woman—not more than thirty
—she lost the use of her limbs, and during the re-
mainder of her life had to be carried or wheeled
about in a large chair. Never being seen, except

sitting, she had the appearance of a queen upon her throne. It will be seen from the following letter, that her strictures on men and morals were as dignified as her appearance. Whatever personal news may come to light in these old letters, is so old that it has now become historical, and merely illustrates the spirit of the time. If there be any survivors, we can only quote Lady Teazle, and say, that "Scandal, like death, is common to all."

Lady Charleville had been a steady protectress to Lady Morgan when she needed friends, and was her admirer now she had obtained a distinguished position in the eyes of the world. Madame Bonaparte's friendship for Lady Morgan was more for her own sake. She found in her a friend with some substance of character, and one who could sympathize with the romantic discomforts of her position.

Lady Charleville to Lady Morgan.

14, TERRACE, PICCADILLY,
November 24, 1817.

I never was more pleased to hear from you, dear Lady Morgan, than in the receipt of yours of 27th of October, as the explanation you gave me of Perney's name sliding (through natural confidence in a decent man's catalogue) into your work, did away a cruel prohibition of the higher powers, who, on their arrival at Worthing, said they knew that author to have written only indecent blasphemy! and that they who approved of it could not be my correspondent. Thank God, you did not do so; such a heart and such talents as yours should not be exposed through the idle vain-glory of seeming to have read everything, to so dreadful an imputation; and it is in the fulness of goodwill and admiration for your talent, which is superior and *improving every year*, that I rejoice all these stern readers can now say is, that you relied too hastily on the bland and decent manners of Frenchmen, and could not conceive, with a pure and honest heart, that any one could recommend an unvarnished tale of indecency to your consideration. Lord Charleville says this wicked man has *never* written but against religion and decency, and that one line of his principal work contains more shocking impiety than the folios of all the encyclopedists; he will not allow that Voltaire's *Pucelle* (giving it up as a work too free, yet rather calculated for the Romish abuses of religion than to impugn the basis of all), or Chaucer's loose tales, should do away their fame, since Voltaire's other works are highly beneficial to mankind, and highly moral; and, at least, old Geoffrey, though a libertine, is not an impious one! The parallel, therefore, he thinks unjust, and yet he would wish, in praising either Voltaire or Chaucer, that a woman should mark something of disapprobation of the loose parts of their writings. Such is the result of all he said to me; and once more your letter of the 27th has set all to right again, and I trust in heaven that your warm and amiable feelings may no more be tortured by the disapprobation of good and stupid men, or the *slanders of ruffians*.

I received your letter of the 7th; you now know why it remained unacknowledged. I knew before I received it that Mr. Croker was the author of the article, in which, some say, he was assisted by Mr. Barrow, Secretary to the Admiralty; but of that I doubt, as hitherto this gentleman has kept to the investigation of science only. I am quite of your opinion that Mr. Croker deserves all the reprobation of candid, honourable men; but I don't think squibs will touch him—his mail of brass, and his heart of adamant secure him; and though I sincerely wish him every mortification, I don't see what can afford it to such a man. I sent the lines to Scotland * to some clever people, who think as I do, about the general merits of *France*. I am sure all the newspaper mention of it was in its favour, for people do love controversy. I hope the next edition may, somehow or other, do away with the mention of Perney's name! which is of more import than you can well believe in respect to society.

The Danish Ambassador, who speaks English as well as we do, said to me the other day, " We, in Denmark, cannot impeach Lady Morgan's politics as being dazzled with Napoleon!"

I agree in *toto* with your feelings of what true religion should be, " to visit the sorrower in affliction, and keep one's self unspotted from the world;" this, with a firm acknowledgment of the great truths of Christianity, would be the perfection of all doctrine!!! To persecute is horrible, and every species of protection

* See *ante*, p. 58.

that law, and liberty, and property inviolable, can bestow, is the indefeasible right of a subject of these realms; but what has that to do with the question of giving legislative rights to Romish persons, insomuch as their fatal superstition has established deism on the continent in all thinking men. We should dread and deplore to encourage a worship of such baleful effect; nor ever give them power to sap the foundations of a pure and holy form of worship, which, allowing of the finest system of ethics for our guide, requires no sacrifice of the understanding.

* * * * *

I have heard since I came into town yesterday, that Walter Scott has given *Rob Roy* to the press as his own, and says he has another novel ready. Sir J. B. Burgess is publishing *The Dragon Knight* (a poem epic). Mr. Ellis has disappointed all his friends by his dull narrative about China.

Sir William Gell is gone back to the Princess of Wales, and those anxious for her honour and security are glad of it, as the wretches in whose hands she is, have already contrived to load her with debt as well as dishonour.—She, who in England (dearer than in any other spot on the globe), did not leave a debt, and refused an augmentation of income. Mr. Brougham tried, but could not break the spell; but Gell has more power with her, and equal goodwill.

M. CHARLEVILLE.

Early in July, Colburn had sold the first edition of *France*, and, on July the 14th, wrote impatiently for the new preface, that he might bring out the second edition, which was to be in octavo. The preface was to explain how the same errors were in that as in the first. He says, "I have announced the work by numerous paragraphs and advertisements, and it shall be *well* advertised *everywhere*." Colburn had always more faith in his own advertisements for the success of a work than in the genius of the author. Since furnishing the work on *France*, Lady Morgan had been busy on a new Irish novel which she had now three-parts finished. Sir Charles had also written a scientific work in his own department. These they offered, in the first instance, to Colburn, who declared he would be charmed to publish them, as he considered "the solidity of Sir Charles would qualify the airy lightness and badinage of Lady Morgan;" but he wanted to have the MS. at a bargain, and offered a thousand pounds for the two. Lady Morgan resented the idea. She hated a bargain, except when she drove it for herself, and she threatened to go to some other publisher. Colburn complained that it would be a bad return for all his exertions, and there was a good deal of haggling, the result of which was that he agreed to give one thousand two hundred pounds for the two. This they accepted. Sir Charles's work has not remained in memory; but the novel, which Colburn called *Florence Macarthy*, is still read and admired.

It is not so romantic as *O'Donnel*; but it hits much harder upon the social and political abuses in Irish Government. In this book, Lady Morgan embodies her own views in the heroine, who is as wild, fascinating, romantic and extravagant as ever trod the stage of theatre or page of romance. Florence Macarthy appears always in disguise and masquerade —flits about like a will-of-the-wisp, mystifying everybody—setting the wrong to rights, "confounding the politics and frustrating the knavish tricks," of all who mean wrong to Ireland. Like all Lady Morgan's heroines, she is endowed with very little money, but no end of beauty, good sense, wit, and the representative of a real *ould* Irish noble family of decayed fortunes.

It is curious that whilst the story is wildly improbable, the accessories are all true, not only in spirit, but in the letter. The heroine, Florence Macarthy, has the mission, (self-imposed and followed, *con amore*) of arousing a charming young Irishman to a sense of what he owes to his country, and to stimulate his indignation against the oppressions and abuses especially crying for redress.

The sketches of character, the pictures of fashionable society in Dublin, the English fine ladies and dandies of the period, the Irish characters, both of the good and of the despicable class—in short, all the shades and varieties of the moral and social influences at work in Ireland at the time, are given with a subtlety and vividness which is wonderful; they are dashed off with vigour; they live, and move, and bear their truth to nature stamped upon them in every line. Mr. Crawley, the Castle hack, and all his tribe, the toadies and servile tools of Government, embody what were then the worst evils of English rule in Ireland. All the Crawley sketches are supreme and inimitable for the racy humour, the genuine fun Lady Morgan has thrown into their portraits. They are etched with a sarcasm that bites like aquafortis; but the humour tempers and mellows the malice. In this family sketch she paid her debt to Croker, who, rightly or wrongly, had the credit of being the author, not only of the attack on *France*, but of all the other assaults upon her in the *Quarterly*.

Lady Morgan was, before all things, an artist, and she did not hate Croker too much to be able to make him amusing to the general reader, who had no cause of offence against him. There was nothing impotent in her revenge; no wish to wound beyond her power to strike; the strokes of her weapon were clear, keen, incisive, and effectual. She got the laugh on her side; she left her critic transfixed on the point of her diamond pen, and she could afford to forgive him, for she had, as children say, "paid him off," and kept a balance in hand against the future.

In the end, the conversion of the hero is rewarded by marrying Florence Macarthy, whom he has loved hopelessly all along, and who has been at once his guardian angel, guide, philosopher, and friend. All Lady Morgan's novels are characterised by the same theatrical construction. Her theatrical descent and early associations account for her use of stage effects and melo-dramatic expedients. This love of mystery, disguise, and rapid changes of scene (for the heroines are all gifted, if not with ubiquity, at least with the power of being in one place in a miraculously short space of time, after having been seen in another, a long way off) give an element of romance to Lady Morgan's novels, which remove them from real life or "the light of common day." It perhaps enables readers to go patiently through political discussions and statistical details of the then existing state of things in Ireland, which otherwise would not have been tolerated, but it gives an air of trick and mannerism which, to say the best, is meretricious; but in spite of criticism and sober judgment, it makes them extremely entertaining.

CHAPTER VI.

OUT OF ENGLAND INTO FRANCE—1818.

LADY MORGAN was still engaged in completing *Florence Macarthy*, when Colburn went to press with it early in March, though it was not more than half finished. He had his own reasons for pressing forwards the publication. He had an idea. This idea was to follow up the success he had had with the work on *France*, by producing another of a similar class upon Italy.

In March, 1818, Colburn wrote to Sir Charles and Lady Morgan, proposing they should pay a visit to Italy that year, and write a work upon that country, similar in scope and design to the one that had been so successful on France; Lady Morgan to write the observations and sketches on men, manners, and the things worthy of note; Sir Charles contributing the chapters on the state of the laws, the influence of politics, and the condition of science and education. He offered them two thousand pounds for the copyright. They closed with the offer, and he wrote to thank them, declaring that their frank acceptance of his offer had put him in fresh spirits. He urged them to come to London immediately, to make their final arrangements. Sir Charles and Lady Morgan left Dublin rather earlier this year, bringing *Florence Macarthy* to be finished amid the brilliant bustle and distraction of a London season.

On their way to London Sir Charles and Lady Morgan remained one night at Holyhead, the spot she had so often visited when going to her old friend, Lady Stanley. The dear friend was dead, and here is Lady Morgan's record of her visit to the empty shrine.

"This is the first time I arrived at Holyhead without the hope of seeing dear Lady Stanley standing at her own gate, with Sir John on one side and Susanne on the other with her shawls and dog. The gates were now closed, and all looked gloomy and desolate."

Colburn had engaged rooms for them in Conduit Street, and they were soon surrounded by all the gaiety of London. Colburn was in high good humour, and so enchanted with *Florence Macarthy*, in reading the proofs, that in the enthusiasm of the moment he rushed out and bought a beautiful *parure* of amethysts, which he presented to Lady Morgan, as a tribute of admiration, and perhaps, with a little hope of keeping her in good humour. The whole of their stay in London and Paris, *en route* to Italy, has been minutely chronicled in the Odd Volume,* and there is no further need to allude to it. It was a pleasant season of visits and

* Published by Bentley, 1858.

friends, old and new; but Lady Morgan wrote to her sister—

"You are not to suppose we spend all our time in idleness, for we study hard in our different departments. I give an hour to Italian every morning, and have began a course of history, ancient and modern, to rub up my memory before touching classic ground."

Italy was not then the accessible holiday tour it has since become. There was enough of difficulty and adventure to give the journey a dash of the heroic to Lady Morgan's imagination, which loved to set all things in theatrical array.

Whilst in London she received the following letter from Madame Jerome Bonaparte. Madame Bonaparte had returned to America, where she must have found her position more irksome than in Paris, if her wrongs had not been too great to leave room for petty vexations.

Madame Jerome Bonaparte to Lady Morgan.

May 23, 1818.

My dear Lady Morgan,

I have not received a line from you since my arrival in America, which I regret more than I can express to you. I wrote you a very long letter describing the effect your work on France produced on its transatlantic readers. The demand was so great, that it went through three editions with us. I assure you that your reputation here is as familiar and as great as in Europe, where you are so justly admired. I wish

I could see and listen to you once more; but this, like all my desires, must be disappointed, and I am condemned to vegetate for ever in a country where I am not happy. My son is very intelligent, and very good, and very handsome—all these advantages add to the regret I experience at the destiny which compels me to lose life in this region of *ennui*. You have a great deal of imagination, but it can give you no idea of the mode of existence inflicted on us. The men are all merchants; and commerce, although it may fill the purse, clogs the brain; beyond their counting houses they possess not a single idea—they never visit except when they wish to marry. The women are all occupied in *les détails du ménage*, and nursing children—these are useful occupations, but do not render people agreeable to their neighbours. I am condemned to solitude, which I find less insupportable than the dull *réunions* which I might sometimes frequent in this city. The men being all bent on marriage do not attend to me because they fancy I am not inclined to change the evils of my condition for those they could find me in another. Sometimes, indeed, I have been thought so *ennuyée* as to be induced to accept *very respectable* offers; but I prefer remaining as I am to the horror of marrying a person I am indifferent to. You are very happy, in every respect, too much so, to conceive what I suffer here.

I have letters from Paris which say De Caze, the Minister of Police, is created a peer, and is to marry one of the Princesses de Beauveau, whom you know. *Qu'en pensez-vous?* It appears very strange to my *recollections* of the state of *political* feeling of the parties, but nothing is too surprising to believe of politicians. He is very handsome, at least, which is not a bad thing in a husband; they say, too, that he has talents, and great sensibility—of the last two I cannot judge, as I saw him only *en passant.*

Paris offers too many *agrémens*, too many agreeable recollections—among the latter you are my greatest—and I think with pain that I shall perhaps never see you again.

Mais cela n'empêche pas que je vous prie de lui dire —that I recollect him with pleasure and regret, and that I beg to be remembered to him. I suppose you will return to Paris, where I hope you will be happy and pleased; it is very easy to be pleased and happy in your situation, because every one is pleased with you, and you are loved whenever you choose to be so. The French admire you so much, that you ought to live with them. Suppose you were to come to this country; it is becoming the fashion to travel here and to know something of us, and I assure you that if you would spend some time here you might find materials for an interesting work—*de toutes les manières*, you would make any country interesting that you wrote about. I wish I could return to Europe; but it is impossible—a single woman is exposed to so many disagreeable comments in a foreign country; her life, too, is so solitary except when in public, which is not half the day, that it is more prudent for me to remain here; besides, I have at present only eleven hundred pounds a-year to spend, which you know make only twenty-five thousand francs—not enough to support me out of my own family, where I have nothing to spend in eating, or in carriages, rent, &c. I wish I could send my son to Europe for his education; I should prefer Edinburgh, but I know no one there to whom I could entrust him. I should write you more frequently were there any incidents in this dull place which might interest you, or any anecdotes that could amuse —there are, alas, none. I embroider and read, *pour me débarrasser de mon temps*—they are the only distractions left me. Do you remember the description Madame de Stael gives of the mode of life Corinna found in a country town in England, and the subjects of conversation at Lady Edgermon's table, which were limited to births, marriages, and deaths? I am so tired of hearing these three important events discussed, and my opinion of them has been so long decided, that it is a misery to be born and to be married, I have painfully experienced, without lessening my dread of death —so you may imagine how little relish I have for the conversation on these *tristes* topics, and how gladly I seek refuge from listening to it by retiring to my own apartment.

Adieu, my dear Lady Morgan—*il ne faut pas que je vous vous ennuye davantage.* Make my best love acceptable to Sir Charles, and ask him to think sometimes of me. Write to me, I entreat you. J'ai plus que jamais besoin de vos lettres pour me consoler de tout ce que j'ai perdu en vous quittant pour revenir dans mon triste pays. Have you a good college in Dublin? I might send my son there in two years, perhaps, as I cannot send him to France, and do not wish him educated in England, where his name would not recommend him to much favour.

I remain, most affectionately yours,
ELIZA PATTERSON.

A letter from Lady Morgan to her sister, written on their route to Paris, is a curious picture of what travelling was in comparatively modern times. We seem to be divided by a great gulf from those days,—as wide as that which separates us from the feudal times.

Lady Morgan to Lady Clarke.

CALAIS,
August 27, 1818.

Here we are, my dear love, after a tremendous expense at the hotel at Dover, where we slept last night, and embarked at twelve o'clock this morning, in a stormy sea. The captain remained behind to try and get more passengers, and the result was, that we remained tossing in the bay near two hours, almost to the extinction of our existence. In my life I never suffered so much. As to Morgan, he was a dead man. The whole voyage we were equally bad; and the ship could not be got into port,—so we were flung, more dead than alive, into a wretched sail boat, and how we got on shore I do not know. It rained in torrents all the time; but the moment I touched French ground, and breathed French air, I got well. We came to our old *auberge,* MM. Maurices, and the first place we got to was the kitchen fire, for we were wet and cold;— and really, in that kitchen I saw more beauty than at many of our London parties. Madame Maurice and her daughter, are both handsome women. We were obliged to have bedrooms opposite to the *auberge,* as it was quite full, but the house, Madame told us, belongs to "*maman.*" She is herself about fifty, so you may guess what "*maman*" is. She is *admirable*— a powdered head, three feet high, and souflet gauze winker cap. Our chamber-maid is worth *anything.* She is *not* one of the kitchen beauties, *par exemple;* but here she is—an ugly woman of seventy, in her chemise, with the simple addition of a red corset and a petticoat, several gold chains, and an immense cross of shiny stones on her neck, with long gold earrings, and with such a cap as I wore at a masquerade. With all this, her name is Melanie; and Melanie has beauty airs as well as beauty name. Whilst she was lighting our wood fire (for it is severely cold) I asked her some questions about the Mr. Maurice. You may guess what a personage he is, for she said—" Ah pour notre Mr. Maurice on ne parle que de lui—partout Madame on ne s'occupe que de notre Mr. Maurice." So much for Miss Melanie and *her* Mr. Grundy. We dined at the *table d'hôte.* We had an Englishman and his wife, and a Frenchman only, for our company. The Englishman was delightful. We had a capital table, with everything good, and in profusion; but the Englishman sat scowling, and called for all sorts of *English sauces,* said the fish was infamous, and found fault with everything, and said to the waiter—" What do you mean by your confounded sour mustard?" The poor waiter to all his remarks only answered in English, " How is dat, sar?" The Burgundy was " such d——d stuff." And the *last* remark, " Why, your confounded room has not been papered these twenty years," was too much for our good breeding; and we and the Frenchman laughed outright. Is it not funny to see our countrymen leave their own country for the sole *pleasure* of being dissatisfied with everything?

We leave this early to-morrow, and shall be in Paris the next day, please God. Lafayette is to come up for us to take us to his chateau; until, therefore, I learn the post town of *La Grange,* direct to the Hotel d'Orleans, where we shall go on our arrival in Paris. I feel myself so gay here already, that I am sure my *elements* are all French. A thousand loves, and French and Irish kisses to the darlings.

S. M.

The travellers passed through Paris and Geneva into Italy. In Florence, they met Tom Moore, then troubled with his leg. In Lady Morgan's papers is a little note which may be given for the sake of the story that follows.

Sunday night, October.

My dear Morgan,

This leg of mine seems inclined to turn out rather a serious concern, and the sooner I avail myself of your skill, the better. Can you make it convenient to call upon me soon after breakfast to-morrow morning?

Yours very faithfully,
THOMAS MOORE.

This "leg" had been an ill of long standing. Moore refers to it in several of his letters to his mother in the previous year.

Lady Morgan used to tell, in a very droll manner, a story about a visit that Sir Charles paid to Moore whilst he was laid up with the leg of which he complains in the preceding note. Moore was a good Catholic, or at least very orthodox in his opinions; Sir Charles was neither. On this occasion, after examining and prescribing for the leg, he sat down on the bedside and entered into a physiological and metaphysical discussion. Moore, for a time, sustained his part, until he became somewhat hardly pressed, when he exclaimed—

"Oh, Morgan, talk no more,—consider my immortal soul!"

"Damn your soul!" said Sir Charles, impatiently—"attend to my argument."

Argument was not the strong point in Moore.

Moore mentions this conversation; but does not make a story of it.

CHAPTER VII.

SOJOURN IN ITALY—1819.

THE ground mentioned in these letters has been constantly travelled over since; but there is a freshness and vitality in Lady Morgan's description which give it a peculiar charm. It is curious to contrast the changes that have come over travelling since those days.

Lady Morgan to Lady Clarke.

MILAN, ALBERTO REALE,
May 1819.

MY DEAR LOVE

By this I trust you have received my letter from Geneva,* which we left with difficulty and infinite regret. We had entreaties and invitations to remain for months to come, and as a temptation to bring us back, we have the offer of a house and garden on the

* Published in "Odd Volume."—*Bentley*, 1858.

Lake as long as we please to occupy it. We were
loaded with books and little presents at our departure,
and letters and notes of adieu, with the most flattering testimonies of esteem and even of affection. They
were all astonishment at what they termed *my simplicity*, as they expected to find me a learned lady at
all points. The day before we departed we dined with
the Prince or Hospodar of Wallachia, who is travelling
with his charming family of three generations, his
Prime Minister, and a number of his court! What I
would have given if you had seen us in the midst of
their turbans and beards! the Princesses and the sweet
little children speaking nothing but Greek, and con-
versing with me by signs, all dressed in Greek costume, and the servants in the beautiful Albanian dress!
The men speak French like Parisians, and we have
made up a great intimacy with Mavrocordato, the minister, who is young, handsome, and pleasant. The
women had eyebrows painted like a horseshoe down to
the nose. They set out for Italy the day after us, and
overtook us on the road with a suite of five carriages.
Our first day's journey from Geneva was through the
lovely valleys of Savoy to Chambery — the capital.
There we had letters, and found green peas, straw-
berries, and kind and enlightened people. Accompanied by learned librarians and professors, we visited
the public institutions, and what interested me more,
the town and country house of Madame de Warrens.
For the whole of our journey, so far, see Rousseau's
Confessions. Here we found my *France* better known
than in Ireland, for although it was *mise à l'Index*,

that is interdicted by the government with Madame de Staël's last work, I was assured that it was to be found in almost every house.

Having passed two or three days in Chambery, which is not much larger than Drogheda, we proceeded the next day through scenes of romantic beauty that defy all description. At a lovely Alpine village —Aquibelle, we were so delighted, that we made a halt, and made some delightful little excursions on foot, where no carriage could penetrate. Here the *snow mountains* rose closely on us. The next day's journey all appearances of spring gradually faded into a perfect winter, the horrible grandeurs of the Alps multiplied around us, and fatigued in spirits and imagination, we reached the dreary little village of Lanslebourg late in the evening, where all presented a Lapland scene, nothing but snow and ice, and a hurricane blowing from the mountains. We found at the foot of Mont Cenis, which we were to begin to ascend the next morning, an inn kept by a good little Englishwoman, and I believe, next to finding myself at your chimney corner, this truly English inn gave me the greatest pleasure I could feel. It snowed all night, and we began our ascent in a shower of snow, with four stout horses and two postilions dragging our light carriage. My imagination became completely seized as we proceeded, and I sat silent for near seven hours, my teeth clenched, my hands closed, my whole existence absorbed in the sublime horror that surrounded me. The clouds that form your sky were rolling at our feet, and the pinnacles of the mountains were confronted with the dark vapours which formed their Alpine firmaments in stormy weather. We had a slight glimpse of what they call "*la tourmente*," which obliges travellers to employ guides to hold down the carriage on each side to prevent its being carried away. We had three feet of snow under our wheels; but the road was otherwise fine. Such a noble work, such a monument of the mighty means and great views of Bonaparte! As we descended, a slow spring gradually opened on us, the snows were melting, the trees budding, and once arrived in the lovely plains of Lombardy, the same glowing summer presented itself we had left in the valleys of Savoy. We passed a day at the first Italian town we reached, Susa, at the foot of Mont Cenis, and with the old Governor, with whom we had a delightful scene. The next day we arrived at Turin—a pretty city of palaces—took a handsome apartment in the Hotel de l'Europe, and sent out our letters of presentation by our Italian *valet de place*. The next day the whole town of Turin was down on us. Some of the *corps diplomatique*, some of the ministers and officers of the Court, the Prussian Ambassador and Ambassadress, the Prince Hohenzollern, the principal physicians and professors;—all left their cards and offers of service. The Countess of Valpergua, one of the leaders of the *haute noblesse*, took us at once to herself, and without the least form or ceremony, told us that in the first place we must command her carriages, and horses, and her box at the opera. The night after our arrival she made a ball for us and introduced us personally to the whole Piedmontese *noblesse*. The palace Valpergua, was the first Italian great house I saw, and the suite of rooms we passed through that night were, I think, more spacious and numerous than the rooms of state at the Castle, though Madame Valpergua told me she had only opened half the suite. A few nights afterwards, the Prussian Ambassadress made a ball for us equally brilliant. She told me that she had lately been at Baden, and that the Princess of Baden, hearing I was travelling, was very anxious to see me and pay us every attention—that they had both spent a night crying over *The Missionary*. But what flattered us infinitely more, was the attention of the Count de Balbo, minister, who, as head of the University, gave orders that all the professors should attend to receive us. At the University, imagine my shame to see all the learned muftis in their robes, each in his department, receiving us at the doors of their halls and colleges. In the Cabinet de Physique, they prepared all sorts of chemical experiments for us, &c., &c. These poor gentlemen were under arms three days for us. I must give you one of our days at Turin. From nine to twelve, morning, we received visits from professors and *literati* who accompanied us to see the sights. Every one dined at two o'clock. Between four and five, regularly, the Countess Valpergua called for us in an open carriage, and we drove to see some villa near the town. By seven o'clock we were back for the Corso, where all the nobility drive up and down till the opera begins. From thence we went to a coffee-house and had ices, and then to the Opera, where, during the

whole night, visits were received, and everything was
attended to but the music; by eleven we were at home.
The Court was at Genoa; but the Master of the Ceremonies showed us the palace from top to bottom.

At last here we are, in the ancient capital of Lombardy, now under the government of the Emperor of
Austria, whose brother, the Arch-Duke Regnier, is the
lord-lieutenant here. Milan is a very fine city, and
as far as we have gone, a delightful residence for us.
The Count Confalonieri, and his lovely Countess, came
to us the moment of our arrival, and from that moment attentions, visits, friendship, and services on all
sides. Madame Confalonieri began by taking us to
the Corso, one of the great places of exhibition, and
introducing us at the Casino, where the nobility are
exclusive, and where even professional men are not
admitted, and then insisting on our considering her
opera-box as ours during our residence here. Thus
presented, our success was undoubted; but we found
it was already prepared for us by the eternal *France*,
and by Morgan's work in French, sent here from
Geneva.* Not only the liberal party have visited and
invited us, but the Austrian Commander-in-Chief and
his wife have been to see us, and we have spent an
evening there. We dined yesterday at the Count de
Porrio's, whose palace is celebrated for its Etruscan
vases, &c., &c. The Italian dinner is very elegant;
the table is covered with alabaster vases, flowers, fruit,
and all sorts of ornaments; the soups and meats, are

* Outlines of the *Physiology of Life*.

served on the side-table, cut up, and handed round by the servants, so all is kept cool and fresh—the great object of their lives here. From the only English residents here, we have received the kindest and most hospitable attentions. These are Lord and Lady Kinnaird, and Colonel and Lady Martha Keating.

The Opera-house is considerably larger than the Opera-house at London, and truly magnificent and imposing; but the stage only is lighted: the women go in great bonnets, and it is, therefore, by no means so brilliant or enjoyable as ours. The orchestra is immense, and the scenery, for beauty and taste, beyond what you can imagine; and the ballet the finest in Europe as a drama, though the dancing is bad; as soon as the ballet begins, every one attends. They have played one wretched opera for these forty nights back, for they don't change these entertainments ten times a year. Last night we had a new one brought out, and helped to damn it. God bless you all, dear loves, and send me safe back to you!

S. M.

Lady Morgan's descriptions remind one of Beckford's *Italy*, and the Italian novels of Mrs. Radcliffe; especially of some of the pages in the *Mysteries of Udolpho*. These scenes had not then been expounded by Murray's *Guide Books*, or hackneyed by "summer tourists." The freshness of "better days" still hangs over them!

Lady Morgan to Lady Clarke.

LAKE OF COMO, VILLA FONTANA,
June 26, 1819.

The attentions of the Milanese increase with our residence among them, and persons of all parties, Guelphs and Ghibellines, have united to pay us attention. The Ex-minister of the Interior made a splendid entertainment for us at his beautiful villa, as did the Trivulgia, and a Marquis de Sylvas, of whose villa and gardens there are many printed accounts. We were told there was no hospitality in Italy. We not only dined out three times a week on an average, but we have had carriages and horses so much at our service, that though we have made several excursions of twenty and thirty miles into the country, we never had occasion to hire horses but once, and that was to go to Pavia, where we spent a few days, and made the acquaintance of old Volta, the inventor of the voltaic battery. We went with the Count and Countess Confalonieri to see Monza, and its magnificent cathedral, where the iron crown of Lombardy is kept. The difficulty and ceremonies attending on this, convince me that the travellers (not even Eustace) who mentions so lightly having seen this relic, have never seen it at all. We had an order expedited the night before from the Arch-Duke to the chanoines of Monza, who received us in grand pontificals at the gates of the church, as did the Grand-Master of the imperial suite at the palace of Monza, where the Arch-Duke resides. We have also been to see the Grand Chartreuse, and in all my life I was never so entertained; but as to churches, and pictures, and public edifices, and institutions, my head is full of nothing else. To tell the truth, we became latterly quite overcome and exhausted by the life we led, for we never knew one moment's quiet, nor had time to do anything. We had been offered the use of two beautiful villas on the Lake of Como, for nothing; one of them, the Villa Someriva, one of the handsomest palaces in Lombardy. We left Milan ten days back, and have since lived in a state of enchantment, and I really believe in fairy land. I know not where to refer you for an account of the Lake of Como except to *Lady M. W. Montague's Letters*. The lake is fifty miles long, and the stupendous and magnificent mountains which embosom it, are strewn along their edges, with the fantastic villas of the nobility of Milan, to which, as there is no road, there is no approach but by water. We took boat at the pretty antique town of Como, and literally landed in the drawing-room of the Villa Tempi. The first things I perceived were the orange and lemon trees, laden with fruit, growing in groves in the open air; the American aloes, olive trees, vines, and mulberries, all in blossom or fruit, covering the mountains almost to their summits. The blossoms and orange flowers, with the profusion of roses and wild pinks, were almost too intoxicating for our vulgar senses.

The next day we set off on our aquatic excursions through regions the wildest, the loveliest, the most romantic that can be conceived. We landed at all the curious and classical points—at Pliny's fountain, the site of his villa, &c.,—and after a course of twenty-five miles, reached *my villa* of Someriva, which we found to be a splendid palace, all marble, surrounded by groves of orange trees, but so vast, so solitary, so imposing, and so remote from all medical aid, that I gave up the idea of occupying it, and we rowed off to visit other villas, and at last set up our boat at a pretty inn on the lake, where we sat up half the night watching the arrival of boats and listening to the choruses of the boatmen. The next day we returned, and after new voyages found a beautiful little villa on the lake, ten minutes row from Como, which we have taken for two months, at six pounds a month. The villa Fontana consists of two pavilions, as they are called here, or small houses of two storeys, which are separated by a garden. In one reside the Signor and Signora, our hosts, with a charming family; in the other reside the Signor and Signora Morgan, with an Italian *valet de chambre*. These pavilions are on the lake in a little pyramid; the vines and grapes festooned from tree to tree, and woven into a canopy above. The lake spreads before us with all its mountain beauties and windings. To the right lies the town of Como, with its gothic cathedral. Immediately behind us, on every side, rise the mountains which divide Italian Switzerland from Lombardy, covered with vines, olives and lime trees, and all this is lighted by a brilliant sun and canopied by skies bright, and blue, and cloudless. We have already made some excursions into these enchanting mountains, which are like cultivated gardens raised into the air; and walked within a mile of the Swiss frontier. We have a boat belonging to the villa anchored in the garden, into which we jump and row off. But of all the delights, imagine that shoals of foolish fish float on the surface of the lake in the evening, and that Morgan, who ambitioned nothing but a nibble on the Liffey line, here catches the victims of his art by dozens! Our villa consists of seven pretty rooms on the upper floor, and four below. The floors are stone, sprinkled with water two or three times a-day, the walls painted in fresco, green *jalousies* and muslin draperies, and yet with all these cooling precautions, the heat obliges us to sit still all day. There is only one circumstance that reconciles me to your not sharing our pleasures, and that is a small matter of thunder and lightning, which comes about two days out of three, and is sometimes a little too near and too loud for the nerves of some of my friends. At this present moment it shakes the house, and the rain is falling as if Cox of Kilkenny was coming again. If, by the time we return, I don't make "Les serpents de l'envie sifflent dans votre cœur" with my Spanish guitar, my name is not Oliver! Morgan is making great progress on the guitar. I think it would amuse you to witness the life we lead here. We rise early, and as our house is a perfect smother, we open the blinds (the sashes are never shut), and paradise bursts on us with a sun and sky that you never dreamt of in your philosophy. We breakfast under our arcade of vines, and the table covered with peaches and nectarines, while the fish literally pop their heads out of the lake to be fed, though

Morgan, like a traitor, takes them by hundreds. Except you saw him in a yellow muslin gown and straw hat, on the lake of Como, you have no idea of human felicity! All day we are shut up in our respective little studies, in which the light scarcely penetrates, for the intolerable heat obliges every one to remain shut up during the middle of the day, and the houses and villages look as if they were uninhabited. At two o'clock we dine, at five, drink tea, and then we are off to the mountains, and frequently don't come back till night, or else we are on the lake; but in either instance we are in scenes which no pencil could delineate, nor pen describe. The mountains with their valleys and glens are covered with fig-trees, chestnuts, and olive-trees, and with the lovely vineyards which are formed into festoons and arcades, and have quite another appearance from the stunted vineyards of France. The other day, after dinner, we walked on till we came to some barriers, where we were stopped by *douaniers*. We asked where we were, and found it was Switzerland. So, having walked through a pretty Swiss village, and admired a sign, " William Tell," we walked back to Italy to tea. We are by no means destitute of society; some of our Milanese nobles come occasionally to their villas on the lake, and we are always asked to join the party. The Commandant de la Ville continues to give us tea parties, and we have three very nice English families, of whom we see a good deal (that is, as much as we like). One consists of three sisters, heiresses, and nieces to the Bishop of Rochester, the Misses King. They are sensible, off-handed women, travel about with no protection but a Newfoundland dog, though still youngish, and are equally independent in every other respect. They were so anxious to know us, and so fearful of intruding, that the youngest (*drôle de corps*) was coming in disguise as an Italian lady (because English women, they said, have no right to force themselves on me), with some story to get admittance! Another family, Mr. Laurie's, English people of fashion, with seven children, a French governess, an Irish tutor, and an English housekeeper. Our last and most delightful is Mrs. Lock and three charming daughters; she is aunt to the Duke of Leinster, being the old duchess's daughter, by Ogilvie. She is connected with all the first and cleverest people in England, and smacks of all that's best in the best way. She was, she said, a long time negociating the business of an introduction to me, and at last effected it by getting a dinner made on the lake, to which we were invited. Since then we are in constant correspondence, either by voyages on the lake or by notes. We dined there the other day, and by way of amusing the sweet girls, who are shut up in the loveliest but most solitary site, I announced a party in my vineyard; and there were the Kings, and my Austrian commandant, and some of his officers and Spanish guitars, and a little band of music and fireworks, provided by the young Signori of my host's family; there was tea, and cakes, and all sorts of things laid on the terrace by the lake; and Mrs. Lock's boat approached in view, and the heavens looked transcendently bright, when lo! up rose one of the lake hurricanes, the lightning flashed, the thunder rolled, tea, cakes, and fireworks were carried into the air, and poor Mrs. Lock, after tossing for five hours in a boat, which at every moment threatened to be overset, was too happy to land at midnight, two miles off, at a wretched little village, and pass the night at a cabaret or miserable public house. So much for my Como news!

The weather has been splendid; the heat was at ninety degrees of our thermometer for some days. In the midst of the glories of this beautiful clime these sudden storms burst forth, and while they last, spoil all. Among our Comoesque amusements, one is going to the festivals of the saints on the mountains, and to the churches. To-morrow we are to have an opera in Como, with a company from Milan, and the Commandant has given us his box. There has been an imperial fête at Milan, called a *carousal*, for which we had an imperial invitation; but as court dresses were necessary, we thought it not worth the expense. We are delighted with the good family of our host here; they are, Don Giorgo and Donna Teresa, the heads; he is ready for the "Padrone," and excellent in his way; she, the best woman in the world; but as they speak Milanese, and very little Italian, we get on as it pleases heaven. The chief beau is the eldest son, a major in the army, and aide-de-camp to his uncle, a general; he is "Don Gallina," and my "poor servant ever," for he absolutely watches our looks and anticipates our wishes. Then two younger sons, handsome lads, come home for their college vacation, and two pretty, brown, black-eyed girls, Donna Giovana and Donna Rosina—nothing can equal their gaiety and noise. They live in the garden, and the young men are delightfully musical. The talent for music here is as common as speech. The children walk hand in hand and sing in parts almost from the cradle. On Sundays, the recreation of the peasantry is to get into boats, and float on the lake, and sing in chorus, which they do wonderfully, but you never hear a solo, though there is nothing but singing from morning till night. Such is our life, circle, and society here! Considering the remoteness of our habitation *ce n'est pas mal.* I forgot to mention we have an ex-ambassador and his gay, French wife, and some Capuchin friars, and that I was most gallantly received by the monks of a most famous college here—one of them, the finest head I ever beheld. Nothing can equal the beauty of some of the fine heads here, of our young hosts in particular; but there is also the most hideous race, called Cretins, that ever nature sent into the world to disgrace her handy works; they are precisely the figure of nut-crackers, that we have in toy-shops, not above two feet high, with the head almost on the knees, but monstrously gay and self-conceited.

I labour, as usual, four or five hours a-day. I think I shall do the best that I have done yet, and that my great glory is to come. Lord Byron is, I hear, at Bologna. We have read his *Don Juan.* It is full of good fun, excellent hits, and *à mourir de rire.* His blue-stocking lady is sketched off wickedly well, but his shipwreck is horrible, bad taste, bad feeling, and bad policy. I see they have put in the French papers that I have left Italy for Vienna. I don't know the motive. What is to be done about Moore? We were going to write to Byron about him, poor fellow!

Love to Clarke; kisses to the children—*sans adieu.*

S. M.

Moore's deputy at Bermuda had, at this time, embezzled a large sum of money, for which Moore was held responsible.

CHAPTER VIII.

LETTERS AND GOSSIP.

A LETTER, from excellent Lady Charleville, carries us back to the time when *Tales of the Hall*, *Mazeppa*, and *Don Juan*, were the "last new poems!"

Lady Charleville to Lady Morgan.

LONDON,
July 13, 1819.

MY DEAR MADAM,

Had I required to learn the uncertainty of all human projects being fulfilled, my now sad tale had taught it me. After a consultation here, a warm climate was held to be good for Lord Charleville, and I had no doubt of quitting England forthwith, but my son's illness forbids our emigration; thus sinks, for the second time, to the ground, my hope of selfish relief for myself, and advantage to my children by foreign travel, and observation of man in other climes. Upon receipt of your kind letter, *I went to Colburn*, whose answer, perfectly unsatisfactory as to fact, was to require your address, which I have sent. *Florence Macarthy* is in the fifth edition, and it has been dramatised with good effect at the Surrey Theatre, where the *Heart of Mid Lothian* was better arranged by far than at Covent Garden! Lord Byron's *Mazeppa* has a beautiful description of wild horses, that makes amends for every line of the other trifles which swell his pamphlet, and Crabbe's *Tales of the Hall* have the nature and morality of his former works, and are still more prosaic. Scott's new tales offer one very beautiful story—*The Bride of Lammermoor*—and one bloody and dull *Legend of Montrose*. Lord Byron's *Don Juan* I have not yet got; but *I hear* it is not personal, but very impious and very immoral; however, this may be as false as the other distorted account of it, and, write what he may, his is a great genius unhappily directed.

Lord and Lady Westmeath's separation for temper, and the overthrow of Lord Belfast's marriage and fortunes, by Lord Shaftesbury having discovered that the Marquis and Marchioness of Donegal were married under age by *licence*, and not by banns, which renders it illegal, and bastardizes their children irreparably, is the greatest news of the upper circles at present. The young lady had said she married only for money; therefore, for her, no pity is shown; but poor Lord Belfast, to lose rank, fortune, and wife at once, at twenty years of age, is a strong and painful catastrophe to bear properly. I hear Mr. Chichester (rightful heir now) behaves well; but he cannot prevent the entail affecting his heirs, nor the title descending to him from his cousin.

There have been half a dozen marriages, and another dozen are about to take place. Lady J. Moore to Mr. William Peele; Lord Temple, Lady M. Campbell; Mr. Neville, Lady Jane Cornwallis; Mr. Packenham, Miss Ponsonby, and so on, &c.

This letter is a true account of a most agitating, frightful state of mind, that required all the effort that I was capable of to enable me to *seem* like other people before my dear child, for he judged his state by my impressions of it as they appeared to him, and I did act a difficult and a cruel part, laughing and telling tales to him when I thought all lost!!

Farewell; and to your better pencil I consign all the glories of Italian scenery; may you, in Sir Charles's health, find a recompence and a joy such as I wish you, to sweeten life and reward your real merits.

PS. I have just finished *Don Juan*—it is beautifully written, not immoral, not personal. Farewell; I am always your Ladyship's sincere friend.

C. M. CHARLEVILLE.

Lady Morgan to Lady Clarke.

MILAN,
September 3, 1819.

Here we are again, and here, owing to the kindness and hospitality of our Milanese friends, we sojourn for two days. You never saw such lamentation as our departure from Como produced. The Locks came over in a storm to see us, and we were obliged to contrive beds for some of them, who remained with us all night. The poor dear Fontanas parted from us with tears in their eyes; the Kings said they would follow us, and we had a little crowd of friends round our carriage. All this is very gracious in a foreign country, and, indeed, without vanity, I must say we have hitherto inspired affection and made friends wherever we have been. The moment we reached our Albergo Reale, we had all our old cronies of Milan. A large dinner party was made to day at Count de Porro's, who has been one of the kindest persons we have met with in Italy; he has two superb villas on the Lake of Como, to which he took us the day before we left Como. It was the festival of the Saint of the Lake; we went to church in the morning where high mass was celebrated by the Bishop; we had the finest opera music that could be selected—I never heard anything so imposing and splendid; in Ireland they have no notion what the catholic religion is. At night we had fireworks on the lake, accompanied by thunder and lightning. There is scarcely a note of printed music, you are obliged to have all copied; but the backwardness of this unfortunate country is incredible. We have just returned from a dinner party, after which we went to pay visits, as is the fashion here, to the Marchesa Trivulgi, who is a patient of Morgan's at present, and on whose account we remain a day longer than we intended. I will describe one visit that will do for all. The palace Trivulgi is a great dark building; we enter the court, which is surrounded by a pillared arcade, and go up a flight of great stone stairs into the waiting-room; the servants permit us to pass in silence, and we continue our route through eight immense and superb rooms, all dimly lighted, the floors marble, and the hangings silk, &c., &c. This suite terminates in a beautiful boudoir, where we found the Marchioness on her *canapé*, with a small circle of visitors. At nine o'clock, the visiting is over at home, and then the whole world is off for the Opera. Direct your next, Florence, *poste restante*.   S. M.

In contrast with the tone of keen enjoyment in Lady Morgan's letters, here is one from Madame Jerome Bonaparte. She has come from America to Geneva, and finds herself almost as uneasy in one place as the other. It was as much the custom then to be ruined in America by "commercial speculations," as it has continued to be since; but whether ruined or prosperous, her letters are always pleasant.

Madame Patterson Bonaparte to Lady Morgan.

GENEVA,
October 1, 1819.

MY DEAR LADY MORGAN,

Your letter from Casa Fontana reached me yesterday. I cannot imagine the cause of this long delay, as it appears, from the direction you gave me for the 1st of September, that the letter was written previously; the date you neglected putting. I am very anxious to see you again, to assure you of an affection

which absence has not diminished, to listen to you once
more, and to relate to you my adventures since our
separation. I had heroically resolved to support the
ennui of my fate in America, and should never have
ventured another voyage to Europe could I have
found the means of education for my son which exist
here; but either he must have remained ignorant or I
was compelled to leave the repose of my *fauteuil*,
therefore, I did not hesitate to sacrifice my personal
comfort for his advantage.

You know we have been nearly ruined in America,
by commercial speculations, and even I have suffered,
as my tenants are no longer able to pay me the same
rents, and the banks have been obliged to diminish the
amount of yearly interest which I formerly received
from them; these inconveniences are, however *momentané*, and I flatter myself that in a year or two, *tout ira
bien*; it is, however, provoking enough to find one's
income curtailed at a moment when I most required
it; my son's education, too, demands no inconsiderable
expense, and as you know, his father never *has* and
never will contribute a single farthing towards his
maintenance. We have no correspondence with him
since the demand I made two years ago, which was
merely that he would pay some part of his necessary
expenditure; this he positively refused, therefore, I
consider myself authorized to educate him in my own
way. I wish I could see you again; it was so unfortunate for me that you had left Geneva before my arrival. I fear, too, that you will not return this way,
and it is impossible for me to leave my son without

protection in a foreign country. Your *Florence Macarthy* is the most delightful creature, and had the greatest success with us; by the way, you should take into consideration with your bookseller in London, the profits which accrue to him from the sale of your works in America, where they are as much sought after as in Europe. This town is intolerably expensive, quite as much so as Paris; there exists, too, an *esprit de corps*, or *de coterie*, appalling to strangers,—I mean to *woman* strangers, for men are *les bien venus partout*; it is quite *à propos* that I did not contemplate amusement, or *petits soins* during my *séjour*, and that I came *seulement par devoir*. They have a custom here *parmi les gens de haut ton prendre à un prix très élevé des étrangers en pension seulement "pour leur agrément."* In these genteel boarding-houses there is no feast to be found, unless it be the feast of reason; the hosts are too *spirituels* to imagine that their *pensionnaires* possess a vulgar appetite for meat and vegetables, tarts and custards, but as I cannot subsist altogether on the contemplation of *la belle Nature*, I have taken a comfortable apartment for six months, *en ville*, where I hope I shall get something to eat. *La belle nature, Mont Blanc, le Lac de Genève, le beau coucher du soleil, le lever magnifique de la lune,* are in the mouth of every one here, and *paraissant tenir lieu de tout autre chose.* I am writing you all this; my letter will, perhaps, never reach you. Adieu, my dear friend; tell Sir Charles everything amiable for me, and be convinced of the sincerity of my affection for you both.

My health is entirely restored, and I am much less

in the *genre larmoyant* than when you saw me,—I was so ill, *physiquement*, that I had not sufficient force to support *les maux morales*. I am so happy that I did not go to Edinburgh; the climate here is finer; living, although dear enough, cheaper, and the language, *French*,—more desirable for my son than English, which he knows; in short, *à tout prendre*, I am better here than I could possibly have been in Great Britain. Why do you persist in living in Ireland? I am sure you would be delightfully circumstanced in any other place.

E. P.

The above would reach Lady Morgan in Florence, at which city she arrived early in October. Before giving her own account of her journey, we present a billet from the Comtesse d'Albany, the widow of Charles Stuart and of Alfieri! The words are little, a mere permission to visit the Ducal library, but gracefully courteous. If we could transfer the autograph to the reader, the clear, firm, round, legible writing, —he would look at it with an interest borrowed from the fortunes of the writer.

The Countess of Albany to Lady Morgan.

Ce Mercredi, Octobre 13, 1819, à 3 heures.

La Comtesse d'Albany n'a pas oublié qu'elle devait procurer à Lady Morgan le plaisir de voir la bibliothèque du Grand Duc. Elle sera la maitresse d'y aller Vendredi prochain 18 de Mai depuis dix heures jusqu'à deux ou bien Lundi si ce jour ne lui convient pas.

Elle est priée de ne pas passer l'heure de deux, le Bibliothécaire étant obligé d'aller à la campagne. La Comtesse d'Albany profite avec empressement de l'occasion d'assurer Lady Morgan de sa considération et de tout ce qui lui est dû.

Lady Morgan to Lady Clark.

FLORENCE, PALAZZO COUSINI,
October 28*th*, 1819.

We left you setting off for Florence. At the opera the Counts Confalonieri and Visconti told us we were mistaken, and that we were going with them the next morning to Genoa! Without more ceremony they ran off with our passport to the police and got it changed, and *finalemente*, as we say in Italy, we set off next day for Genoa. Our journey lay partly over the Apennines; we began to ascend them a little before the purple sunset of Italian skies, and pursued our route by moonlight, and never did any light shine upon scenes more romantically lovely. Nothing was wanting. In the cleft of a mountain we heard a funeral chaunt, and the next moment appeared a procession of monks, their faces covered, and only their eyes seen,—horrible, but strange and new to me. We slept that night on the top of the mountain, and the next day, having walked more than we drove, we beheld "Genoa the superb" at the foot of the Apennines, and the Mediterranean spreading far and wide. Our hotel lay on its banks, and we had scarcely dined, when we were invited to go on board a British ship of war that lay in the bay (the Glasgow, Captain Maitland). Accompanied by our Italian friends, off we sailed. There never was anything to equal the *empressement* of the officers and their kindness to me. I left them my fan, and they gave me one. They had tea for us, and I was so delighted with this most magnificent spectacle, that I went down between decks and saw three hundred sailors at supper, notwithstanding the heat was at one hundred degrees. The result was that the next day I was seized with rheumatism, &c., and never knew one hour's health during the fortnight I remained there; still, I struggled against it, as I had so much to see, to learn, and to hear,—went about to visit all the palaces,—oh, such ancient splendour! Churches, hospitals, and institutions!—All the learned professors, head physicians, &c., waited on Morgan. The Commander-in-Chief himself, who came to us the moment we arrived, with his aides de camp, accompanied him to the different hospitals, and he was solicited to give his opinion of the disorder of a young heir to a great family, which he did with success. This family, and that of the Marchese Pallaviccini, are the first in the town; they were among the first also to come forward. They asked us to a splendid ball and dinner, and we took so well that they insisted on our considering their table as ours, and dining with them every day. We did so as long as my health and the fatigue of going to their villa would admit of the thing. But oh, that you could see us going! You must know that the old republican streets of Genoa are so narrow, one excepted, that carriages cannot ply, as the town is built up against the Apennines, and the villa Pallaviccini is perched on the steepest; there is no going there, but being carried in sedan chairs, and this is the way Morgan and I went every day; for nothing but a goat and a Genoese chairman could scale those precipices. The night of the ball, all the officers of the Glasgow went in this manner. *A propos*, one of the officers came on shore to see us, and sent up his name, Mr. Marcus Brownrigg. It was no other than "I am your man, and I'll carry your can," thrown into a very charming and gentlemanly young man. I never saw so kind a creature. He said he had orders to bring the Captain's boat and ten men for me as often as I pleased. He came with this set-out twice, and was in despair that I could not go. He wrote me an elegant note to tell me so, but alas! after near a fortnight's struggle, and going out every day sick and weary, I was knocked down fairly, or rather foully, with a bilious complaint that threatened fever. There was no getting a breath of air,—I suffocated; however, Morgan was nurse, doctor, all, and himself far from well. In fact, in despair of my recovering in this scorching climate, he wrapped me up one fine morning and threw me from my bed to the carriage, and set off with me for Bologna. The moment we began to descend the mountains and get into the fresh, delicious plains of Lombardy, I recovered, and we both got well by the time we reached Parma, where the late empress of Europe reigns over a dreary, desolate, and gloomy country town. Her only amusement is the opera, and such an opera! a narrow lozenge box, lighted with five tallow candles. We staid to see the churches and Correggio's paintings, and would have staid longer, but we were entirely hunted out by the bugs. Modena, though a royal residence, is a sad set out, and the whole of this earthly paradise broken up into little states, neglected, poor, melancholy, presents but one great ruin. We gladly escaped from these little capitals to the lovely magnificent country. The vines festooned from tree to tree, present their luxurious fruit to any hand that will pluck them. It was the vintage, and I never saw such contrasts as the comfortless aspect and misery of the people, and the enchantment and plenty of the scenery.

Arrived at Bologna, we sent out our letters, and the next day were visited by all that was delightful and distinguished in the town. The Countess Semperiva, a young, pretty, clever widow, took us at once under her wing; her carriage was at our door every morning to take us to see the galleries, palaces, &c. She made a delightful dinner party for us, so did our banker, at his villa; a Madame Martinelli, the Beauty and Wit of Bologna, was equally kind, and made two very elegant evening parties for us; at the last we found Crescentini, singing some of his own delightful compositions at the piano, and Sir Humphrey and Lady Davy; nothing could be more cordial than he was, though he is completely turned into a fine man upon town. All the cleverest professors called on Morgan, and when he went to the hospitals he was complimented on his work (*Outlines of the Physiology of Life*), which, by-the-bye, has taken wonderfully in Italy, and procured him infinite fame; a second edition of the French translation has appeared. When we arrived at Bologna, they recommended us our apartments by telling us they were well aired, as Lord Byron only left them the day before. You may suppose he came to Bologna to visit the learned body of that ancient university, or consult its famous library. Not a bit of it. He came to carry off a young lady.

The hotels at Florence are handsome, comfortable, and expensive. We set up at the Nova-Yorka, kept by an Englishwoman. Our arrival being known, some of the principal persons came to visit us *instanter*; the Prince Corsini (minister of the interior), Prince Borghese (Bonaparte's brother-in-law), the Countess D'Albany, widow of the last Pretender, and the fair friend of Alfieri. Several of the learned came to see Morgan,—Lord Burghersh, the Ambassador, and Lady Burghersh, Lady Florence Lindsay, and her charming daughters, and lots of my Paris Wednesday evening acquaintances of all nations. The Countess D'Albany, who never goes out, asked us immediately; she is "at home" every evening, and holds quite a royal circle. All her fine gold plate, the finest I ever saw, was displayed. The circle is most formal, and you will scarce believe, and I am ashamed to say, she kept the seat of honour vacant for me, next herself. It was in vain, last night (for we go to her constantly), that when ambassadresses and princesses were announced, I begged to be allowed to retreat, she would not hear of it. You have no idea the sensation this makes among the folks

here, as she is reckoned amazingly high and cold. She
has remains of the beauty so praised by Alfieri. But
the kindest of all persons is the minister, Corsini. He
made a splendid dinner for us at his most magnificent palace, to which he invited all the noted literary
characters in Tuscany; a *réunion*, they say, almost
unknown here. We were invited to dine at the English Ambassador's, where we had a large party.
Last night we went to Madame D'Albany's full of
your letter, delighted with its dear, welcome contents,
but quite *tristes* about Moore. I had scarcely taken
my seat by the legitimate Queen of England, when
Lord Burghersh brought up a dashing beau, who was
no other than "brave Colonel Camac," who told me
that he had been all day roving about looking for us,
for a friend who had just arrived;—it was no other than
Anacreon Moore! Accordingly, while we were at breakfast next morning, enter brave Colonel Camac and
Moore! By the advice of all friends he has taken a
trip to Italy, till something can be done to better his
affairs; he travelled with Lord John Russell, but parted
company with his lordship to visit his friend Byron,
at Venice. Moore said we were expected at Venice,
and that he had heard of us everywhere. Lord Byron
bid Moore tell Morgan he would be happy to make his
acquaintance, but not a word of encouragement to his
"lady intellectual." I never saw Moore gayer, better,
or pleasanter. We have begged of him to come and
breakfast with us every day, and he goes with me the
day after to-morrow, to the Comic Opera, where I have
Capponi's box. He then runs off to Rome, Naples, and

returns to Holyrood House, Edinburgh, where he settles down to write and arrange his affairs. What elasticity and everlasting youth! Pray call on his excellent mother and tell her all this; she will be delighted to hear of him. He feels about Italy much as we do. He told us Morgan's work, though attacked, has been treated with the greatest respect as an extraordinary though a dangerous book.

You will now like to know how the deuce we have got into a palace, into a suite of elegant and spacious apartments, filled with flowers such as are only found in Italy. (Moore says "how are we ever to leave it all.") The fact is we are here in the thraldom of a fairy. Everything has been prepared for us; we want for nothing. A few days after our arrival, when we were sick of the expenses of our inn, comes a gentleman to say he is the Marquis de Capponi's *homme d'affaire* that he has an apartment ready for us, an opera box, &c., &c., and here we are in a palace once belonging to the Prince Corsini. The palace Capponi is the finest I have seen, except the great Orsini, and a much more extensive building than Carlton House. There are apartments for every season: those of summer open into an orangery. The actions of its historical lords are painted on the walls of the great saloon. They have eight villas round Florence, at one of which we breakfasted the other day: one immense room laid out with curiosities and antiquities. Should the handsome Marchese Capponi call on you, (for he is now on his way to Ireland), tell him how gratefully I express myself. All the English

say, we are the only strangers for whom the Italians
make dinners. We were the other night at a party at
Mrs. Mostyn's, (daughter of Mrs. Piozzi), where we met
Lord and Lady George Thynne. Mrs. Piozzi is in
high health and spirits at eighty. Meantime, in spite
of all my friends can say, I am growing old, and now
look forward only to living in your children, to whom I
trust I shall be restored early in the spring, for the
moment the Alps are open we set off, please God. I
think half the Irish reform is owing to *Florence Macarthy*. I expect a statue from *that enlightened and grateful people*. The first thing I saw here in all the
booksellers' windows was my picture stuck up with a
good translation of *Florence Macarthy*. It is well
done, and the picture pretty, but not like. Bartolini, the famous sculptor, has shown us great civility.
He has dedicated to me one of his best statues, a boy
pressing grapes; the original is bought by Lord Beauchamp, and a cast done by himself is to be packed up
and sent to Ireland for me. I shall be like the Vicar
of Wakefield and his picture. I would willingly have
made a visit to Italy blindfolded to have seen only
the Gallery at Florence;—we go there every day. I
read to Moore *Lady Belvidere*, and it made us all die
laughing. We leave this for Rome on the 2nd of
November.

S. M.

Lady Morgan did not in the least exaggerate the
attention she received; for Moore in his diary, dated
Florence, October 17, 1819, confirms every word.

A little note from Moore, pleasant, and by no means romantic for a poet.

Thomas Moore to Sir C. Morgan.

Rome,
November 7th, 1819.

My dear Morgan,

I have only time for a line; but a line from Rome is worth a hundred from anywhere else. This place does not disappoint. There are some old brick walls to be sure, before which people stand with a delight and veneration in which I cannot sympathize; but the Coliseum is the very poetry of ruins. My leg, thanks to you and Goulard, arrived quite sound and well, and has never troubled me since.

I think of being off from here the latter end of this week. It was my intention at first to go to Naples, but Cannæ was by no means tempting, and then there is such talk of escort, &c., &c., that, what with the Colonel and the guards, I thought it much too dilatory a proceeding, and gave it up.

Love to Lady Morgan.

From hers and yours truly,

Thomas Moore.

The "son of Hortense," so slightly passed in the next letter from Lady Morgan to her sister, was no other than Louis Napoleon, now Emperor of the French.

Lady Morgan to Lady Clarke.

ROME, VIA DEL ANGELO,
December 17, 1819.

MY DEAR LOVE,

I received your letter at the foot of Antonines' Pillar, and have seen nothing at Rome pleased me better— and now for our journey of seven days in the middle of December. We travelled in furs and rugs like Russian bears; but the climate softened as we proceeded—we found the trees in full leaf, and the enchanting, lovely, and diversified scenery wore a fine October appearance. The romantic views are beyond description—all the towns dreary ruins, too much for English spirits to stand; we ascended to many of them (Cortona and Perugia particularly) up perpendicular mountains, and the horns of the oxen that drew us, were on a level with the top of our carriage; but oh, the inns!!! We travelled with *tea, sugar, tea-things and kettle*, but from Florence to Rome we could get neither *milk* nor *butter*. There was but one fire-place in each inn, and that kept in the heat and let out the smoke. Our precious servant (*a treasure*) took care of us as if we were children, and made a fire in a crock in our bedroom, which, with *stone floors, black rafters*, and a *bier* for a bed, and the smell of the stable to regale us (for it generally opened to it) was quite beyond the reach of *his* art to make comfortable. We always set off before daylight and stop before dark. Thirty miles from Rome begins that fearful desert the

Campagna, and then adieu to houses and population. We arrived, however, safe and sound, without even a cold; but the fatigues of travelling, and I think the *climate*, is terribly consuming. I think I look twenty years older than when you saw me. However, I am in excellent spirits and health, *odds wrinkles ! ! !*

The kindness of our Florence friends pursued, or rather *devanc/'d* us here. The Princes Corsini and Borghese, who have the two finest palaces at Rome, wrote to their librarians and agents to be of use to us in every way. The Countess D'Albany wrote to the Duchess of Devonshire to say we were expected, and yesterday (the day after our arrival) are their invitations sent to us. The Princess Borghese (Pauline, Napoleon's beautiful sister) has written to invite us to spend the evening, and the Duchess de Braciano, has asked us for every Thursday evening whilst we remain in Rome. To night we go to the Duchess of Devonshire, and after her *soirée*, to a concert at the Princess Borghese's. The former wrote us the kindest of notes. I think you will like to hear something of Pauline. She is separated from Prince Borghese, who was so civil to us at Florence; but she lives in his superb palace here quite like a little queen! Nothing could equal her reception. She said it was noble in me not to *fall heavy* on the *unfortunate*, &c. I confess I do not see that exquisite beauty she was so celebrated for. She is, she says, much altered, and grown thin, fretting about her brother. Her dress, though *demi-toilette*, very superb; and the apartments, beyond

beyond! She had a little circle, and she introduced
us to the son of Hortense (the ex-Queen of Holland),
her nephew, and to a daughter of Lucien Bonaparte;
when we were going away she put a beautiful music-
book of the Queen of Holland, into our hands, to copy
what songs we pleased.

The Eternal City disappoints at first entrance. I
thought it mighty like an Irish town, shabby and dirty
—we have yet seen nothing save St. Peter's, to which
we ran like mad the moment we arrived. The first
impression of that disappointed too; the interior overwhelmed me! but not as I expected—but of such
places and things it is impossible to speak with the
little space a letter affords. The climate heavenly—
orange trees in boxes out of every window, migno-
nette, &c.; young lamb, chickens, and salad every day.
We have got into private lodgings, lots of visitors—
Lord Fortescue and Lady Mary, Sir Thomas Lawrence
(who has just shown us his picture of the Pope, that
has left all the Italian painters in despair). I have two
cardinals on my list of visitors. The Italian ladies
dress as we do—the French toilette—some of them
very fine creatures, a *rich beauty*, all glowing and bright
—the most good-natured, caressing creatures. We get
on famously with our Italian. I spoke all along the
road to the common people, and got lots of information.
Did I not tell you that Bartolini, of Florence, has done
my bust in marble?—just as I had written so far,
Canova called on us. He is *delightful*, and recalled
Dénon to our recollection.

December 18.—We had a delightful party at the

Duchess of Devonshire's last night; divine singing; Lord John Russell was introduced to us (brother of the Duke of Bedford), and I flirted all the evening with the Prince of Mecklenburgh! On my return home to old Dublin, I shall feel as Martha did about sifting cinders. I have had a visit from the daughter of *Monti*, the famous poet.

Adieu, S. M.

The following amusing account of a visitation from two bores is written in a journal of scraps kept whilst on her journey—this is the only finished entry. There are other things which, if finished, might have been entertaining, or if legible; but they are jotted down in memoranda as indications for her own memory, and are unintelligible to any one else. The present sketch of a morning with two Bores, has been recovered from MS., compared with which, ill-written Greek characters, or a cuneiform inscription, would be legible as fair Italian text-hand!

Bores and Prosers.

Enter Mrs. B—— and her brother, who prosed me out of Spa, begged me from Lausanne, and hummed me into such a lethargy at Geneva that it is a mercy I was not buried alive! They are the best poor dears on earth—and there's the worst of it.

I had my cheek kissed by the sister, and my hand by the brother, for ten minutes at least, by the town clock—not rapid electrics, but long-drawn kisses, against all character of kissing, which, if it be not electric, is nothing.

The kissing over, the prosing began.

Mrs. B—— took the lead, *comme de raison*, opened the campaign *d'ennui*, with unwonted vigour; the fun was to see her brother deliberately taking up his posture of patience, like a general on active service, his heavy lids gently falling over his heavy eyes; his very nostrils breathing stupefaction.

Observe, for it is good to know the outer and visible signs of our natural enemies, Bores have noses peculiar to themselves. The nose of a German Bore is a sort of long, broad, romantic, rather aquiline, and rather drooping nose—the drooping nose characterises invariably the nosology of a bore—in a word, it is the leading feature.

But to return; Mrs. B—— began with an account of her journey. Not a stage, not a turn in the road, not a cross that I had gone over six days before but was described to me, first *en gros* and then *en détail*; but this was nothing—at least it was fact, topographical fact—but to my utter despair, every village, town, and house, "put her in mind" of some cottage, town, road, street, or something, in Ireland, Scotland, or England—something had happened to her in one or all of the aforesaid places. But still *this* was nothing; they were graphic pictures, however ill-drawn—it was the *moral* demonstrations, the particular parentheses, which left me without hope, help, or resource; every beggar, post, landlord, or landlady, "put her in mind" of her mother's housemaid, who used to say when called to warm the bed, &c. Boots put her so strongly in mind of her grandfather, by having a wart on his left cheek, that I trembled lest the course of association should carry us back to the founder of the family of Bores, which would have thrown us back to the memories of the Pre-Adamites, had not the entrance of a *gouté* cut her short, for ah! there is nothing short about bores but stopping their mouths by filling it with ice-cream. This was the moment for her brother, who cut in nobly to open his entrenchments. The whole family are of the breed of those dealers in art, science, and literature, who gave rise to the caution, " Drink deep or taste not."

The dear B——'s have drunk like sparrows and swelled like crows, but drunk a little of everything, " from humble port to imperial tokay," and it is this that renders them more tiresome in their prosy scraps than the most obdurate ignorance could ever make itself. No one could be in the room a moment after Mr. B—— came in, without knowing that he was a geologist, botanist, archæologist,—everything. He began by complaining of all he had suffered from heat, and I gave him my whole share of sympathy! But when he got upon the *causes*, and talked of the fundamental laws of nature, I started up in the midst of a diatribe on cosmogony, and in despair, exclaimed, " My dear Mr. B——, you are aware that God made the world in six days, and did not say one word about cosmogony!" It might be thought that was a hard hit;—not at all, he took it gravely and began a disquisition on the Mosaic account. The word Moses over-

came all my power of face, and I burst out in a fit of
laughter, for by one of Mrs. B——'s "put-me-in-
minds," Moses put *me* in mind that in Ireland we call
a bore "a Mosey," and there was something so utterly
Moseyish in the look and manner of the proser, that
the ridiculous application was too much for me, and I
owed him, perhaps, one of the pleasantest sensations in
the world, that of laughing, not wisely, but too well.
I have now made out my case of bore-phobia.

CHAPTER IX.

STILL IN ITALY—1820.

Lady Morgan to Lady Clarke.

ROME,
February 4th, 1820.

DEAR LOVE,
YOUR letters have given us great uneasiness about our house; but I have no room for any feeling except joy and gratitude that you are well out of your troubles, and that the young knight promises to do honour to his people.

Now for Rome, and our mode of existence. Immediately after breakfast we start on our tours to ruins, churches, galleries, collections, &c., &c., and return late; dine, on an average, three times a week at English dinner parties; we are scarcely at home in the evenings, and never in the mornings. The Duchess of Devonshire is unceasing in her attentions to me; not only is her house open to us, but she calls and takes me out to show me what is best to be seen. As Cardinal Gonsalvi does not receive ladies, she arranged that I was to be introduced to him in the Pope's chapel; as he was coming out in the procession of cardinals, he stepped aside, and we were presented. He insisted upon calling on me, and took our address. Cardinal Fesche (Bonaparte's uncle) is quite my beau; he called on us the other day, and wanted me to drive out with him, but Morgan looked at his scarlet hat and stockings, and would not let me go. We have been to his palace, and he has shown us his fine collection (one of the finest in Rome). Lord William Russell, Mr. Adair, the Charlemonts, &c., are coming to us this evening. Madame Mère (Napoleon's mother) sent to say she would be glad to see me; we were received quite in an imperial style. I never saw so fine an old lady,—still quite handsome. She was dressed in a rich crimson velvet, trimmed with sable, with a point lace ruff and head-dress. The pictures of her sons hung round the room, all in royal robes, and her daughter and grandchildren, and at the head of them all, *old Mr. Bonaparte!* Every time she mentioned Napoleon, the tears came in her eyes. She took me into her bedroom to show me the miniatures of her three children. She is full of sense, feeling, and spirit, and not the least what I expected—vulgar. We dined at the Princess Borghese's,—Louis Bonaparte, the ex-king of Holland's son, dined there,—a fine boy. Lord William Russell, and some Roman ladies in the evening. She invited us all to see her jewels; we passed through eight rooms *en suite* to get to her bedroom. The bed was white and gold, the quilt point lace, and the sheets French cambric, embroidered. The jewels were magnificent.

Nothing can be kinder than the Charlemont family. We were at three *soirées* all in one night. With great difficulty I at last got at Miss Curran, for she leads the life of a hermit. She is full of talent and intellect, pleasant, interesting, and original; and she paints like an artist.

God bless you. S. M.

A letter from Lady Charleville contains some very amusing contemporary gossip. The charitable reader will be glad to see authentic instances of generous feeling in King George the Fourth, not generally known.

Lady Charleville to Lady Morgan.

BRIGHTON,
18*th February*, 1820.

A long and severe attack of my spasmodic affection, dearest Lady Morgan, must excuse and account for my silence. I am now as well nearly as before it happened; and I delay not to thank you for your very kind letter from Florence, which I received here in January. Let me assure you of the unwearied solicitude I feel that your progress through Italy, nay, let me say conclusively, through life, may be as successful and as well spent as its commencement. You know me too well to take pleasure in fulsome compli-

ment, if I knew how to address it you; but I shall not
doubt that you know I value the feelings that fill your
heart—its tenderness—its fulfilment of close domestic
duties—and also its deep sense of all Ireland has had
to suffer, though we may differ in the causes; in
short, that I admire the natural patriotism and love
of liberty which inspires your lively imagination and
throbs at your heart, and without which your writings
had never attained their just celebrity. I understand
and like you the better even when the scale and compass may not strictly bear you out; and in full sincerity I will always speak when I think they do not,
because however ungifted I am, yet I am true and
unprejudiced, which is the best light to common
minds. I suppose you at Rome are steeped in classic
lore; and I fain would know whether the remains
of the glorious dead do not fill you with something
more than contempt for our moderns? This and
other absurd questions I would ask you, but that I am
sure you would rather hear what we are about here.
Well, we are going on dully enough, our Regent in
love like a boy of sixteen, and the marchesa, after
eight years' attempts on his person, I believe in full
enjoyment of her base ambition. We dined twice, by
royal command, and were several evenings in a party
of about twenty, where she was awkwardly enough
situated, and certainly without tact or talent to get
out of the dilemma. His royal highness had very
cleverly left the pavilion unfit to enter, and therefore
stuffed into a common lodging-house in Marlborough
Row, with his one sitting-room about twenty-four by

eighteen, his suite next door; and no party of the Lord Chamberlain Hertford, or Cholmondley, &c.; thus he escaped at once from the societies of eighty and their *sposas* to those of his own age, and twenty years difference, *se compte pour quelque chose*. So there we were singing, and he as gay and as happy *singing second, à gorge déployée* to the musical misses, and making love, *tout son saoul*, when his brother's death struck him to the heart;—for a heart he has depend upon it, and a generous one too. The Duke of Kent had behaved to him basely, yet he wrote tenderly to him, and forgave him. It is strange to say how much he felt the death of his father, always unkind to him; and a fact it is that he was thrown into fever by these events, and a cold brought on inflammation of the chest. Tierney saved his life by courage. One hundred and thirty-six ounces of blood were taken from him at four bleedings, and he is safe and well now. As soon as he was out of danger, *he sent for the Duke of Sussex*, and said, "My father and brother dead, warns his family to unite and live as they should do. I can forget everything!" The duke wept much, and the world is pleased with the king, and does him justice. Again, the late king's Will is unsigned, and consequently all his money-wealth goes by law to the Crown. When the Chancellor told him so, his reply was, "No, my lord, I am here to fulfil my father's wishes, not to take advantage of such a circumstance; therefore the Will will be executed as if it had been signed." Of another amiable trait you will think as I do. Walker, apothecary and surgeon, who has attended him since his childhood, failed to open the vein; and as Sir Matthew Tierney had been a surgeon, and the danger of an hour's delay was great, he took the lancet, and failed also; upon which His Majesty said, "Demm it, I'm glad you fail, for it would have vexed Walker," and turning to whom, he said, "Come man, tie up the other arm."

Observe, if you please, the excellent feeling which, with his life dependant on the operation, animated him to forget himself for the old man who had often sat up in his nursery, and you will allow it was very fine. The report of all travellers who have had any knowledge of the Princess of Wales, renders it imperative that such a woman should not preside in Great Britain over its honest and virtuous daughters, and something is to be done to prevent it. The king's wish is, that she should be handsomely provided for; and he fain would divorce her, but the Chancellor and others wish only to save England from the disgrace of such a queen, and themselves the unpleasant work of unsaying their rash acquittal. There are only foreigners to witness her dreadful life on the continent; and John Bull thinks a foreigner would lie for sixpence, so a middle line will be pursued, I imagine, on the opening of the new parliament in May.

February 18th.

The Duc de Berri's murder; I have had such an account of it from the Col. de Case himself to his nephew. All parties, of course, abhor the act; but it is feared by all wise people it will be made use of as a plea to deprive the people of the benefit of some law resembling our *Habeas Corpus!* All this you will hear of better than my defective information can apprise you. In the way of literature, we have been all busied with Mr. Hope's *Anastatius; or, Memoirs of a Greek*, which certainly has a great deal of excellent matter in it; but, upon the whole, it is a heavy book, and one which bespeaks a most unhappy feeling in its author. Walter Scott's *Ivanhoe*, with his Jewess Rebecca is worth a world of Christian damsels. He has got nine thousand pounds for that, and his novel not published. Mr. Chamboulan's book is read and admired, and Murray has given him one thousand two hundred pounds for it. He has nobly fulfilled his duty to Napoleon. Napoleon's own work is only worth much as a military notice upon the battle of Waterloo. The writing I doubt being his own, because the extreme vanity of epithet is entirely unworthy of so great a man. Yet there is something fine in the avoidance of complaint against the party who betrayed him in that senate which owed its existence to him, &c., &c. Farewell; I hope Sir Charles Morgan is quite well; and tell him from me not to expose himself to visit the catacombs, where malaria prevails at all seasons.

Mr. Becher has married Miss O'Neil, and she has nobly provided for her whole family out of thirty thousand pounds she had accumulated.

February 25.

It is now known that Leach, Vice Chancellor, persuaded the Regent there could be no difficulty in the divorce of his wife; but that upon proposing it to Lord Howe, he persisted that two ocular witnesses of English birth would be required by John Bull to divorce an English queen; and that fifty foreigners would not suffice to satisfy the country. The point is, therefore, given up, and a legal separation only resolved on. Her life might be taken for forgery; but I understand she is to be let off cheaply, and her income of fifty thousand pounds given her. Farewell. I wish you a most happy year, and as many as may smile upon you.

C. M. CHARLEVILLE.

Lady Morgan, once more in Rome, writes as indefatigably to her sister as though she had no other correspondent in the world, nor any book to prepare for nor any travelling, or sight-seeing, or visiting.

Lady Morgan to Lady Clarke.

ROME, PALAZZO GIORGIO,
April 2, 1820.

MY DEAREST LOVE,

Here we are again, safe and sound, as I trust this will find you all. We were much disappointed at not finding a letter here on our return, and now all our hopes are fixed on Venice, for which we should have departed this day but for the impossibility of getting horses; the moment the Holy Week was over, there was a general break up, and this strange, whirligig travelling world, who were all mad to get here, are now all mad to get away. Before I place myself at Rome, however, I must take you back with me for a little to Naples. Just as I despatched my letter to you, with the account of my February summer, arrives the month of March with storms of wind, a fall of snow on the mountains, and all this in an immense barrack, called a palace, without chimneys, or doors that shut, or windows that close. In short, as to climate, take it all in all, I am as well satisfied now with my old, wet blanket, Irish climate as any other. I had nothing to complain of, however, at Naples, but the climate—nothing could exceed the kindness and politeness of the Neapolitans to us both. Every Monday we were invited to a *festino* given by the Neapolitan nobility to the English, and our time passed, in point of society, most delightfully. There is less to be seen than at Rome; but those few sights are more curious and more perfect than anything at Rome except the Coliseum. The buried town at Pompeii, for instance, is unique,—a complete Roman town as it stood two thousand years ago, almost all the furniture in high preservation; but this is beyond the compass of a letter. We left pleasant, brilliant Naples with infinite regret, and our journey here was most curious. Notwithstanding we were five carriages strong, yet at each military post (and they were at every quarter of a mile) two soldiers leaped upon our carriage, one before and another behind, with their arms, and gave us up to the next guard, who gave us two more guards, and thus we performed our perilous journey like prisoners of state. You may

guess the state of the country by this. At Rome,
however, all danger from bandits ends, and when I
caught a view of the cupola of St. Peter's rising amidst
the solitudes of the Campagna, I offered up as sincere
a thanksgiving as ever was preferred to his sanctity.
We arrived in Rome in time for the first of the ceremonies of the Holy Week. All our English friends
at Naples arrived at the same time; but after the
Holy Week at Rome, never talk of Westminster elec-
tions, Irish fairs, or English bear-gardens! I never
saw the horrors of a crowd before, nor such a curious
mélange of the ludicrous and the fearful. We had a
ticket sent us for all by Cardinal Fesche, and saw all;
but it was at the risk of our limbs and lives. Of all the
ceremonies the benediction was the finest, and of all
the sights, St. Peter's illuminated on Easter Sunday
night, the most perfectly beautiful. We were from
eight o'clock in the morning till two o'clock in the
afternoon in the church; all the splendour of the earth
is nothing to the procession of the Pope and Cardinals.
Morgan was near being crushed to death, only he cried
out to Lord Charlemont to give him some money (for
he could not get to his pocket), which he threw to a
soldier, who rescued him. I saw half the red bench
of England tumbling down staircases, and pushed back
by the guard. We have Queen Caroline here. At
first this made a great fuss whether she was or was
not to be visited by her subjects, when lo! she refused
to see any of them, and leads the most perfectly retired life! We met her one day driving out in a state
truly royal; I never saw her so splendid. Young

Austen followed in an open carriage; he is an interesting-looking young man. She happened to arrive at an inn near Rome, when Lord and Lady Leitrim were there; she sent for them and invited them to tea. Lady Leitrim told me her manner was perfect, and altogether she was a most improved woman; the Baron attended her at tea, but merely as a chamberlain, and was not introduced. Before you receive this, if accounts be true, Her Majesty will be in England. I think you will not be sorry to hear that if we live and do well, our next letter will be dated from Paris.

S. M.

Sir Charles and Lady Morgan returned home in the course of a few weeks after the above letter. They arrived at their house in Kildare Street safe and well. The following extract from a letter of Lady Morgan to Mrs. Featherstone gives in a few lines a picture of herself and her husband settled down to their ordinary avocations, and engaged on their great work, the record of all they had dared and seen during their travels.

Lady Morgan to Mrs. Featherstone.

KILDARE STREET,
September, 1820.

MY DEAR MRS. FEATHERSTONE,

I really was rejoiced to see your pretty hand-writing once more. The recollections of old friends are to me infinitely more precious than the attentions of *new*, and though the latter days of my life are by far the most prosperous, yet I look back to the first (adverse though they were), and to those connected with them, with pride and affection—you and Mr. Featherstone are two of the oldest friends I have. I thank you for the expression of friendship contained in your kind letter.

Our journey to Italy has been most prosperous, as well as the pleasantest we ever made. Nothing could equal our reception everywhere. We were particularly fortunate in such a long journey as we have made throughout Italy, not to have met with an accident, and in a country, too, part of which is infested with banditti; but the fatigue was *killing*, accommodation wretched, and expense tremendous.

Imagine, on our reaching home, we found the tenant who had taken our house during our two years' absence, had gone off with the *rent*, destroyed and made away with our furniture, and left our house in such a ruinous condition that we have been obliged already to spend three hundred pounds to make it *habitable*. I have brought many pretty things from Italy, so that we endeavour to console ourselves for our loss by enjoying what is left and what we have added. I am now writing eight hours a day to get ready for publication by December, and endeavour to keep out of the world as well as I can, but invitations pour in. People are curious, I suppose, to hear some news from Rome, and I want to keep it for *my book*. And now, dear Mrs. Featherstone, believe me,

Truly and affectionately yours,

S. MORGAN.

The following letter from Madame Bonaparte shows that lady devoured by energy and *ennui*.

Madame Patterson Bonaparte to Lady Morgan.

GENEVA,
September 30th, 1820.

MY DEAR LADY MORGAN,

I wish they would give us your work on Italy to rouse me from the lethargy into which I have fallen. It is only you that have both power and inclination to make me forget the ennui of existence, and only in your society that I am not entirely *bête*. What shall I do with the long mornings in Geneva? You know you laughed me out of my *maître de litterature*, which, *par parenthèse*, was very inconsiderate, unless you could have pointed out some more amusing method of killing time. Baron Bonstettin came to see me to-day; you were the subject of our conversation, nothing but admiration and regret when we talk of you.

How is dear Sir Charles? He is the only man on earth who knows my value, which has given me the highest opinion of his taste and judgment.

The Marchioness de Villette wishes me to spend a month with her in Paris. I cannot go, although it would be a great *soulagement* to converse with a person who loves me, one has always so much *sur le cœur*, and in this country they are so heartless. I do *dédomager* myself a little by uttering all the ridiculous things which come into my brain, either about others or myself. *A propos*, how do you like the Queen's trial? the newspapers here are worn out in passing from one prude's hand into another's; they are so much inquired for that the *loueurs des Gazettes* have raised their price.

Do not let me forget to tell you that Mr. Sismondi has made my acquaintance—he is married, too; I wonder that people of genius marry; by the way, I recollect that you are an advocate for *le mariage*. Oh! my dear Lady Morgan, I have been in such a state of melancholy, that I wished myself dead a thousand times—all my philosophy, all my courage, are insufficient sometimes to support the inexpressible *ennui* of existence, and in those moments of wretchedness I have no human being to whom I can complain. What do you think of a person advising me to turn Methodist the other day, when I expressed just the hundredth part of the misery I felt? I find no one can comprehend my feelings. Have you read *Les Méditations Poëtiques de Lamartine?* There are some pretty things in them, although he is too *larmoyant*, and of the bad school of politics. Miss Edgworth is here; I visited her; she came to see me with Professor Pictet, and we have never met. She has a great deal of good sense, which is just what I particularly object to, unless accompanied by genius, in my companions. It is only you that combine *tous les genres d'esprit*, and whose society can compensate me for all the losses and the mistakes of my heart; but I shall never see you again, those whom I love and who love me are always distant; I am dragging out life with the indifferent. They are so reasonable and so unmoved in this place, their mornings devoted to the exact sciences, the evenings to whist, that in spite of myself I am obliged to read half the day. There have been some English, but I have seen little of them—they would not like me, I am too *natural où naturelle.* I believe that women are cold, formal, and affected—just my antipodes, therefore we should not be agreeable to each other, besides, they require a year to become acquainted, and I have too little of life left to waste it in formalities.

Do hurry, then, with your work on Italy, *pour maintenir vôtre* reputation, and to give me pleasure— my pleasures are so few that my friends are right to indulge me when they can.

I have seen a German Countess;—that means, seen her every day during three months; she is a practical philosopher of the Epicurean sect, a person just calculated to make something of life—unlike me as possible —she has a great deal more sagacity; to do her justice, she tried *de me débarrasser* of what she called *mes idées romanesques et mes grandes passions;* but I am incorrigible, and go on tormenting myself about things which I cannot change. She had more coarse common sense, with greater knowledge of the world, than any person I have ever known. I wish I resembled her, because I should be more happy.

Adieu, my dear Lady Morgan, write me frequently; your friendship is among the few comforts left me.

E. P.

CHAPTER X.

THE BOOK ON ITALY.

The book on Italy was advertised to appear simultaneously in London and Paris on the 15th of June, 1821. The English edition was announced in two volumes quarto. There had been some difficulty in completing them together. In Colburn's letters, there is a curious incidental mention of there being no post to go out to France between Friday and Tuesday! The French edition was published by Dufour, who is several times mentioned by Lady Morgan in her *Odd Volume*. Dufour found great favour with Lady Morgan. Colburn, in one of his letters, expresses himself hurt that she should consider Dufour's gratitude as something wonderful compared with the insensibility of English publishers. He says, "Ought not Dufour to have an exuberance of gratitude, considering he has got the publication without paying anything for it? Now though *I* am paying two thousand pounds for it, which Lady Morgan calls 'a paltry sum,' but at the mention of which every one held up their hands in amaze, yet I declare that I feel happy that my sanguine temperament has enabled me to go so far towards a remuneration for a species of labour, which is, after all, not to be remunerated by publishers, but by the more pleasing acquisition of *Fame* "

Lady Morgan, however, did not consider fame any substitute for that payment; and Colburn expressed himself much hurt at a jest of hers about " authors and publishers being natural enemies."

Italy appeared nearly on the day appointed. It produced a greater sensation than even the work on France.

Comparatively little was known of Italian society, or the condition of the country. Italy had just passed from the despotic but intelligent sway of Napoleon to the blessings of the " right divine to govern wrong " of the Bourbons; and Lady Morgan's work is full of eloquent lamentation and description of the change for the worse that had come over everything. It is the work of a woman who could see what passed before her eyes, and could understand the meaning of what she saw. There are several chapters on the state of Medical Science and Jurisprudence—contributed by Sir Charles Morgan—marked by solid judgment and good sense.

It is still the best description of the state of Italy, moral and political, as it was at the period of the restoration of the Bourbons.

Her ladyship's criticisms on the public buildings and pictures may lie open to question; but the spirit of the book is noble, and its fascination is undeniable.

To the last, Colburn considered it one of the most valuable of his copyrights.

In his letters, there are curious indications of the state of journalism in those days; except the great reviews, which were governed by party politics, the literary papers were entirely in the hands of those publishers who advertised largely.

Colburn wrote with great satisfaction to Lady Morgan to tell her that the *Examiner*, the *New Times*, and the *John Bull*, had abstained from saying anything against the work, adding naïvely, " I am intimately acquainted with the editors; and *advertising with them a great deal, keeps them in check.*" Criticisms and reviews went more by clique than merit. Colburn's indignation when journals "in which he advertised largely" ventured to say a word in blame or even in question of one of *his* publications, would be comic, if it did not reveal the entire abeyance of moral courage and independent judgment on the part of those who were presumed to guide public opinion in literary matters. The machinery of literary journalism has since then undergone a change.

A letter from Colburn, three weeks after the appearance of the work, reports progress.

Mr. Colburn to Lady Morgan.

LONDON,
June 27, 1821.

DEAR MADAM,

I have forwarded to you some papers, in which the book is mentioned after a fashion,—to call them criticisms would be a misnomer. The *Times* has acted the part of traitor, after getting two copies from me. However, it only confirms me in the opinion that the *Times* is certainly the most illiberal of journals. I was much amused with the *Literary Chronicle* making a heinous offence in me keeping my author before the public! The *Press, Globe, Herald,* and *Statesman,* all speak handsomely; and whether others do so or not, will not affect the sale, which must go on according to the principles laid down for all my publications, or rather yours. It will be well, however, to hear all the remarks before the second edition goes to press. Indeed I hardly knew what I was saying when I talked of commencing immediately, as if the knowledge of a second edition got abroad (as I fear it has in Dublin), it will materially tend to *delay* the publication of it.

I had the pleasure of receiving from Lover the miniature, which is certainly well done. It was necessary to have a fresh background, made the proper size. Meyer is engaged upon it. He will take every pains. It is a pity I had it not three months ago.

The public will be quite ready for a new work in January or February next. But it is high time, I should think, of settling my account, fifteen hundred pounds; the other five hundred to remain open a little while, if you have no objection. I assure you I always wish to be square. If agreeable, instead of giving my bills, I will pay into any banker's in town.

Dear Madam, yours most obediently,

HY. COLBURN.

In another letter of later date, Colburn mentions his delight at Byron's notice of *Italy*, as he declared he saw in it "a great and profitable effect upon the sale."

Lord Byron, writing to Murray, August 24, 1821, said, "When you write to Lady Morgan, will you thank her for her handsome speeches in her book about *my* books? I don't know her address. Her work is fearless and excellent on the subject of Italy. Pray tell her so; and I know the country. I wish she had fallen in with me, I could have told her a thing or two that would have confirmed her positions." His Lordship had been at the pains to defend himself to Murray from the charge of plagiarism in general.

He says, "Much is coincidence; for instance, Lady Morgan (in a really *excellent* book, I assure you, on Italy) calls Venice an *ocean Rome;* I have the very same expression in *Foscari,* and yet *you* know that the play was written months ago, and sent to England; the *Italy* I only received on the 16th instant."

Amongst Lady Morgan's correspondence at this time, extending over a period of several years, are a series of letters, all more or less long and sorrowful, from Italian and Spanish refugees. Even clever people cease to be capable of writing amusing letters when they are in distress.

These "refugees" were men who had been mixed up in plots to attempt to gain political freedom and enlightened laws for their country, which had been condemned by other nations to return to the old Bourbon rule. Some of these men had suffered imprisonment, and, after many trials and tortures, had escaped to England to lead a life of exile in poverty, worse to bear in England than elsewhere. Sir Charles and Lady Morgan were much in advance of the political opinions of their time. They sympathised with the Italian people in their struggles, when there was as yet no public interest for them; when England cared little for these things, they nobly repaid all the kindness they had received during their sojourn in Italy, by patient untiring zeal in behalf of the Italian refugees, who came over in shoals after the unsuccessful rising of 1821. All who came addressed themselves to Lady Morgan; appealing to her to obtain for them money, employment, advice, assistance; in short, for every conceivable service which one human being can require from another.

To those who know what it is to endeavour to serve to the utmost, with necessarily limited powers, which every one persists in believing to be *unlimited*, Lady Morgan's unflagging, cheerful, exertions on behalf of the Italian and Spanish refugees will be at once a matter of surprise and admiration. The mere reading of these letters, to say nothing of paying the postage, must have been no slight effort to a woman naturally so impatient of dulness and expense as Lady Morgan.

Archibald Hamilton Rowan was a gentleman of family and fortune. In 1791 he was Secretary of the Dublin Society of United Irishmen. He was prosecuted for a seditious libel in 1794, and sentenced to two years' imprisonment in Newgate, with a fine of five hundred pounds. Curran made a celebrated speech on Rowan's trial. The principal witness against him was a worthless and disreputable man, named Lyster. There is a life of Rowan by Dr. Drummond. Rowan's fortune was originally five thousand pounds a year, on which, however, his philanthropy made heavy draughts. "He had always," says his friend, Lord Cloncurry, "some adventure on his hands, and two or three of these in which he rescued distressed damsels from the snares and force of ravishers, made a deal of noise at the time." During the period when he was in America, he was often in want of money, his remittances from home being uncertain. He was indebted for a livelihood to his mechanical skill, which enabled him to take charge of a cotton factory at New York. In his youth he was eminently handsome, remarkable for his noble stature and bodily strength. He was proud of having run a foot-race in the presence of Marie Antoinette and the whole French Court in jack boots, against an officer of the *Garde du Corps*, dressed in light shoes and silk stockings; he won with ease, to the great admiration of the Queen, who honoured him with many marks of regard. He kept up his strength and remarkable appearance to the last; he might be seen in the streets of Dublin, a gigantic old man, in an old-fashioned dress, followed by two noble dogs, the last of the Irish race of wolf dogs.

The following letter from him to Sir Charles Morgan was written during the period of George the Fourth's visit, and alludes to some royal *gentillesse* not acceptable to the lady.

Hamilton Rowan to Sir Charles Morgan.

September 14th, 1821.

MY DEAR SIR CHARLES,

I did my duty to my Sov—— no, to my family. I kissed the lion's paw, but did not attempt to pull the tail of the beast. I have seen my caricatures, which are strong likenesses of the original, but until I saw George the Fourth, I never met a person who in features, contour, and general mien out-did their caricature. Hone's likeness in the House that Jack Built is a flattery.

I shall be well pleased to hear that the charms of the Hermitage give way to the boudoir and library in Kildare Street. I really am not fit to leave home for more than a few hours. I even cross the bridge with reluctance. Yet I rowed my boat down to the bay, expecting a noble assemblage of vessels of war, but I was disappointed; probably because when soldiering on South Sea Common, I had repeatedly seen the British fleet riding at Spit Head. You have heard how Mrs. Dawson drove his Majesty from her society, and Mr. Dawson, I hear, says he is not surprised at it, as she is so old and ugly, that he has not kissed her himself these seventeen years. I hear he does not think the Irish ladies remarkable for their beauty. There are to be *six feasts* a year, &c., &c., &c., which, however, are at a stand, for Hercules is cleansing the prisons.

A letter from London of the 11th, says the King is

at Milford, and proceeds by land to London, where, I believe, other greetings will meet him, than he found on this side of the channel. Will all this end in smoke?

Two bad days after what we have had are bad omens for rents. Yet, I cannot think with Mr. Attwood, that an issue of notes would cure short payments. I do think the monied interest should bear a proportion of the incumbrance, but really, the taking off duty on the manufacture of grain, and supplying the deficit by seven-and-a-half per cent. on poor devils who receive one hundred pounds a-year as compensation for their services, and letting contractors for loans, &c. go free, is not fair play.

I am yours sincerely,
A. H. ROWAN.

I am lithographising Mr. Wolff's prayer over the corse of the persecuted—injured Queen of England.

CHAPTER XI.

LIFE AND TIMES OF SALVATOR ROSA.

A SECOND edition of *Italy* in two volumes octavo had been put into the press as early as August of the preceding year, but the publication had, for trade reasons, been delayed. It came out in January, 1822; Colburn going to immense expense in advertising it. During her sojourn in Italy, Lady Morgan had become enthusiastic about Salvator Rosa, both as a hero and an artist, and had collected many materials for writing the history of his life and times. The work on Italy had to be completed before she began any other work; but no sooner was *Italy* through the press than she was busy with *Salvator Rosa*. After a long correspondence Colburn agreed to her terms for the copyright of this new work. He engaged to give her five hundred pounds, and entreated her to get on with it as quickly as possible.

With liberal good sense he sent her as a present all the books that he conceived would be useful to her in the course of her work. He also pathetically entreated her to take care of her eyes, and to have green cloth upon the table where she wrote.

In addition to her swarm of Spanish and Italian refugees, Lady Morgan had, at this time, an Irishman on her hands: a man of genius, and as difficult to help as all the rest put together. It was the Reverend Charles Robert Maturin. This gentleman was the author of a tragedy, called *Bertram*, in which Kean had appeared at Drury Lane, and of a romance called *Melmoth*, which had made a sensation, and for which he had received five hundred pounds. He was not an unsuccessful author, for Colburn, writing to Sir Charles Morgan, in 1818, says, "Maturin's tragedy has run through many editions, and has certainly made him a great name." Maturin had, since that time, fallen into great distress; he had written another tragedy and another novel, which neither managers nor publishers would take; and he wrote quires of letters to Lady Morgan entreating her to use her influence with Kean and Elliston to take the tragedy, and with Colburn to bring out his new novel. To those asking assistance and patronage, it seems very hard that they who have succeeded for themselves should fail in their attempt to help others; but neither the success nor the qualities that earn success can be transferred. On the contrary, the ill fortune seems to re-act on those who try to help them.

The difference between the position of Maturin and that of Lady Morgan was the result of the difference in their characters. That fetish of Ireland "good luck," had befriended him once. His early chances in life had been far better than Lady Morgan's; but he could not use them. Sir Charles raised a subscription for him, amounting to fifty pounds. The first use he made of it was to give a grand party. There was little furniture in the reception room, but at one end there had been erected an old theatrical property throne under a canopy of crimson velvet, where he and Mrs. Maturin sat to receive their visitors.

Once, when Mrs. Maturin was confined, Lady Morgan called to enquire after her and the baby—the Irish servant who opened the door took the enquiry to her master, and returned with the message, "Plaze, my Lady, the masther says, 'My angel is better, but my cherub has flown!'"—a piece of "good luck" for the cherub.

Melmoth the Wanderer, and another romance called *Woman*, or *Pour et Contre*, had each a success in its day. A search in any old circulating library would disinter them, and they would repay perusal. Isidora, in *Melmoth*, and Eva, in *Pour et Contre*, are female characters which deserve to be recollected amongst the ideal women who inhabit the pages of romance. A man who had made such a success ought not to have required any further help.

Maturin subsequently wrote a tragedy which was accepted at Drury Lane—called *Manuel*—Kean taking the part of the hero. Its success was not equal to that of *Bertram*—which is still played occasionally. After *Manuel*, he wrote another tragedy, which was played at Covent Garden, called *Fridolfo*. We remember to have read them both, but can only testify to the blankness of the impression they have left. Maturin also published a volume of sermons which were entertaining.

He died in great poverty, feeling resentment equally against those who helped him and those who had not.

In December 21, 1821, Colburn wrote a formal proposal to Lady Morgan, offering two thousand pounds if she and Sir Charles would write a work on Germany, similar in design to her books on France and Italy. This proposition, however, never came to anything, Lady Morgan being at that time engrossed with her *Life and Times of Salvator Rosa.*

If Colburn's letters and memoirs were published, they would form a chapter in the secret history of English literature. His letters to Sir Charles and Lady Morgan abound in curious details of his method of making "his authors," as he always styled them, and their books successful. After Sir Richard Phillips, Colburn was the person most connected with Lady Morgan's literary life; and he was as much fascinated by her wit and grace as a woman, as Sir Richard Phillips had been; but, like Sir Richard, he was afraid of letting his admiration interfere with a good bargain. Lady Morgan, on her side, was perfectly indifferent to all flattery from her publishers which did not tend to profit.

Here is a note from Lord Erskine, who, in his turn, had been flattered by Lady Morgan's compliment on his style.

Lord Erskine to Lady Morgan.

13, Arabella Row, Pimlico,
October 11*th*, 1822.

Dear Lady Morgan,

A long time ago, in one of your excellent works (all of which I have read with great satisfaction), 'I remember your having expressed your approbation of my *style* of writing, and a wish that I would lose no occasion of rendering it useful. I wish I could agree with your Ladyship in your kind and partial opinion; but as there never was an occasion in which it can be more useful to excite popular feeling than in the cause of the Greeks, I send your Ladyship a copy of the second edition, published a few days ago.

I have the honour to be,
With regard and esteem,
Your Ladyship's faithful, humble servant,
Erskine.

In her search after materials for her *Life of Salvator Rosa*, Lady Morgan applied to Lord Darnley, who was known to possess a number of the painter's noblest works. Lord Darnley at once replied to her request for information as follows:—

Lord Darnley to Lady Morgan.

Berkeley Square,
October 30*th*, 1822.

Lord Darnley presents his compliments to Lady Morgan, and loses no time in returning an answer to the letter with which he has been honoured by her ladyship.

The *Death of Regulus*, by Salvator Rosa, is, and has been for some years, in Lord Darnley's possession, having been purchased by him, together with another very fine picture by Guido, from an Italian of the name of Bonelli, who had brought them from Rome, where they were both in the Colonna Palace, till the Prince was compelled to sell them (as Lord Darnley has been informed) to enable him to pay the contribution levied by the French. The *Regulus* was always esteemed. It is believed to be Salvator's finest work. The exact price paid for it Lord Darnley cannot ascertain, as there are other things included in the bargain. It was certainly very large, but not so much as generally supposed.

There is also in Lord Darnley's collection at Cobham Hall, another Salvator Rosa, inferior in merit only to the *Regulus*, representing *Pythagoras teaching his doctrine to Fishermen*.

There is an etching of the *Regulus*, by Salvator himself, which Lord Darnley believes may easily be obtained, and which will give a much better idea of the picture than any description can afford.

Whenever Lady Morgan again visits the Continent, she will find these pictures exactly in her way; and Lord Darnley hopes she will take the opportunity of convincing herself of their merit, and that their common friend, Mr. Porri, will be her *cicerone*.

Lord Darnley is rather surprised that Lady Morgan should have heard nothing of the *Regulus* in Italy, as the place it occupied in the gallery of the Colonna Palace, at Rome, is pointed out.

A letter from an old Irish gentleman who had "registered a vow;" marks the spirit of the times, and may wind up the letters of this year.

Sir Capel Molyneux to Sir Charles Morgan.

MERRION SQUARE,
24th *December*, 1822.

MY DEAR SIR CHARLES,

I think it necessary to inform you that when the Union Act passed, a few patriots, with myself, invoked the most *solemn imprecations on our heads* if we should ever attend levee, ball, or dinner, at the Castle until its repeal should take place!!! I have great respect for Lord Wellesley. I admire his liberality. I did all I could, leaving my ticket at the Park at Woodstock. You will explain this, if agreeable to the gentlemen of the household. With compliments to Lady Morgan,

Yours very truly,
C. MOLYNEUX.

CHAPTER XII.

WRITING THE LIFE AND TIMES OF SALVATOR ROSA—1823.

LADY MORGAN was searching in all directions for information about Salvator Rosa's pictures. Amongst others, she wrote to Lady Caroline Lamb, who interested her brother in the subject, and to the Duchess of Devonshire. The Duchess's answer contains gossip about pictures and other matters. The writer of this letter was not Georgiana, the beautiful, electioneering Duchess, but the second wife of the Duke (Lady Elizabeth Foster) who died in 1824.

The Duchess of Devonshire to Lady Morgan.

ROME,
March 22nd, 1823.

MY DEAR MADAM,

I should not have delayed so long answering your interesting letter, if I had not been almost in daily expectation of some part of the information which you was so anxious to obtain on the subject of Salvator Rosa's writings and musical compositions. All that I have yet received was, the day before yesterday, in a letter from the Abate Cancilliari to M. Molagoni, one of Cardinal Gonsalvi's secretaries. I enclose you what he says. The answer from Baini, about his musical compositions, I have not yet received. Cammuccini told me that there only remained at Rome two undoubted pictures of Salvator Rosa, and that there were two small landscapes at Palazzo Spada. The picture which you mention at Palazzo Chigi, they seem ignorant of, or to doubt its being what you represent it. The same of *La Lucrezia*. I wish that I could have been of more use to you; and I shall be anxious to see the *Life of Salvator Rosa* when it is published. General Cockburn is still here; and I have told him how difficult it is to obtain any of the works which you mention. I was told that some sonnets were published; but I went to De Romani's, and he had them not. If anybody can procure the music, it is Baini. I am very glad that you are not unoccupied; and I can easily conceive the interest which you have taken in writing the life of so extraordinary a genius.

We have had a severe winter for Rome; and even to-day, though very fine here, we saw snow on the Alban Hill. A Marchesa Farra Cuppa has begun an excavation at Torneto, ancient Tarquinia, which has excited a great degree of interest. A warrior with his lance and shield was discovered entire, but the first blast of air reduced it to dust. She gave me part

of his shield. A small vase of a beautiful form and two very large oxen are, I believe, coming to the Vatican Museum. The antiquity of them is calculated at three thousand years. Other excavations are making by some proprietors at Roma Vecchia. The first *fouille* produced a beautiful mosaic statue of a fine stag, in black marble. I feel gratified that my Horace's satire is approved of. Pray are there in it two of Pinelli's engravings and compositions to the Latin text? If not, I will send them you by General Cockburn. I beg my best compliments to Sir Charles,
    And am, dear Madam,
        Your ladyship's very sincerely,
            ELIZABETH DEVONSHIRE.

PS.—A fine statue of a Bacchus has been discovered, about four days ago, not far from Cecilia Metella's tomb.

Lady Caroline Lamb had written to her brother, the Honourable William Ponsonby, to ask him for information about Salvator Rosa for Lady Morgan. The information contained in his letter is interesting to those who admire, or collect, his pictures.

The Honourable William Ponsonby to Lady C. Lamb.

BRIGHTON,
April 20, 1823.

DEAREST SISTER,
  I send you all that I can recollect about Salvator Rosa's pictures. I must have some account in town

of all those I have seen, or liked, abroad; but now I can only quote from memory. Lady Morgan will, of course, have much better information, both from books or her own observations, than any I can send. Boydel's engravings, and Richardson's and Pond's, give some of the finest pictures in England. With respect to the Duke of Beaufort, he has no pictures of any kind now (but family portraits); and I much doubt any of any great reputation having, at any time, been purchased in Italy, unless Lady Morgan is very sure of the fact. I could easily find out by applying to the Duke, if she wishes it. The second and third Dukes of Devonshire were both great collectors of gems, precious stones, books, pictures, drawings, prints, &c., and the Salvators at Devonshire House were bought by them: I think by the third. *Jacob's Vision* is, I believe, reckoned the finest; but I like the large landscape at Chiswick, which was bought by Lord Burlington, the best. It is the fashion now to run down all the pictures at Devonshire House and Chiswick; but I do not believe justly. Amongst the number, there may be some bad; but I would back Sir Joshua Reynolds' and West's opinions and my own eye, though I am no judge, against modern critics. My brother had two, *Zenocrates and Phryne*, still at Roehampton, and a smaller one, which you must recollect, *Jason and the Dragon;* the figure in armour, spirited and graceful, like all Salvator's, and the rocks almost as natural as at Sorrento, and the cave where he studied; both have been, I think, engraved by Boydel. The former was bought by my grandfather, at the sale of the old Lord Cholmondeley; the *latter* has had rather a remarkable fate, having belonged to two of the richest men in England, in the possession of both of whom it seemed likely to remain; and, indeed, in my grandfather's it seemed tolerably secure, though he was not quite in that predicament. He bought it at the sale of the Duke of Chandos, in Cavendish Square. It was afterwards sold to Mr. W. Smith, and, at his sale, travelled back again in the possession of Watson Taylor to its old habitation in Cavendish Square,—likewise purchased by Watson Taylor. It is now shortly to be sold again with his pictures; but I hope Lady Morgan will not puff it before its sale takes place, as I have great thoughts of squeezing out all I can possibly afford, to try and get it back again, though it does seem to *porter malheur*. She, of course, knows of the *Belisarius* still at Raynham. It was given by the King of Prussia to Lord Townshend when Secretary of State. There were formerly two (if not three) very large pictures by him at Lansdowne House, left by the late Lord Lansdowne to the Dowager, and sold by her. I have some idea the present Lord Lansdowne bought them back. I only remember the subject of one of them,—*Diogenes:* fine, but not a pleasing picture. It has been etched by Salvator Rosa himself, together with three other large ones; but I forget whether either of the other two I mentioned at Lansdowne House are amongst them. The four are these,—*Diogenes; Regulus*, formerly at the Colonna Palace, at Rome, but not there now. I have seen it, but forgotten where; *the Battle of the*

Giants; and the Child exposed, hanging on a most beautiful tree. They are generally bound up with his etchings of groups and single figures. Lord Ashburnham has, I believe, *St. John preaching in the Wilderness.* The *Prodigal Son* travelled to Petersburgh with the Houghton collection. Two very fine sea views at the Pitti Palace, and the *Witch of Endor,* formerly at the Garde Meuble et Versailles, and now, I suppose, in the Louvre. I find one at Lord Derby's. Prince Ramoffski showed me a card at Vienna, in the lid of a snuff-box, on it a very pretty sketch by Salvator Rosa, which he is said to have done one day that he called on a friend who was out, to show him he had been there. They tell pretty much the same story of Michael Angelo at Rome. There is, at Rome, a painter who paints Claudes and Salvators for the use of the *forestieri* in a most extraordinary manner, and has taken in numbers of us.

Your affectionate brother,
WILLIAM PONSONBY.

A letter from General Cockburn to Lady Morgan, with the result of his enquiries about Salvator Rosa's works; he was the author of a dissertation on the Passage of Hannibal over the Alps.

General Cockburn to Lady Morgan.

ROME, *May 24th,* 1823.

MY DEAR LADY MORGAN,

I have at last got into the Chigi palace. The Duchess of Devonshire was there the same day, and took Camacini with her (a first rate artist), and we saw the picture of the *Satyr and Philosopher*, and formed the following verdict—

> Done by Salvator Rosa no more
> Than by Jacky Poole or Lord Glandore.

From Croker's ill-natured lines on one of our poor friend J. Atkinson's plays. The *Philosopher*, not like any print I ever saw of Rosa, and there is no other picture in the palace or in Rome even reported to be a portrait of him.

The Duchess also took Camacini to the capitol to see the Magi, called Salvator Rosa's; our verdict, *a vile performance*, not worth sixpence, and certainly not done by Rosa,—and appeal against this if you please. There are two magnificent and genuine pictures of his here, one in the Colonna Palace, *Prometheus chained to the Rock*, and the Vulture devouring him, horribly well done. The other is an altar-piece in the church of St. John, Dei Fiorestini; namely, the Martyrdom of Sts. Cosmos and Damian on the pile, but the fire, instead of burning them, by a miracle, burns their persecutors, which it would not have done, had such unbelievers as you and Sir Charles been on the pile; and old *Sardinia* would willingly have you both on such a pile if he could, and *en attendant*, he *burns* your Italy whenever he can lay hold of a copy. I wish the old rascal and the two Ferdinands, Naples and Spain, were to suffer martyrdom,—but I should be content to hang or throw into the sea,—not liking torture. I saw the librarian this day, at the Vatican, and he swears as hard as any

Pat ever did before *Baron Boulter*—that Salvator Rosa left no music, at least, none in the Vatican.

Now you have got all the information which Rome can produce on the subject, so go to press as fast as you can. We shall remain in dear Rome another month; if you answer this, direct—*Venice, poste restante.* I shall not be more than three weeks going there, from hence, and that will just give time for you to receive this, and for us to hear you are well, wicked, and radical as ever.

I remain,
My dear Lady Morgan,
Most sincerely yours,
G. COCKBURN.

From Lady C. Lamb and her brother, William Ponsonby, there is a joint letter, containing further information about Salvator Rosa's pictures.

Lady Caroline Lamb and Hon. Wm. Ponsonby, to Lady Morgan.

19, ST. JAMES'S SQUARE,
May 27th, 1823.

I hope you will not impute it to me that your questions are not answered; the truth is, I am in the country, enjoying this most beautiful time of year, and my brother has written me word that he will make all the inquiries you desire, but how soon this may be I cannot tell. Lord Cowper will write down on paper *about one only.* The two at Panshanger are landscapes in the usual dark, abrupt style. The one at Chiswick, much larger, is reckoned very fine; there is a famous Belisarius there, but I do not think they know who it is by; the Soldier in Armour and the old Belisarius are quite beautiful,—can this be a Salvator? The Phryne you name, has reddish, or rather, yellow hair, and is by no means decent in her drapery. I never could endure that picture; it is not, I fancy, at Rochampton now; there was a very fine one there besides, which my brother will name to you. I must try and see the one you mention; but it is not this month that I can do anything beside staring at the flowers and trees. All this is very unsatisfactory, therefore, only consider this letter as a kind of apology for my delay. You shall hear more soon.

Dear Madam,

My sister sends me this letter to forward to you, and apologizes for not having done your commission earlier, because she was in the country. I must do the same, because I am in town, and really have had my time completely taken up by business; besides, as you must know, the great houses from which our information is to be obtained, are not always the most easy of access. Not to lose more time than necessary, I thought it better to write direct to you and recall to your recollection our old Dublin and Priory acquaintance, than send any little information I might be able to glean round by Brocket. As for *Phryne*, I cannot say I ever was much struck with the modesty and decency of her attire and countenance. She and the philosopher appear to be engaged in a very warm argument, but she does not exhibit herself as she did to the Grecian painter on the sea shore, nor has she recourse to the expedient she made use of to melt the stern hearts of her judges. There is nothing eloquent in the picture, however, and it is not one which I ever thought very pleasing; this is still in Lord Bessborough's possession at *Roehampton.* The *Jason was sold,* and was a most beautiful picture, full of all the bold and wild character of Salvator's landscapes, and the grace which I think he usually shows in his figures, though Sir Joshua Reynolds says no. The Russian prince's name is Ramoffski. The Duke of Beaufort has a curious picture by Salvator Rosa, at Budminton, but I do not recollect seeing it, though I have often been there. I will enquire more particularly as to the subject the first time I see him, but the story is that it was painted to ridicule the pope and cardinals, and that he was banished from Rome in consequence. I think Phryne's hair is light. The Belisarius is still in Lord Townshend's collection at Raynham, and was given to the Secretary of State of that family, by the King of Prussia. The Belisarius my sister mentions at Chiswick, is of doubtful origin, but never claimed Salvator Rosa as brother, and could not be listened to in any court if sworn to him. It has been sometimes said to be by Vandyke (and is stated so in the engraving I think) sometimes by Murillo, and is a very fine picture. I do not know where the Giants are, nor the Child Exposed, whom I believe to be Œdipus. I will make enquiry concerning Lord Lansdowne's, Lord

Ashburnham's, and Lord Morpeth's pictures. Those at Devonshire House are the *Jacob's Vision*, with the angels ascending and descending by the ladder to and from heaven, one of *Jacob and the Angel wrestling;* and another, landscape, with huge trees and rocks, with soldiers reposing on them. There is a large landscape at Chiswick. His letters are curious, and I believe rather difficult to be met with now. Would not a new edition, with some observations on them, form a good second volume of his life. I fear I have but very inefficiently executed your commission, but beg leave to assure you that it is not from want of inclination.

Yours, most truly,
W. S. PONSONBY.

The Duchess of Devonshire, along with much kind interest expressed in Lady Morgan's work, gives a little grave remonstrance on her Ladyship's habit of hasty judgment and rash assertion.

The Duchess of Devonshire to Lady Morgan.

ROME,
May 31st, 1823.

DEAR LADY MORGAN,

I send you a list of the pictures which are known to be Salvator Rosa's, and those that are attributed to him. You will see what you attribute to the ignorance or indifference of Prince Chigi to the treasure which he possesses, is a proof of his being neither ignorant nor indifferent, but convinced that the picture did not deserve to be classed as the performance of that great painter, and discouraging its being called his.

I have taken with pleasure all the pains necessary to procure you the information which you wanted, but do not be offended if I say that I should have felt still more pleasure in doing so were you less unjust to this country; fallen they are certainly in power, but not in intellect, or talent, or worth of every kind; and your stay in Italy was far too short to admit of your appreciating them as your own undoubted talent would have enabled you to do, had you staid longer and derived your information from other sources. You said to me once, that were you to write your journey in France again, that you should write it very differently. I am sure you would say the same were you to come again into Italy; every monument of antiquity is attended to with the greatest care, and every picture that requires it is either cleaned, or noted down to be so. The commission of five attend on every new discovery to give their opinion as to the merit of what is found, and most productive have this year's excavations proved to be in sculpture. Mosaic repairs go on, and new buildings in every part of Rome, and the Braccio Nuovo alone merits, in the Duke of Devonshire's opinion, that one should come from London to Rome were it only to see that beautiful new museum, begun and completed by a pope from the age of seventy-nine to eighty-two!

I know not any capital so adorned by its sovereign as this is. To know with certainty the different objects, there is a catalogue by Signor Camacini; of all the classical pictures in the churches, and galleries, and palaces,—of all those that deserve citation,—of all the frescoes, outward and inward,—of the different houses which are classical or rare. We are often apt to think things are unknown because we have fancied them valuable on the authority of Vasi, or a *lacquey de place*, and find the owner scarcely knowing of their existence; Vasi and the *lacquey* having given an assumed name, and the proprietor, like Prince Chigi, who is a man of taste, of science even, and of elegant literature, is called ignorant because he disclaims the assumed merit given to his picture. Prince Chigi has a small gallery of excellent pictures and statues, and the Filosofo was shown me on my request, because *put by as not Salvator's*. He has the famous Cicero, and a cameo with the last battle of Alexander the Great; these the Prince shows himself.

Baini is living, he is a man of great musical science, he composed a fine *Miserere*, which was sung this year; but Salvator improvised his compositions, and no written ones can be found. Monseigneur Mai made diligent search for me, but in vain. If I can be of any further use to you, pray write to me. General Cockburn is still at Rome.

Events of the day are passing which may deserve blame, but the efforts,—the heroic efforts which the Greeks have made and are making, are worthy of all our admiration, and will end, I hope, by restoring that interesting country to its situation in Europe. There is matter to animate your genius, and I hope you will turn your thoughts to something that may tend to do justice to this long oppressed and calumniated pople. And, my dear Lady Morgan, I must add, in praise also of my dear Rome, that the Greek fugitives were received in Ancona, and fed and lodged there. This is true tolerance.

Once more adieu, my dear Madam, and pray let me know when your life of Salvator Rosa will appear; I have no doubt of the success which it will meet with.

Very sincerely yours,
E. DEVONSHIRE.

So much for Salvator Rosa and his pictures. Whilst Lady Morgan was busy rehabilitating the name and character of a man of genius, she was undergoing a very unpleasant ordeal herself.

Sir Charles Morgan had been knighted by an act of personal favour, before he had done any thing ostensibly to merit the distinction, and it had been made a handle for ill-natured sarcasm; but vague ill-nature gave place to special hostility. Lady Morgan had made herself too marked a personage in the liberal interest to escape the hatred of the opposite party. The Tory clique desired to mortify her by any means, they were not particular about their weapon, and they certainly hit upon a method which was likely to mortify her to their heart's content.

The right of the Lord-Lieutenant to confer the honour of knighthood was impugned. It was speciously argued that since the union, the king alone in person could confer honours. The titles of several

of their own partisans were at stake as well as Sir C.
Morgan's; but they were willing to sacrifice a few of
their friends to their hatred of Lady Morgan. The case
was argued in England before the judges at the house
of the Lord Chief Justice Dallas. Legal opinion was
favourable to the privilege, and the following letter
conveyed the intelligence to Sir Charles Morgan. Lady
Morgan cared for the title a great deal more than her
husband did; but it would have been a mortification
to him to have had it declared an illegal possession.

J. Rock to Sir Charles Morgan.

OFFICE OF ARMS, WESTLAND ROW,
June 30, 1823.

In the absence of Sir William Betham, I beg leave
to state for your information, that on Tuesday last the
judges of England assembled at the house of Lord
Chief Justice Dallas, in London, in pursuance of the
royal mandate, to take into consideration and decide
upon the disputed power of the Lord-Lieutenant of
Ireland to confer the honour of knighthood. Two of
the number were unable to attend from illness; but
the other ten were of opinion unanimously that the
Lord-Lieutenant did possess the power, and that knights
created by him were knights throughout the world.

I expect the return of Sir William Betham from
England in the course of this week, when the above
solemn decision will be given to the public in a man-

nor equally *notorious* as the doubts of the Lords of the Admiralty which originally occasioned the discussion.

I have the honour to be, sir,
Your most obedient,
Very humble servant,
F. ROCK.

Amusing letter from Lady Caroline Lamb, complains of false reports. She suffered more than most persons from this "common lot," though "candid friends" would have told her she brought it on herself.

Lady Caroline Lamb to Lady Morgan.

August 8, 1823.

I have been much annoyed to-day by a paragraph in two papers about my turning a woman out of doors —pray if you see or hear of it, contradict it. As I hope for mercy, it is a most shameful falsehood made by a very wicked girl, because I sent her away. She came to me as Agnes Drummond, a spinster, and ten days after hid a man in Brockett Hall; the servants, in an uproar, discovered him in the evening; he said first his name was Drummond, then Fain—it was natural we should desire him to walk out, in particular as Agnes Drummond had confided to me, only the day before, that she had been married, when sixteen, to a thief of the name of Fain, who had married her and carried away her watch and property. I trouble you with this, as I see my name as having *beaten* her and turned her out of doors *without clothes*, in the night; instead of which, my coachman conveyed her to an inn, and had great difficulty in making her sleep there. She took my clothes away and seal, which were taken from her. She now calls herself Fain,—her own clothes were marked *E. M.* She left them wet in the laundry or they would have been sent to her that night.

I have, I think, the very person Lady Cloncurry would like; she is about twenty-two, very clever, good, and with a good manner, writes a beautiful hand, knows music thoroughly, both harp and pianoforte. She is attached to an old mathematician in Russia—a Platonic attachment; his name is Wronsky, so that as they are not to marry or meet for ten years, she is very anxious to go into any respectable and comfortable family where she will be well treated; she draws, paints uncommonly well, and, provided she had a room to herself, a fire, pen, ink, and paper, or a book, I dare say she will make herself comfortable anywhere; how far she would like Ireland, I guess not, as her views turned to Italy or Paris: if, however, your lady will communicate with her herself, I will send you her answer; she is a person of strict morals and great propriety—a little high, but excessively sweet-tempered. She is by no means expensive, yet to go to Ireland I think she would ask eighty guineas—is that too much? She would dedicate all her time to the children after ten in the morning to six at night;

she would play also on the harp of an evening, read to the lady if she were ill, or write her letters for her.

Ever yours,
CAROLINE LAMB.

There are other letters from the same fascinating and gifted, but most unhappy, lady. They are full of a whimsical grace, and might have been written by a bird of Paradise for all the practical sense they evince. Lady Morgan was very much attached to her, and tried to inspire her with common sense; but of that it holds good, as Rubini said of singing, "*Monsieur, le chant ne s'enseigne pas.*" She was full of generous impulses and good instinct; but she was too wilful either to hold or to bind. More than most women, she needed to be wisely guided, and this wise guidance was precisely the "one thing lacking" to her brilliant lot.

Lady Caroline Lamb to Lady Morgan.

September, 1823.

MY DEAR AND MOST AMIABLE LADY MORGAN,

I thank you from my heart for what you said Sir Charles would do; and now, as you say, for business. It is a disagreeable thing to recommend any one, and in particular when the education of children is a point at stake. I therefore shall write you word for the inspection of Lord and Lady Cloncurry, all I know of Miss Bryan, although the knowledge that my letter is to be seen by strangers will prevent my writing as fully as I otherwise should. Pray tell me something of Lady Charlemont. I feel very much interested for her. My dearest mother liked her. Lady Abercorn admired her, and so did Lord Byron. She has, I am sure, suffered very, very much. Sometime or other, tell me how Lord Caulfield came to die, and how Lady Charlewood is. Pray, in your prettiest manner, remember me to her. I enclose you, upon trust, a letter of Miss Bryan; but as there are two or three trifling mistakes in grammar, do not show it. Only see what her feelings are. I feel interested for her; yet she and I are not "congenial souls." She is more dignified, tranquil, calm, gentle, and self-possessed, than I am; and therefore, if she is made to be all she can be, she will do better to bring up others. Now as every one must, will, and should fall in love, it is no bad thing that she should have a happy, Platonic, romantic attachment to an old mad mathematician several thousand miles off. It will keep her steady, which, in truth, she is—beyond her years. Added to this, she plays perfectly; can draw quite well enough to teach; do beauty work; paint flowers; write and read well; and teach the harp. For manner, dress, arrangement, appearance, exactness,—do well. What I do not know about her is this,—I do not know if she is able to impart her knowledge. I do not know if she is religious, although I presume she is. Lady Cloncurry must guide her; she is yet but young, and I advise most particularly that she should begin as she intends to proceed. Miss Bryan is very gentle, although proud, and can bear being spoken to; but she requires to be told the plain truth, whole truth, and all the truth.

She has, certainly, good abilities and considerable knowledge. Of the latter, perhaps rather too much, as it makes her somewhat positive; but there is no conceit: her presumption is in her manner. It appears to me that there is a good chance of her doing well; but Lady Morgan must be aware that the power of instructing is almost a gift of nature; that many of the best instructed themselves are very deficient in it. She must also be aware that much temper and management is necessary to enable a person to like well the situation of a governess, which, in every family, will be beset by some of the difficulties and annoyances which Lady Morgan has well described in *O'Donnel*.

With great regard,
CAROLINE.

Lady Caroline's story of a Governess is continued in her correspondence along with other stories, not so positive in their human interest.

Lady Caroline Lamb to Lady Morgan.

October, 1823.

MY DEAR LADY MORGAN,

Thank you and thank Sir Charles for all his kindness about my fairy tale, *Ada Reis*, although I think he uses a rod even whilst he is merciful. I must now tell you about Miss Bryan. She has caught cold, and been very, very ill. I would not, for the world, have Lady Cloncurry wait for her; but if she chances to be without a proper person when well, Miss Bryan would assuredly go. However, it is no loss to the girl, as I feel sure she wishes to die or to marry Wronsky, and therefore do nothing further about her. She is sensible, handsome, young, good, unsophisticated, independent, true, ladylike, above any deceit or meanness, romantic, very punctual about money, but she has a cold and cough, and is in love. I cannot help it; can you?

Whoever has reviewed *Ada Reis* must not think me discontented, neither unhappy. The loss of what one adores affects the mind and heart; but I have resigned myself to it, and God knows I am satisfied with all I have and have had. My husband has been to me as a guardian angel. I love him most dearly; and my boy, though afflicted, is clever, amiable, and cheerful.

Dear Lady Morgan, let me not be judged by hasty works and hasty letters. My heart is as calm as a lake on a fine summer day; and I am as grateful to God for his mercy and blessing as it is possible to be. Tell all this to Sir Charles; and pray write to me. Your letters amuse me excessively. I would I had anything clever or pretty to pay in return.

CAROLINE.

Joseph Hume, then M.P., for Middlesex, was a correspondent of Sir Charles. The present generation may not know so much of Joseph Hume and his economies as the one that has just passed away. He was a man who did his duty sturdily, and was a thoroughly honest man, of the stuff that builds up a nation.

Joseph Hume to Sir Charles Morgan.

LONDON,
December 19th, 1823.

DEAR SIR,

As it is my intention to bring the Church Establishment of Ireland before the House of Commons in the ensuing session, I shall be obliged by your sending me any authentic accounts of the value of the Church property, *i.e.*, of the bishops, deans, and chapters of any diocese, that I may lay it before the public as completely as possible.

The cause is so good a one that I wish to be in moderation, and within bounds, as exaggeration always hurts our cause.

The system of tithes ought to be entirely abolished, as every attempt, like that of the last session, to bolster up so preposterous and a bad system must tender to render the change too violent when it shall be made; and the late conduct of some of the church militant will only hasten the event.

Until a radical change takes place in the Church establishment and Church property, there will be no peace in your wretched country, and every aid to affect these changes will be a real benefit to the country.

To expose these evils of the system of tithes as it has been working in the last year, it would be of great use to me if you could cut out of any newspapers all the cases that can be depended upon, where burnings, murders, the interposition of the military, the destruction of cattle, &c., &c., have taken place on account of the tithe system, that they may be brought into array at once; also the conduct of such of the clergy as have taken the law into their own hands, or have behaved harshly so as to produce disturbance or mischief.

Can any account be obtained of the number of persons who have been murdered, hanged, and transported in the last year in Ireland on account of the tithes' disputes?

All these, with documents to enable me to prove them, will be most valuable in forwarding the object I have in view, *an exposure to effect a complete change.*

I shall want as much information of that kind as you can collect for me before the middle of January, to be prepared to agitate the subject by the middle of February. Callous as the ministers are to proceedings that disgrace the country, and regardless as they are to the misery produced in Ireland by their conduct, and indifferent as they are also to the enormous charge on Great Britain to keep a whole nation under military power, I am confident that nothing will rouse the public indignation so much as a proper exposure of all these evils and their causes.

If you will zealously aid me, you will, I trust, aid the best interests of your own country; and in your desire to do that, I hope there cannot be a doubt.

I shall, therefore, expect your early attention to my requests, whilst

    I remain,
      Your obedient servant,
        JOSEPH HUME.

P.S.—I this day delivered to the charge of Mr. Felix Fitzpatrick a copy of Mills' Essays on Government, on Jurisprudence, and the Liberty of the Press, of which we have printed one thousand for circulation; and I hope you will approve the sound doctrines they contain.

In October 1823, the *Life and Times of Salvator Rosa* appeared in two volumes octavo. Lady Morgan said she wrote the work to the sound of Rossini's music. It was her favourite of all her works, and was written because she thought Salvator Rosa had never received justice from posterity. In her preface to the first edition she says, "should it be deemed worthy of enquiring why I selected the Life of Salvator Rosa as a subject of biographical memoir in preference to that of any other illustrious painter of the Italian schools, I answer that I was influenced in my preference more by the peculiar character of the man than the extraordinary merits of the artist. For admiring the works of the great Neapolitan master with an enthusiasm unknown perhaps to the sobriety of professed *vertu,* I estimated still more highly the qualities of the Italian patriot, who, stepping boldly in advance of a degraded age, stood in the foreground of his times, like one of his own spirited and graceful figures when all around him was timid mannerism, and grovelling subserviency. I took the opportunity of my residence in Italy to make some verbal enquiries as to the private character and story of a man whose powerful intellect and deep feeling, no less than his wild and gloomy imagination, came forth even in his most petulant sketches and careless designs. It was evident that over the name of Salvator Rosa there hung some spell, dark as one of his own incantations. I was referred for information to the Parnasso Italiano, one of the few modern works published ' with the full approbation of the Grand Inquisitor of the holy office.' In its consecrated pages I found Salvator Rosa described as being of ' low birth,' indigent circumstances—of a subtle organization, and an unregulated mind, one whose life had been disorderly, and whose associates had been chosen among musicians and buffoons.' This discrepancy between the man and his works awakened suspicions which led to further enquiry and deeper research. It was then I discovered that the sublime painter was in fact precisely the reverse in life and character of all that he had been represented. * * * * As I found, so I have represented him, and if (led by a natural sympathy to make common cause with all who suffer by misrepresentation) I have been the *first* (my only merit) to light a taper at the long neglected shrine, and to raise the veil of calumny from the splendid image of slandered genius, I trust it is still reserved for some compatriot hand to restore the memory of Salvator Rosa to all its original brightness."

Having begun her work with this intention, Lady Morgan carries it through. She has produced a very clever, romantic biography, obscured by fine phrases and lighted up by exaggerated antitheses, but she has collected her materials with industry, and put them together as carefully and brilliantly as a Roman Mosaic. She is too much of a partisan to carry her hero out of the quagmire in which she found him, for she fights at every body and every thing that strikes her imagination by any association of ideas, so that Salvator is generally thrown down and lost in the fray. A more tranquil style and a simpler statement of her facts, with less colouring, and fewer epithets, would have given her testimony more weight, and effected her object better, if that were a single-minded desire to write the true biography of a calumniated man of genius. But Lady Morgan could never forget or efface *herself*. In her novels that did not signify; she kneaded together her characters and her story, and each had a suitability which gave a charm to the whole. When she meddled with history and facts she wrote of them as though they possessed no more substance than scenes in a novel, and this takes away from the dignity and reality of her historical facts, and hinders the reader from doing justice to the ardour and industry with which she sought materials to support every assertion on which she ventured, in spite of the rash rhetorical exaggerations which marked her style,—when she was *not* writing works of fiction.

Those who wish to obtain the facts of Salvator Rosa's life, to form a judgment of his life and labours, will find Lady Morgan's life of him a good handbook, for she has bestowed great industry upon it, and she always gives her authorities and the sources of her information.

Some of the incidental observations in Salvator Rosa are amusing, as for instance, when speaking of Louis the Fourteenth, who pensioned Bernini and neglected Poussin, she said, " this idle prodigality of kings is the result more of ignorance than of vice. If they usually know little of the arts, they are even still less aware of the value of money."

Lady Morgan received five hundred pounds for the copyright. It went into a second edition in 1825, when it was reprinted in a single volume. It was the intention of Colburn to have prefixed a portrait of Lady Morgan; she sat to Lover for the miniature, which has been before referred to. It was to be engraved by Meyer, but between the painter and the engraver, the result was such unmitigated *ugliness*, that Colburn would not let it appear, and he presented Lady Morgan with a beautiful velvet dress, as a peace offering for the annoyance. Colburn and Lady Morgan had many quarrels about this time, chiefly occasioned by Lady Morgan insisting that Colburn made "great gains" out of her works, and did not pay her in proportion,—an imputation which Colburn highly resented. He complained much of her "hard thoughts" of him, and he stoutly maintained that although Lady Morgan had wonderful genius, yet it was to his own good publishing that her works were indebted for their great success; nevertheless, he was dreadfully jealous lest she should leave him for any other publisher.

In spite of the high prices he paid, Colburn seemed to justify Lady Morgan's suspicions of his "great gains," for he this year separated his circulating library from his publishing business, and took a house at No. 8, New Burlington Street, next door to Lady Cork, "who, he feared would be rather angry at his presumption, coming next door to her, shop and all!"

CHAPTER XIII.

CONNEXION WITH THE NEW MONTHLY—1824.

COLBURN was very anxious to obtain Sir Charles and Lady Morgan as contributors to his Magazine, *The New Monthly*. He wrote to them to say that although the highest terms he gave were fifteen to sixteen guineas a sheet; yet, to her and to Sir Charles he would give "a bonus of half as much more, according to the quantity." Lady Morgan consented, and set to work on an essay on *Absenteeism*, which the enemies of Ireland were always declaiming against, as the source of all the woes of Ireland. She set herself to show that Absenteeism was but the effect of ill-government and unjust legislation from the earliest period of England's rule.

She began to read up for her materials and she found much help from the *Pacata Hibernia*, of which mention is made in her letters to Sir Charles, when she ran away to Dublin during her engagement, and would not return till she had almost driven him past his patience!

Lady Morgan had seen in her youth so much of the misery of financial irregularity, that she had a sacred horror of all debt; she kept her accounts with a punctuality that would have been creditable to a Chancellor of the Exchequer. One entry has an interest, as showing that literary labour, when well done and industriously followed, is *not* the ungrateful, ill-requited task it has been the fashion to represent it. Lady Morgan worked hard and *drudged*, without feeling degraded by the process.

May 9.—This page is from an old Account-book.—By my earnings, since April 3, 1822, I have added to our joint-stock account, such sums as makes the whole £5,109 7s., from £2,678 11s. 6d., as it stood on that date. The several sums, therefore, vested in the Irish and English Stocks, and *which, being my earnings,* I have disposed of according to my marriage settlement, are—

£	s.	d.	
5,109	1	1	Reduced 3 per Cent. Annuities.
680	0	0	Irish 3½ per Cent.
32	13	9	Irish 5 per Cents.
600	0	0	Loan at Interest.
6,421	14	10	

The above is not a despicable sum to have made by her own industry, and saved by her own thrift.

Lady Morgan used to tell an anecdote, that she once took with her to one of the vice-regal balls, during Lord Wellesley's administration of Ireland, a small packet containing a letter of Lady Mornington. She took the opportunity when his Excellency addressed her, to say—

"I have brought your Excellency an offering, a letter of the woman you loved best in the world, a letter that will interest you." Lord Wellesley took it, but not without a look of slight surprise. The packet was not of course opened then, but the next morning, before she was up, Lady Morgan received the following letter, accompanied by the gift of a beautiful silver case to hold perfume bottles.

The Marquis of Wellesley to Lady Morgan.

April, 1824.

I am very grateful to Lady Morgan for the perusal of this letter. It is written by Prudentia Trevor (sister to my mother) who was married to Charles Leslie, of Monaghan; it is franked by my grandfather, Arthur Trevor, the first Lord Dungannon. It must have been written from Bryntrinalt, in North Wales, in the year 1761. I was born in Grafton Street, Dublin, 1760, in a large, old house, afterwards pulled down, opposite the Provost's house. I was taken to England, 1767, where my family attended the coronation.

The above note is written in pencil. The essay on *Absenteeism* had become a more important work than Lady Morgan at first contemplated, and she was unwilling to allow it to appear as a mere magazine contribution; but Colburn, after some correspondence, persuaded her to let him have it. On the 10th of May, 1824, he wrote very gratefully to thank her for her acquiescence in his proposal to let it appear in his magazine, expressing a hope that the *notes* would not be too long or too numerous, it being her peculiar tendency to pile up all her loose lying materials into notes as long as the text. *Absenteeism* appeared in the June number of the *New Monthly*. It is written in a florid, declamatory style. It begins with the ancient glories of Ireland, reflecting mournfully on the times "when all in Ireland who were not saints were kings, and many were both, while none were martyrs." In those true Church and State times, the Irish kept in their own country,—a pilgrimage to St. Patrick's purgatory—a royal progress of some Toparch of the South to some " Dynasty " of the North, or a morning visit from King MacTurtell to his close neighbour, King Gillemohalmoghe, (which occasionally resulted in broken heads to both parties) was all the 'absenteeism' of Ireland until the period of our Henry II. King MacTurtell was king of Dublin; and not far from Dublin there lived an Irish king named Gillemohalmoghe. Of the territories of this prince, Michael's Lane, in Dublin, formed a part; and his kingdom extended as far as Santry, the seat of Sir Compton Domville. Dermont Macmurrough O'Kavenagh, king of Leinster, is the first Irish absentee on record. He took refuge in the court of Henry II., of England; hence the invasion, &c., &c., &c " Sir

Charles Morgan, in his preface, gives the pith of the whole book, and says, with a tone of apology, "In taking up the subject of absenteeism, the peculiar bent of Lady Morgan's mind has given a picturesque turn to her ideas, and induced her to view the matter less as an economist than as a poet and as a woman. But the great truth has not escaped her that absenteeism is less a cause than an effect." The whole of Lady Morgan's work goes to prove that English treachery and tyranny first made Ireland uninhabitable, and then punished its inhabitants for trying to leave. Like a true apologist and partisan, whilst she cannot deny the fact of absenteeism, nor the evils which the absence of a resident gentry entailed upon the country, she argues away the blame from the natives and lays it upon the English government. As a treatise of the hour *Absenteeism* did its duty, but it is of little value otherwise.

Sir Charles and Lady Morgan came over to London for the season of 1824; and Lady Morgan described the incidents of her life in letters to her sister.

Lady Morgan to Lady Clarke.

LONDON,
12*th July*, 1824.

Imprimis,—We have three and ninepence to pay for the last packet, charged overweight; but as I suspect it was the "*chillies bulletins*" that kicked the balance, I am quite satisfied to pay any sum for the productions of the most original writers of the age, only I beg to put my dear little bevy of correspondents on their guard in future. I see you are sick of my *routs and riots*, and, in truth, so am I. The heat is more oppressive than I ever found it in Italy. I have passed such a curious morning that I must describe it to you whilst I remember it. I sat to three artists from ten to one o'clock; then came a delightful person, Mr. Blencoe, by appointment, with a collection of original letters by Algernon Sydney (in his own precious handwriting to his father, Lord Leicester), models of style and full of curious facts that throw new glory on his character, and new light upon the times of Cromwell and Charles II. Mr. Blencoe found also at Penshurst, a journal kept by Lord Leicester which, with Sydney's letters, he is going to publish. He was scarcely gone, when Lord Byron's letters to his mother and others were confided to me. I shall only say, *en bref*, that though Cicero was to rise to plead for him to public opinion, he could say nothing in his behalf so powerfully favorable to his character as these *natural, charming*, and interesting letters: warm affections and high morality in every line. Poor fellow! He says, on the death of his mother, "Now she is gone, I have not one friend on earth, and this at twenty-three! What could I have more to say at seventy?" Just as I had devoured them (as I did in a great hurry), came in a packet of Mrs. Piozzi's MSS. letters; but after Byron's, they were sad namby pamby stuff. She says, crying down the French Revolution in 1797, "What do you think, the women have absolutely left off hair-powder! I see nothing but ruin for this unfortunate country!"

We have just got notice that Lord Byron's funeral takes place on Monday. Morgan is to go. His name is on the list; so are all the Whig lords. We could not bring ourselves to go and see him laid in state.

Our dinner at Dick's *(Quintin)* was sumptuous. We had the house of Mulgrave, Lady Cork, Lord and Lady Dillon, Sir Watkin, and others,—Lord Mulgrave's daughter, Lady Murray, is a charming person. They are particularly civil to us, and we dine there next Friday; and, on Wednesday, we are to meet the Duke of Wellington and Lord Hertford at Lady Cork's.

Campbell came to breakfast with Morgan, and they went *together* to the funeral of poor Lord Byron. The public wish was that he should be buried in the abbey, but his sister would have him buried in the *family vault*, and insisted on his funeral being a PEER's funeral, from which the *vulgar public,* the *nation,* was to be excluded. There would not have been a single literary person there, but Rogers and Moore (his personal friends), had not Morgan and Campbell, at the *last moment,* suggested others. All was mean and pompous, yet confusion: hundreds of persons on foot, in deep mourning, who came to pay this respect to one of the greatest geniuses of the age. Thomas Moore takes tea with us this evening, before we go to Lady Cork's *Whig* party. Did I tell you of the *gentillesse* of some of the managers of the theatres? They have sent me *keys* of private boxes?

VOL. II.   O

I can no more. God bless you all, good people; and love me as I love you. S. MORGAN.

In allusion to Lady Morgan's love of general society, her political friends looked doubtingly on her London season of this year; her friend, the Honourable Mrs. Caulfield, niece of Sir Capel Molyneux, the fine old Irish gentleman and "patriot," who had registered a vow not to encourage Lord Lieutenants until the act of union should be repealed,—this daughter, as great a patriot as himself, wrote to Lady Morgan,—" I will not affront you by supposing that you will suffer by the ordeal your patriotism and your radicalism are undergoing. I will only say that I shall congratulate you and human nature if you end your gaieties among the Tories without a slight degree of contamination. I am alike enraged at your abuse of Dublin (though as to society, it is just) and at your idea of adding to the number of those *you yourself* write against by becoming an *absentee*. True friendship shows itself most in misfortune; and the riches, the society, the comforts, of London and of England should only attach an Irish patriot more strongly to his country,—the land of sorrow and suffering. I trust neither the variety, scenery, wealth, nor society afforded on the Continent or in England, will ever tempt us to have a *home* in either, but that like a captain to his ship, we shall not abandon poor old Ireland so long as our rulers allow our lives to be safe and of any use to it."

The *tone* of the "friends of Ireland" was then little

less dangerous to the true welfare of the country than the ultra-Protestant bitterness of the Tories, who did not know how to manage either the country or the people; it is difficult in these days of tranquil politics to realise how "all faces gathered blackness" when they touched upon them.

The following letter from Lord Cloncurry is given as containing the views of an Irish landlord on the subject of poor laws for Ireland.

Lord Cloncurry, when the Honourable Valentine Lawless, had been mixed up very actively with the proceedings of the "United Irishmen." He was arrested in May, 1798, confined for about six weeks in the house of the king's messenger, in Pimlico, and then set at liberty with an admonition. On April 14, 1779, he was again arrested "on suspicion of treasonable practices." The "*Habeas Corpus*" was at that time suspended. He was examined before the Privy Council, was committed to the Tower, where he endured a somewhat rigorous imprisonment, until March, 1801, when he was discharged on the expiration of the "suspension;" without having had any regular trial. He suffered much in health; and domestic afflictions fell heavily upon him during the twenty-two months of his imprisonment. The lady to whom he was engaged to be married, died of sorrow and anxiety on his account, his father also died, and to avoid the contingency of confiscation, left away from him the sum of seventy thousand pounds; this, together with the disorder that his affairs fell into, made his loss in a pecuniary point of view a sufficiently heavy fine.

Lord Cloncurry to Sir Charles Morgan.

TORQUAY, DEVON,
October 6, 1824.

MY DEAR SIR CHARLES,

I see by the papers that I owe you sixteen shillings and eight pence on the Greek account, which you can either receive from Val. or hold over *in terrorem* against me. Your observations on the Poor Laws, and the prospect of introducing them into Ireland, are founded on the best principles of human political philosophy, and I would only act in opposition to them from a feeling of the utter hopelessness of our situation, and from the idea that they may ultimately be one means of bringing about that change which all parties allow to be necessary. The case of Ireland is so different from that of any other country, that as a mere Irishman I think quite differently from what I would as a citizen of the world. What could be more silly or atrocious than the Corn Laws? An Englishman voting for them should have been sent only to Bethlehem or the hulks, yet I voted for them, as I knew my countrymen *never taste* bread, and the same, bad as it was, gave *us* much English money. Now the Poor Laws will not, I think, ruin the price of land as you expect, but will lower it, and perhaps cost me twelve or fifteen hundred per annum; but as no tenant can pay more than he already does, the landlords must be answerable, as in the case of tithes—thus the Poor Laws will be an indirect absentee tax—the desire to abolish it will join the upper orders to the *corps réformateur*, and ultimately the whole system of iniquity must be put down.

I am truly sorry Lady Morgan should feel one moment's illness. I am interested for her as an Irishman as well as a sincere and grateful friend. We have got a capital house here, and the place is beautiful and pleasant; if you could come to us for a couple of months we could make you and your dear lady very comfortable.

I want to consult you as to an application from Staunton for an advance of one hundred pounds on his security, for the purpose of re-establishing the *Morning Herald*. I would most willingly give one or two hundred pounds for a clever, thorough-going Irish paper, to be managed by a committee; but though I always take the *Evening Herald*, it is too polemical and too personal, and too full of long, drawling, priest-written stuff to do any real good. I have no objection to aid Staunton with fifteen or twenty pounds; but for any farther advance I should like the security of a committee. I wish you and Curran would turn this in your minds, and see whether we could not establish what is so much wanted.

Yours ever,
Most faithfully,
CLONCURRY.

PS. Our M.D. here is an Irish Papist, brother to Councillor Scully. Balls and cards here every week, to the great comfort of Miss Brynn.

CHAPTER XIV.

LORD BYRON AND LADY CAROLINE LAMB.

The correspondence between Lady Caroline Lamb and Lady Morgan, on the subject of Lord Byron, together with the noble poet's last letter to Lady Caroline, may now be given. In a rough memorandum, written by Lady Morgan on a loose sheet of paper, in the year before she commenced to keep a regular diary, there is some account of Lady Caroline, taken down from her own mouth. The sentences are but fragments, yet they make a very sad and singular picture of this gifted woman in her youth and early married life. Lady Caroline's account of her first introduction to Byron, and of the impression made on her by the noble poet, will be read with universal interest. The lady's words must be set down in their rough state, exactly as they appear in Lady Morgan's journal.

"Lady Caroline Lamb sent for me. Her story: Her mother had a paralytic stroke: went to Italy: she remained there till nine years old, brought up by a maid called Fanny. She was then taken to Devonshire House, and brought up with her cousins. She gave curious anecdotes of high life,—children neglected by their mothers—children served on silver in the morning, carrying down their plate to the kitchen—no one to attend to them—servants all at variance—ignorance of children on all subjects—thought all people were dukes or beggars—or had never to part with their money—did not know bread, or butter, was made—wondered if horses fed on beef—so neglected in her education, she could not write at ten years old. Lady Georgiana Cavendish took her away, and she was sent to live with her godmother, Spencer, where the housekeeper, in hoop and ruffles, had the rule over seventy servants, and always attended her ladies in the drawing-room. Lady Georgiana's marriage was one *de convenance*. Her delight was hunting butterflies. The housekeeper breaking a lath over her head reconciled her to the match [to become Duchess of Devonshire]. She was ignorant of everything. Lady Spencer had Dr. Warren to examine Lady Caroline. He said she had no tendency to madness,—severity of her governess and indulgence of her parents. Her passion for William Lamb—would not marry him—knew herself to be a fury—wanted to follow him as a clerk, &c. Ill tempers on both sides broke out together after marriage—both loved, hated, quarrelled, and made up. 'He cared nothing for my morals,' she said. 'I might flirt and go about with what men I pleased. He was privy to my affair with Lord Byron, and laughed at it. His indolence rendered him insensible to everything. When I ride, play, and amuse him, he loves me. In sickness and suffering, he deserts me. His violence is as bad as my own.'"

Her account of Lord Byron:—

"Lady Westmoreland knew him in Italy. She took on her to present him. The women suffocated him. I heard nothing of him, till one day Rogers (for he, Moore, and Spencer, were all my lovers, and wrote me up to the skies—I was in the clouds)—Rogers said, 'you should know the new poet,' and he offered me the MS. of *Childe Harold* to read. I read it, and that was enough. Rogers said, 'he has a club-foot, and bites his nails.' I said, 'If he was ugly as Æsop I must know him.' I was one night at Lady Westmoreland's; the women were all throwing their heads at him. Lady Westmoreland led me up to him. I looked earnestly at him, and turned on my heel. My opinion, in my journal was, 'mad—bad—and dangerous to know.' A day or two passed; I was sitting with Lord and Lady Holland, when he was announced. Lady Holland said, 'I must present Lord Byron to you.' Lord Byron said, 'That offer was made to you before; may I ask why you rejected it?' He begged permission to come and see me. He did so the next day. Rogers and Moore were standing by me: I was on the sofa. I had just come in from riding. I was filthy and heated. When Lord Byron was announced, I flew out of the room to wash myself. When I returned, Rogers said, 'Lord Byron, you are a happy man. Lady Caroline has been sitting here in all her dirt with us, but when you were announced, she flew to beautify herself.' Lord Byron wished to come and see me at eight o'clock, when I was alone; that was my dinner-hour. I said he might. From that moment, for more than nine months, he almost lived at Melbourne House. It was then the centre of all gaiety, at least, in appearance. My cousin Hartington wanted to have waltzes and quadrilles; and, at Devonshire House, it would not be allowed, so we had them in the great drawing-room of Melbourne House. All the *bon ton* of London assembled here every day. There was nothing so fashionable. Byron contrived to sweep them all away. My mother grew miserable, and did everything in her power to break off the connexion. She at last brought me to consent to go to Ireland with her and papa. Byron wrote me that letter which I have shown you. While in Ireland, I received letters constantly,—the most tender and the most amusing. We had got to Dublin, on our way home, where my mother brought me a letter. There was a coronet on the seal. The initials under the coronet were Lady Oxford's. It was that cruel letter I have published in *Glenarvon*: it destroyed me: I lost my brain. I was bled, leeched; kept for a week in the filthy Dolphin Inn, at Rock. On my return, I was in great prostration of mind and spirit. Then came my *fracas* with the page, which made such noise. 'He was a little *espiègle*, and would throw detonating balls into the fire. Lord Melbourne always scolded me for this; and I, the boy. One day

I was playing ball with him. He threw a squib into the fire, and I threw the ball at his head. It hit him on the temple, and he bled. He cried out, 'Oh, my lady, you have killed me!' Out of my senses, I flew into the hall, and screamed, 'Oh God, I have murdered the page!' The servants and people in the streets caught the sound, and it was soon spread about. William Lamb would live with me no longer. All his family united in insisting on our separation. Whilst this was going on, and instruments drawing out—that is, in *one month*—I wrote and *sent Glenarvon to the press*. I wrote it, unknown to all (save a governess, Miss Welsh), in the middle of the night. It was necessary to have it copied out. I had heard of a famous copier, an old Mr. Woodhead. I sent to beg he would come to see Lady Caroline Lamb at Melbourne House. I placed Miss Welsh, elegantly dressed, at my harp, and myself at a writing-table, dressed in the page's clothes, looking a boy of fourteen. He addressed Miss Welsh as Lady Caroline. She showed him the author. He would not believe that this schoolboy could write such a thing. He came to me again in a few days, and he found me in my own clothes. I told him William Ormond, the young author, was dead. When the work was printed, I sent it to William Lamb. He was delighted with it; and we became united, just as the world thought we were parted for ever. The scene at Brocket Hall (in the novel of *Glenarvon*) was true. Lord Byron's death—the ghost appearing to her—her distraction at his death. Medwin's talk completed her distress."

We may now proceed with the correspondence.

Lady Caroline Lamb to Lady Morgan.

MELBOURNE HOUSE,
June 2.

MY DEAR LADY MORGAN,

I have sent for, and I know not if I shall receive, the portrait you wished to see. I am afraid you have seen me under great irritation, and under circumstances that might try any one. I am too miserable. You have not yet advised me what to do—I know not, care not. Oh, God, it is a punishment severe enough; I never can recover it; it is fair by William Lamb to mention, that since I saw you he has written a kinder letter; but if I am sent to live by myself, let them dread the violence of my despair—better far go away. Every tree, every flower, will awaken bitter reflection. Pity me, for I am too unhappy; I cannot bear it. I would give all I possessed on earth to be again what I once was, and I would now be obedient and gentle; but I shall die of grief.

Think about Ireland—if only for a few months—yet what shall I do at Bessborough alone? God bless you; thanks for your portrait; hearing this, is a sad ending to a too frivolous and far too happy a life. Farewell; if you receive the portrait, return it, and send the letter; it is his parting one when I went to Ireland with mamma (*I mean Lord Byron's*). She was near dying because she thought I was going to leave her. William, at that time, loved me so much that he forgave me all, and only implored me to remain. My life has not been the best possible. The slave of impulse, I have rushed forward to my own destruction. If you like the drawing of me, which Pickett did before he died, I will try and have it copied. I trust faithfully to your returning my letter and both pictures.

Ever with sincere interest,
and affection,
CAROLINE.

Lord Byron's Parting Letter to Lady Caroline Lamb.

(Enclosed in foregoing.)

MY DEAREST CAROLINE,

If tears which you saw and know I am not apt to shed,—if the agitation in which I parted from you,—agitation which you must have perceived through the whole of this most nervous affair, did not commence until the moment of leaving you approached,—if all I have said and done, and am still but too ready to say and do have not sufficiently proved what my real feelings are, and must ever be towards you, my love, I have no other proof to offer. God knows, I wish you happy, and when I quit you, or rather you from a sense of duty to your husband and mother, quit me, you shall acknowledge the truth of what I again promise and vow, that no other in word or deed shall ever hold the place in my affections, which is, and shall be, most sacred to you, till I am nothing. I never knew till that moment the madness of my dearest and most beloved friend; I cannot express myself; this is no time for words, but I shall have a pride, a melancholy pleasure, in suffering what you yourself can scarcely conceive, for you do not know me. I am about to go out with a heavy heart, because my appearing this evening will stop any absurd story which the spite of the day might give rise to. Do you think *now* I am cold, and stern, and wilful? will ever others think so? will your mother ever—that mother to whom we must indeed sacrifice much more, much more on my part than she shall ever know or *can* imagine? "Promise not to love you," ah, Caroline, it is past promising. But I shall attribute all concessions to the proper motive, and never cease to feel all that you have already witnessed, and more than can ever be known but to my own heart,—perhaps to yours.

May God protect, forgive, and bless you ever and ever, more than ever

Your most attached,

BYRON.

PS.—These taunts which have driven you to this, my dearest Caroline, were it not for your mother and the kindness of your connections, is there anything in earth or heaven that would have made me so happy as to have made you mine long ago? and not less *now* than *then*, but more than ever at *this time*. You know I would with pleasure give up all here and beyond the grave for you, and in refraining from this, must my motives be misunderstood? I care not who knows this, what use is made of it,—it is to you and to *you* only that they are, *yourself*. I was and am yours freely and entirely to obey, to honour, love, and fly with you when, where, and how yourself *might* and *may* determine.

From the confession of Lady Caroline, previously given, it will have been seen that Byron continued to write to her while she was in Ireland. How the unhappy woman quarrelled in the last degree with her indulgent husband is not told in these papers. That she parted from him and went abroad, are facts involved in the statements which ensue. The letters must be given without comment.

Lady Caroline Lamb to Lady Morgan.

[*No date.*]

No, no, not that portrait out of my hands—I cannot bear. I will have it copied for you. I must take it with me to Paris. Thank you, dear Lady Morgan, for your advice, but you do not understand me, and I do not wonder you cannot know me. I had purposed a very pretty little supper for you. I have permission to see all my friends here; it is not William's house; beside, he said he wished me to see every one, and Lady —— called and asked me who I wished to see. I shall, therefore, shake hands with the whole Court Guide before I go. The only question I want you to solve is, shall I go abroad? Shall I throw myself upon those who no longer want me, or shall I live

a good sort of a half kind of life in some cheap street
a little way off, viz., the City Road, Shoreditch, Camberwell, or upon the top of a shop,—or shall I give
lectures to little children, and keep a seminary, and
thus earn my bread? or shall I write a kind of quiet
every day sort of novel, full of wholesome truths,
or shall I attempt to be poetical, and failing, beg my
friends for a guinea a-piece, and their name, to sell my
work, upon the best foolscap paper; or shall I fret,
fret, fret, and die; or shall I be dignified and fancy
myself, as Richard the Second did when he picked
the nettle up—upon a thorn?

Sir Charles Morgan was most agreeable and good-
natured. *Faustus* is good in its way, but has not all
its sublimity; it is like a rainy shore. I admire it
because I *conceive* what I had *heard* translated elsewhere, but the end particularly is in very contemptible taste. The overture tacked to it is magnificent,
the scenery beautiful, parts affecting, and not unlike
Lord Byron, that dear, that angel, that mis-guided
and mis-guiding Byron, whom I adore, although he
left that dreadful legacy on me—my memory. Remember thee—and well.

I hope he and William will find better friends; as
to myself, I never can love anything better than what
I thus tell you:—William Lamb, first; my mother,
second; Byron, third; my boy, fourth; my brother
William, fifth; my father and godmother, sixth; my
uncle and aunt, my cousin Devonshire, my brother
Fred., (myself), my cousins next, and last, my *petit*
friend, young Russell, because he is my aunt's godson;

because when he was but three I nursed him; because he has a hard-to-win, free, and kind heart; but chiefly because he stood by me when no one else did.

I am yours,
C. L.

Send me my portrait. I trust to your kindness and honour.

Lady Caroline Lamb to Lady Morgan.

[*No date.*]

DEAR LADY MORGAN,

You know not what misery and illness I have suffered since last I wrote to you. My brother William—my kind guardian-angel—informed me to-day that you were in town, and as I am too ill to go out, and wish to consult you about publishing my journal, and many other things, would you do me the favour to call here to-morrow evening, or any time you please, between eight and eleven? Unless you meet my brother you will find no one, and, as I have four horses, I can send for you, and send you back when you like.

Yours most sincerely,
CAROLINE.

PS. I was rather grieved that you never answered my last imprudent letter; fear not, they have broken my heart—*not my spirit;* and if I will but sign a paper, all my rich relations will protect me, and I shall, no doubt, go with an Almack ticket to heaven.

Lady Caroline Lamb to Lady Morgan.

October 16.

MY DEAR LADY MORGAN,

I have a great deal to say to you, and to explain to you, and I will write soon; but I have not been well. Lady Cowper called soon after you left me at Thomas's Hotel, and promised to call on you and say that I could not. I have seen her since, and found she did not; but she wished to do so much, and I now send you her card; pray see William and my son, and write and tell me all you think about them, and Ireland, and when you next will be out. I write this solely to fulfil my engagement—saying, I leave *you when I die Lord Byron's picture*, now under the care of Goddard —the original by Saunders. Pray excuse one more word until I hear from you, and believe me

Ever most sincerely yours,

CAROLINE LAMB.

Lady Caroline Lamb to Lady Morgan.

DOVER.

MY DEAR LADY MORGAN,

It would be charitable in you to write me a letter, and it would be most kind if you would immediately send me Lord Byron's portrait, as far more than the six weeks have expired, and I am again in England.

If you will send it for me to Melbourne House, to the care of the porter, I shall be most sincerely obliged to you. My situation in life, now, is new and strange—I seem to be left to my fate most completely, and to take my chance, or rough or smooth, without the smallest interest being expressed for me. It is for good purposes, no doubt; besides I must submit to my fate—it being without remedy. I am now with my maid at the Ship Tavern, Water Lane, having come over from Calais. I have no servants, page, carriage, horse, nor fine rooms—the melancholy of my situation in this little dreary apartment is roused by the very loud, jovial laughter of my neighbours, who are smoking in the next room. Pray send me my invaluable portrait, and pray think kindly of me; every one in France talked much of you, and with great enthusiasm. Farewell; remember me to your husband and family, and believe me

Most truly yours,
CAROLINE LAMB.

PS. Direct to me care of the Honourable William Ponsonby, St. James's Square, London.

I hope you received a letter from me written before I left England.

Lady Caroline Lamb to Lady Morgan.

MY DEAREST LADY,

As being a lady whom my adored mother loved, your kindness about Ada Reis I feel the more, as everybody wishes to run down and suppress the vital spark of genius I have, and, in truth, it is but small (about what one sees a maid gets by excessive beating on a tinder-box). I am not vain, believe me, nor selfish, nor in love with my authorship; but I am independent, as far as a mite and bit of dust can be. I thank God, being born with all the great names of England around me; I value them alone for what they dare do, and have done, and I fear nobody except the devil, who certainly has all along been very particular in his attentions to me, and has sent me as many baits as he did Job. I, however, am, happily for myself, in as ill a state of health as he was, so I trust in God I shall ever more resist temptation. My history, if you ever care and like to read it, is this— My mother, having boys, wished ardently for a girl; and I, who evidently ought to have been a soldier, was found a naughty girl—forward, talking like Richard the Third.

I was a trouble, not a pleasure, all my childhood, for which reason, after my return from Italy, where I was from the age of four until nine, I was ordered by the late Dr. Warre neither to learn anything nor see any one, for fear the violent passions and strange whims they found in me should lead to madness; of which, however, he assured every one there were no symptoms. I differ, but the end was, that until fifteen I learned nothing. My instinct—for we all have instincts—was for music—in it I delighted; I cried when it was pathetic, and did all that Dryden's ode made Alexander do—of course I was not allowed to follow it up. My angel mother's ill-health prevented my living at home; my kind aunt Devonshire took me; the present Duke loved me better than himself, and every one paid me those compliments shown to children who are precious to their parents, or delicate and likely to die. I wrote not, spelt not; but I made verses, which they all thought beautiful—for myself, I preferred washing a dog, or polishing a piece of Derbyshire spar, or breaking in a horse, to any accomplishment in the world. Drawing-room (shall I say withdrawing-room, as they now say?) looking-glasses, finery, or dress-company for ever were my abhorrence. I was, I am, religious; I was loving (?) but I was and am unkind. I fell in love when only twelve years old, with a friend of Charles Fox—a friend of liberty whose poems I had read, whose self I had never seen, and when I did see him, at thirteen, could I change? No, I was more attached than ever. William Lamb was beautiful, and far the cleverest person then about, and the most daring in his opinions, in his love of liberty and independence. He thought of me but as a child, yet he liked me much; afterwards he offered to marry me, and I refused him because of my temper, which was too violent; he, however, asked twice, and was not refused the second time, and the reason was that I adored him. I had three children; two died; my only child is afflicted; it is the will of God. I have wandered from right, and been punished. I have suffered what you can hardly believe; I have lost my mother, whose gentleness and good sense guided me. I have received more

kindness than I can ever repay. I have suffered,
also, but I deserved it. My power of mind and of
body are gone; I am like the shade of what I was; to
write was once my resource and pleasure; but since
the only eyes that ever admired my most poor and
humble productions are closed, wherefore should I indulge the propensity! God bless you; I write from
my heart. You are one like me, who, perhaps, have
not taken the right road. I am on my death-bed;
say, I might have died by a diamond, I die now by a
brickbat; but remember, the only noble fellow I ever
met with is William Lamb; he is to me what Shore
was to Jane Shore. I saw it once; I am as grateful,
but as unhappy. Pray excuse the sorrows this sad,
strange letter will cause you; could you be in time
I would be glad to see you—to you alone would I give
up Byron's letters—much else, but all like the note
you have. Pray excuse this being not written as
clearly as you can write. I speak as I hope you do,
from the heart.

C. L.

CHAPTER XV.

THE YEAR 1825.

In the year 1825, Lady Morgan, for the first time, began to keep a diary, and from this date the account of her life will be chiefly drawn from the entries in her diaries. For a year or more, these entries are somewhat barren of incident; they are occupied with mere reflections, and with the rough draft of an autobiography afterwards more fully developed, and given in the first volume. A brief extract from the diaries 1825, 1826, will suffice for the general reader—the paragraphs, like so many others of Lady Morgan's papers, have no date. The first would appear to have been written in April, or early in May, of the year 1825.

Letters from Italy state that the tribunals of Austria have just condemned to death Count Confalonieri, the Marquis Pallavicini, M. Castiglioni, Colonel Moretti, and three young students. The crimes imputed to these individuals, who are held in the highest estimation in Italy, are not even looked on as faults there, as, according to the letters alluded to, they consist only in the explicit manifestation on their part of the aversion which all Italians entertain for the domination of Austria as their country. My poor Confalonieri! how little, when I knew him bright and brilliant in Italy, did he dream of this day of darkness in store for him! Even if his doom be commuted into *carcere duro*, it will be almost worse than death.

May 4.—Received the affecting news of Dénon's death, he was only ill fifteen hours. He was nearly eighty.

Lord Archibald Hamilton is dead. I first met him *chez* the Duchess of Sussex, 1811. He was then rather a *ci-devant*, but an epitome of rank and fashion. He was much in love with the sister of the Duchess of Sussex. His mind was enlightened, his spirit independent, and he was full of integrity. He was a man of kindly temperament, and he will be much missed, especially in Scotland.

Journey to London.—Struck by the changed physiognomies of the population—more intelligent-looking and less well fed. Blessings of science and all-pervading illumination staring one in the face at every mile through the Welsh mountains—their romanticism disappearing—their civilization increasing.

St. Albans and its delicious abbey!

London.—Curious visitors—General Pepe, the Neapolitan chief, and all the young revolutionary leaders of Piedmont and Lombardy,—the eldest but twenty-nine,—with me every day, and talking of erecting a statue to me when Italy shall be free—*hélas!* Sir Robert Wilson called on me; mild and interesting-looking; speaking well, but with gravity; must have been, and indeed is still, very handsome. General Pepe most affected of all the Italians I have seen by the disasters of Naples. Lady Caroline Lamb called,—quite comical, talking religion, and offering me half-a-dozen of her Pages. Went to Miss White's assembly; found her in the midst of a brilliant crowd, dying of the dropsy. Many persons presented to me of notoriety, Washington Irving, author of *The Sketch Book;* the Magnus Apollo of the *bas bleus*—Hallam, author of *The Middle Ages.* Moore (Anacreon) called to-day; said " Murray raves of you, not as an author only, *entendez-vous,* but as a woman." When I told this to Colburn, he looked aghast. I said to him, "Colburn, I observed to Mr. Moore, that I hoped my conquest would get me a good price for my next book." "Did you say that?" exclaimed Colburn, in a pathetic tone. His fear of *his* author, is like the Irish Quaker's complaint, of "somebody having taken his drumstick from him."

Went to St. James's Palace to see Mrs. Boscawen, the Queen's maid-of-honour. [The Mrs. Boscawen referred to was Anne, daughter of General the Honourable George Boscawen, and grand-daughter of Hugh, first Viscount Falmouth. She was born in 1744, and died in 1831.] Found her niched in the old court garret with a most fantastical little balcony, and terrace full of plants, flowers, and foreign birds. She was de-

lighted to see me; talked of my books, and offered me
a bouquet in return for all the charming things she
had read of mine;—full of old court news, and of the
King's going to throw down her apartments;—could
talk of nothing else, and of her waylaying the King on
his departure for Ireland. Spoke of nursing him in
his youth;—knew Mrs. Delany;—told me she had a
great desire to go to Lady Pepy's blue-stocking parties.
Her companion is Miss Tickell, descendant of the poet.
Collation at St. James's, with Mrs. Boscawen,—went
through the palace. I met Mrs. Boscawen a fortnight
after;—took up the account of the rooms; she called
Lady Cork "her fellow-servant." Miss Porter, mild
and unaffected; Mr. Place, the Templar, worth all the
rest;—Holland House, the school of political corruption, spoilt all the young men;—Miss Benger, tall, thin.

At Miss White's dinner;—Porson (not the author
of the *Parody*) and Milman were there;—W. Spencer
reminded me he knew me at Lisburne;—Mrs. Somerville, a celebrated mathematician, young and prettyish;
—Mrs. Marcett, the political economist, getting hold of
W. Spencer and preaching Christianity to him, wishing
him to go to church at Geneva, that he might be converted through the pretty women;—General Church
there, it is well I had not Pepe with me!

Ugo Foscolo dined with us at Mrs. Brown's;—full
of paradoxes,—hated Italian music,—cried over my
Irish song;—his account of his novel *Jacopo Ortis*, all
true;—was six times more in love than he described;
—defended England's conduct to Italy;—cried down
the Whigs for originating the present system. He

despised the society *du bon ton* of London;—it only gave him the trouble of writing apologies.

Went with Lady Caroline to Miss White's.

London, Bury Street, St James.—June 15.—Yesterday's campaign we had thousands of Italians who came to pay their *devoirs*, amongst others, Castiglione, as handsome as ever;—the Marquis de Prie, a very elegant young man. At seven o'clock we set off to our dinner-party at the Macneil's. The company were, the Hon. Charles Brownlow, M.P., who made the famous Protestant speech a little while ago; Mr. and Mrs. Horace Twiss, the nephew to John Kemble; Mr. Douglas Kinnaird, brother to Lord Dunsancy; Mr. Edwards, son of Lord Kensington, and Miss Alexander, daughter of the Bishop of Meath. A few people came in the evening; we left at past eleven o'clock, and set off for Lord Listowel's Kensington Gore, which we did not reach till near twelve. Their company had left, and they were all dressed themselves to go to a ball; we staid a little time, and then went on to Lydia White's, and although it was long past twelve, we found the invalid lying on her couch in the midst of her party; Sidney Smith, of the *Edinburgh*, and *the* wit, *par excellence*. What a difference in the political thermometer? our dinner red-hot orange, and our *soirée* of the coolest *green*, where it was not *blue!*

June 17.—To-day, dinner at Lady Cork's; there never was anything to equal the splendour of her entertainments and her rooms. In the evening we went on to Lydia White's, thence to Mrs. Burton's.

Carlton House was on fire the other night; there was one roomed burned, but they succeeded in extinguishing it before it did any more mischief.

The King was in the house at the time, and he held a levee the next morning.

I saw a warming pan at Strawberry Hill, the other day, which had belonged to Charles II.; there is on it the following motto, "Sarve God and live for ever;"—the date 1660—the period when his love for Barbara Palmer, afterwards Duchess of Cleveland, was in its first bloom.

This is all of the diary 1825, which the general reader will perhaps care to have. The following letters from Colonel Webster, son of Lady Holland, and aid-de-camp to Lord Wellesley, the other from the ever attractive Madame Jerome Bonaparte, continue the amusing gossip of the day.

The chief event in her affairs of this year was, that in August 22, 1825, *Salvator Rosa* came to a second edition; but Lady Morgan and Colburn had many squabbles together—she complaining of his shabbiness, and he complaining that she was "very hard upon him;" but neither of them wished to separate in their business transactions. He was looking anxiously forwards to a new Irish novel from her, and she was meditating how to make him pay the interest on her increased popularity. She and Sir Charles were, at this period, regular contributors to the *New Monthly* and the *Metropolitan*.

Captain Webster to Lady Morgan.

Park, Ampthill,
September 11, 1825.

My dear Lady Morgan,

It is an age since I have heard of you, and I really was in hopes when you arrived safe and sound on the other side of the water, that you would have sent me some news of you and yours.

Colonel and Mrs. Dawson are on their way to Buxton to visit Mrs. Fitzherbert, who would not be present at the marriage, but sent her a thousand guineas; the morning after the event, Miss Seymour received a packet from the King, enclosing a charming letter, begging her to be kind to her best friend, Mrs. Fitzherbert, and enclosing a draft for two thousand pounds; after Buxton they go to the Continent. I fear that Uxbridge and his wife will be separated—his temper is too violent, and she does too little to please him; they say that Uxbridge intends to keep the pretty little children, of which he will be heartily tired in six weeks.

I shall hope to hear of you, if you send your letter to Castle it will be forwarded to me; let me know what is going on among you all. I hope you are in your own house again, and that it is done to your satisfaction.

Adieu, pray make my remembrances acceptable to Sir Charles, and believe me

Very sincerely yours,

Henry W.

Madame Patterson Bonaparte to Lady Morgan.

PARIS,
November 28.

MY DEAR LADY MORGAN,

Mrs. Evans has given me your welcome letter; I cannot express to you how much I was delighted at hearing that you had not forgotten me. I passed only a few months in Italy, where I saw the most beautiful woman in the world, who since died in her *husband's* palace at Florence, surrounded by friends, and conjugally regretted by Prince Borghese! He buried her in the handsomest chapel in Europe. She left a legacy to my son of twenty thousand francs. Voila en peu de mots ci que j'ai a dire de la Princesse Pauline. I have been *pour mes péchés*, a great deal in Geneva—that centre of prudery, heartlessness, and illiberal feelings. I left it with pleasure, and hope that I never shall return to it. I have paid a short visit to America. "Aux cœurs bien nés la patrie est *chère*," which does not mean that one should not prefer the *séjour* of Paris to that of the dullest place on earth. Lafayette was caressed, adored, and substantially rewarded. I saw him in Baltimore, and talked to him of you, whom he loves and admires, *malgré le temps et l'absence*; Miss Wright was with him, or near him, all the time he was in America. She intends writing *something* of which he is to be the *hero*. Why did Moore destroy Lord Byron's memoirs? It was a breach of confidence—they were intended for publication.

You are very kind in inquiring after my father and my son. The former is living, the latter has grown up handsome—a classical profile, and *un esprit juste.* He is in America. My health is, as usual, neither good nor bad—nerves very tormenting, mind, as formerly, discontented, although I flatter myself that I am growing more patient of injustice and egotism. What do you say of De Genlis? Her memoirs are said to be *peu véridiques.* People seem to be disappointed that she does not relate her gallantries; but of course she thinks, *que cela va sans dire.* One of her *truisms* is, that Madame de Villette was convinced of the truth of the Christian religion—a conviction that our poor dear friend certainly imparted to none of those who lived with her. Genlis has pleased no one by the publication of this work of imagination—the drippings and last squeezings of her brain. She lives at Mantes, with Casimir, the boy whom *elle avait ramassé en Allemagne.* He is infected with her *devotion,* or her hypocrisy, or both.

Poor Dénon is dead; Madame D'Houchin is, I hear, dreadfully grieved at her deplorable *veuvage du cœur.* Nothing can, I think, console for the loss of a person whom one has loved and been loved by. Madame Capodoce is here, regretting poor M. de Brito, who died some time since; she looks dreadfully ill—her husband now lives with her after an absence of thirty years. "Un mari suffit rarement pour remplir le cœur" was said to you by Madame Suard—this *agreeable* person is still living, and *folle comme autrefois.* Do you know a dull writer called Julien, who publishes

a periodical paper. I thank Sir Charles for his kisses,
which I reciprocate at the same time; but I send my
love to him. I hope the gloves fitted—wedding gloves,
sent by the Lord-Lieutenant of the Marchioness of
Wellesley!!! Was the Duke, Great Bolingbroke, at
the wedding? Do contrive to get a letter to me by
une occasion particulière. I do not like the idea of
the police, your readers, receiving what was intended
for me. Pray let me know what you are doing, &c.,
&c. Be assured I shall not slip through your fingers
through my negligence. Adieu,

   Believe me,
  Ever most affectionately, yours,
     E. PATTERSON.

P.S.—Warden is as usual; he never leaves the Faubourg St. Germain. I have no doubt that he has *un sentiment*—nothing else could keep any one there. What do you think of Miss Harriet Wilson's life, written by herself? Every one reads it. She is living in Paris, which seems to be the favourite residence of all naughty English women. Miss Harriet is married to a very handsome man, who was willing to make an honest woman of her. I have fifty scandalous things to tell you; but I write in haste that I may send my letter to England by a friend. I have been in Paris only a few days; I have seen no one. All the people whom I knew are dead or absent.

CHAPTER XVI.

THE YEAR 1826.

DURING this year, Lady Morgan's chief employment was upon the Irish story which Colburn had been looking for so long, *The O'Briens and the O'Flaherties.*

A great Protestant petition to Parliament for the repeal of the political and religious disabilities which in Ireland pressed so heavily on the Roman Catholics, was got up in the early part of this year. It was intrusted to the hands of Sir Charles Morgan to receive the signatures, and most of the leading nobility of Ireland came forward to the appeal, and signed it. That petition was a great incident in the battle for Catholic Emancipation—a battle which is still faintly echoed in the periodical squabbles about the Maynooth grant. It cost more moral courage to be a liberal in those days, or rather to have the courage to be *just*, especially in Ireland, than can now be understood; to be liberal then, needed a very earnest conviction. We return to the diaries:—

March 13.—My novel of *The O'Briens and the O'Flahertics*, is announced as much nearer finished than it really is.

I was last night at a private party at the Castle. I was (as of late I have constantly been) the centre of a circle. It changed its character very often, at first; the courtiers, chamberlains, and aides-de-camps, all waiting near the door for the Vice-Regal entry, and as the circle widened, I found I was the nucleus of the falling set; on one side O'Connell, Lord Killeen (the Catholic chief), and my ultra-liberal husband—on the other side, stood North, whose gentle, temporising, Whig-Toryism, places him with the Doctrinaires of our country; Dogherty, the ministerial *enfant trouvé*; Col. Blacker, Grand Master of the Orange Lodge, commonly called "the roaring lion;" and Joy, the Solicitor-General, the *oriflamme* of every species of intolerance and illiberalism, all standing amicably side by side, like the statues in the "Groves of Blarney," though *not* "naked in the open air"! Thirty years ago the roof would not have been deemed safe which afforded O'Connell, and such as he, a shelter.

That—

> First flower of the earth,
> First gem of the sea,

O'Connell, wants back the days of Brian Borru, himself to be the king, with a crown of emerald shamrocks, a train of yellow velvet, and a mantle of Irish tabinet, a sceptre in one hand and a cross in the other, and the people crying "Long live King O'Connell!" This is the object of his views and his ambition. Should he ever be king of Ireland, he should take Charley Phillips for his prime minister, Tom Moore for chief bard, J. O'Meara for attorney-general, and Counsellor Bethel for his chief-justice. O'Connell is not a man of genius; he has a sort of conventional talent applicable to his purpose as it exists in Ireland—a *nisi prius* talent which has won much local popularity.

November 27.—Darby O'Grady, the Chief Baron's brother, is *impayable;* he walks about the street in tight yellow buckskins and a dandy hat.

Here is a picture of O'Connell "in his habit as he lived," or rather as he lives, which almost realises my fancy portrait! It came to-day in a letter from William Curran.

"The only country news I have is that some rain has fallen, and the fields are beginning to look almost as green as O'Connell, for he walks the streets here in the full dress of a verdant liberator—green in all that may and may not be expressed, even to a green cravat, green watch-ribbon, and a slashing shining green hatband, and he has a confident hope that 'the tears of Ireland will prevent the colours from ever fading.'"

Sir Charles Morgan's daughter by his first marriage, Annie, was about to be married, and Sir Charles came to England to arrange preliminary business with her m.... ther's family. By the marriage settlements, his own fortu.... was to revert to her on his death.
It was the first time Sir Charles and Lady Morgan

had been separated since their marriage, as on this occasion Lady Morgan did not accompany him. The following letter gives Sir Charles' account of his doings in London.

Sir Charles Morgan to Lady Morgan.

FLADONG'S HOTEL, LONDON,
May 29, 1826.

DEAREST SYD.,

I have this moment received your two letters and enclosures. The latter I will get set up in type, and correct before I leave town. *I* think it good and amusing; but I fancy Colburn will be frightened to death at its boldness.

I have written to Count Porro. Ugo Foscolo is in *quod*, cut by his friends and countrymen, after diddling Lord John Russell out of a thousand pounds. I dined yesterday with Harry Storks; he was talking of some reprobate Roman Catholic who would eat a horse on Ash-Wednesday, upon which, says I, "not unless it was a *fast horse!*" "Ah, ah, ah." (This is for Livy's tender ear) there never was Clarke's equal on the floor of creation; it is a great misfortune he has never turned his mind to the philosopher's stone, I am sure his perseverance would discover whether such a thing is catalogued on the book of nature or no. The children shall have new silver nothings of some sort.

Oh this London! this London!! here have I been on my legs all day, like a penny-postman. I went to Lydia White's last night, who was lying on the same sofa, in the same drawing-room, with the same blue furniture and blue hangings as usual—she was precisely what you know her. I only spoke to her and Moore, and went away in half-an-hour, in the *blue devils*. Moore is rapidly undergoing that transformation which will qualify him for a place in Hallam's book. He is not going to Ireland. On Saturday, I dined at home, and went to the Opera. I have just opened a new mine for magazine writing; but this is a secret. Colburn wants me to write a *political* novel —for God's sake make me out a *canevas*, and I shall try my hand at it. I have just got a kind note from *Madame Patt.*, wanting me to fix a day for dining with her; but I do not think I shall have one to spare. I did not tell you how Pasta charmed me in the *Romeo* the other night. She sang "Ombra adorata" *divinely*. They played, also, an act of *Teobaldo ed Isolina*, in which Velluti sang "Notte tremenda," in a style of which I had no idea, still, however, he does not please me. The ballet, *La Naissance de Venus*, was better, and I believe now I have done with operas. You must not mind that lying old witch Madame de Genlis' attack on you in her book. I thought she would not let you off easily; you were not only a better, and younger (and *I* may say *prettier*) author than herself, but a more popular one.

I have seen the Charlemonts, the Charlevilles, and the old lady of Burlington Street, and most of your friends, and am charged all over with kindness to you, and regrets that you are not with me. Parliament will be up in a few days, and then all will be off. Here goes my tenth day, and that is half-way through this tiresome job. I think you may begin to feed the calf, as I shall be off the moment my business is settled. Oh this cursed wilderness of a town; you may guess how bad it is when a man sits down to write to his wife, *à l'heure qu'il est*, Regent Street like a carnival. Now I'll trouble you to guess what I am going to tell you; but I'll be d——d if you do, so to save you the trouble of making a judy of yourself, I may as well tell you at once that Capel is going into Parliament to teach the Premier his "*reading made easy*," and set the finance at rest. He is to represent Queensborough with its mayor and freemen. These old boys beat us hollow. Think of his encountering the heat and fatigue of late House of Commons work? By-the-bye, I met at breakfast, in the coffee-room, this morning, our old Italian friend, Dr. Clarke. He is a good specimen of our good Italians. He told me news of many of our old friends at Rome and Naples, which I shall keep for you till we meet. Fashions!! heavens if I have not forgotten to tell you, from that queen of fashion, Mrs. M'Neil! *bonnets* the size of *my* umbrella; your gigot sleeves as full *as you can make them*. I am reading *Vivian Grey*, at night, and in bed in the morning. Colburn gets twelve hundred pounds per annum for the *Sunday Times*, eighteen hundred pounds on the *New Monthly*, and shared eleven hundred pounds this year on the *Literary Gazette*.

Ever yours, whether you believe it or not,

C. M.

PS.—If ever I am caught in this region of smoke again "all alone, *proudie*," I'll be ——!

In the mention of Lady Morgan by Madame de Genlis, there was nothing to break any bones nor even to give a scratch to the most ardent self-love. Madame de Genlis writes in the character of a Minerva, and expresses herself as though Lady Morgan were one of her *élèves*, in the *Tales of the Castle*, who required a gentle admonition.

"Lady Morgan," says Madame de Genlis, "is not beautiful; but there is something lively and agreeable in her whole person. She is very clever, and seems to have a good heart: it is a pity that, for the sake of popularity, she should have the mania of meddling in politics [of course it was natural that Madame de Genlis who, as she boasts, had educated two princes and one princess of the blood, should think small things of Lady Morgan's liberal ideas]. She says gracefully, that "her vivacity, and rather springing carriage, seemed very strange in Parisian circles. She soon learned that good taste of itself condemns this kind of demeanour; in fact, gesticulation and noisy manners have never been popular in France. When people go to the promenade it is to take a chair. When she came to me one day, she told me she had a very interesting lady in her carriage who was desirous of seeing me—this was Mrs. Patterson, the first wife of Prince Jerome Bonaparte. Lady Morgan pressed me very much to receive her; I consented. I saw a very fine woman—mild, melancholy, and quiet, who was worthy of a better fate."

Of course there is an air of affable superiority in

the above which is very amusing, but not calling for any sympathy, and certainly cannot be called "an attack."

The following scraps of diary complete the year 1826.

October 27.—Poor Talma!! one of the earliest and kindest of my French acquaintance. The account of his death has just reached me. Of all the eminent men I knew in Paris in 1816, there now only remain Lafayette, Jouy, and Humboldt. Talma died of intestinal schirrus. Monsieur Du Puytren was desirous to perform an operation which he was convinced would have saved him if he had had strength enough to undergo it, but he was deterred from resorting to it by the extreme weakness to which he was reduced. The Archbishop of Paris repeatedly called at his house, but Talma declined to see him. Talma did not suffer any acute pain, he only complained of having a cloud before his eyes. Talma refused to see the Archbishop or any priest, saying that he would not deny the forty brightest years of his life, nor separate his cause from that of his comrades, nor acknowledge them to be infamous. The present Archbishop has endeavoured to obtain the repeal from the Court of Rome of the excommunication pronounced against actors. Talma was born in Paris, in January, 1760. His father was a dentist, who afterwards exercised his profession in London with great success.

October 30.—A ballad singer was this morning singing beneath my window, in a voice most *unmusical* and melancholy; my own name caught my ear, and I sent Thomas out to buy the song, here is a stanza:—

> "Och, Dublin city there's no doubtin'
> Bates every city upon the say;
> 'Tis there you'll hear O'Connell spoutin',
> An' Lady Morgan making tay;
> For 'tis the capital of the finest nation,
> Wid charming pisantry on a fruitful sod,
> Fighting like divils for conciliation,
> An' hating each other for the love of God."

Just received the following note from Archibald Rowan, sending me the history of the "United Irishmen" for my "O'Briens and O'Flaherties."

H. Rowan to Lady Morgan.

Tuesday Evening.

As there is no certainty from what seeds or flowers the bee extracts its sweets, H. Rowan sends Lady Morgan a book, which, it seems, was published after he left Ireland, and, till he met with it the other day, he did not know it existed.

CHAPTER XVII.

THE O'BRIENS AND O'FLAHERTIES—1827.

EARLY in 1827 the novel of the *O'Briens* and the *O'Flaherties* was complete. There was a long negociation about the price. Lady Morgan had a perfect conviction of her own value, and she stood out for terms. Colburn wrote pathetically that no other publisher ever would or could feel the interest he did in her works, or make so many sacrifices to insure their success, and as those things did not move Lady Morgan, he wrote on May 7, 1827, and made an offer of one thousand two hundred and fifty pounds, to be paid by instalments. This, Lady Morgan refused, and after some further correspondence, Colburn, sooner than see a rival in possession, agreed to her terms, which were one thousand three hundred pounds down for the copyright, one hundred pounds on the second edition, and another hundred on the third edition, with the stipulation that no edition was to exceed three thousand copies.

The work was more popular than any of her former

tales. The pictures of Irish society immediately before and after the Union, and the characters of the vice-regal Court under the Duke of Rutland, had a peculiar interest at the time the book came out, which has now evaporated; but there is still the perennial interest of human nature, dashes of Irish humour and Irish pathos, and traits of manners not now to be found,—for the Irish peasant of the present day is quite a different creature. As a repertory of the manners, customs, grievances, and society as it existed both in Dublin and the provinces in the time when Ireland was the seat of misgovernment and mistake, the *O'Brien's and the O'Flaherties* will always be a standard work of reference. As a tale, the plot is too confused, and the interest too much diffused; the whole story is rambling, but detached portions of it are inimitable; for instance, the account of the Miss Mc Taafs and their "Tea Day," which we have quoted elsewhere, and which was drawn from the life. It is a portraiture perfect in its kind, and like a picture by Hogarth in words. The Lord Aronmore is not so interesting a personage as *O'Donnel*, but any one wishing for a book full of scenes of racy Irish fun and delicate satire would find these in the pages of the *O'Brien's and the O'Flaherties*. The first volume which is occupied with an account of an Irish feud, might be omitted, as it damps the reader's interest by too long a prelude.

A certain rebel, General Aylmer, offers the type for her hero. The real General, driven from his own country after the troubles of '98, entered the Austrian service; distinguished himself; became a general; was selected to accompany the Emperor of Austria when he visited England, and, at the special request of the Prince Regent, he was left behind to teach the sword-exercise to the British Army. His special pupils were the 10th Dragoons, and he performed his task so well that he received a free pardon and a handsome sword from the Prince Regent himself. He tried to settle in his native land; but, all patriotic as he was, he could not be happy in peace and retirement. He headed a band of Irish sympathizers, and joined the South American patriots, then in the beginning of their struggle under Bolivar. He fought hard, of course, and received a wound in one of their battles, from the effects of which he soon after died. Some idea of a *real* Irish hero may be formed from the incident that once having got into a squabble with the Duke of Leinster's gamekeepers, he called on His Grace to complain, attired in his full Austrian uniform, with sabre and helmet complete!

February.—Death of Lydia White; I received the account this morning. Poor Lydia had asked a party to dine with her on Friday,—on Wednesday she was dead! From economy of eyes and lights, she used to sit when alone to a late hour without lights. Her servant having placed candles on the table in the front drawing-room waited for his mistress to ring to light them. He thought he heard something fall, but as the bell did not ring he did not go up, till surprised at her remaining so long in the dark, he entered, and found her lying on the floor. Dr. Holland was sent for, but medical aid was too late. When some of her party arrived to dine on the Friday she was lying dead. Poor Lydia! before she was buried she was forgotten!

The Lydia White so often referred to was a personage of much social celebrity in her day. She was an Irish lady of large fortune and considerable talent, noted for her hospitalities and dinners in all the capitals of Europe, particularly London and Paris. She had remarkable quickness at repartee. At one of her small and agreeable dinners in Park Street (all the company except herself being Whigs), the desperate prospects of the Whig party were discussed. "Yes," said Sidney Smith, who was present, "we are in a most deplorable condition, we must do something to help ourselves; I think," said he, looking at Lydia White, "we had better sacrifice a Tory virgin." "Ah!" replied she, "I believe there is nothing the Whigs would *not* do to raise the wind."

There are several incidental mentions of her in the diaries of Lord Byron and Moore. Byron seems to have been inclined to shy at what he calls her "*purple parties*," but he does not speak ill-naturedly, though he rather makes fun of her. He tells Moore in one of his letters that Lydia White was in Venice, and had just borrowed his copy of *Lalla Rookh*.

For some time before her death she was in a languishing state of health, but it provoked witticism rather than compassion. Moore says in his diary, May 7, 1826:—"Called upon Rogers; found him in

high good humour. In talking of Miss White, he
said, 'how wonderfully she does hold out; they may
say what they will, but Miss White and *Missolongi*
are the most remarkable things going.' "

In consequence of disease she became of a great
size during the latter part of her life; and the best
her friends could find to say of her was, that she would
" leave a great gap in society." For a woman who
was so well known in the world, she has passed singularly out of remembrance.

March 8.—Last night, Laporte, the celebrated
French actor from the Vaudeville, delighted a very
chosen society at our *petite soirée* by his reading of *Les
Precieuses.*

In the dawn of refinement there is always a tendency to the *Précieuse-ism* of the Hôtel Rambouillet.
Louis XIV., that most illiterate of men, was bored
alike with the real and affected superiority of some of
his courtiers; he was protector of Molière, and even
the Jesuits could not hunt down *Tartuffe.*

May 9.—Received in Kildare Street the Duke de
Dalmatia, son of Marshal Soult, and his friend de
Visconti. They were sent to me by the Duc de
Montebello.

The diary is resumed in London.

July 27.—Lady Charleville was pre-eminently
agreeable to-day,—we talked over Lady Cork; she is
eighty-one, and gave a dinner to twenty special guests

the other day. Her last intrigue "*aux choux et aux raves*" was driving a hard bargain with the Tyrolese to sing at her party. She picked them up in the Regent's Park, and brought them down to thirty shillings, which she was heard wishing to beat down to eight, when she stood with them where she thought there was no one to listen, but they held out for the thirty shillings.

At the Duke of St. Alban's, where there were all the opera people, she said, "Duke, now, couldn't you send me the pack for my evening?" "Certainly," said he, and they were sent with a grand piano forte. When they came to her, Lady Cork got frightened, and said " Je suis une pauvre veuve, je ne saurais payer de tels talents, mais vous verrez la meilleure société, la Duchesse de St. Albans, &c., &c." The Primo Amoroso bowed, and acknowledged the honour, but intimated that the Duchess always paid them.

Lady Cork went to the Duke and accused him of taking a word at random, *tout de bon.*

The Duchess overhearing, came forward in a rage, and scolded the little Duke like a naughty schoolboy. The angry Duchess took all upon herself. Lady Cork was very angry at "the show up."

Talking this morning with Lady Charleville on the report of my having found assistance in Brownlow's conversations. "Not you, child," she said, "you have a splendid imagination, but you have no powers of argument." She was right as to the fact, but wrong as to inference. Men are always more easily convinced by images presented to their senses, than by arguments offered to their reason. Images are facts, arguments are but words, and impressions are more rapidly conveyed than ideas. I have often failed to excite an interest by argument,—I have always succeeded by a scene.

There is nothing less amusing than writing for the amusement of the public.

Lady Cork said to me this morning, when I called Miss —— a nice person. "Don't say *nice*, child, 'tis a bad word. Once I said to Dr. Johnson, ' Sir, that is a very nice person.' ' A *nice* person,' he replied, ' what does that mean? *Elegant* is now the fashionable word, but will go out, and I see this stupid *nice* is to succeed to it; what does nice mean? look in my dictionary, you will see it means correct, precise.'"

Lady Cork also told me that on one occasion when Croker was dining with the King, the Duke of Clarence was present, who was always indignant at the insolence of office displayed by Croker in the Admiralty. "When *I* am king," said he, " I will be my own secretary of the Admiralty." The King overheard them and said, "What nonsense is that you are talking, Croko?" "His Royal Highness is mentioning what he will do in case he should become king." The next morning the King sent for Croker to his bedroom, and reproached him for exposing his brother, and he was *never invited to dinner again*.

The following note from Lady Caroline Lamb contains the announcement of the unexpected death of Canning.

Lady Caroline Lamb to Lady Morgan.

Brockett Hall,
Wednesday.

My dear Lady Morgan,

In consequence of a carrier coming this way, I have heard to my excessive horror that Mr. Canning is either dying or dead. I am coming to town in consequence to know the truth, and if I can, to see the Duke of Devonshire; in the mean time, will you call upon me to-morrow (Thursday) the moment you are up, and pray let it be early; you never said good bye, you never said thank you for my sweet scent. You never brought me the portrait. I take this note to town to-night, scarcely hoping to see you. I have two or three notes from William, evidently not knowing this disastrous news.

Yours most truly,
C. Lamb.

To return to the diary again—

Canning's death makes less sensation than might have been expected; he had no hold on the convictions of society. His one absorbing idea was to be the political Atlas of England, to raise her on his shoulders. His vituperative eloquence, his wit, his *aplomb*, his humour were exquisite. When I wrote my first *France*, and attacked the Bourbons in my tiny way, Canning was at the feet of the restored despots, and called Bourdeaux *Le Temple de Madame D'Angoulême.*

Lady Cork once took me to visit him, but he was out.

Dublin again.—We have busied ourselves very much upon the occasion of Talbot's election, and wrote all sorts of squibs, some of which were sung in the street the next day.

October 19.—We dined at our new Secretary's to-day (W. Lamb). We had Curran and Grattan, names new to the salons of our Irish Secretary.

I was telling Henry Grattan and Mrs. Blachford that I had introduced their father in my *O'Briens and O'Flaherties* at the head of his volunteer corps in the park. Mrs. Blachford said that her father one day marched his company into the middle of the sea. On another occasion he was reviewing them with his glass to his eye, and Mrs. Blachford was near him; he asked her, "Mary Ann, are their backs or their fronts towards me?" He was very blind and very absent, and his mind full of anything but military evolutions.

Crumpton told me that a man repeating to him an observation of a clever person who had said "such a one's mind is still in full force, but he must die, his *physique* is quite worn out," he said Dr. B—— says, 'Mr. —— must die for his physic is out!" * * * The Hon. George Keppel, aid-de-camp to Lord Wellesley, became an *habitué* of our house in Kildare Street. *Il n'en bougait plus*—at last it came out that he had a manuscript by him of his journey through Persia—in a word, he wished me to *blanchir son linge sale*, or rather to sell his book for him. I always like to encourage the young rising aristocracy to work, for a thousand reasons, so I took his MS., read it, and sold it for three hundred pounds to Colburn, who, but for me, would not have given him three hundred pence. After it was out, his vanity got alarmed lest I should arrogate to myself the "best passages in it!"

November 12, *Sunday.*—At my once-a-fortnight's Sunday dinners yesterday, I had a strange *olla podrida* sort of gathering. Bunn, the lessee of the theatre; Calcraft, the manager; Sir Charles Malcolm, just appointed to his first place at Bombay; Mr. Cuthbert, and one or two others. In the evening, Sheil, Curran, Crampton (Surgeon-General), Mrs. Corregan, the *prima donna* (who sang charmingly); some of the old Court, an American Corinne, Miss Edgeworth, and the Lakes of Killarney.

Bunn's anecdotes were some of them very amusing. Talking of Theodore Hook, Bunn said (though Bunn is by way of being his friend and disciple) "No friendship can bind him, he will show up a friend in his writings all the same as his foe. He is said to make three thousand a-year by the *John Bull* and his other writings. He lies on a sofa and drinks claret all day, and has a face like a grenadier's cap. He was the confidential friend of Lord Bathurst."

Here he was interrupted by the frank indignation of Sir Charles Malcolm.—"He is one of the greatest rogues that lives unhanged! When Lord Bathurst engaged him to write the account of Bonaparte's detention at St. Helena, there were among many gross falsehoods, a calumnious attack upon my uncle, Sir Pultney Malcolm. He heard this, and said to Lord Bathurst, 'I hear that there is such a work coming out; the moment it appears I will publish a counter statement, in which I will tell the whole truth—*I will spare none!*' The work, on the day it was to appear, was suppressed; Lord Bathurst bought it up from Colburn."

The John Bull, The Age, The Beacon, The Satirist, and such works may be called into life, and men may endorse their opinions. They may have partisans, readers, and patrons. Despotism in politics, corruption in morals, calumny in conversation, degeneracy in taste, bigotry in religion was "the badge of all their tribe."

[NOTE, 1847.—In looking over this book I find all my opinions justified by time. Where now are the *John Bull, The Age, The Satirist? The Quarterly* is so reformed, its name alone remains unchanged.]

The O'Briens and the O'Flaherties. In the dialogue and tone of manners given to my fair oligarchs in the second and third volumes, I was dreadfully afraid there was *de quoi choquer les Prudes,* and I suppressed many droll things that had been related to me. I was murmuring my fears to Lady Cloncurry—severe upon *mœurs* and a model of propriety. Lady Cloncurry set my mind at rest by answering me that I had kept clear of extremes and dwelt more in the decencies than was at all characteristic of the time I described. Her mother, the beautiful Mrs. Douglas, had lived in the thick of the world in the times I had mentioned; she had taken the governess of the Duchess of Rutland, Madame Delval, to educate Lady Cloncurry. They had many curious anecdotes from her, more curious than edifying. The Duke had in his route brought over with him a certain handsome Mr. Bathurst, who, to the amazement of the Irish ladies, used to enter the drawing-room in a succession of somersaults, which he performed with singular agility. Under the lieutenancy of Lord Hardwicke and the commencement of the Duke of Richmond's, there were in the Castle circle a *posse* of titled women of bold reputation, who had the uncontrolled sway in everything. These ladies introduced a kind of savage dance, or rather romp, called "Cutchakutchoo;" this was performed by the parties squatting themselves on the floor, both their arms underneath their legs, and changing places with their partners as well as they could in such a posture. In short, the Dublin court of that period was like the manners described in *Grammont's Memoirs*.

Morgan has just been in to show me this letter from O'Connell.

Daniel O'Connell to Sir Charles Morgan.

MY DEAR SIR,

The *Freeman* is a slave, that is plain; he is a mean and paltry dog, also—but that is of course.

I have got your manuscript, but do not leave it because I hope you will allow me to transfer it to committee, which, on the late occasion, has shown some symptoms of reviving honesty.

Faithfully yours,
DANIEL O'CONNELL.

Poor Lady Caroline is worse; here is a note just come.

Mrs. Hawtre to Lady Morgan.

BROCKETT HALL,
November 22.

I am much grieved that I cannot give you a better account of dear Lady Caroline's health. Since the operation, her symptoms have assumed such varied appearances that at this moment we have no confidence of an ultimate recovery; the natural strength of her constitution is very great, and we have all ardent hopes much good may result from that favourable circumstance. The situation is most distressing to the many kind friends that are interested for her recovery, and we must derive consolation from witnessing her perfect calm resignation. Lady Caroline expressed much pleasure at receiving a very feeling letter from you this morning. Mr. Lamb is cruelly situated to be separated so far at this moment. Trusting I have given you a correct account of my kind friend, though a very unhappy one,

Believe me,
Yours truly,
GEORGINA M. M. HAWTRE.

November 23.—Yesterday I went to see Lord and Lady Howth. Howth Castle stands as it did in the time of General Wade, and seems a mansion of Queen Elizabeth's day—not, I should think, older, except one high square tower, within an enclosure—a method common in old Irish castles. This tower appears of great antiquity. The general mansion is a long, low building of many gables, ascended by broad, sheltered, stone steps; the offices spacious, low-roofed—they stand on the ground-floor. The huge metal bells that have stood there from time immemorial, till the date of their being placed there, has escaped all memory. At either extremity of the hall are a few black oak and balustraded stairs—that to the right leads to the state bedroom, a curious and charming old apartment, breaking out into little turret-closets and recesses that are now alcoves and dressing-rooms for the lords and ladies of the day; that to the left is called the haunted chamber, a formal room said once to have been King William's bed-chamber. Opposite the door of entrance in the hall is a little ante-room leading to the grand stairs and to the drawing-room, a long, low-roofed, narrow room, with a fine, carved ceiling, carefully white-washed, a superb mantel-piece of grey marble, rising in a succession of stories to the roof, each storey set off by a profusion of old china. Then there are coffers, cabinets, japan-screens, and other old relics of old houses and old families that one is ready to fall down and worship. Above are corridors, with dear old bedrooms, odd nooks, and niches for nothing at all; then narrow and winding passages and stairs, popping upon one at every turn; the whole is a perfect picture of the dreary, unconnected style of domestic dwellings,—the comfortless, unaccommodating reality of those times which paint and write so well, but which one would not wish to have lived in. There is a curious picture which represents the great front of the old castle and part of the rock on which it stands. The famous female pirate, Gran O'Neile, is mounted on horse-back, holds a faulchion, with her long, silk mantle drawn decently round her stout limbs, her head well formed, her shoulders and arms are bare, her yellow drapery seems to have fallen off; she has a sort of white veil or bandeau on her head; she is issuing orders to several men, all employed in carrying off plunder from Howth Castle; some are rolling up casks, others throwing about domestic utensils, others are loading asses with difficult piles of luggage which they are conveying towards the shore; but the most remarkable person is the young heir of Howth, an infant child, which one of Gran O'Neile's female followers is holding up to the fair pirate, who is about to place it on horseback before her, at the moment she is issuing her last commands, and leaving the castle for her ship, which was at anchor near. Over all, emerging through a cloud, appears the head and bust, beautifully painted, of some saint. While I stood gazing on this curious picture, I held the present heir of Howth, Lord St. Lawrence, in my arms; beside me stood his young and smiling mother, not yet of age; on the other side, his French nurse, herself a descendant of Gran O'Neile.

In Howth Castle, as elsewhere in secluded places,

there were two state bedrooms, rich, cumbrous, and spacious; all the rest were hovels.

November 27.—Yesterday, we had a dinner-party, the Honourable William Lamb, Lord Cloncurry, Mr. Blake, Chief Remembrancer Curran, Mr. Evans, of Portran, &c., &c. Mr. Lamb was in the lowest spirits from the bad accounts that had come of poor Lady Caroline.

Poor Lady Caroline, her life was fast ebbing; but she had kind friends round her. Here is a letter from her husband, more than a fortnight later.

W. Lamb to Lady Morgan.

DUBLIN CASTLE,
December 12.

DEAR LADY MORGAN,

I have been very neglectful lately in not sending you the accounts which I received. It is with great pain that I now send you the enclosed. It is some consolation that she is relieved from pain; but illness is a terrible thing. Send them me back, that I may forward them to Lord Duncannon.

Yours faithfully,
WILLIAM LAMB.

The following is the letter alluded to; it is endorsed, "Dr. Goddard's letter, sent me by Mr. Lamb."

December 13, 1827.

My dear Sir,

I regret very much that I have but a melancholy account to give you to-day of Lady Caroline's health. Saturday she seemed in good spirits; but on that night she began to complain of pain in her side, accompanied with cough and shortness of breath. These symptoms are, I think, partly accidental, and may not continue; but should they, they will certainly give us great cause of alarm. There is another change, also; she is inattentive to what is going on. She speaks with difficulty, and seems unwilling to see many people. You may gather too plainly from all these symptoms the unwelcome news that her ladyship is getting worse; her sufferings she still bears with fortitude, and complains but little.

I remain, dear Sir,
Your obedient and humble Servant,
G. Goddard.

Lady Charleville to Lady Morgan.

December 30.

You are so kind in the expression of an interest for my recovery, that I must thank you, *au risque*, to take up valuable time with reading a very dull letter. I have suffered from an attack of the chest; a blood-vessel I broke thirty years ago seemed inclined to go over its old train of pain and disease; but it has stopped; and I think if I had air and absence of coal sulphur, I should be well.

Now you know as much as I do myself of "*mon physique et mon moral;*" and I rejoice that you are content with the success of your novel and of the profits. People have more time to read away from this town, I believe, and think more about books of amusement; but I am quite sure the reviews prevent three parts of society from going through any book in London. I fear it will make enemies amongst the survivors of the cabinet of 1786. You have written powerfully, and many of great judgment say so when they dare; but the ladies are vociferous in condemnation of what they call blasphemy and indecency, and conceive me very atrocious for not having discovered either the one or the other defect in the book. The king, I find, was interested in the lighter parts; but some of the charges against the Irish government, he said, were too bad, while God knows they were not half bad enough to my mind. Now, what I like best in the whole was Shane; he beats Eddie Ochiltree off the ground. I wish he had not killed anybody, nor been killed; but all the poetical fancies will fix upon him, if he had murdered all the excisemen in Europe. In short, I love him so that I think he is the hero of the tale, and the Miss Mac Taafs the heroines. I must, however, tell you that I am so miserably convinced, by all I have ever read or SEEN, of the tendency of Roman Catholic tenets to put down human intellect, to control and guide all human interests to their own profit, and to create control even in the heart of every private family, that even independent of Jesuitism, I cannot like any amiable abbess, or allow of any stratagem, that holds forth one of those traps for us to put ourselves and our spirits into the hands of their church.

Our own church has preserved too many Catholic trappings, which common sense must reject. I regret, so far as Ireland is concerned, that at the time we had our volunteers, our patriot hands were not strengthened to make a division of church lands, which would have afforded proper provision both for Protestant and Roman Catholic pastors of all ranks; neither of them could then have stripped the peasant of his mite,—the first by impoverishing him, and the other by superstitious rites.

I think my dear Mr. Grattan was short-sighted in not getting us over this step when we had *arms in our hands*.

My Lord (who when he was sixteen was generalissimo of volunteers for the King's County) says, "you have underrated the whole force by two-thirds;" and also, he says, "there was not one Roman Catholic received into the original institution." He was also deputy to the Convention from the King's County.

We had been so enslaved and so impoverished, that even men like Grattan thought wonders were accomplished in 1782, by hearing us called free, and having a ship or two allowed us, and being permitted to decide finally upon our own cause and in our own parliament.

They ought to have foreseen that with revived energies Ireland should naturally become a still greater object of distrust and jealousy to her *marâtre*,—that a union would be her best policy. Our private securities and our people's comfort should have been looked to when government dared not have refused us the proper and liberal position which the church lands would have afforded for the priests, while enough would have been left for the ascendancy of the religion of the State.

Whatever objections philosophical inquiry may incline to make, the Church of England is pure in its precepts, and does not, by oral confession, put us into the hands of creatures as fallible as ourselves; whose interest it is to subdue our energies and destroy our judgment, in order to direct into one channel the exercise of intellect and property. But this opportunity is past; we can do nothing now but look on; I hope times will mend, as the old phrase says.

I hear from authority, Sir William Knighton now settles all things here. It is certain the king said he loved Lord Holland as his brother, but it is a new question for a British king to ask what the Emperor of Austria and King of France would say to a Whig ministry! Objecting to Lord Holland is objecting to one of the best friends of Old England. I am, and always was, for liberty, for law, and for full exercise of religious opinion; *but* I would have no man a legislator who was bound to follow the direction of his priest; consequently, no Roman Catholic in either house of parliament.

Many people fancy your enlightened Catholics do not confess or would allow of political control; if they do not, why not conform at once? Their opinion on the metaphysics of religion could not be an objection to their sitting in parliament to legislate for us; but a majority, governed by the Jesuits, would soon put out the sun of England.

Lady Anglesey, I think, will never be able to go. I hope Mr. Lamb will stay. You are right, Lady Caroline was scarcely accountable, and is to be pitied; but better her poor heart ceased to beat than stand in the way of the good he may do.

I am, ever yours affectionately,
M. C.

My little grandson is JEAN JACQUES!! *Viva!* compliments to your *sposo*.

Hon. W. Ponsonby to Lady Morgan.

ST. JAMES'S SQUARE,
January 26.

MY DEAR MADAM,

The interest which you have felt for my dear sister, makes me anxious that you should not hear from common report the termination of her long and severe sufferings. From the beginning of her illness, she had no expectation of recovery, and only felt anxious to live long enough to see Mr. Lamb once again. In this she was gratified, and was still able to converse with him and enjoy his society; but for the past three days, it was apparent that her strength was rapidly declining, and on Sunday night at about nine o'clock, she expired without a struggle. A kinder or a better heart has never ceased to beat; and it was to her a great consolation, and is now to us, that her mind was fully prepared and reconciled to this awful change. She viewed the near approach of death with the greatest calmness; and during the whole of her severe sufferings, the patience with which she endured them, or her kind and affectionate feelings for those about her, never failed for one moment. Mr. Lamb has felt and acted as I knew he would, upon this sad occasion.

Believe me, dear madam,
Very faithfully yours,
W. PONSONBY.

Diary resumed :—

January 30.—Received this morning a letter from the Honourable William Ponsonby, announcing the death of his sister, my poor dear friend, Lady Caroline Lamb. She expired on the evening of the 26th. She was tall and slight in her figure, her countenance was grave, her eyes dark, large, bright; her complexion fair; her voice soft, low, caressing, that was at once a beauty and a charm, and worked much of that fascination that was peculiarly hers; it softened down her enemies the moment they listened to her. She was eloquent, most eloquent, full of ideas, and of graceful gracious expression; but her subject was always herself. She confounded her dearest friends and direst foes, for her feelings were all impulses, worked on by a powerful imagination; all elements of great eloquence, but not good for guidance; one of her great charms was the rapid transition of manner which changed to its theme. The chief cause of the odd things which she used to say and do, was, that never having lived out of the habits of her own class, yet sometimes mixing with people of inferior rank, notable only by their genius, she constantly applied her own sumptuous habits to them. Here is a specimen :—she called on me one day in London, and struck by my servant, who announced her, being in livery, she said, in her odd manner, as she was going down stairs, " My dear creature, have you really not a groom of the chambers with you? nothing but your footman? You must let me send you something, you must indeed. You will never get on here, you know, with only one servant—you must let me send you one of my pages. I am going to Brocket, to watch the sweet trees that are coming out so beautifully, and you shall have a page while I am away!"

I am sick of the jargon about the idleness of genius. All the greatest geniuses have worked hard at everything—energetic, persevering, and laborious. Who has worked so much and so well as Bacon, Kepler, Milton, Newton? it is the energy that gives what we call "genius;" that leaves its impression on all it touches. Nothing but mediocrity is slothful and idle.

Dr. Goddard to Lady Morgan.

February 10, 1828.

It was the wish of Lady Caroline that the portrait of Lord Byron in the morocco case should be given to your ladyship after her death. The picture at present is in my keeping; and if your Ladyship would let me know where you are, and how to send it you, I would take care it is properly packed up and forwarded according to your directions.

I beg to be,
Your Ladyship's obedient,
B. GODDARD.

At this time, the Beef Steak Club—a high Tory political gathering in Dublin—invited Lord Anglesey to dinner, and there was a rumour that he was inclined to accept it.

Lady Morgan wrote the following letter to Lord Aylmer, to induce him to use his influence with the Marquis to keep him from attending.

April 18, 1828.

DEAR LORD AYLMER,

The esteem and admiration I have heard you express for Lord Anglesey, and the generous sympathy I know you have always felt towards Ireland, induces me to state to you, *sans préambule*, the following facts. A rumour prevails at present in Dublin, that Lord

Anglesey means to accept the invitation to be given to
him by the *Beef Steak Club*. The circumstance is apparently so insignificant, so utterly unconsequential
that it is necessary to be utterly Irish, and to know
thoroughly the state of this unhappy country to attach
the smallest consequence to it, or for a moment to
suppose that the well merited and universal popularity
of Lord Anglesey could for a moment be shaken by
such an event. The fact, however, is so much the
contrary, that should Lord Anglesey take his place in
a Society which has so long offended the nation, and so
utterly insulted the King in the person of his representative, the Marquis of Wellesley, not all the efforts
of the Catholic leaders now disposed to support and
uphold the popularity of Lord Anglesey's government,
would suffice to keep quiet that nest of hornets the
Catholic Association, who, emblematic of the rest of
this susceptible but injudicious nation, are more willing to submit to injuries than to insult. I need not
tell you, my dear Lord, the effect of the unlucky facility of Lord Wellesley in yielding to the request of
the Beef Steak Club, impeded his subsequent efforts
at tranquillising Ireland, nor into what annoyances it
betrayed him. For the party to whom his unguarded
concession was so flagrant a triumph, has acted more
like a froward child, that pouts the more it is petted.
With respect to the liberty I have taken, and the mode
I have chosen to communicate this to your Lordship
in preference to any person in an official position about
Lord Anglesey, my selection has arisen from your
holding no place, and from knowing that you are

equally the friend of Ireland and of its gallant and excellent chief governor. I leave it entirely to your Lordship's judgment and kindly feelings to act as your excellent judgment may dictate, and

I am,
Your Lordship's very truly,
SYDNEY MORGAN.

The letter effected its purpose, and Lord Anglesey did not go to the dinner.

The diary returns to the subject of Byron and Lady C. Lamb:—

I was showing my picture of Byron, this morning, to Mr. Lovett, of Lismore, of literary notoriety, and the conversation naturally turned on the extraordinary *liaison* of Lady Caroline and Lord Byron *à propos* to which, Mr. Lovett told me the following anecdote.

"One morning I sauntered into Scroope Davis' lodgings, and threw myself on a sofa; but finding both ends full of heaps of books, I said, 'Why the devil don't you put up shelves, and leave your friends a place to sit on?' 'Oh,' he said, 'those were books left me by Byron, when he was going away, and I have not yet disposed them.' I took up some of the volumes with interest, and lighting on *Vathek*, I said, 'Oh, you must lend me this, I have never had it;' and turning over the leaves, I found a poem in MS. addressed to Lady Caroline Lamb, with some allusion to her conduct to her husband. I read it aloud, and Scroope Davis, snatching the book from me, said, 'No, you must excuse me, I cannot let you have that.' He would not even permit me to read the poem a second time. It was atrociously bitter and cruel. A woman was never so treated in poetry or prose.

Thou false to him, thou fiend to me.

This is the only line I can recollect."

By-the-bye, Lady Caroline assured me, last August, that Byron's last letter to her was sealed with Lady Oxford's coronet and crest. That she had a presentiment, on receiving it, of its contents, and that having read it she fell into a swoon, and took to her bed in a wretched hotel in Dublin; and that her head and heart never recovered the shock, and never would.

August 10th.—Olivia and her three girls still at Jenkinstown, Kilkenny—well for them! whilst I am perched up in my two-pair-of-stairs dressing-room, breathing dust, and seeing nothing but neighbour Sweeney's old house, and the carpets up and the curtains down, all ready for the workmen and our departure. What a pickle to receive Prince Pickle Mustard in, and on dreary Sunday evening, too, that direful day in Dublin!

We had just returned from a long, dreary drive, tired, cold, covered with dust, when a thundering knock came to the door—J. Thomas flew to open it; enter a creature, fine and foppish—a sort of a tartar turned dandy—who asked, in a foreign accent, for Lady Morgan.

Thomas, sulky as a pig, because he hates "my lady having them furriners," cried, "I don't think my lady is at home; but I'll thry, sir. Who shall I say, sir?"

"The Prince Pucklau Muskau"!!!

Away went Thomas, tumbling down the kitchen stairs—

> Jack fell down and broke his crown,
> And Jill (Morgan, with a bottle in his hand)
> ——came tumbling after.

I, like Miss Polly, tumbled up stairs to the drawing-room and stood in all my dust and dowdiness to receive l'Altezza, whom *le cher J.*, announced as "Prince Pickling Mustard," (just as last summer he persisted in calling Prince Cimatelli, "Vermacelli;") Well, I put on the best face (a dirty one) I could on it, and endeavoured to excuse things. The Prince put me at once at my ease. He is a most *finished* fop. *Hélas!* I shall have to unpaper and unpack my room and ask him to dinner when he returns from Wicklow.

Thomas Campbell, who had recently lost his wife, wrote to Lady Morgan:—

Thomas Campbell to Lady Morgan.

10, UPPER SEYMOUR STREET WEST,
LONDON,

August 15, 1828.

DEAR LADY MORGAN,

Will you and Sir Charles do me a kindness, though I am sensible that in spite of the best feelings towards you, I have no great claims upon your favour? It is to receive my young friend Mr. Macdonald, with the usual attention which you are known to show to respectable strangers. Mr. Macdonald is the son of a gallant and distinguished General, who has more of the aspect and character of the true Highland chief than any man I know. Young Macdonald is, of course, a Tory, from his Jacobite family, deadly enemies of the Campbells, by the way; but he is liberal and sensible, and, therefore, I wish him to see the true-blue liberals of Dublin under your kind auspices.

I long to see you and Sir Charles once more in London. Of my dreadful domestic calamity, you must have heard some time ago. The decline of my Matilda's health was very rapid, and the afflicting blow, as you may suppose, was agonisingly stunning. It is impossible to divest the dissolution of a beloved being of pain and horror to those who watch it; yet thank God, I had no conception that death could be apparently so little painful to a sufferer. At first her illness threatened to be exactly like that of four of her sisters, who died before her, after lingering for four or five years in pangs of body, not unmixed with mental alienation. But thanks to heaven, my poor Matilda had a shorter and gentler fate.

My son continues better, and is so companionable that I feel his society a great blessing to me in my lonely house. I have fitted up, since I saw you, a small and beautiful adjoining cottage into a library, which opens from my parlour. You must come over from Ireland for the purpose of seeing me in this retreat, reading your works, and enjoying the self-complacency of an old and comfortable author.

I have long intended to send you a copy of my last

edition; but I have always a latent distrust that if I gave the commission to Colburn, he would neglect it, like everything else. Mr. Macdonald has promised to charge himself with delivering it. Deign to accept, and with best regards to Sir Charles,

Believe me,
Dear Lady Morgan,
Your obliged and sincere friend,
T. CAMPBELL.

The diary continues—

August 19.—What a pleasant evening I have spent with my dear friends the Hamilton Rowans. Captain H——, the gallant commander of the Cambria, was there; he is just returned from Greece, and told me many curious facts. What added to the interest was, that there lay on the sofa his dog Caroline, which had been present at the Battle of Navarino. He brought over with him a little boy who had been saved out of the Capitan Pacha's ship when he burnt it.

I heard a great deal of Mavrocordato, my old travelling acquaintance in Italy.

August 21.—We were engaged to go, last evening, to Maritimo, to Lord Cloncurry's, but Morgan had to dine previously at the Mechanics'. I requested permission to bring Prince Pucklau Muskau with us, which was granted. Whilst I was dressing, I dispatched Thomas and the carriage for his master to the Mechanics', with directions to proceed thence to fetch the Prince. Poor Thomas was kept an age waiting for his master, and he wrote him a note in the hall, which Morgan gave me. It is *à mourir de rire*.

"*Sir Charles!* Me lady will be very unhapy and seriously blame me, for ye not forthcoming.

"Ye most obedient and very humble servant,
"THOS. GRANT."

When they went for the Prince, after waiting an hour, word came out that His Highness had disappeared—where, nobody knew; and it was near twelve o'clock before we arrived at *Maritimo*. I made the Prince my excuse, and as there were a number of Englishmen by, there was a general laugh; and they said, "What! is poor Prince Pickle come *here?* Oh, he will have you down in his '*morgen blatt*'—he will *pounce* on you." In short, I saw there was a ridicule about him, or a something, but it shall not deter me from being civil to him. He is a stranger and a foreigner, and recommended to me by Mrs. Beauclerk—sufficient causes. He comes to visit "remote Ireland," and if I shut my door, what house will receive him? He has the eye of a cat—a sort of mild roguish look, like his master of Austria.

There is nothing so extraordinary as that the nobility of England should have produced so few geniuses. Who but Lord Byron? I know not one. Lord Peterborough, perhaps, comes nearest; but he was too wild and extravagant. The Dukes of Buckingham and Rochester were wits, not geniuses; and their talent, developed by the civil wars, gave them the advantage of middle life, necessary for exertion. The sharpening of the faculties, by exercise and exertion, are advantages denied to the great. The Lord Keepers, and Lord Chancellors, and other law lords, were clever men, but they were many of them *la lie du peuple*, and none of them of noble blood. What a sad show up of pretension and mediocrity is Walpole's work of royal and noble authors!

August 22.—What a splendid head of Arthur O'Connor, painted by Hamilton, I have just been looking at! This noble and unfinished picture represents him at full length, with very scanty drapery, and as Demosthenes. He looks like a noble Irish savage of the sixteenth century, with his blanket, mantle, and skewer. There were four of those O'Connors, all fine men as to the *physique*. They were Arthur, and Roger, and Roderick, and—I forget the other name. The two elder full of talent, and champions of Irish independence. They never crouched to power. Lord Longueville, their uncle, put Arthur into the Irish parliament to uphold the Government of the day, and to speak against the Catholics. He took the direct contrary line, and he was disowned and disinherited by Lord Longueville. When the *Press*, an Irish newspaper of 1797, was burnt by the common hangman, and Peter Finerty, the printer, was pilloried for seditious libel, published in that paper, Arthur O'Connor stood beside him upon the scaffold, and held an umbrella over his head.

I have so little confidence in the certainty of this life, that I always live as if I were going to die. I never stir from home for more than a month without settling my little affairs and altering or adding to my *Will*, as circumstances direct.

I never am in debt one shilling. Poor people ought always to pay ready money, by which means they live as if they were rich. By not doing so, the rich often live as if they were poor and die insolvent.

August 23.—I received a letter, signed James Devlin, which has made me laugh; a blessing, any how! He says he is come up from the country to settle in Dublin; "but being unable to get into any but a beggarly employ," he has, "as his only alternative, and with a boldness, under such circumstances, he hopes pardonable," written a poem; and "snatching fortitude from despair," he sends it to me to get published. I read the poem—*Recollections of a Patriot*—not worth recollecting, and I have written at once to tell him so.

August 25.—Here is a letter from my poet showing a degree of sense that is wonderful in a poet who is also an Irishman. Here it is. What a contrast between the humble confidence that he can make good boots and shoes for gentlemen and the "fortitude from despair" with which he wrote his bad poetry! Oh! why will not every one find out his "last" and stick to it. How much more pleasantly the world would jog on!

James Devlin to Lady Morgan.

DUBLIN,
Thursday.

MADAM,

Finding that I may expect no benefit from my poetry, and feeling that I must use some exertion to get myself out of the difficulties my want of employ has involved me in, I again take the liberty of troubling your Ladyship, requesting, should Sir C. Morgan want any articles in the way of my business (a gentleman's boot and shoe-maker) that he would do me the kindness of favouring me with a trial, confident, should he do so, of my ability to give satisfaction.

I remain, your Ladyship's
Obliged and most obedient servant,
JAMES DEVLIN.

Thursday, November 19.—To-day, is the Public Dinner given by the friends of civil and religious liberty, and got up at our house on Wednesday.

November 20.—I must get an account of the Dinner. It went off splendidly, but there was some *démêlé* about Prince Pucklau Muskau: first, he was not wanted there; and next, he desired Morgan to find out, if he went, whether the health of the king his master would be drunk (at a dinner given to celebrate freedom!); and next, if he would have the precedence of an Altezza granted to himself. There was a burst of "*noes*" when Morgan read the proposition.

Morgan had the indiscretion to advise the Prince *not* to go. He seemed to be struck and mortified. I tremble for the consequences. It is just as well not to be married, for marriage is but another name for suffering.

The conjugal anxiety of Lady Morgan on the subject of the Prince's wounded susceptibilities, was a source of great fun to "the darlings in Great George Street," who wickedly amused themselves with writing challenges to their uncle, with caricatures of "the event on the turf," coming off at "Goose Green," the favourite locality in Dublin for "affairs of honour," as Chalk farm used to be for London. But Lady Morgan's anxiety was *tout de bon*—Sir Charles was the most peaceable man in the world; but she was in continual dread lest "Morgan should be called out;" à *propos* to his strong politics. On this occasion, however, the Prince was quite innocent of any intention to challenge any body.

The next entry in the diary is, " *The Prince is gone, thank God ! ! !* "

November 22.—Sheil this day from England, after his triumphal dinner and noble speech. At night he was at my tea table, full of fire, fun, spirits, and energy —what a *physique!*

Cobbett, he says, overpowered him with praise in the waggon at Penenden Heath. It was not until he saw five columns of his speech in the papers that his honey turned to gall. It was like Majesty against the *Register*. He cannot bear to be out-printed. Sheil's manner of speaking startled his sober auditors at the London Tavern; he is extremely theatrical in his delivery, and as he says himself, it is too like the stage.

This meeting on Penenden Heath had an immense political importance at the time.

A meeting of the landed proprietors, clergy, and freeholders of the county of Kent, was summoned for the 24th of October, 1828, to petition against Catholic Emancipation. The place appointed for the meeting was Penenden Heath, in Kent, and from the rank and influence of its promoters great importance was attached to it. Mr. Sheil conceived the bold idea of attending the meeting, and making a few statements on the opposite side. He qualified to become a freeholder in the county, that no legal objection might be taken against his right to address the assemblage. He kept his intention a secret, except from a few intimate friends, and presented himself to address the meeting. His appearance caused the greatest excitement and uproar. No one could hear a word of his speech; but he delivered it steadily to the end, and then sent an accurate copy of it to one of the evening papers; and every part of the kingdom thus heard his arguments and was penetrated by his eloquence. It was an admirable speech, marked by the soundest judgment in the selection of its topics, and it was as eloquent as the man's whole heart could make it. It produced a great impression in all quarters. A public dinner was given to him, at the City of London Tavern, by four hundred friends of civil and political liberty. Jeremy

Bentham, who was prevented attending, expressed in his letter of apology his admiration of the speech as "a most masterly union of logic and rhetoric."

November 30.—Sir Walter Scott's sermons. What twaddle! what logic! what common places given in the commonest pitiful platitudes! Oh, genius! these are the things that bring you into disrespect.

December 4.—Dinners in old times! The joyous, brilliant tables of the Powers, the Grattans, the Bryans, &c., &c., compared with the sumptuous dulness, and expensive *menu* of the present style of dinner, what a difference? I am led to this reflection from the accident of meeting Harry Bushe, this morning, in the street, just arrived from the south; and having persuaded him to come and take *la fortune du pot*, at five o'clock, in Kildare Street, and go with us to the play. We sat down to a little round table, barely within the rule, of not more than the Graces. Coffee was served, and the carriage at the door before seven, so that there was not time for much more than a *causerie de dessert*, but I was struck by the humour, memory, reading, and knowledge of past Irish life and Irish manners displayed; yet Harry Bushe was merely a man of fashion in that brilliant circle in which we moved twenty years back; well-educated, and well-bred, full of life and spirit, fun and frolic, as were all the gentlemen of that day. His brother, Parker Bushe, the last of the pleasant gentlemen of Ireland, had more *wit*, tact, and keen relish of humour than any man I ever knew.

The account of his death recently reached me in London. I exclaimed in the selfishness of my own social loss, and in the words of Madame de Villette, on the death of Chamfort, "J'ai perdu en lui mon meilleur causeur." I might have added, *mon meilleur lecteur*, for he was one of the men of Ireland *at whom* I wrote my Irish novels; there were *hits*, and touches, and traits in *O'Donnel* and *Florence Macarthy* which none but such as he could appreciate and feel. These two gentlemen are the nephews of the late Mr. Grattan, and brothers-in-law to that most perfect of Irish gentlemen, Richard Power, of Kilfane, a class of men now become extinct in Ireland, they are replaced by a dull and dogged set.

I was in all the *prémices* of my passion for an antique lamp, which Hamilton, the painter, had got in the tomb of the Cæsars, and I from his daughter, when Mr. Wyse dropped in. I turned his attention to my lamp, which I held in my hand. He observed it was a true antique—a heathen and not a Christian lamp. The heathen lamps, he said, are all of a finer and lighter earth than those made after the Christian era, when all the arts degenerated. They generally bear the impress of a dove, or cross, or olive branch, whilst those of the antique bore the head of a Jupiter or Mercury.

Poor Wyse! with a woman of taste and intelligence and domestic habits, how happy he might live; but I doubt if a woman of feeling would be happy with him; he married one without either, and whose whole existence was *une sotte vanité*.

CHAPTER XVIII.

LETTERS AND DIARIES—1829.

ALTHOUGH Lady Morgan lived through such stirring times there is very little said in her journals about politics. She and Sir Charles were much mixed up in the movement for Catholic Emancipation, and Lady Morgan's drawing-room, in Kildare Street, was the *foyer* of liberalism; her influence over the young men who frequented her house was great, and all the leaders of the liberal party recognised her as a staunch and effective ally. Her salon was a rallying-point where people of all sects and shades of opinion met; she received alike dandies, women of fashion, political agitators, and members of the Government.

No two persons could have been more entirely opposed to each other in their nature, taste, and character, than Lady Morgan and Mrs. Hemans. With all her celebrity, Mrs. Hemans shrank from publicity, to which Lady Morgan had been inured, until it had become her second nature. They had no point of personality in common, except that both of them

were women of genius. It is very pleasant to see
them meeting on the mutual ground of womanly
kindness. The following letter from Mrs. Hemans
must, in great measure tell its own story. It would
appear, that an impression had gone abroad that the
circumstances of Mrs. Hemans were the reverse of
comfortable, and it had produced a desire amongst
many of those who admired her genius and respected
her character, to help her in any mode that might be
the most acceptable. Lady Morgan, in her genuine
kind-heartedness, came forward to do as she would
have wished to be done by; her letter is not on record; but the reply of Mrs. Hemans is at once dignified
and grateful.

Mrs. Hemans to Lady Morgan.

WAVERTREE, NEAR LIVERPOOL,
January 2, 1829.

MADAM,

I beg to acknowledge, with sincere thanks, the very
kind interest expressed towards me in your letters,
both of which, after considerable delay, occasioned, I
imagine, by my late change of residence, I have just
received. It is indeed, pleasant to be the object of
feelings so cordial, to hear of unknown friends so zealous; nor do I the less gratefully own the services
thus frankly offered, because it is not necessary that
I should avail myself of them. I have recently met
with a very liberal publisher in Mr. Blackwood, and
he has just brought out new editions of two volumes,

The Records of Women, and *The Forest Sanctuary*, in which most of the pieces originally sent to the *New Monthly*, and other periodical works are collected. I will order copies of them to be sent to Mr. Colburn's, for Lady Morgan, who will, I hope, honour me by her acceptance of them, and believe me, with a sincere feeling of her kindness,

           Very truly
              Her obliged servant,
                   FELICIA HEMANS.

In February, 1829, Parliament having been invited, in the Speech from the Throne, "to consider the condition of Ireland," proceeded to introduce a Bill for the summary suppression of political societies under whatever name they might exist. The duration of the Bill was limited to twelve months; it was passed without opposition, in order that the course might be cleared for the great impending struggle for Catholic Emancipation. It was well known amongst the friends of emancipation, that one of the Duke of Wellington's great difficulties, was the powerful body of the Catholic Association, as a word either of triumph or of threat from that body, would have rendered the King entirely intractable. This Association had been revived in 1827. It was a signal example of the faculty of organisation, and of the all but omnipotence of Association as an engine to carry any object it may have in view. The Catholics in Ireland had attained the perfection of national organisation; they had almost reached the discipline of a regular army. Perhaps the Anti-Corn Law League, many years later, is the only other organised popular machinery which can be compared to it.

The Catholic Association had done its work when the English Government had been induced to consider the best mode of granting political justice to the Roman Catholics. The friends of religious liberty felt that any sacrifice must be made to prevent the least pretext for revoking the good intentions formed with so much difficulty. Lord Anglesea, who had been won over to the cause of emancipation, used all his influence to induce the leaders of the movement to suspend their proceedings. But the members of the Association were somewhat reluctant to give up their position. There were meetings of the leaders, and many hot discussions; the prospect of public affairs was ominous and unsettled. It is mentioned in the *Life of Sheil*, by Torrens McCullagh, that at a party at Lady Morgan's, a letter from Mr. Hyde Villiers, (brother of the present Earl of Clarendon, then Commissioner of Customs to Dublin) was shown to one of the leaders of the Association. This letter reiterated all the pleas put forth by Lord Anglesey, for the suspension of the proceedings of the Catholic Association. Coming, as it did, from one who was supposed to know the intentions of the Government, it produced a great effect. Mr. Woulfe, the member to whom the letter had been specially shown, requested leave to show it to Sheil. A private meeting assembled at Sheil's house, where the important step was resolved upon; and when they separated, Sheil undertook to propose the dissolution of the Catholic Association, at the next meeting. Accordingly, on the 12th of February 1829, Mr. Sheil moved, "that on its rising that day, the Association should stand perfectly dissolved." "The object of this body," said he, "was, and is, Catholic Emancipation; that object, in my judgment, is already attained. Nothing, except our own imprudence, can defeat it. The end being obtained, why should we continue to exist? In a few days the Act of Parliament will put us down. Let us determine to dissolve, and declare our motives for so doing."

The motion was carried, after some debate, and the Confederacy, which had existed under various forms for six years, separated to meet no more.

February 12.—I am just returned from the meeting of the Catholic Association, and faithful to its fire; for so great was the heat, and crowd, and excitement, that I nearly died *under harness*. *The great question*—the dissolution of the Catholic Association, was the subject of debate; and every ardent mind came worked up to the contest. All the best feelings, cool judgment, and tact, was evidently for the prompt and voluntary extinction of this great engine of popular opinion.

February 13.—Yesterday was memorable for our great meeting at the Rotunda of the friends of civil and religious liberty—the first great thing of the kind since the great era of the northern volunteer martyrs, recalling the public spirit of 1782; there were fourteen peers present; but, for the account, see the newspapers of the day.

The *élite* of the *élite* dined with us the same day. Lords Miltown, Cloncurry, George Villiers, Henry Greville, Charles Brownlow, R. Sheil, John Power, Lord Clements; Lord W. Paget, and Lord Bective were invited, but were engaged, so they came in the evening with Wyse, and others of the notables. Since the Union, no such re-union has been in Dublin.

February 15.—I was at a party last night of the *débris* of the ascendancy faction; but the Orange ladies all looked *blue*, and their husbands tried to look green.

Very shortly after this event, Lord Anglesey was recalled from his Viceroyalty, to the great regret of all the liberal and enlightened portion of the Irish public. Lady Morgan wrote to him the following letter.

Lady Morgan to the Marquis of Anglesey.

KILDARE STREET, DUBLIN,
February 24, 1829.

MY LORD,

While your Lordship is still occupied in receiving testimonials of national gratitude and regrets, it is almost presumptuous in an individual to make claims upon time so importantly devoted; still I cannot resist the desire of soliciting your notice to the little *sketch* of vice-regal popularity in Ireland that accompanied this—for I am neither of a sex nor a country to permit discretion to wait on feeling; and I should be sorry to be the last (however least) of the many whose offerings of respect and admiration are about to follow the ex-Lord Lieutenant of Ireland in the privacy of domestic life. It is a proud, and I may say rare privilege, to be so followed. How few of your Lordship's predecessors have won it, and how dearly they have purchased it, forms the subject of pages which had probably never been written had this unfortunate country never benefitted by your government.

I have the honour to be, with deep sentiments of respect,

    Your Lordship's
      Obliged and obedient servant,
        SYDNEY MORGAN.

This letter followed Lord Anglesey to England, whence he replied—

Marquis of Anglesey to Lady Morgan.

      UXBRIDGE HOUSE,
       February 28, 1829.

MY DEAR MADAM,

I have this moment received your flattering effusion of the 24th.

I never could bear to keep the ladies waiting, even for one moment, and therefore hasten to tell you, that as my hour of trust is so near its close, I issue no more proclamations.

Why, *the Percy* might take me, and with his two pocket justices commit me summarily! *Gare*, then, your coteries. There may be treason in tea drinking. I advise you to look to it.

But, surely, *you* did not suspect *me* of inditing in rhyme? *You must* have found out that *I* am the most prosaic, perhaps the most *prosy* (I leave you two full months to decide this latter point) of *all* representations of royalty.

Be this as may, I will not shine in borrowed plumes any longer. No, my dear Madam, I am as incapable of making a rhyme as of effecting the quadrature of the circle, or of speech making, and this latter misery is daily inflicted upon me.

March 4.

MY DEAR MADAM,

My dismay is great at finding this scrawl amongst my papers. I really thought that it had gone, and been long since committed to your flames.

I now send it as I found it, merely to show, that if I had forgotten my letter, I had not felt indifferent to yours.

Do not let all my good friends quite forget me, and I beg you to

Believe me,
Very truly yours,
ANGLESEY.

Lord Anglesey was replaced by the Duke of Northumberland; hence the allusion to "the Percy."

March 11.—Sunday, dressing room, 12 o'clock. What an age since I put anything into this book! Christmas festivities at Lord Miltown's, Lord Cloncurry's.

My article on "Irish Lord Lieutenants" was sent off yesterday at two o'clock for the *New Monthly*. For five days I had been working against time and scarcely drew breath. To-day I am a lady at large (if not a large lady), and now for my own amusement and edification. Feet on fender—fire blazing away—snow falling—nothing but discomfort without and comfort within! soon will come my darling children and their good little father and dear little mother; and oh, the merry day we shall have in spite of wind and weather! And so please God we begin the new year; for this is our first family *réunion* in 1829.

The letters which follow relate mainly to the Irish politics of the year.

Lady Charleville to Lady Morgan.

My Lord has given the Roman Catholic Committee two hundred feet on the side of the Grand Canal, for two schools and a house, for the Sisters of Charity. As the population of Tullamore is about six thousand, our school (on the Lancastrian principle) holds one thousand, and is never half full, which does not suffice. To read, write, and cypher, and work, is good, come as it may; I will not consider it as an attempt to extinguish mine, but rejoice that anything is about to be done for the lower classes.

Farewell, and always believe how much I am
Yours faithfully,
C. M. C.

Richard Sheil to Sir Charles Morgan.

MY DEAR SIR CHARLES,

Pardon me for not having immediately answered your kind invitation. I intended to pay my respects to-day, and to say that I should wait on you. I saw Colonel Gosset, this morning, who says that Lord Anglesey goes on Monday. Lord Melville has refused the Government of Ireland. It is not known who will be appointed. Brougham omitted, from bad health, to attend two meetings of the Opposition. Lord Holland has written to Blake to say that the lukewarm are excited by Lord Anglesey's recall. It is considered a most improper proceeding. Lord Holland has written a tract on Lord Bexley's attack on the Catholic religion!

Present my compliments to Lady Morgan, and believe me,
Most truly yours,
RICHARD SHEIL.

March.—So the *Quarterly* has let loose its dogs of war again on me, under the new groom of the kennel, Mr. Lockhart, of John Scott celebrity and Walter Scott's auspices. The Scotch reviews accuse my poor innocent *O'Briens and O'Flaherties* of being blasphemous and indecent—the old charge newly tagged up.

Now I have a right, like other British subjects, to be judged by my peers, and I summon a jury of matrons, of the most intact reputation, mothers "who wear pockets, and don't hold opera-boxes signs of inward grace," to say if they detect in my pages one line that tends to make one honest man my foe. Why, then, if they do, I submit to be branded with that horrible stigma with which a modest woman and a moral writer is now impugned withal. But I have been tried already before that truly Grand Jury, the PUBLIC, from which there is no appeal, and acquitted; and I have before me a letter from Mr. Constable, offering me the same terms as Sir W. Scott.

I see in the papers, to-day, the death of Mr. Gifford—the direst, darkest enemy I ever had. We never saw each other; he hated me for my success and my principles.

Mort la bête, mort le venin,

at least *esperons!*

Gifford was, it is said, in the receipt of a large income. During the time that he was editor of *The Quarterly Review*, Mr. Murray paid him nine hundred pounds a year. He received annually, as one of the comptrollers of the Lottery Office, six hundred pounds. He had a salary of three hundred pounds as paymaster of the band of Gentlemen Pensioners, two hundred a year as clerk of the Estreats in the Court of Exchequer; and, in addition to all these sums, he enjoyed a pension of, we believe, four hundred pounds per annum from Lord Grosvenor

April 4.—Just dispatched to Colburn my preface to the *Book of the Boudoir*, which is to appear immediately. We are off to England, ourselves, and thence shortly to France.

April 6.—Adieu to care and home, to some whom I love, and to all whom I hate! I leave my trash bag behind me.

The *Book of the Boudoir* succeeded *The O'Briens and the O'Flaherties*. Her own account of it is given in the Preface, as follows:—

"Whilst the fourth volume of the *O'Briens and the O'Flaherties* was going through the press, Mr. Colburn was sufficiently pleased with the subscription (as it is termed in the trade) to desire a new work from the author. I was just setting off for Ireland—the horses literally putting-to—when Mr. Colburn arrived with his flattering proposition. Taking up a scrubby MS. volume, which the servant was about to thrust into the pocket of the carriage, he asked, what was that? I said it was one of my volumes of odds and ends, and read him my last entry, made the evening before. "This is the very thing," said he.

It was as Lady Morgan says, published in April, 1829. It contains short articles, essays, and observations, such as she was in the habit of writing in her diary—a little enlarged and put into shape; but it is the book that exhibits all her faults of style, and manner, in an exaggerated form. It was bitterly reviewed in *Blackwood*, where she was accused of all the sins the Tory party could find to lay to her charge—the worst she deserved to have said of the *Book of the Boudoir* was, that it was careless, flippant, and egoistical; it ought to have none but friends for readers; the public is not accustomed to be treated in the free and easy tone of this work, and as sins of taste are always more resented than sins of principle, it is no wonder that her enemies and detractors found an opportunity for being ill-natured, and availed themselves of it. There are some admirable articles in *The Book of the Boudoir*; but it is not the work on which Lady Morgan's admirers would take their stand.

There is no journal of her visit to France, this year, nor of her stay in London. There is the following entry in her journal after her return to Dublin.

September 1.—After a most delightful and triumphant visit to France, and residence of three months in Paris; after a most prosperous journey through the Low Countries and Holland, an excellent and agreeable voyage from *Ostend to London*, and business-like and satisfactory residence in London, and a detestable passage across the Herring Pond, we arrived at our own dear but dirty little home, and a most joyous meeting with our family in Great George's Street.

Lady Morgan, during her visit to London in 1829,

made the purchase of her *first carriage*, and took it back to Dublin with great complacency.

Neither she nor Sir Charles knew any difference between a good carriage and a bad one—a carriage was a carriage to them. It never was known where this vehicle was bought, except that Lady Morgan always declared, "it came from the first carriage builder in London."

In *shape* it was a grasshopper—as well as in colour. Very high and very springy, with enormous wheels, it was difficult to get in and dangerous to get out. Sir Charles, who never in his life before had mounted a coach-box, was persuaded by his wife "to drive his own carriage."

He was extremely short sighted, and wore large green spectacles when out of doors. His costume was a coat, much trimmed with fur, and braided. James Grant, their "tall Irish footman," in the brightest of red plush, sat beside him, his office being to jump down whenever anybody was knocked down or run over, for Sir Charles drove as it pleased God. The horse was mercifully a very quiet animal, and much too small for the carriage, or the mischief would have been more. Lady Morgan, in the large bonnet of the period, and a cloak lined with fur hanging over the back of the carriage, gave, as she conceived, the crowning grace to a neat and elegant turn out.

The only drawback, to her satisfaction, was the alarm caused by Sir Charles's driving; and she was incessantly springing up to adjure him "to take care," to which he would reply, with warmth, after the manner of husbands.

September 11.—This day sat alone clearing out the dust traps, refitting up from kitchen to garret, working myself like a galley slave, removed between two and three thousand volumes, cleaned and varnished thirty pictures, washed all my old china and knick-knacks, worked with my servants and the char-women for three days successively. Talked much to the two char-women—*such misery!!* Told them how to make a bouilli instead of eating salt bacon, when they *did* get meat. One of them, a half naked creature, was a sentimentalist. I heard her say, in her slang brogue, to her comrade, "Kitty, dear, did iver ye read Caroline and Lindor? its an illegant story!" This must be *Caroline of Litchfield*. One of the painters said "Did you get a sup of 'By yer leave, Charley?" (*read* whiskey!)

September 12.—Went to Portran (Mr. Evan's) to get rid of the smell of the paint.

September 14.—Returned to town; house finished and beautiful. Received a splendid present from the Baron Gérard, of his picture of Henry the Fourth entering Paris, the Tomb of Bonaparte, and Cupid and Psyche, all framed and hung up along with my other presents from eminent artists.

September 25.—Received my first invitation from Duchess of Northumberland. Received a deputation of weavers in their misery; they presented me a petition to assist them. I wrote them an answer.

September 24.—Dinner party at home; little *soirée*

in the evening. Brought in some improvements in the *menu* of my table, which I have gathered in my travels. A *plombière*, first made known in Ireland; great success. Busy all day for my weavers.

September 30.—Begun my new work on France—out of materials in journals; don't in the least know what I shall make of it; interrupted by a *cours de toilette;* an hour *bien sonnée* in my dressmaker's hands. She is making up a fine tabinet dress for the Duchess of Northumberland's party on Thursday.

The Duchess of Northumberland, it should be said in explanation of the above, was a great patroness of Irish manufactures; she made all the ladies of her court live in tabinet dresses. The Duke endeavoured to develope Irish resources, and Tory as he might be, he made himself beloved during his vice-royalty.

CHAPTER XIX.

THE SECOND WORK ON FRANCE—1830.

SCRIBBLING all day; called down to the drawing-room at near five o'clock. "It's *Counsellor Curran*, my lady!" Morgan, invalided, came up enchanted to see his friend Curran, though they are at the antipodes of human feeling—my own Morgan being all heart, &c.

Morgan said, "Curran, we are quite alone, do stay and dine with us."

(Now this is a most unfair thing in husbands—this asking to dinner à *l'impromptu*, particularly a man like Curran, who likes a good dinner). Clever Curran, who knows all the little *plis et replis* in the human character better than the great, looked hesitatingly at me. I laughed, and said, "It is not fair to take you in; we are invalids; our dinner is an invalid dinner; *soupe, bouilli* and a roast fowl, except we order up the kitchen *pièce de résistance*—but I dare not mention it."

"If it is not a leg of beef smothered in onions," said Curran, laughing.

"No; but is almost as bad—a leg of pork and pease-pudding," said I.

Quoth he, "The thing in the world I like best." So he ran home to dress, stipulating we should let him off the moment we had dined (an old trick of his); but I chose to make the agreeable, so did he, and he staid with us, *en tiers*, till midnight. He was, as he can always be, most clever, amusing, and rational. He gave us anecdotes and imitations of Steele, the Catholic demagogue, admirably, particularly his *whacking* the editor of the *Morning Herald* three several times, each time observing, "*There!* I don't think I had complete satisfaction!"

We talked of the good, but coarse Irish novel, *The Collegians*. The story is a fact, and not only a fact, but the trial of the hero, and the whole melancholy event, was given by Curran in the *New Monthly Magazine*, just after it happened—in much finer style than in the *Collegians*. The hero was a Mr. Scanlan, a dissipated young man in the county of Limerick; his family are what the peasants call, "small gentry," we, "gentry." His uncle, Mr. Scanlan, was High Sheriff last year; Curran dined with him the day of the hero's execution. Curran said the uncle's *sang-froid* and indifference were frightful; he shrugged his shoulders, tucked his napkin under his chin, said "it was a sad business," and called for soup. In this, one may discern the same temperament as in the nephew, the murderer.

The fair, frail girl, whom this Munster Lothario

had seduced, robbed her uncle of eighty pounds at his suggestion—satiety and avarice were his motives to murder her. She had given him forty pounds, he wanted the rest, and to get rid of her.

When he had sent her off in the boat with his servant, who was first to shoot and then fling her into the Shannon, he lurked about the shore waiting his return. To his dismay, he saw the party row back—she, all smiles and fondness, extending her arms to him. The servant, taking him aside, said, " I cannot kill her! Sure, when I had the pistol raised, she turned round with her innocent face, and smiled so in mine; I could not hurt a hair of her head, the crathur."

Scanlan took him to a public-house; primed him with whiskey, gave him a fresh bribe, and sent him off once more, with his victim, to sail on the Shannon —waited his return on the shore, and *saw him come back without her*.

The other anecdote was this:—The jailor of Limerick had been an old and confidential servant in the Scanlan family, and had nursed this young man on his knee.

When the moment of execution arrived, and he knelt down to knock off the irons, his tears dropped on every link, and looking up in the young man's face, said, " Ah, Masther John! when I nursed you in these arms, in your father's house, little ever I thought this would be the office I should do for you."

Scanlan died with a lie on his lips, denying the crime. He had been condemned on the strongest circumstantial evidence; but shortly after his death, the servant, who had murdered the girl at his command, was taken up for another murder and hanged. He gave every link that was wanted in the chain of evidence, and related the whole story a little before his execution.

The Prima Sera, as the Italians call it, is very agreeable. It begins immediately after dinner, or siesta; it includes the drive on the Corso, and the visit before the Opera. *We* have a prima sera that is suited to our climate and is very agreeable. It has the freedom of evening society with the sociability of morning visits. I mean the two hours which intervene between the fall of evening at four o'clock, and the dressing or dinner-hour—the hour when the pleasant visitors drop in—when the fire burns brightest, and the lamps are few, and one is still in one's morning-dress, and men put their splashed boots, without let or hinderance, where an hour or two afterwards it would be *outlawry* to appear in clean ones [*shoes* were, at that period, *de rigueur* in the evening], and the feet are put on the fender, and the shoulders find a resting-place in the luxurious arm-chair. The news comes fresh in from the ride or the club; the anecdote is still new from the ball or the *soirée*, where nothing is presumed and everything is ventured; when the story of the diner-out is not yet made, nor the sally of the professed wit held back for its *à propos;* when one talks nonsense *best* and laughs at it *most*. It is enough to know there is an epoch of the day when one may be agreeable without stimulus, and enjoy without effort.

17th *January.*—Just heard of the death of Sir Thomas Lawrence and of Mr. Monkton, Lady Cork's brother.

January 20.—Yesterday we dined at Lord Dungarvon's, at Fairfield. Our party, Marquis and Marchioness Clanricarde, Earl and Countess of Howth, Lady E. St. Lawrence, Master Townsend and his daughter, Mr. Blake (Chief Remembrancer) and his wife; Colonel Cruise, and *Dan O'Connell;* this being the second time in my life that I ever met the redoubtable Dan. Dan is not brilliant in private society, —not even agreeable. He is mild, silent, unassuming, apparently absorbed, and an utter stranger to the give-and-take charm of good society; I said so to Lord Clanricarde, who replied, " If you knew how I found him this morning; his hall, and the very steps of his door crowded with his *clientèle*—he had a word or a written order for each and all, and then hurried off to the law courts, and from that to the Improvement Society, at the Royal Exchange, and was the first guest *here* to-day, when I arrived. Two hours before, he was making that clever but violent speech to Mr. La Touche, and now no wonder he looks like an extinct volcano."

Lady Clanricarde is the only and much-loved daughter of Canning, and is quite worthy of being so, *quelle tête,* inside and outside! beautiful and clever, every word an epigram or a thought, pleasant and amusing with it all!. The dinner was charming, with sweet Lady Dungarvon's warm, cordial manner of doing the honors in her own pretty house. I had lots of Irish *shanaos*

(Anglice, gossip), with these first-rate Irishmen. Lord Clanricarde told us of the burning down of his beautiful castle.

Feb. 28th.—Poor Molly! I cannot drive her or her situation out of my head. She is dying, but well cared for at my dear sister's.

Molly, as the reader may recollect, was the old nurse; one of the heroines of Lady Morgan's autobiography. She retained to the last her fine Irish black head of hair, and a few teeth as white as ever. She had become very *exigeante* and rather given to whiskey in her declining years; but she was still a specimen of a faithful retainer as distinguished from modern servants.

April 28th.—Joseph Lefanu, son of Sheridan's excellent sister, my old, kind friend, came to-day. It is the wreck of a dear old friendship. His visit to Kildare Street marks an epoch; he is broken down in health and spirits,—a premature old age. Dublin is a tomb to him,—all his friends dead. He spent the evening with us, and we gave up going to the birthnight to stay with him. The tint of intellect over all he says is very Lefanu-ish; he told me an anecdote of his uncle Sheridan missing a legacy of ten thousand pounds from a point of honour, refusing to go and see a man in his last illness lest he should suppose he was actuated by mercenary motives. I said, I believe that anecdote is in Moore's *Life of Sheridan*. "Oh, no," he replied, bitterly, " *this is authentic !* "

The following is an interesting notice of an excellent

actress and good woman, who still lives warm in the memory of all who knew her, and who will always be a name of mark in the annals of the English stage.

Miss Huddart (Mrs. Warner) was associated with the best efforts of Macready and Mr. Phelps to renew the drama and render the stage all that in certain conditions of society it is capable of becoming as a powerful engine for good.

Lady Charleville to Lady Morgan.

MY DEAR LADY MORGAN,

I beg to offer you and your nieces my tickets for Miss Huddart's benefit; she is the meritorious and amiable daughter of a lady of real merit, who was well known to me, and moved in the best society, at one time in Dublin. I am told this young actress is very promising, and I can only answer for her being the best of daughters, and having met with the heaviest affliction lately by the loss of her father.

A show of patronage from persons of talent would do much for a *debutante*, and I know you will lend yourself for a few hours to serve this friendless young creature on my account.

I beg Sir Charles to join you, and write me a few lines with your opinion of her. If I could have gone to Dublin to wait on the Duchess of Northumberland, I should have been happy to have taken a box and gone to see this young creature, for her mother's sake, but *four* deaths have shadowed over my thoughts for some time, and left me no joyous fancies for the present. I hope the saints may not shut up the theatre, for it is literally true that I dare not speak of going to a play to the few I am acquainted with in Dublin of my lord's family.

I know how pleased you must be with the Relief Bill, and I trust in God it may promote general prosperity in this country.

Yours,
C. M. CHARLEVILLE.

The reader will not have forgotten Mr. Wallace, the old friend and correspondent of Lady Morgan. His wife, who had long been an invalid, died some time previous to Lady Morgan's marriage, and whether Mr. Wallace had himself been a pretender to her favour, or whether, without having made any declaration of his intentions, he still felt aggrieved that another should be preferred before him, there is no evidence to tell; but the acquaintance ceased after Lady Morgan's marriage. He was now a second time married; and the following note is endorsed by Lady Morgan:—"Mr. Wallace sent this note on the 27th, 1830, after an interruption of friendship from the year 1811." The month is not mentioned, but it was about this period.

Thomas Wallace to Lady Morgan.

Monday Morning.

MY DEAR LADY MORGAN,

I was greatly mortified yesterday at finding you and Sir Charles had called at Belfield, and departed without asking for me. I was at home, and should have been very much gratified indeed to have seen you and him, meaning as you did such very kind things towards us. Of those kind intentions I most cheerfully shall avail myself, and shall participate gladly in the hospitable and *spirituel* gratifications which are always, I know, of olden time, to be found with you and in the society which you select.

Mrs. W. will wait upon you.

Yours most truly,
THOMAS WALLACE.

May 20*th*.—Off to-day for Shangana and my dear General Cockburn. I am breaking down again under close air and want of exercise. Morgan, I declare, loves me very well, but not well enough to break through his usual habits of indolence, so he don't walk, and hates driving,—so I have no resource.

May 30*th*.—Returned home the 27th—Shangana is a divine spot! how I enjoyed its scenes! I used to reproach the General for leaving it in these very words—

"Oh, how canst thou renounce the boundless store
Of charms which nature to her votary yields,
The warbling woodland, the meandering shore,
The pomp of groves, the garniture of woods;
All that the genial ray of morning gilds,
And all that colours to the song of even,
All that the mountain's sheltering bosom yields,
And all the dread magnificence of heaven;
Oh, how canst thou renounce and be forgiven?"

Gray says, "this of all others is my favourite stanza; it is true feeling, it is inspiration!" How can *I* "hope to be forgiven?"—saying this at the grove every day as I returned from my walk before breakfast, when I yielded to a vice-regal mandate, and came back to town for the fête of the king's birthday at the park! It was, however, a splendid scene. I had a deal of funny chat with the lord-lieutenant; what made it most droll was that two orange bishops were looking on; here was part of our talk—

Quoth I, "Lord Anglesey! some admire you as lord-lieutenant, some for your heroism, but I admire you for—

Lord A. "What, Lady Morgan? pray shock us!"

Lady M. "For the cut of your coat; who is your tailor? or is all this your own order?"

Lord A. (laughing) "Oh, I never give an order, I have an old model coat, the great great grandfather of this; I always say 'make it like this coat,' that is all *my* order."

Lady M. "The fact is, you dress better than any one, *et je m'y connais bien!*"

Lord A. "Well! I *did* dress well when I was young, *so well*, that my early and kindest friend, the late king, did me the honour to enter the lists with me; I remember his saying, at a ball at Devonshire House, 'There is that d——d Paget, better dressed than ever.' He went further than this. One day I went to Carlton House, by appointment; we were to go together, the prince and I, to some morning fête, I forget where. I had waited some time in the drawing-room, when a groom of the chambers put in his head, looked earnestly at me, and retired. Presently the valet of H. R. H. put in *his* head, stared, and retired. I began to get a little impatient, when a page entered, walked round, and followed the other two. The prince then made his appearance, *dressed exactly like myself!* I heard afterwards that he was dressed when I arrived, and had sent to see how I was dressed, successively changing every article, till he was told he was my double! All this *now* appears ridiculous, but *then* it was *tout de bon.*"

LADY M. "I don't think he would have taken your excellency *now* as a model in anything."

LORD A. "No, he hated me, at least, he could never forgive me my conduct in Ireland. I grieved at this, for up to my first Irish vice-royalty, he was the kindest of the kind, and I loved him much."

LADY M. "Well, but to go back to the toilette, don't you think one gets more *soigné* as one gets older?"

LORD A. "I really think one does; in fact, one owes it to society to make amends for the defects of time; we ought to shock the younger world as little as possible."

Morgan joined us, and we got into politics.

Lord A—— said, "Much has been done in the way of reform, but the Tories *must swallow more yet,* the Church establishment must retrench. If those gentlemen would save anything, they must give up much. If the king had lived a year longer, you would have had a revolution, nothing could have stopped it."

June 17.—Off to Lyons.

June 27.—Returned from Lyons—Lord Cloncurry's,

a long, large party—the first day good—Sheil, Curran, and Jack Lattan. I never saw him in such force; he thanked me with all the gallantry and enthusiasm of youth for my allusion to him in the *Book of the Boudoir*. "Forty years back," he said, "it would have driven me mad, and even *now* it makes my head turn." His brilliancy overwhelmed all the wit present; Sheil was silent, and Curran dull. All sat staring and listening. He is part of a bygone generation,—his wit was, perhaps, *trop fort*. His wit put me in mind of poor Grassini singing in Paris last year, —it would be invidious to say why. After all, Lord Cloncurry is the drollest of the droll, he makes me laugh more than any one. We had the Jocelyn, Percys, and others very charming. Lord Cloncurry made me die, by the simple way he told me that when the Duke of Northumberland was coming to stay a few days at Maritimo, he said to Lord Cloncurry, "Do not put yourself to any inconvenience for my people, (his servants), they never drink either port or claret." "Upon my word," said Lord Cloncurry, "I am very glad to hear it, for with me they will only get very small beer."

July 1*st.*—I had a few people last evening,—my own family, Curran, General Cockburn, and the ex-judge Johnson; Johnson is a fine specimen of the old wit, talent, and literary condition of Ireland. He was the intimate friend of the celebrated Curran, to whose son he is much attached. Though eighty-five years of age his conversation is full of force, humour, and gallantry, scarcely a trace of age. He told me in the morning he should give up a dinner-party and box at the theatre to come to us.

Captain Arthur Wellesley (the Duke of Wellington's nephew) dropped in. In the course of the evening Johnson told him an anecdote of his illustrious uncle that amused him.

"I dined," he said, "about forty years ago with old Colonel Ross, of Gloucester Street, Dublin; Ross's nephew, a college boy, (the late General Ross,) dined with us; in the middle of dinner, a little aide de camp, a playfellow of Ross's, came in. They amused each other at dinner with running pins into each other, and made such a noise that the old Colonel, starting up, cried, " G—d d—n it, boys, if you cannot be quiet, go out into the yard and play ball, but don't disturb the dinner." The boys, were the Duke of Wellington and General Ross.

Judge Johnson was a judge who was prosecuted for a seditious libel; it was an attack on Lord Hardwicke, when lord-lieutenant of Ireland (published in *Cobbett's Register*), at the moment when he had a seat on the Bench. The jury found him guilty of the libel; but an opportune change of ministry between the verdict and the sentence, allowed a *nolle prosequi* to be entered. He retired from the Bench, on a pension, in 1806. He had a most unprofessional taste for military affairs, and held some peculiar theories; amongst others, that pikes and arrows were better weapons than muskets or bayonets; and he prided himself on having invented a pike with a hollow staff, to contain arrows, and a leg to support the weapon, and side traces to unite it with others, so as to form a *chevaux-de-frise!!*

July 5th.—Left town on Friday for Morris Town, the seat of Jack Lattan, County Kildare; he carried us off *vi et armis* in his old French *calèche*, with his old French horses, and his French cook driving us. He comes yearly from his hotel in the *chaussée d'Antin* to his old seat in the Bog of Allan; what a transit! As we passed that vast ruin, the palace built by Lord Stafford, near Naas, (one of the items in his indictment), he pointed to a field under the window of the ruin. "There," he said, "begins my estate, we held it under King John, and never lost or added an acre; we must have been very mediocre people." Lord Stafford, in one of his letters, describing this palace as having been built with the hope of having the king's majesty his guest, observes, "My close neighbour is one Lattan, an Irish Papist." The Wentworth property is now Lord Fitzwilliam's. The traditions of this country are all in Lord Stafford's favour, he did no violent things here. Lattan said his memory fatigued him by its redundance. What myriads of anecdotes! Here is a funny one. The Duc de Laval said to him, one day, on the subject of England—"Écoutez mon cher, je connais l'Angleterre au fond, les fils aînés sont tous riches et ivrognes, les cadets sont pauvres et volent sur le grand chemin!"

Lord Cloncurry in his *Life and Times,* mentions Mr. Lattan having been in the French service, 1793; he describes him as one of a race, now extinct; a genuine Irishman, in heart and purpose; his service in France, as an officer in the Irish brigade, had added the polish and gallantry of a French gentleman, while his manly figure was set off in full perfection by the air and habits of a soldier of the old school. The brilliancy of his wit was never clouded, nor his enjoyment of present mirth ever damped by thoughts of to-morrow. When his purse was full, he drew upon it without scruple, for self or friends, and when it was empty he would sit down to translate the *Henriade*, to help an *émigré* friend with the proceeds of its publication.

French Revolution.

September 5th.—Since I last scribbled in these pages, what events! I have lived in them, for them, and with them, even at this distance from the scene of action! My life, made up of sensations, will be found in the postscript of my new *France*, the publication of which was retarded for the purpose of inserting it. I shall not say a word of this great subject here.

September 8.—The arrival of Moore and his family has *fait epoch*. We had to meet him at dinner yesterday,—North, Sheil, Curran, and my own family; all his old cronies in the evening, and his old love, Mrs. Smith, to whom he addressed the song "If in the dream that hovers." He sang as well as ever, but it made us all sad; all he sang had reference to the past. I felt when I went to bed as if I had been at the funeral of old friends.

Moore refers to this dinner in his diary, September 7, 1830. "Desperate wet day; dined at Lady Morgan's—company, Edward Moore, North, Curran, Sheil, the Clarkes."

Great delay about the appearance of my book, it takes six days to receive and return each proof sheet. It ought to come out to-morrow.

The second *France* was published on the 7th of September, 1830. It is in every respect superior to the first, except that the continent having now been open for fourteen years, the present work had not the peculiar zest of novelty. To the present generation of readers, however, the *France* of 1829-30 belongs as completely to a time gone by as the Gaul of the days of Cæsar. *France* of 1829-30 is a very brilliant book, and it is not so flippant as its predecessor. There is much less self glorification about social flatteries and attentions; Lady Morgan had become more accustomed to such things, and her own position in society was both higher and better defined. The points where she produces herself in the present work, are precisely those on which her own sympathies and associations appeal to the reader, and give a special interest to the topic in hand. Each chapter makes a charming *feuilleton*, abounding in wit and shrewd observation. If we had to point out the work in which Lady Morgan has given herself and her peculiar genius the fairest play and the fullest development, we should take our stand upon her second work on *France*.

The political and social shades of society in France immediately previous to the revolution of 1830, "the three glorious days" which have now passed into oblivion along with much other "pomp and glory of the world," are caught like a rainbow at the brightest moment. The men and women of the time,—the politics, the pictures, the music, the drama, the shrines of historical interest and of social associations—may be seen as in a magic mirror. The chapter on the drama brings back the faint echoes of names which in our youths filled the public ear. When Mademoiselle Leontine Fay was the young, handsome, charming *jeune première* of the Théâtre de Madame, "drawing fast-falling, unconscious tears and half-stifled sobs from all Paris in the *Mariage d'Inclination;*" and when Dumas' *Henri III.* was a new piece, with Mademoiselle Mars for its heroine, Rossini is spoken of as "overwhelmed with his professional labours," putting the finish to his *William Tell*, which had been for the last two months the topic of conversation and expectation in the musical world of fashion. The chapter on romanticists and classists is very amusing. Lamartine, Victor Hugo, St. Beuve, were then *faisant leurs épreuves*, and are noticed as new authors. The chapter on modern literature contains some excellent criticism and sound remarks. The chapter called "Mornings at Paris" is a charming *resumé* of people and things. Names appear on each page with a personal sketch or a *mot*, which makes the reader at once of their society. There is a visit to Béranger in the prison of La Force; and there are two memorable dinners; one at the Comte de

Ségur's, with a record of the conversation as fresh and as amusing as if it were not on topics half a century old; the other is a dinner at Baron Rothschild's, dressed by the great Carême, who had erected a column of the most ingenious confectionery architecture, on which he had inscribed Lady Morgan's name in spun sugar. What woman would not have been flattered by such a tribute! The chapter on *The Archives of France* contains a lively account of her pilgrimage to shrines, dear from historical associations, but not set down in any guide book, and disappearing under the march of imperial improvement. It would be impossible to give a detailed criticism on these two charming volumes, but we would advise our readers in their own interest to send for them, instead of "something new from Mudie." The chapters by Sir C. Morgan consist of articles on philosophy, public journals, primogeniture, and public opinion. They are good, and the conscientious opinions of a man whose indorsement is worthy of respect.

This work was, however, destined to cause Lady Morgan more trouble and annoyance than she met with in the whole of literary life put together. It made an event in Lady Morgan's life, and was in itself a curious illustration of the laws and customs of the republic of letters, as it existed in the year of grace, 1830.

Sir Charles and Lady Morgan had gone to France entirely *propria motu*, without any bargain or understanding with any bookseller.

On their return, Lady Morgan set to work to write

her scenes and impression. Colburn took it for granted that she neither could nor would leave him for any other publisher; he considered that Lady Morgan was bound to him in literary matrimony for better and worse, and he behaved to her with a cool security which was not altogether suited to her character. She wrote to tell him she was writing a second work on France. Colburn, who was always in arrears with his correspondence, did not reply. Lady Morgan wrote again, and as her letter produced no answer beyond a lazy request to be told the size, title, and topics of the new work, with no definite offer. Lady Morgan then opened a negociation with Messrs. Saunders and Otley, just, as years before, when Sir R. Phillips refused, in the matter of the *Wild Irish Girl*, to give the price she demanded, she wrote to Johnson, a rival publisher, as the reader may remember. She wrote again to Colburn to tell him what she had done. Mr. Colburn wrote an indignant letter to Sir Charles Morgan, July 4, 1830, the very handwriting of which testifies to his rage at her ladyship having opened a correspondence with another house:—" I can only *now* say, that if Lady Morgan does not break off the negociation (which is simply done on the plea of a misunderstanding) it will be no less detrimental to her literary than to her pecuniary interest. As to myself, it is a very different feeling, and not my pecuniary interest that makes me urge this matter, as I can prove, if necessary, I have lost considerably by the last two or three works; but I am ready, and always have been, to give Lady Morgan more than the value of her works when I know *what I am to bid for*—pray recollect, that Lord Byron used to send his works to Murray without hesitation."

This *sourde* threat was not likely to intimidate an intrepid woman like Lady Morgan, who had stood fire so many years, and who loved a fight like a true Milesian. The bargain with Messrs. Saunders and Otley was concluded. The terms were to be a thousand pounds for the copyright; five hundred pounds to be paid down on the publication of the work, the other five hundred by four bills at different dates.

The work was published in two volumes, the type and paper were unexceptionable, the appearance of the volumes was handsome, and a spirited portrait of her ladyship, as a frontispiece. The first payment was duly made—and then—there came a full stop! The new work by Lady Morgan instead of being received with a lively sensation as usual, encountered a dead silence. Messrs. Saunders and Otley writing to Lady Morgan, September 23, 1830, say, "In reply to your inquiry respecting the sale of the work, we are sorry to say it has been anything but encouraging; the booksellers having taken very sparingly, and we have had but a small demand, although much had been previously done in the way of advertising, &c., the effect of which must, no doubt, have been greatly impeded by the opposing system practised. The notice in the *Chronicle*, slight and incidental as it is, is the most favourable that has yet appeared. A system of indiscriminate censure appears to pervade all others, while the more influential remain silent."

Colburn had proved what he could be as a friend, and he was now showing what he could be as a foe. Not only was he enraged at losing "one of his authors,"—his favourite one, too, but he was also exasperated at the audacity of any other publishers in entering into competition with him, and he proceeded to let them see how he could punish them, and to teach Lady Morgan that her success had been less owing to her own genius than to his own skill as a publisher.

"The opposing system," referred to in the letter from Messrs. Saunders and Otley was a series of manœuvres and advertisements by Colburn, on the announcement of the new work by Lady Morgan on France. The newspapers of the day appeared with this advertisement,—LADY MORGAN AT HALF PRICE. The advertisement stated that in consequence of the great losses which he had sustained by Lady Morgan's former works, Mr. Colburn had *declined* this present book on France, and that all the copies of her books might be had at half price. Nothing more insulting to Lady Morgan or more damaging to the success of the new work, could have been contrived. Sir Charles and Lady Morgan were powerless to combat this state of things; and Messrs. Saunders and Otley wrote more and more piteously about their own loss, entreating to have a modification of their contract. They proposed to give up their copyright, to receive back their bills for the second five hundred pounds, and to bring out a second edition (so called) of the twelve hundred copies on hand, Lady Morgan sharing the profits.

Lady Morgan offered to give them an extension of

time, but declined to let them off their bargain, saying, that a contract was a contract. Her second edition, as it was called, answered no better than the first; and Messrs. Saunders and Otley were losers upon every item,—printing, paper, advertisements, &c., in addition to the five hundred pounds in cash they had paid to Lady Morgan, and the further sum for which they were liable. Sir Charles and Lady Morgan obtained Counsel's opinion as to the chance of making Colburn amenable for his proceedings. Mr. Wallace, Q.C. (Lady Morgan's old lover,) gave it as his opinion that a case would lie against him, as it could be proved he had used threats; but Saunders and Otley did not choose to send good money after bad, and declined a lawsuit. After a tedious correspondence, which extended over a year, they declared their intention, on the 1st of September, 1831, to go to law to get their contract cancelled. Eventually, the whole affair came into court. The curious and peculiar feature in the case was, Colburn's own admission that he had been so enraged at losing Lady Morgan's work, that he had done everything he could to injure her literary reputation, and to damage the sale of Messrs. Saunders and Otley's publication; that he much regretted what he had done under the influence of wounded feeling; and he took that opportunity of retracting whatever he had said in her disparagement. Speaking of his magazines, he said that he paid his other contributors according to a fixed tariff; but that to Sir C. and Lady Morgan he gave whatever price they demanded. Lady Morgan, in relating this history, always said, that Colburn behaved like an angry lover seeking a reconciliation with his mistress. The matter was at length arranged; Colburn made some proposal that satisfied Messrs. Saunders and Otley. But Lady Morgan was not to be so easily appeased. She was sorry to have been the cause of loss and annoyance to Messrs. Saunders and Otley, instead of the goddess of good fortune, which she had hitherto been to all. To compensate in some degree to them, and to show that she was perfectly satisfied with their conduct, she allowed them to publish *Dramatic Scenes and Sketches from Real Life.* But neither did they make this work answer as a literary speculation. We shall speak of it in its proper place.

Thomas Campbell was at this period the editor of Mr. Colburn's magazine, the *New Monthly.* Being the friend of Lady Morgan and of her husband, he was naturally in an embarrassing position, for at this time the quarrel between Colburn and Lady Morgan was at its bitterest. The following letter shows that he did his best to act uprightly towards all parties.

Thomas Campbell to Lady Morgan.

MIDDLE SCOTLAND YARD,
September 8th, 1830.

MY DEAR LADY MORGAN,

I write to you under the depression of a most miserable bad cold, but so impatient am I to communicate the sum and substance of what I have to say, that I was determined not to delay my answer till the cloudy atmosphere of head should clear up.

The sum and substance is, that dexterous as the little man is, he will be cleverer than even himself at mischief, if he contrives to make the *New Monthly* a vehicle for his further malignity towards you. I will watch every sheet and sentence that goes to press, and nothing, with my permission, shall go to press that is in the least disrespectful to you.

If I followed the impulse of my own feelings, I should not limit myself to *negative* conduct in this business. You may easily imagine what I think of Colburn's conduct to you. It shocked and disgusted me when I heard of it, and, moreover, it astounded me, for his conduct to myself has, on the whole, been very fair and liberal. I thought him incapable of such an action as the advertisement, and if he ever enters upon the subject with me, I will tell him my mind in the strongest reprehensive terms. But my interests are, unfortunately, for the present, involved with his, and I have disagreeable subjects enough to discuss with him without entering on that point. On this, however, you may rely, that he shall not get the *New Monthly* to be an engine of his hostility.

God knows when I may be able to accomplish my long-thought-of jaunt to the Emerald Isle. I trust, however, ere long, to see you or Sir Charles, or both of you, on this side of the Channel; you will surely visit us this year. Here you will find me in a far more liveable part of London than I lived in before, which was so remote that it almost kept me out of society. I am now within a bow-shot of what Dr. Johnson called the full tide of human existence at Charing Cross. I beg my best regards to Sir Charles, and not forgetting to congratulate you both on the late glorious events,

I remain, my dear Lady Morgan,
With respect and regard,
Yours truly,

T. CAMPBELL.

September 17*th*.—Moore brought a delightful man to us yesterday, the fashionable wit, Luttrell, of the Lady Cork and Charleville set, and author of the *Advice to Julia*. The moment Moore got in, he tried, as usual, to get out. Morgan said, "I beg pardon for the proposition, but do sit down if you can." "Oh, you have *found him out*," said Luttrell; "I have rarely seen him stay so long anywhere." He got upon the public journals: Luttrell said the *Court Journal* was the standard of bad taste, and cited its calling Lady Londonderry "our own Emily." Talking of Hazlitt, my old critic, and of his special dirtiness, Moore told the anecdote of Charles Lamb, saying to him when they were playing cards nearly as dirty as his hands, "Hazlitt, if dirt were trumps, what a fine hand you would have!" Our wits belong to the last century.

My husband wished to get up a dinner for Moore, at his club, here is his answer:—

Thomas Moore to Sir Charles Morgan.

September 20*th*, 1830.

My dear Morgan,

I need not say to you how much I feel both the honour and kindness of the invitation which you propose to me, but the fact is, my mind is now wholly set upon getting away as soon and as safely as these equinoctial breezes will let me. Having the nervous task of transporting women and children, at this time of the year, either by Bristol or Liverpool, I am preparing to take advantage of the very first appearance of more settled weather, and, therefore, could not form any engagement that would be likely to interfere with this purpose, nor, indeed, enjoy it at all as I ought, if I *did* form it. It is my intention, however, to be here again before the end of next spring, and then (if my kind friends of the Dawson Street Club continue still in the same disposition towards me) it will give me the most sincere pleasure to accept their invitation. I write in a hurry, but you will, I know, have the kindness to convey all this to them in a way that will best do justice to my feelings, and believe me,

Ever, my dear Morgan,
Most truly yours,
Thomas Moore.

Moore mentions this dinner in his diary, and says, "It is the *third* dinner that has been in contemplation for me, one of them being a mob feast at six shillings a head; which Jack Lawless wants to get up for me."

October 29th.—O'Gorman Mahon is not a charlatan, but a mountebank—a mountebank on wire. When asked to dine at the chief secretary's, the other day, he arrived when dinner was nearly over, in a chaise and four horses, two postilions, &c., &c., and entering the room, where he was an utter stranger, exclaimed, on seeing Sheil at the further end of the dinner table, "Ah! ah! my little friend, so you are here!" my blood ran cold, thinking what would come next. I blush for my countrymen.

November 23rd.—A *delightful* letter and pretty present of tablets from dear Lady Emily Hardinge.— A letter from the editor of the *Athenæum*, offering me liberal terms—altogether a pleasant post.

This is Lord Anglesey's day of entry! What an apotheosis! O'Connell has organised all that is false, bad, and ungrateful in the country against him. All through the town are placards ordering "All who love Ireland to stay at home." Some of O'Connell's "two thousand gentlemen" took their stations in different places, and endeavoured to harangue the people against this once idol of the nation; but in spite of this, Lord Anglesey had with him all the intelligence, wealth, rank, and respectability of the country. The cries of "O'Connell for ever!" "Down with dirty Dogherty!" were abundant. Morgan got out of a sick bed to go and meet him (much to my anxiety and apprehension). Lord Cloncurry came home with Morgan after the swearing in of the lord-lieutenant, and afterwards dined at the state dinner at the castle. Amongst some of the odd and pleasant things Lord Cloncurry told us, was, that Billy Murphy wrote to him to say that O'Connell would call on him at Maritimo on Tuesday last, to offer him all the trades to walk in procession, to meet Lord Anglesea on his entry. Lord Cloncurry waited at home all day, but the "Liberator" never came—*en attendant*, he had changed his mind, and absolved the people from all gratitude to their true friend. Ireland seems now organised for revolution. The government has not one periodical organ,— O'Connell's party has all, save the Orange papers, who are equally factious. It is very disheartening. Meantime, parliament at this most critical moment is prorogued.

The "letters" alluded to in the ensuing note from Lord Anglesey, were in all probability contributions from Sir Charles or Lady Morgan herself, to some liberal journal. Contributions of common sense, and a little tranquil stupidity, administered with discretion, were, doubtless, the best possible remedies for the restless cleverness of the Irish character. There is a great virtue in stupidity, it gives cohesion, and is a necessary quality before cleverness can attain the breadth and solidity of wisdom.

Marquis of Anglesea to Lady Morgan.

UXBRIDGE HOUSE,
December 3rd, 1830.

DEAR LADY MORGAN,

I have been favoured by the receipt of your obliging letter of the 28th of November, and have also received the letters you were so kind as to send. These had already attracted my notice, and very able productions they are. The subject is admirably handled, and cannot fail to do infinite good.

Oh, that Ireland would try the effect of a little quiet! From mere curiosity she should try it. Granted, that bustle and agitation are very charming, but *toujours, toujours perdrix!* is too much. Do let us be very still and stupid, I am fit for that state of things, and for that only, for I am a sad sufferer, and nothing but the restless desire I have to contribute my mite to help you all, could have induced me to quit my arm-chair. You must all compassionate me, and be very good.

Believe me,
Dear Lady Morgan,
Very truly yours,
ANGLESEA.

The following letter from Thomas Moore to Lady Morgan, is about literary matters. Incidental mention of an offer he had once had "to conduct the *Times*."

Thomas Moore to Lady Morgan.

SLOPERTON COTTAGE,
December 22*nd,* 1830.

MY DEAR LADY MORGAN,

As you seemed to think it better that I should commune *direct* with the publisher, and I had a prospect of being shortly in town, when I could deliver my answer in person, I deferred writing to either you or them till that opportunity should occur. I have now seen your messengers, at least, one of them; a very grave, respectable bibliopolist as I should wish to meet with, and have given him my answer (as I feared all along I should) in the *negative.* I was glad, however, to see that he had not much set his heart upon the plan, and I shall hope that neither have *you* been very desirous of it, as I hate to refuse anything that *any* body (how much, therefore, such a luminous lady as yourself) wishes me to do. The fact is, it would not be worth a publisher's while to give me such a sum as *alone* would make it worth *my* while to put myself so much out of my way. I was once offered at the rate of one hundred pounds a month to conduct the *Times* for a certain period, and at another time had a proposal from Croker to edit the *Quarterly Review,* at a thousand pounds a year, but neither tempted me. Talking of the *Times,* I have no conception of who was the author of that malignant attack upon you, but meant to have asked the editor, had I seen him when I was in town. That great machine and I have long parted company;

their politics under the Duke of Wellington (as I took care to tell them), being everything that I most detested. I shall be always glad, however, when they are in the ways of orthodoxy (as they seem to be just now), to put a helping hand to the lever, for such it is of the most massive kind.

Mrs. Moore begs to be most kindly remembered to you and Sir Charles, who is, I trust, by this time, quite himself again.

Ever yours, most truly,
THOMAS MOORE.

PS.—People express a little alarm about my *Life and Death of Lord Edward*, and I get hints from all sides that it would be prudent to defer its publishing; but I shall not mind them.

Christmas-day.—My birth-day—*à quoi bon?*—still I have great cause to be thankful whilst all I love live. What a cordial greeting from the Clarkes; how soothing! how cheering! what a beautiful aspect of life! Love and the arts—I found them all round the round table; the blackest frost without; all warm and sunshine within. Flaxman's illustrations of Dante on the table, Morgan strumming Rossini at the piano, Josephine with her pencil, sketching the group, &c., &c. Alas! how long will this last? We returned home better in health, feelings, and spirits, forgot O'Connell and the Irish Rebellion, the calumnies of authors, the envy of critics, and soon the whole world, in the calm, deep sleep of temperance and kindly feelings.

CHAPTER XX.

LAST YEARS IN DUBLIN—1831.

THIS note from Lady Morgan to Moore, at the period when there was an Irish Coercion Bill in prospect, gives a picture of a state of things which we hope is never likely to return.

Lady Morgan to T. Moore.

KILDARE STREET, DUBLIN,
January 2nd, 1831.

DEAR MR. MOORE,

I am tempted to put your *good nature at rest,* with respect to the *refusal* of the *editorship.* Your friend Crampton (whom I met at dinner yesterday) has offered to forward a note to you by *his* packet. So I am tempted to write. *My* opinion is, that it would be for the advantage of literature if *periodical* publications were put down for ever. Mr. Crampton and I agreed last night that we should be inclined to "put on the *list of friends those whom you say have advised you not to publish* your *Life of Lord Edward,* at this most *mal à propos and inauspicious moment. Ireland* is no more the *country you left* three months ago than it is *Cochin China!* To judge by the outline and aspect of things, a *connoisseur* in *revolution* (and I am *pas mal* in that species of *virtù*) all would say we were on the eve of the worst and most perilous political commotions *one* coming from *below,* and such elements! Imagine countless thousands of the lower classes pouring through the streets, silent, concentrated, *worked* by a nod, a sign; and this, the day after a proclamation from the government, forbidding *all* meetings.(!) All other classes are *paralysed;* government is without *one* organ to address to public *opinion; not one newspaper* in its service—*terrorism* the order of the day, and a parliament *dispersed* for six weeks at least, and the nation left to the prayers of the Archbishop of *Canterbury* and the black *Pasto* of Mr. Percival. It is clear that they know nothing about us in England; by this time, however, Lord Anglesey has probably *given* them a *hint; his reception* is a stain upon the country, which can never be effaced; peace or war (*civil war and extending woes*) now lies in the influence of O'Connell over the passions of the people; "*to this complexion are we come at last.*"

    In haste,
      Dear Mr. Moore,
        Yours truly,
         S. MORGAN.

January 26th.—I made a very agreeable sort of

Donnybrook fair party on Friday last,—20th. My women were all pretty, and my men all pleasant, and *pour comble* we got up a proverb *en action*, in very good style, all *à l'improviste*, and though almost strangers to each other in this line, they were acted *à merveille*.

The proverb—" Poverty comes in at the door, love flies out at the window."

What shouts of laughter and fun!—our audience—Lord Douro, Lord Headford, Sir Guy and Lady Campbell, Sir E. and Lady Blakeney, Augustus Liddle, Colonel Bowater, Lord F. Paulet, Mrs. Caulfield, Miss Armitt, and Miss Crumpton.

Had a letter to-day from David, the sculptor, sending me my own bust in marble, and that of Lafayette!

February 15th.—Sitting all alone to-day; just before dinner enter T. Moore! *pardi!* I could not believe my eyes. "Why, what on earth brings you here? is it to dine with me to-day?" "No, I'll dine with you to-morrow." "My mother was dying, I was sent for, she has seen me, and has revived." Morgan came in. Moore sat all the time; I never before saw him sit for ten minutes together; he was cordial, and pleasant, and confidential. He told us many strange things. Poor fellow, he has never been able to get out of debt. He told us Rogers had expended three thousand pounds on the publication of his dandy book. Oh, these amateur authors who write for fashion, while *we* write for fame or famine! Moore says he thinks Murray would like to publish for me.

February 17th.—I had a little dinner got up in a hurry for Moore, yesterday; it was got up thus. I threw up my windows, and asked the inmates of the cabs and carriages of my friends as they passed the windows, and sent out some penny porters, and lighted up my rooms. Moore was absolutely astounded when he saw my party! He sang some of his most beautiful songs in his most delightful manner, without stopping; some of them twice over, and all of them as if every word was applicable to the people around him. Many of his old friends were around him; I said, " if you stay a day or two longer, I'll do better than this." "No, no," he said, "never again can such a thing be done. This is one of the few happy accidents which occur rarely; besides, I don't want to efface the impression even by something better.'

I never saw him more natural or agreeable. He praised Murray to the skies, and said he was princely in his conduct to authors. Moore disliked me in my youth; he told me at Florence that he thought Byron did not wish to know *me*, and *did* wish to know Morgan.

April 1st.—Poor Molly! I went to see her, and the whole was too much for me—my dear Morgan just returned from her—we are with her every day! What a scene! her whole anxiety is about her funeral, her coffin, &c. I have promised her to do all, and now she is at peace, although her drunken sister (who is looking forward to a glorious wake) has brought her priest, who told her she could not be saved. My sister is all goodness to her, and nurses her like a mother!

Morgan and I have just had a *battle royal!* The subject was, as usual, one of my improvements in the house. All, however, of my improvements have been made at *long* intervals; the *last* I was five years working at. The present point at issue is, *I* want a little *greenhouse* to put my plants in on the *open space* at the back of the stairs; I want this done, and have offered to pay for it. Morgan vows I never shall have it, and is gone out in a passion; but I don't despair. Upon this occasion I am a bore, and he is—a bear.

Mrs. Hemans had at this period settled in Dublin. Friendly acquaintance and interchange of well disposed civilities went on between herself and Lady Morgan, in spite of the differences of their habits, for Mrs. Hemans was then an invalid, and inclined to withdraw from general society, in which Lady Morgan found her element. These distinguished women regarded each other with high consideration.

From Mrs. Hemans to Lady Morgan.

Upper Bagot Street,
May 7th.

Mrs. Hemans presents her compliments to Lady Morgan, and returns the "Metropolitan," with many thanks for all the pleasure it has afforded her. She trusts that her little messengers may be able to bring her an improved account of Lady Morgan's health, and that the particulars of the *Macaw's début* in fashionable life will not be long withheld.

This Macaw was the pet of Lady Cork and Orrery, and Lady Morgan was writing a *jeu d'esprit*, called *Memoir of a Macaw of a Lady of Quality.*

A letter marked private has always an attraction; the present note from Sheil is about public affairs, and though time has deprived them of all the uncertainty that gave them their emphasis, at the moment it is interesting to see events as they pass in incidents day by day. Lady Morgan was always deeply in earnest about politics. Parties were running fearfully high upon the Reform Bill.

R. Sheil to Lady Morgan.

Tuesday, July, 1831.

My dear Lady Morgan,

Your letter to me is most gratifying; it is another and a greener leaf in my parliamentary chapter, a thousand thanks to your good heart. Believe me you mistake me much if you try me by my observance of the rules of etiquette; I know how to value your faculties and your character. There is no one whose friendship and praise I prize more than yours and Sir Charles's. I have received a series of kindnesses from both, which I cannot readily forget.

There is no news here in the political circles to which I can give implicit confidence. It is *said* that there are dissensions in the cabinet, and that the king has had a fit of apoplexy. Party runs so high that I can attach no credit to what I hear, even from the *highest* quarters on *both* sides. I *believe* that there has been a great defection among the Lords, but that it is quite possible that some of the ministers may ultimately become terrified at their own reform. Lord Melbourne was great. Charles Grant did not speak with the cordiality of strong conviction.

Lady Cork was last night making special inquiries about you; she asked me whether it was true that you were writing the adventures and observations of her Macaw. It lately bit off the toe of a countess, but on the calf of a minister it could make no impression.

I met Jeffery and Macaulay here at dinner; Jeffery has the most astounding volubility I ever witnessed; he will not do in the house, I fear. I witnessed at Sir J. Mackintosh's his introduction to Wordsworth, for the *first* time. The latter grinned horribly, a ghastly smile.

Remember me to Sir Charles, and believe me,
Yours most truly,
R. SHEIL.

August 13*th*.—We are invited to the regatta; but we shall go to Lucan instead [Lucan was a watering place near Dublin, fashionable, and much frequented at that time] to repose from country house dissipations, and then I shall set to work at my Irish histories. My dirty house is to be given up to workmen, and I am to have a French window at the head of the stairs, opening on the balcony; the greenhouse question is still laid on the table, but I will have that too before I die, but not long before, I fear.

The review mentioned by Lord Anglesea in the ensuing letter was an Irish one, written to serve some question of the moment; the times, both in England and Ireland, were threatening, and every small contribution of common sense was thankfully received by those who had the guidance of public affairs.

Lord Anglesea to Lady Morgan.

BLACK ROCK,
September, 12, 1831.

MY DEAR LADY MORGAN,

I ought to have thanked you sooner for the Review you sent me, and for calling my attention to the well-written article in it by Sir Charles Morgan. I had already seen *extracts* from it, with which, to be honest, I was better pleased than with the *whole,* for it happens that I go the full length with him in what I had before met with, whereas, in part of that which was new to me, I differ. I am sorry—you, probably, glad —that I have not time to explain myself.

Lady Anglesea showed me your note regarding an Italian opera, in Dublin, during October and November. If the thing is likely to take, I shall be delighted to promote it, and all my family will join. I think every encouragement should be given to those who will render Dublin gay. We want a little *dégourdissement*, because too much entangled in sombre politics. We may be vastly good patriots, and yet be always lively and good humoured; but before Messrs. Calcraft and de Bégnis embark in this undertaking, they should well calculate their means.

    Believe, me,
     Dear Lady Morgan,
      Very faithfully yours,
       ANGLESEA.

October 1st.—I thought the child's ball, at the Stanley's, a *triste* affair, or the contrast with Lady Emily's child's ball made it appear more so.

They were very civil; and Mr. Stanley seemed as if he wished to be as unlike a *minister of state* at a child's ball as possible; he ran about and was even *frisky*, and at the ponderous supper (where there was a smoking sirloin of beef at the head, and a cold round at the foot, two turkeys and ducks at the side); he kept crying, "Why don't you eat; pray eat," as if he was feeding the poor Irish at a soup kitchen.

October 16th.—On my return from Lucan, I find *mon bon ami* the black volume, my journal white or blue, and unwritten still, on the writing desk in my dressing-room; there it has lain for a month, and it actually requires an effort of will to open and scribble in it. My life at Lucan was an odd one, I was placed in a set I never was in before, such a place is the mutual rendezvous of quizzeries of all sorts, and I should have died of it, but for my Dominican monk, Father

Fitzgerald, of Carlow (of whom and our romance more hereafter), and his friend the head of the Dominicans, Father Harold, and our own odd, clever, paradoxical friend, Professor Macartney. We made a delightful little coterie, and all the mediocrities were frightened out of their stupid wits. Holy St. Francis! what a conclave in the midst of their sanctity! for they were all saints, and vulgar saints My arrival caused universal dismay. Miss M——, the archbishop's daughter, ran away, others were about to follow her, but I turned them all. No Lady Huntingdon, had she dropped among them, could have been more in the odour of sanctified popularity than I was, after a while, and my life there was, in some respects, most delectable,—air, health temperance, and occupation. I wrote there my two most arduous Irish articles for the Metropolitan. Since our return, we have been in perpetual agitation about the Reform bill, but I picked one gay, light-hearted, agreeable evening out of the bustle,—a dinner and soirée for Paganini. I asked him, not as a miraculous fiddle-player, but as a study. He came into the drawing-room in a great coat, a clumsy walking stick, and his hat in his hand (quite a Penruddock figure), and, walking up to me, made a regular set speech in his Genoese Italian, which I am convinced was taught him by his secretario; it abounded in *Donnas celebritissimas*, and all the superlatives of Italian gallantry. At dinner, he seemed wonderfully occupied with the dishes in succession, and frequently said, "*ho troppo, mangiato!*" at each dish, exclaiming, "*bravissimo! excellentissimo!*" The fact is, I had copied a Florentine dinner as closely as I could, having had a Florentine cook all the time we were in Italy; so, we had a *minestra al vermicelli; maccaroni*, in all forms, &c., &c. I asked him if he were not the happiest man in the world, every day acquiring so much fame and so much money. He sighed and said, he should be but for one thing "*i Ragazzi*," the little blackguards that ran after him in the streets. In the evening, I took him into the boudoir; we had a *tête-à-tête* of an hour, in which he told me his whole story; but in such an odd, simple, Italian, gossiping manner, half by signs, looks, and inflections of the voice, that though I can take him off to the life verbally, I can give no idea of him on paper;—still here is the outline. His father and mother in humble life in Genoa, fond of music—no more. At four years old, he played the guitar, and, untaught, attended all the churches to sing, and at seven years of age, composed something like a *cantata;* then he took up the violin and made such progress, that his father travelled about with him from one Italian town to another, till he attracted the attention and attained the patronage of Élise Bonaparte, then Grand Duchess of Tuscany. He was taken into her family, and played constantly at her brilliant little court; there he fell in love with one of her *dames d'honneur*, who turned his head, he said, and he became *pazzo per amore*, and found his violin expressed his passion better than he could. Mademoiselle B—— became his guide and inspiration; but they had a terrible *fracas*, they fought, fell out and separated. One day, in his despair, he was confi-

ding his misery to his beloved violin, and made it
repeat the quarrel just as it happened; he almost
made it articulate the very words, and in the midst
of this singular colloquy, Mademoiselle de B——
rushed into the room and threw her arms round his
neck and said, " Paganini, your genius has conquered;"
their reconciliation followed, and she begged he would
note down those inspirations of love; he did so, and
called it, *Il Concerto d'Amore.* Having left it by accident on the piano of the grand duchess, she saw, and
commanded him to play it; he did so, and the dialogue
of the two strings had a wonderful success. He married
afterwards a chorus singer at Trieste, and she was the
mother of his little Paganini, whom he doated on.
The mother, he said, abandoned them both, and that
he was now no longer susceptible of the charms of the
" *Belle Donne.*" His violin was his mistress. While
telling me all this, he rolled his eyes in a most extraordinary way, and assumed a look that it is impossible
to define — really and truly something demoniacal.
Still, he seems to me, to be a stupified and almost
idiotic creature.

Here is a letter from the Countess of Cork and
Orrery, still harping on her macaw.

Lady Cork to Lady Morgan.

TUNBRIDGE WELLS,
October 25.

It is actually nine months since I received a letter
from dear Lady Morgan. I immediately conceived a

letter of thanks, but never had it in my power to bring it to light. Lucina is not at hand, nor any other friendly assistant.

The bantling with bright thoughts is quite decayed, and I remain your stupid old eighty-six, without a second idea.

I should not venture to intrude upon you to-day; but that I really am anxious to be regaled with one of your pretty greetings. Tommy Moore told me my macaw had spoke both witty and clever. Bulwer, &c., &c., said the same, and that they would send it to me. I have never seen it. When can I hear of it—answer this, and tell me, when you come to England. I don't wish it till April, when I promise you constant, pleasant *réunions*. I am more *chez moi*, and go out less than ever. I collect pleasant people, and like this last act of the play as well as any part of my life. I am in good health, and have many kind friends, among whom I trust you'll allow me to set you down in the first class.

For I am, very truly,
Your faithful and obliged servant,
M. C. O.

A true Whig.

PS. You must write some beautiful panegyric on my sweet friends, Miss Foleys.

This macaw, which has been several times alluded to, who spoke both witty and clever, was a bird of wisdom belonging to Lady Cork, and Lady Morgan wrote a charming paper entitled *Memoirs of a Macaw* of a *Lady of Quality*, which first appeared in the *New Monthly*, and afterwards was republished in *The Book without a Name*. It is a model for the kind of writing; it is full of good feeling, and has caustic, lively touches of society which give a pleasant sharpness; and there is a sketch of a poor " Younger Brother," that is quite touching; altogether, it is one of Lady Morgan's happiest efforts.

October 30.—In that coarse, dashing, but not altogether ill-written novel the *Staff Officer*, there is a picture from the life of my dear old friend Joe Atkinson. The author wrote me a fine letter under the signature Oliver Moore, presenting me his book and saying lots of civil things.

This moment the news came in that our excellent friend, Wallace, is returned at last for Drogheda. I worked hard at this, and wrote to all whom I thought could or could not, assist him. Poor Wallace is very ill, and got his fever at his odious election.

November 2.—My poor dear old friend, Hamilton Rowan, is fast going; Morgan saw him the day before yesterday, lying in his chaise-lounge, feeble, but still full of spirit and interest in the passing events.

November 7.—The cholera is approaching. I proposed to Morgan that we should retire from Dublin; he stopped me short by saying, that where there was most danger that was his post. His view of the case changed my whole feeling on the subject; *he must* stay, and, therefore, *I* will stay, so last night we set about thinking what was wisest and best to be done for the preservation of the poor prisoners of the Marshalsea. We think we have succeeded. He has gone to examine the state of the prison, and then to make his proposals to the Lord Lieutenant.

A letter from one of the horse-riders of the Royal Arena, to beg I will command his benefit and give him my name; of course I refused. How people mistake my energy for influence!

November 14.—Yesterday was a day of offerings. Robertson presented me with a good miniature of myself. It is a nice picture; but much thinner, graver, and more sharp and *collet monté* than I ever was, or ever shall be *secula seculorum*. Offering the second— A fine bronze medal of Walter Scott, brought me from Edinburgh. Third—a brace of superb pheasants from Capt. Jekyll, of the Grenadier Guards. Lady Elizabeth Clements and Mrs. Caulfield have just walked in with a present of twelve yards of white satin, embroidered in flowers by the late Countess of Charlemont for a court-dress. They made me swear that I would act a *proverbe* for them in it some evening. This is the fun of the thing—the philosophy of it is the embroidery; it must have taken a life to do, and is a fine illustration of the life to which ladies of quality were put to formerly to get rid of their time. I have been thinking to what use I can put it—as curtains for the boudoir it would have no effect, except that of soiled, flowered linen. Draperies of white satin, embroidered in flowers, sounds "sweetly" in a novel; but for effect, masses both in colour and material, an adaptation of light and shades are the things; thus, some fifty yards

of scarlet or rose-coloured moreen, at two or three
shillings a yard, would have more effect than all the
embroidered satins in the world. Furniture should
be rich, simple, voluminous, and capable of falling, or
rather melting, into deep folds; the effect of the rich
masses and lights and shades produced by a drapery
of this texture is surprising. I think I shall make a
douilliette for my French bed, dye it green and stuff
it with eider down.

November 27.—All the early part of the day
house-keeping, looking over table-cloths, cutting out
dusters, and what not of the huckaback order.

Prince Pucklau Muskau's book just come! I am
properly trotted out in it. It is too horrible to think
there is no doing good without paying the penalty.
The prince's book, the Prince of Darkness, I should
say, if it did not bear the name and impress of the
Prince Pucklau Muskau. At the very time we were
showing him hospitality, he was concocting this book,
in which I was to be misrepresented and belied. The
conversations he describes, was utterly false. I never
again ought to receive a foreigner into my house; this
is the fourth time I have been the subject of attacks
written by such guests. It is rather curious that at
this particular moment another foreigner should be
presented to me, Count Charles O'Haggerty, *écuyer* to
the duchess of Angoulême, at Holyrood; but I am
sick and weary of it all.

December 20.—I cannot endure the sight of this
book (my diary), I have nothing but botherations to
enter. But what a glorious triumph! The Reform

Bill passing through the House, two to one against the Tories.

December 25.—Christmas-day, my birthday. Hélas!!

December 26.— Yesterday I dined with my own dear family; what a cluster of clever, handsome and beloved heads!

To-day, off to Malahide Castle, where we spend our Christmas.

CHAPTER XXI.

A FLYING VISIT TO ENGLAND—1832.

January 2.—Kildare Street. We had a cordial household, hospitable time at Malahide—all old friends—the Talbots—the Evans of Portran, my old lover and friend, Edward Moore. The fine old Castle is always my delight. I finished my article on it, for the *Metropolitan*, in the old library, with a Grant of Edward IV. lying beside me, bearing his own signature. Drove to Howth Castle—more antiquities—promised Lady Howth we would dine and stay there next Thursday, then to General Cockburn's for the rest of the holidays.

So enchanted to get back to our snuggery in Kildare Street, with all its warmth, comfort, and enjoyment. Those great castles are so cold and dreary, one has so many miles to walk between drawing and dressing-room that the contrast to my little china closet is very great, and then my agreeable droppers in, from three to five.

January 4.—A pleasant levee to-day, clever Mrs.

Caulfield, and wild, but pleasant Edward Bligh; a tremendous set-to in politics.

January 5.—Working hard at old chronicles for my intended new novel, *Grace O'Mally.*

January 16.—Went to see the lions and boa constrictor figuring away at the theatre, most wonderful! Martin played with the lion, or rather, the lion with him like a great Newfoundland dog romping with a child. Martin has been predestined by his temperament to tame savage beasts, and to be eaten by them some fine day.

January 24.—All going on cheerily, good company and good spirits, when arrived the last number of the *Quarterly.* The acrimonious spirit of old Gifford still survives, and all the bitterness and weakness it exhibited against me twenty years back, more violent than ever. Prince Pucklau Muskau's vile book furnishes forth this new attack on me; the worst thing they can find to say against me is that my father was an actor, the miserable creatures!

January 27.—By-the-bye, this has been a merry week—a gay ball at Lady Kingsmill's; yet a more brilliant assembly at the Marquis of Headford's. I flirted with Sir Harcourt Lees, and Lambert of Beaupark, the high priests of Orangeism. One of them told me that the *cicerone* of the cathedral of Cashel, showing it to him the other day, said, "And here, sir, is the ould part, built by the pagans, and these statues were the *pa*-gods!"

Our new Archbishop Whateley has astonished, outraged, maddened the clergy by advising in his last sermon that some passages, and *some* only, be selected from the Bible and given to the people. They left the church in convulsions, exclaiming, the Bible, the *whole* Bible, and *nothing but* the Bible!"

January 28.—Last night, sitting with the Earl of Rosse, he told me many strange stories, picked up when he was a child from his father, who lived to be a hundred. He described a ball at the great O'Moore's, where the company, exceeding the number of beds, the ladies lay down round the capacious hearth, their feet pointing towards the fire. An old woman came in with an immense quantity of woollen cloth, which she flung over them, and so they slept!

The "madder," so often mentioned in Irish song, was a wooden tankard, made square; there were then no tools for turning. Wooden noggins and wooden dishes were universal; they are still much used in country parts.

When Lord Rosse was Sir Lawrence Parsons, he wrote some learned works on Irish antiquities; his son, Lord H. Oxmantown, is a great mechanician, he is now occupied on a telescope of great power.

February 1.—I began another new work to-day on *The Ignorance of Women,*—shall I ever finish any? I doubt it, the motive no longer exists, and perhaps, too, the working material is worn out—this frittering away of mind is very like it.

February 20.—The Whigs and the ministry going the way of all flesh; these mongrel Liberals will never do,—never did do.

Lord Grey's speech on the enforcement of the tithe

is conclusive. Lord Plunkett is at the bottom of this one of the old set of Irish politicians, *rompus et corrompus*. Family aggrandisement is his great motive in all. Somebody said to old Norbury some time before he died, " It is odd that Plunkett cannot see his way clearly about the tithe. " Sir," said Lord Norbury, " he has the *son* in his eyes."

Lord Plunkett is an acute, eloquent, and clear-sighted man, to the extent of his views; but they are not extensive. His politics are simply, rigorously *British*, not European.

Lord Grey is the screw loose.

February 27.—Parties and balls galore this last week—no need to specify.

March 23.—Ever since my last entry, " with darkness compassed," shut up, a dark room, a horrid state, a tax upon those whose charity leads them to come to me. The kind Talbots carry me off to Malahide on Saturday.

April 8.—The other day I took a party to see Malahide Castle. As Lady Chapman's carriage had been broken at a *soirée* the night before, I drove her in my phaeton. Compare this with my *début* in Dominic Street, when I went to be hired as a governess! I did the honours of the castle in my old quality of *Custoda*.

We had an excellent luncheon, and we came home loaded with flowers and vegetables, *à l'ordinaire*. In short, nobody can grow old more agreeably than I do; I sit with the picture of the immortal Ninon de L'Enclos hanging over my head, a sort of votive shrine raised to the art of remaining young through mind, when youth has passed away!

I am getting on with the learned opening of my new book on Woman.

April 19.—The cholera is making fearful strides among the filthy dens of the wretched lower orders! many of the higher are panic-stricken.

May 17.—Tory ministry out! just as Lord Anglesey was packing off.

What emotions this event has raised in my mind! and what an interval! Yesterday—Europe—mankind seemed thrown back on the horrors of past and dark ages; and now they are not only restored, but advanced by centuries. I could not resist writing to Lord Anglesey. Here is a rough draft of my letter.

Lady Morgan to Lord Anglesey.

May 17, 1832.

MY DEAR LORD,

In moments of great commotion and great emotion, all forms of etiquette must yield to the expressions of strong feeling which acknowledge no masters of ceremonies. My husband and I were at the Park a day or two back, to pay you our deep regret at your leaving. To-day, under a far different excitement, I venture to obtrude the expression of our congratulations on the greatest triumphs that freedom and knowledge ever obtained over despotism and bigotry. England is saved, and great and good men again take those high positions in which they may best serve the interests of mankind. Of course, your excellence is left with us to revive hopes for Ireland, who, like a capricious mistress, although she may sometimes *bouder*, the object of her passion has no desire to change.

I am, my dear Lord,
 With sincere respect and congratulations,
  Your Excellency's devoted subject,
   SYDNEY MORGAN.

I have just had a letter from Moore, proving that it is equally true of one who becomes rich, as of a poet, that he must be *nasciter non fit.*

Thomas Moore to Lady Morgan.

May 24th, 1832.

MY DEAR LADY MORGAN,

At the time I received your letter, I was not very well able to answer it, and, indeed, till within these two days, have felt by no means well, or like myself. I am, however, now much better. I have been in correspondence, during part of the time, with your friend of the *Metropolitan*, Captain Marryatt, and if the most cautious and flattering liberality, on his part, added to your kind persuasions, could have made a contributor or editor of me, I should have been one at this moment. But I hate to be *tied;* it is this, far more than what you call my aristocratic (God help me) prejudices, which makes me reject so often the golden

bait flung at me. If I were to judge, indeed, of the
state of literature from my own experience, I should
say it never was more prosperous, as I have actually
turned away from my *door* (as the shop-keepers say)
fifteen hundred guineas and a thousand pounds a year
within the last three months; all the time, too,
wanting money most pinchingly. From what you
said in your letter I took for granted that Campbell
had intimated some intention of abdicating the editorship; but this I find not to be the case, and if I were
ever so disposed to accept of the chair, I should shrink
from the slightest step, on my part, that could be con-
strued into a wish to supplant him. I lament to hear
of his present state, but he *has* been a noble fellow.
You will think it looks very like contributorship when
you come to see some verses of mine announced for
the next number of the *Metropolitan;* but, besides my
wish to show, by some trifling mark, how much I felt
the kindness both of Captain Marryatt and Dr. Saunders, these verses were of a kind that would not *keep*,
being a good deal circulated, or, at least, shown about
by those who are interested in them, and, therefore,
likely to get into print. All I have told you about
shop business here is for your private self alone; for,
though vain enough, God knows, at being praised so
much higher than I am worth, I think it, in general,
not right to proclaim the particulars of my negociations with the bibliopolists.

Give my best regards to Morgan,

And believe me, very truly yours,

THOMAS MOORE.

May 27.—A bright summer morning. Morgan took up his guitar at breakfast, and began to *frédoner La Biondina, in Gondoletta*, and an hour afterwards, under the combined influence of sunshine and green tea, Morgan, who is in as high health and spirits as I am *out* of both, ran up to my dressing-room, where I was prosing over my *Women of the Church*, with a handful of MS. music. "See what I have composed," said he, and laying it down on my tiresome writing-desk, he played and sang a pretty *cavatina*.

May 28.—I am suffering beyond all conception from want of air and exercise. My house is small and confined; there is no thorough air, and I am never allowed to open a window to obtain it. When summer comes, Dublin is a dreary desert inhabited only by loathsome beggars, and I feel suffocated; I complain, and think and say, "this is a hard fate." My complaints are met with ridicule and vehement argument—sometimes with harshness; they are not borne with, because their cause is not felt, and all that makes *my* misery makes the happiness of one who, by law and custom, is the master of my actions, while books and easy chairs make up his whole wise scheme of happiness! All he says *may* be true, and I *may* be wrong; it *may* be weakness, caprice, an appetite for excitement; but still it is misery, and there is no reasoning with sensation. Men feel this, and plead it for the indulgence of their own whims—poor woman is commanded to suffer, and be silent, if she is so weak or wicked as to have no control over her sensations. This has been and will be my little personal narrative *in secula seculorum*.

[There is the following note at the bottom of this page of the diary, which is an amusing commentary on the above. *October* 29, 1832.—Looking back on this page, I can scarcely believe I am the person who wrote it; for *now* I am in high health and spirits, and in great vigour of body and mind. My trip to England, and air and exercise, have restored the balance of affection between us!]

London, July 1.—I thought I was past all enjoyment; but well may I enjoy so cordial and gracious a reception from all my old and new London friends. These pleasant and fresh apartments in St. James' Place, close to the parks, and within reach of everything that is best, is very enlivening. My visitors begun at ten o'clock this morning—authors, publishers, booksellers, and artists; afterwards, some new and old cronies—Campbell, Captain Marryat, Bulwer, Dilke, and Wentworth Dilke; Lardner, Miss Sheridan, Sir M. Shee, Valpy, and Bentley; then in the afternoon, Ladies Charleville and Charlemont, Lady Stepney and others. This is pretty well for one day. Perhaps what is most delightful of all, is to find the old friends I had early made in my youth still at their post. Lord Nugent was one of my visitors, and more agreeable than ever.

I was carried off to the parks and zoological gardens, by Mrs. Webster, and have now a late eight o'clock dinner to dress for. In short, this is a second spring, an after crop!

July 2.—Yesterday, a charming dinner made for me at Mr. Dilke's. Amongst many celebrities, Hood (of the *Comic Annual*) a very grave person, looking the picture of ill-health, was presented to me. Morgan quite happy—good music in the evening. The cordial hostess, full of kindness—pretty house—full of good pictures and old curiosities.

Lady Cork still in town, still well disposed, but is so *bent* on *getting up a dinner*, that all her lingering forces are summed up in that.

Mrs. Charles Gore, the authoress of the thousand and one fashionable novels (her last, *Pin Money*), and a very successful writer; is herself, a pleasant little rondelette of a woman. I found her something of my own style. When I went to pay her a visit, I found her preparing for a dinner party in a pretty little bit of a boudoir house; we talked and laughed together as good-humoured women always do, and agreed upon *many points*. She made some *clever hits*. Trelawney, D'Orsay, and some other brilliant villains were to have been presented to me to-day, but I was out when they called.

I have little time to write my journal, and so merely *jot down* people and things *as a reminder*. As thus: Lady Aldborough has just been—wonderful still—her own hair, graceful figure, and *such a toilet!!* her wit (*un peu trop fort*) most racy, she might *almost* be my mother!!

The following note from Countess Guiccioli is very interesting in its broken English; she had not yet become a great lady at the French court, nor taken up the dropped stitches of her " respectability."

The Countess of Guiccioli to Lady Morgan.

July 9th, 1832.

[With Lord Byron's hair and autograph.]

The Countess Guiccioli presents her compliments to Lady Morgan, and sends to her some lines of Lord Byron's hand-writing, together with some hairs of him. She adds to that a ringlet of her own hair, only because Lady Morgan asked it. But she cannot do that, without a sort of *remords*, as it was a profanation to put together in the same shrine so holy relics with so trifling a thing as it is; for the rest, the few lines of Lord Byron's writing hand are directed to the Count Gamba, Countess Guiccioli's father, and are written in a playful style, as he did frequently, and always when he talked about the laziness and not extraordinary cleverness of his minister, Mr. Sega.

The Countess Guiccioli wishes and hopes that a better opportunity will be presented to her, in order to show how high is her esteem and admiration for the illustrious and amiable Lady Morgan.

August 16.—At last arrived at the original part of our pilgrimage, *Leamington!* found it a twaddle—people taking physic to slow music, and returning to quick; but oh, for Warwick Castle! and Guy's Cliff! enchanting! My old flirt in my priory days, "the lord of the castle," was not at home; the Bertie Percys were, and they were all kindness and hospitality.

August 30.—We are now back to dull, dusty Dublin; we have been to pay our respects to the vice-royalties, and saw Lord Anglesey and Lady Mary Paget, and had a long and pleasant confab. Lord Anglesey said, "will you dine with me to-day, to-morrow, or Monday." We said, "Monday, if it suits your Excellency." Lord Anglesey.—"Who will you have to meet you?" I was *going* to say, "Pat Costello and Dan O'Connell;" but thought that would be *too* agreeable, so, said, "your Excellency's family." Lord Anglesey.—"Oh, poh, you must have somebody!" At this moment, in came Mr. Secretary Stanley. Lord Anglesey said, "You shall have him." Stanley bowed and smiled, and so it is settled we dine at the Phœnix on Monday.

Tuesday.—Our dinner was rather *triste*, *dull*, and *fine*. Lord Anglesey not in spirits, one of his bad days.

Lady Morgan piqued herself on her influence over the young men of her circle. She always endeavoured to rouse them from their desultory habits of amusement, to a sense of their duties as land owners and Irishmen.

October 25.—I have just got a fine new cloak, and am so smart! Went to Riversdale, to see Lady Guy Campbell in it. [Lady Guy Campbell was the daughter of Lord and Lady Edward Fitzgerald.] She had just got a picture of her old granny, Madame de Genlis, and of her mother, Pamela, which had belonged to the ladies of Llangollen, and which I put her in the way of getting.

Lady Guy Campbell told me some curious anecdotes

of her mother's birth. She has no doubt that Pamela was the daughter of Egalité and Madame de Genlis, and she told me that she has a paper signed by them both, being a contract of adoption of the child Pamela by both. She recollects an angry dispute between her mother (Lady E. Fitzgerald), and Madame de Genlis, when the latter said, "*ne vous vantez pas d'être ma fille vous ne l'êtes pas.*" "*Pardi,*" replied Pamela. "*Il n'y a pas de quoi s'en vanter!*" Pamela was born whilst Madame de Genlis was in the West Indies. She sent for the child to London to speak English with Mademoiselle D'Orleans, and Lady Edward said that when she arrived in her little English Red Riding Hood cloak, Madame de Genlis was sitting with the D'Orleans family, and surrounded by the court. The child looking about it, and astounded by so fine a party, flew to Madame de Genlis's arms, whom she had never seen since she was a baby. "Such was her sagacity," said Madame, "that she knew me from my reputation!"

I see a great likeness in the upper part of Lady Campbell's face to Madame de Genlis; but *en beau*, very pretty from expression and movement of countenance. The King of France was present at her mother's marriage with Lord Edward Fitzgerald, at Tournai; he was *then* the Duke de Chartres, and Fitzgerald was in Dumouriez's army.

November 2nd.—Just returned from Bray Head, its delicious scenery, and its beneficent mistress. But what a neighbourhood to live in with its *cagoteries!* What society! all effete races worn out. The very air breathes Methodism, and every tree looked like a preacher. I walked in the sweet Dargle, but not before the evangelical gate-keeper received half-a-crown from Mrs. P—— for letting us into Powerscourt. I went to Holly Brook to see my old friend and Livy's old schoolfellow (Lady Hudson still deep in mourning for her favourite child, Sir Robert); I was delighted with Holly Brook. The old tottering mansion full of the tippling memory of *Robin Adair*. His glass, half a yard high and half a yard round, was shown to me, and his drinking bout with a Scotchman related. The low, dark room is covered with divine pictures. Lady Hudson was Miss Nevil. We have often spent our holidays together.

William Plunket (the hon. and reverend), who sat beside me at dinner to-day, at Bray Head, told me he had been with his father, Lord Plunket, at Holland House, which was almost their home when in London. "One day," he said, "we were the only guests at Holland House, when Prince Talleyrand came in." "Where do you think I come from?" he demanded of Lord Holland. A hundred vain guesses were made. "Well, then, from dining and passing the day *tête-à-tête* with Jeremy Bentham."

I have often thought of this *tête-à-tête*. How could they understand each other? The extremes of sensibility and insensibility, of honesty and roguery—philosophy and philanthropy against diplomacy and villany!!!

November 28*th*.—Just returned from Lord Cloncurry's, a vastly gay party for Lyons. "Dear Lady

Morgan" and her "agreeability," all the rage once more. Why? *Dio lo so!* Why did she *lose* her popularity? I know not. Take the world as it runs, it is never worth a thought; whims, passions, interests, *any* thing but feeling, truth, reason. Lord Brabazon was deputed my cavalier—a cold, sensible, travelled, electioneering young gentleman, far better than his race. I was thought quite charming! "Adieu, dear Lady Morgan, and may you long continue the agreeable creature you are now!" The other day only, "the agreeable creature" was *toute au contraire!*

November 30th.—Met a poor starved beggar child, and gave him a penny. "Och, the Lord pour a blessing on your honour!" "And how does your poor mother live?" I said, among other things. "Och thin, by ating cowld victuals, marram!"

By-the-bye, this reminds me of a blessing I once received from an old beggar woman, to whom I had given a sixpence. "Och thin! the Lord bless yer sweet honour, and may every hair of yer head be a mould four, to light yer sowl to glory!" What an imaginative race they are, (!) would sixpence ever have stimulated an English beggar to such an invocation!

A note from Mrs. Hemans, endorsed by Lady Morgan, "she would and she would not."

The friendly relations of Mrs. Hemans with Lady Morgan were maintained to the last. Lady Morgan's high spirit delighted and attracted the more delicate and reserved lady.

Mrs. Hemans to Lady Morgan.

December 3rd, 1832.

DEAR LADY MORGAN,

I would have come to you *for pleasure* on Saturday evening, but nothing that is not brilliant ought to enter your boudoir, and my eyes and intellect grow so dim together as evening approaches, that I could only take the refuge of an *owl*, in the shade. To-morrow evening, not for business, but for pleasure, I will come if I can; but I must tell you how I am situated. A gentleman was engaged to pass the evening here, and I must either beg your leave to make him my escort, or give him his *congé* till another time. If neither of these expedients will do, you must again kindly excuse me. You are very good for including my little artist in your invitation; the last time I called upon you, I brought with me some of his drawings from the antique to show you; I will beg your acceptance of one, should you think it worth receiving, the next time I have the pleasure of seeing you.

Believe me,
Dear Lady Morgan,
Very truly yours,
FELICIA HEMANS.

December 6th.—So ends my hospitalities for the year 1832. The thousand details necessary for getting up a recherché dinner with few servants is Herculean labour, and, besides, I have to empty my room for space, and yesterday I had upholstery to put up myself, and pictures to move and change, and poor old Mrs. Casey *broke down* from nervousness (*or whiskey*) in the kitchen, and I had to dress *half* the dinner myself, which every body allowed was supreme, particularly my *matelote d'anguille*, and my *dinde farci à la daube!* It matters little how *great* dinners are dressed, but *small* ones should be *exquisite*, or not given at all.

To-morrow we dine with the gay young Vaughans in Merrion Square (he is brother to Lord Lisburne). We are to be few and merry. Last Monday we dined at the P——'s, and were many and dull. Society here is all bad: dearth of mind, and want of Europeanism everywhere, to say nothing of party faction and religious acrimony. Miserable country!

December 10.—Yesterday we were at an *amateur concert*, at the castle. Lord Anglesey and I fell to discourse as usual—politics and *badinage*. The Duke of Leinster played his "big fiddle," and looked happy and amiable, and after each act, pottered about, gathering together the music, settling lights, and, in short, enacting the part of "property man" in a theatrical orchestra *to the life*.

I had the pleasure of taking my two girls with me after a *long dispute* and *struggle* (and a *little intrigue*) with their mother *as usual*.

December 14*th*.—Dined last evening at Mr. Stanley's, the Secretary of State, Phœnix Park. A large official party. It would have been a heavy one, but I put my shoulder to the wheel, and away it went! It turned out a most joyous good humoured party. Stanley was sharp and *mordant*, though agreeable.

He said in the midst of a silence, with a half sneer on his face, "Oh, Lady Morgan, you are a great Irish historian, can you give me a census of the population of Ireland in the reign of Henry II."

I affected confusion, and said, "Well, no, Mr. Stanley, not accurately; but may I presume to ask *you* what is the census of the English people in the reign of William IV. ?"

CHAPTER XXII.

DRAMATIC SCENES AND SKETCHES—1833.

THE work on *France*, in 1829-30, was followed by *Dramatic Scenes and Sketches*, which were also published by Messrs. Saunders and Otley. Lady Morgan gave the work to them in the hope that it would prove some compensation for their disappointment about *France*, but they had not Colburn's genius for making books sell, and though the *Dramatic Scenes* are amongst Lady Morgan's best works, they had not the brilliant success which they deserved. The sum she received and the terms on which the work was published are not on record, but she retained the copyright for herself.

These *Dramatic Scenes and Sketches* are written in a very forcible and effective manner. They show the condition of Ireland as a country, and the state of the Irish peasantry, their sorrows and ignorance, the evil influence of agents and middlemen in the absenteeism of the landlords; the clashing pretensions of the High Protestant Church party with the priests, are excellently shown. The chief aim is to show the ignorance and misconception which prevailed in England of the real condition and necessities of the country; the difficulties, almost impossibilities, thrown in the way of Irish landlords wishing to do their duty and to see with their own eyes what measures of reform and relief were urgently needed. The first *Dramatic Sketch* is called Manor Sackville, and the dramatic form of scene and dialogue allows every shade of character and situation to pass as over a magic lantern. For vigorous delineation and dialogue, it excels her novels,—the form gave her free scope. The dramatic sketch of Manor Sackville is the longest and the most important. It gives a lively picture of Irish country life, an old Irish mansion unexpectedly visited by its proprietor, an enlightened and benevolent man, accompanied by his wife, an amiable, fine lady, and a party of fashionable friends from London. The politics, cliques, and condition of the country, from the Honourable and Reverend Dr. Polypus, rector of Newtown, down to Cornelius Brian, a leader of White Feet, with agents, tithe proctors, Catholic priests, &c., are all vividly described and put into action. The result is, a picture of Ireland as it then existed.

The Irish politics and grievances make rather heavy metal for a book of amusement, but it is enlivened with some of the best touches of Lady Morgan's Irish fun and humour. The other dramatic scenes are shorter, and are illustrations of different phases of English fashionable life.

Lady Morgan was peculiarly skilful in her delineations of English fashionable life. Her "great ladies" have all a *cachet* of belonging to the class for which they are intended; and there is, in all Lady Morgan's "fine ladies," an air of good breeding which distinguishes her fashionable scenes from the ordinary type of fashionable novels, and gives them all the air of scenes of real life. Although *Dramatic Scenes and Sketches* had not the high tide of success which attended the *O'Briens and O'Flaherties*, it is a work which deserved it.

Here is a letter from M. Prosper Merrimé.

The graceful turn of the original is lost in the less flexible power of an English translation; but the style of M. Merrimé has a charm of its own, which cannot be altogether disguised by any disadvantages.

M. Prosper Merrimé to Lady Morgan.

January 2nd, 1833.

I feel very guilty, Madame, for not having sooner replied to your charming letter, brought to me by Mr. Chapman. Believe, however, that although I may have been slow to thank you for it, I have not felt the less sensible of your kind remembrance. I could have wished to be able to go in person and lay my works at your feet, to beg that you would grant me at once your pardon for my idleness, and your protection to travel in the route of Erin, of which land you are the fairy. Unhappily, bonds which are neither of silk nor of gold retain me in Paris. I can scarcely leave it, even for a day, to breathe the fresh air of St. Germains or St. Cloud. For the last three months I have been a creature half a man, half an arm-chair, feeding upon *bulletins des lois*, gravely renewing solicitations, and laughing sometimes when alone at the strange administrative face which is the result!

Public affairs will, however, Madame, leave leisure to read your works upon the present state of Ireland. The form you have given to it confirms me in an opinion I already held, that true talent can apply itself to every species of literature, and that you are as sure to charm your readers by your dramas as by your romances or your travels. Accept, I beg, Madame, all my own congratulations, and permit me to be the interpreter of those of my countrymen who have not, like myself, the honour of knowing you, but which they would address to you if they had.

I beg you to recall me to the remembrance of Miss Clarke, and of Sir Charles Morgan, and pray except the expression of my respectful homage.

Pr. Merrime.

The following notes of good-humoured *badinage* explain themselves. It must have been a great relief to the thorny State kept by a lord-lieutenant to be treated occasionally like a natural human being. The joke about Cæsar alludes to a "command night" at the theatre, where the play had been very hazardous, from its allusions.

The Marquis of Anglesey to Lady Morgan.

[*No date.*]

DEAR LADY MORGAN,

I beg you to thank Mr. Bate *doubly* for me, as well for his having presented me with a portrait of my favourite boat, as for having sent it through your hands.

As you say he is an artist, may I not be permitted to remunerate him for his skill, and can you not help me to guess what will be acceptable?

But why quarrel with *Cæsar?* Cæsar *was* borne out by the results of last night. Cæsar took the bull by the horns, and he vanquished him. Depend upon it, it is the only *safe* way. See how the bull was tamed! He made no fight at all. But I must again defend Cesar from the imputation of *imprudence.* He really, strange to say, knew nothing of the gist of the piece. Knowing it, however, he could not have chosen better; he gave his enemy fair play—fought him, as it were, upon his own ground, and beat him.

Seriously, I never was more surprised than last night. I own I fully expected a most tumultuous uproar, and lo! all was good humour, loyalty, and almost *couleur de rose,* as I shall be when I get my *soirée.*

I remain,
Dear Lady Morgan,
Very faithfully yours,
ANGLESEY.

Lady Morgan to Lord Anglesey.

KILDARE STREET,
Wednesday.

Cæsar is a very dangerous person to engage with, whatever ground he takes! His *desperate pas de charge* is sure to be borne out by the consciousness of his old "*veni, vidi, vici;*" and "*aut Cæsar, aut nihil!*" turns out in the end, to be a very discreet determination; Cæsar must therefore (to borrow his *own favourite* image), "like the *bull* in the china shop, *have it all his own way.*" So much for Cæsar! Now for the Lord-Lieutenant.

Lady Morgan assures His Excellency that Mr. Bate will feel himself *overpaid* by an acceptance of his sketch of the Pearl, and by an approbation so flattering; to offer any other remuneration would wound rather than gratify the feelings of the venerable artist. Mr. Bate is an eminent *enameller,* and should His Excellency ever desire to bequeath to posterity one of the "*thousand and one*" beauties of his *own private collection,* after the manner of Charles II., or Louis XIV., some little order to *eternize* eyes that once *conquered* the *conqueror,* will *faire les délices* of one of the best artists in his line, that England has produced. With respect to the *couleur de rose* passage, in Lord Anglesey's note! Should it *really* be the intention of His Excellency to honour the *thatched roof of an Irish cabin* with his presence, the mistress is ready to *receive* him with that *hearty*
Cead mille falthae,

which he so well deserves from every Irish heart. It is, however, for *him* to *command* the evening. His Excellency's secretary mentioned last night, that every night in the ensuing week was taken, except that of *Monday next*, the 11th. On *that* or any other *evening*, Lady Morgan is sure to be "*at home*" to so illustrious a guest.

For this year, the only diary of any general interest was kept during her visit to London, and her sojourn at Brussels. It begins abruptly:

June 18.—Arrived in London on Monday 10th, by Liverpool, a prosperous passage of eleven hours. From Liverpool to Leamington, where we rested two days, the country one continued garden; no beggary, no poverty. It struck us that the face of the country was much improved since we last travelled this way. We found invitations waylaying us on our arrival.

June 24.—To-day had a visit from Madame Pasta, more naïve than ever; she told us she was near getting into prison at Naples, for singing out of *Tancredi, Cara Patria;* and she said orders were given to omit the word "liberta" in all her songs. Her happy temperament shows itself most in her tender affection for her mother and her daughter; she says that nothing, neither fame nor money, consoles her for their absence.

Bellini came in, and Pasta, Bellini, and José went through one act of his *Norma*. Bellini was charmed with José's voice.

I had a curious scene yesterday: Bentley and Rees

(of the long firm, Longman & Co.), at the same time, one in the back, the other in the front drawing-room. Each came to negotiate about my next book; Bentley is to have it.

Pasta and I were disputing to-day about reputations, I spoke of her *Gloire*, she said, "*Gloire passagère*, it is here to-day and gone to-morrow, your's endures." I said, "*Je voudrais bien troquer mes chances avec la posterité, pour la certitude de vôtre influence avec les contemporains*."

June 28.—To-day, took my girls to Lord Grosvenor's gallery. At night we went to a literary party at Lady Charleville's. Campbell, the poet, said to me, "I am copying out my *Life of Mrs. Siddons*, for which I am to get a price, which, if any bookseller had offered me a few years back, I would have flung in his face, and the MS. into the fire."

The party at Lady Cork's had some curious contrasts. There was Lady Charleville herself, the centre of a circle in her great chair. Lady Dacre, author of —everything; plays, poems, novels, &c., &c. Lady Charlotte Campbell, author of *Conduct is Fate*. Miss Jane Porter (*Thaddeus of Warsaw*), cold as ever, though the muse of tragedy in appearance. Mrs. Bulwer Lytton, the muse of comedy. Lady Stepney, author of the *New Road to Ruin*; lots of lay men and women, a crowd of saints and sinners. The men were still more odd. Sir Charles Wetherell, Prince Cinitelli, D'Israeli, who run off as I skipped in, some other remarkables, and one young man, Lord Oxmantown, an impersonation of a "Committee of the House."

July 1.—Pasta and Bellini jumped out of a hackney-coach at our door to-day, with a roll of music in their hands,—it was the score of the *Norma*, they came, Pasta said, from the second rehearsal. Bellini scolded his great pupil like a *petite pensionnaire*.

July 6.—Days later. Till this morning I have not had a moment to spare to fill up my journal. What a loss! Pleasure, business, folly, literature, fashion! Pasta often calls on us; this is her own account of herself. "I was a *petite demoiselle*, playing and singing in the amateur theatre at Milan. Pasta and I played the Prince and Princess di Jovati, fell in love, and married. Paer, who heard us, or one of us, wrote to us to come to Paris, and play in the theatre of Madame Caladoni. I so wished to travel,* *que j'aurais allé même à l'Enfer! mes parens étaient desolés!* I went on the stage, and was engaged for London: came out in *Télémaque*. I was so ashamed at showing my legs! Instead of minding my singing, I was always trying to hide my legs. I failed!"

"Do you," I asked, "transport yourself into your part?" "*Oui, après les premières lignes. Je commence toujours en Giuditta* (mon nom) *mais je finis toujours en Medea ou Norma!*"

July 14.—I had a peep at club life,—the Travellers. It is the perfection of domestic life! Every comfort at once suggested and supplied; good reasons for not marrying! Women must get up to this point, or they

* Mr. Sterling, of the *Times*, told me, that when Pasta was playing Cherubino, fifteen years ago, in London, she could not procure an order for a friend to the pit!

will only be considered as burthens. Some of the young husbands of the handsomest wives live at their clubs.

Went to see the hydro-oxygen microscope, which has extinguished the solar light. It shows the objects in a drop of water magnified 800,000 times. The wonders of the microscopic world illustrate all the base passions of the whole great system. The animalcules tear each other to pieces, and are agitated by all the worst passions; they are of monstrous and disgusting forms, the water devil, the water lion, with their great heads, and the strange motions of others, are all images of crime and weakness; to illustrate the same state by this exhibition, would be a sermon and a bore; to illustrate the world by the microscope would be an epigram.

July 16.—Amongst the notabilities who have sought us out, are Gabussi and Vaccai, the composers, and Taglioni, *la déesse de la danse,* she was brought to us by her husband, who is the son of a peer of France, and ex-page to Bonaparte. She was quiet, lady-like, and simple, her dress elegant, but simple. She told me her father was *maître de ballet,* and had early instructed her; but she had so little vocation, that when she came to Paris, she had no hope of success. Of her habits of life, she said, she lived temperately, dining on plain roasts, at three o'clock, never sleeping after dinner, nor taking anything till after her exertions at the theatre were over, then, she supped on tea. She practices two or three hours a-day. She said that the moment force was introduced in dancing, grace vanished; her rule was never to make an effort, but to give herself up to nature, and the great delight she had in dancing. She said she never was so happy as when dancing. The moment she comes off the stage her ancles are wrapped in woollen socks, and when she goes home her feet are bathed in arrow-root water.

Last Monday we went to the British Institution, a very mixed society, everybody coming to be seen, and nobody to see the pictures.

After the gallery, we went to a select *soirée* at Lady Cork's. All dukes, duchesses, lords, ladies, and bores; the dresses were bad. D'Israeli shuffled along with his ivory cane, like the ghost in *Hamlet*, and the only amusing thing was a little boy from Ireland, who attacked us all at the door.

July 29.—Yesterday we went to the House of Lords to hear the last debate on the Church Temporalities Bill. We sat in the Peeress's box. The first thing that struck me, was the theatrical set out of the place. The stage below, the gallery above, the dropping in of the actors. To the right from the gallery, in the centre of the lower bench, sat the Dukes of Wellington, Cumberland, Newcastle, and Lord Winchelsea; behind them, Lord Ellenborough, Lord Wicklow, Lord Aberdeen; opposite were Lord Grey, the Duke of Rutland; opposite to us, on the woolsack, sat Lord Brougham, bound up like an Egyptian mummy, his countenance as impassible as Talleyrand's. When a note was presented to him he drew his hands out of his sleeves, in which they were folded, and used glasses. The debate opened with the Duke of Newcastle, who stuttered, stammered, and looked frightened. Lord Winchester followed, who roared and bellowed; he addressed the Bishop of London, whose manner, in reply, was cold, collected, but quite as mad; no eloquence, wit, energy, or originality. Lord Eldon, an old state-property actor, with a conventional manner; his speech was gag—all referred to himself; he was of the people once—he was still of the people, though now he was a peer of the realm! He had filled the woolsack for twenty years; he respected and admired the Duke, but he was angry with him for emancipating the Catholics; he would soon appear before the throne of Heaven (and he took out his blue pocket-handkerchief and wept through the rest of his speech); *he* must soon die; but dying, he foresaw the fall of that glorious assembly; if the bill passed, it must be swept away, it could not last, except on the stability of compacts (for compacts are made for man, not man for compacts) &c. &c. The whole speech, that of an old rogue, but a very good actor. "Pity the sorrows of a poor old man."

In the box with us was the Duchess of Richmond, who never misses a debate. She had been here since five o'clock, and desired her daughter to keep her place when she went home for an hour to meet the Duke of Gloucester; the box holds twenty-five.

The Duke of Wellington's manner and matter were equally bad. He spoke so low and indistinct, I scarcely heard him. The effect produced by these scenes was, the error of erecting a barrier against progress by giving sanction to an assembly, composed principally of old and infirm men. The number of young men is so small as to make every man under fifty conspicuous. Nearly all, as I looked down, seemed bald; many were infirm, and walked with an arm—Lord Holland was wheeled in; they were all men without fathers—consequently, of a certain age. Lord Ellenborough, and two or three others of his standing, represented the middle-aged.

Monday.—Last night, at Mr. Perry's, son of the editor of the *Morning Chronicle.* House after Louis XIV. style; company, Fonblanque, of the *Examiner;* Kenny, the dramatist, &c., &c. The manner of all the men cold and languid; reserve, shyness, and *morgue* make up the character and manners of English society.

Mrs. Bulwer Lytton, handsome, insolent, and unamiable, to judge by her style and manners; she, and all the *demi-esprits,* looked daggers at *me;* not one of them have called on me, and in society they get out of my way. How differently I should behave to them if they came to Ireland!

July 31.—Last night an agreeable party at the Countess of Montalembert's. Renewed my acquaintance with the once famous Lady Clare; Lady Dudley Stuart (Lucien Bonaparte's daughter), in the most extravagant of dresses; but *très aimable.* That egregious coxcomb, Disraeli, was there, too—outraging the privilege a young man has of being absurd.

August 4.—We have had a cordial visit from Captain Marryatt—there had been a coldness since we withdrew from the *Metropolitan.* After dinner, we lounged in the Park, and then took a walk, then home to dress for Lady Cork's, where we met and chatted with all sorts of old acquaintances, Lady Marybrough, Lady Darlington, Lady Augusta Paulet, Rogers the poet, Lady Davy, Lady Caledon, &c.; the Duchess of Cleveland is a very pleasant woman, full of spirit and spirits. It was curious to see that handsome head encircled with diamonds, which first attracted notice under a basket of onions and salad. She was a garden girl, attending the London markets. What a romance was here!

Rogers said, that Moore's book *The Gentleman in Search of a Religion*, was a failure, and that Moore was much disappointed, though he did not expect a very brilliant success.

Yesterday Bellini and Gabussi came, and sang and played like angels. Lucien Bonaparte came in as they were singing—

"O bella Italia che porte tre color,
Sei bianca e rossa e Verde com 'un fiore!"

Lucien exhibited a supressed emotion that was very touching. How honest and clever he is! He said, what I have often preached, "nations that *deserve* to be free, *are* free!" He blamed Lafayette in the late events of France—elect a Bourbon to the throne—and talk of the voice of the people in this election! The people who forget and who bled, were *consulted*, but betrayed. We talked of Ireland. I said, "The Irish have no idea of liberty, they want a king of their own. Come and present yourself, and I will promise you a crown." He laughed, but said, "Point de couronne, point de couronne."

I said "Voilà donc encore une couronne que vous refusez!"

It is well known that he did refuse a crown at the hands of his brother. He and his brother Joseph have only just enough to live upon; Lucien is lodging in a little bit of a house in Devonshire Street (No. 50); Joseph has a *toute petite campagne*, where he lives with his daughter, whom he insists on calling la Princesse Charlotte.

Lady Cork has just written to beg I will name a day to meet the ex-majesties of Spain at dinner! I have been obliged to refuse, as we are off to Belgium this month. What strange things do come to pass in this tragical fever called life!

I am always studying eminent persons. Women above all—eminent no matter for what, De Stäel, or Taglioni, *c'est égal*. Talking with Pasta the other day, I cross-questioned her about her diet. I said, " I remember, one night, being with you in your dressing-room when you had just come off the stage in your highest wrought scene, (the quartetta 'Come o Nimé,') your woman had a bit of cold roast beef ready to put into your mouth, and some porter."

"Ah si," was her reply, "mais je ne prends plus la viande—et pour le porter, I take it half-and-half." This bit of London slang, from the lips of Medea, and in her sweet broken English, had the oddest effect imaginable.

Saturday.—Yesterday was a curious day. I went

with dear Lady Charleville and Mrs. Marley to see some original pictures of Nell Gwynne, at the Duke of St. Albans. The Duchess received us in a superb morning room; her dress was ridiculously fine for the morning—rich white silk trimmed with white lace; a quantity of gold chains, bracelets, &c. She had black ringlets, surmounted by a black lace veil, which fell over on one side. She is a coarse, full-blown, dark-complexioned woman, about fifty. The last time I saw her, was as Miss Mellon, in the *Honey Moon*, when I came over to London to sell my *Wild Irish Girl*. She was then a model of beauty, symmetry, and grace. As I stared at her now, surrounded by ducal coronets, even on her footstools, the pretty poem of *Le Tu, et le Vous*, of Voltaire, came into my head. She accompanied us to her dressing-room, where she showed us two pictures of Nell Gwynne, not original; the one, a beautiful woman wearing a jewelled carcanet, by Sir P. Lely, a copy of an original in the possession of Mr. Calcraft, the Duchess believed; the other, was a miserable thing in the dressing-room.

The Temple and the Idol, were the most interesting things to me; the magnificence and taste of all the mirrors, gilding, pictures, furniture—the profusion of flowers, and, above all, the attending priestesses, the abigails, all over-dressed and ugly, such as any young Duke might be trusted with. The robust Duchess complained all the time of ill health, and said she would hand us over to her housekeeper after she had shown us over the ground-floor.

In the Duke's sitting-room, she pointed out a picture of herself as Miss Mellon, in Mrs. Page—" Very beautiful, done," said she, " for my dear Mr. Coutts, and the Duke will hang it up, you see, as a match for his father, the late Duke, and here is a bust of Mr. Coutts; you will see a statue of him up stairs," and so we did, at the head of the drawing-room—an awful figure! We were shown by the housekeeper into her Grace's second dining-room, almost as magnificent as her first. She said her Grace dressed here in the morning and below in the evening, to save her the trouble of going up stairs. I was thinking of the Polly Peachum Duchess of Bolton, and Nell Gwynne, and her descendant marrying another Nell Gwynne. The whole of this day was amusing. I dined at Lord Charleville's, the company, the old Tory Duchess of Richmond, enjoying the honours founded by Mademoiselle de Querouille (Duchess of Portsmouth), Sir Charles Wetherell, lovely Lady Antrim, young Lord Tullamore and his beautiful wife. After dinner went to a dance with my girls.

August 15, *Monday.*—Yesterday was curious and interesting; people coming to take leave of us. We had at the same moment, Moore, Madame Pasta, Bellini, Gabussi. And now for writing letters, apologies, &c., and off to-morrow for the Rhine.

Monday night.—The eve of our departure for the Rhine. All packed up and ready for the Tower stairs except my stomach. Oh, the horrible sea, and steam-packet!

Tuesday morning, 6 *o'clock.*—Half inclined not to go. London, hot rooms, and late hours have nearly killed me, and yet there is but one place in the world, and that is—dear London!

Everybody has been up the Rhine; and everything worthy of note about Antwerp, Liege, and Cologne, has been written, and may be read in the guide book; but Brussels, at that time, fresh from its revolutions, has a charm that cannot be repeated. We may, therefore, give a few patches from the diary kept during her sojourn in Brussels after they had finished their tour.

September 7th.—After our charming tour through Belgium, here we are settled for some little time. We had scarcely arrived when the French ambassador and his lovely young wife (the *La Tour Maubourgs*) and her charming sister and brother-in-law, Count and Countess D'Oraison came in what they called *conspiration*, to lay violent hands and detain us here, and we, nothing loath, have consented,—my two girls in the third heaven!

Received visits from Monsieur and Madame Engler. The Frekes, Seymours, Dr. Bowring and Count Hompèche. The latter dined at the *table d'hôte* with us, and sat beside me, and had we not fun! An English family at the *table d'hôte impayable*. Mr. J—— turned up his nose at the French wines, "sour stuff, monsieurs," and called for brandy and water. "I'll lay you a cheney tea pot," said he, "they have no melted butter for the salmon."

Thursday—Dined yesterday at the Engler's, a magnificent dinner, and music in the evening, met and chatted a good deal with the Minister of the Interior, Monsieur Rogier, sensible, modest, and high-minded. He is to come and see us to-morrow.

Thursday 15.—What a *levée* to-day of all nations!

Foreigners complain here that there is no society, each *menage* suffices to itself, and when amusement is to be sought, it is bought ready made. The lower orders fly to their cabarets in the environs, the middle class have their *cafés* and *estaminets*, and the highest rank go to their box at the opera; and this with the diversity of a ball in the season and the court ceremonies makes up the whole of their social existence, (very like our own), but there is no house open to receive either morning or evening visits, as there are in Paris. There is no intellectual society as in England; there is no material for it. The women are sedentary and silent, domestic and *devote*, and resemble the mass of our female English society, but without their habits of intellectual cultivation, which brings ease, grace, and courtesy along with it.

September 17.—We shall have to leave this hotel, as it is *all taken* for the great *fêtes*.

September 18.—Hardly got into our pretty apartments in the Rue de la Regence (with our books, flowers, piano, drawings, &c., &c.), when enter Lady Clare, and Lady Isabella Fitzgibbons, and Sir Robert Adair. What a pleasant chat of times and people, past and present! How they recall the bright days of the Priory to me!

September 18.—We dined yesterday at the Palace; great simplicity, with just as much splendour as any nobleman of good taste and wealth might indulge in, but nothing more. The Queen—young, fair, simple, and more than courteous—reminds me of our English girls of rank: a little shy and very graceful, but nothing of the *morgue* of our belles of quality. I looked about me for a ribbon. I spied a gentleman in black, with the broadest blue scarf from shoulder to flank. I thought he represented some ancient order of chivalry, *pas du tout*. It was an *English knight* of the Guelphic Order. The Grand Maréchal, a very agreeable Count, asked me what Order that was. I could not help saying, *L'ordre de tout bête*. Strange to say, here was a royal company of forty persons; there was not one Prince amongst them. There was all the intellect and manhood of the present administration. The Belgian Lafayette, Baron De Hoogoorst, the brave, the patriotic commander of the National Guard; there was Charles Rogier, the Minister of the Interior, who, in the most awful moment of political fermentation at the time of the revolution, flung himself into the very gap of anarchy, and established that character of dauntless devotedness to a great cause which may be deemed the chivalry of politics; Monsieur Le Beau, Ministre de Justice, the prose, as Rogier is the poetry of the revolution; Monsieur Northomel, Secretary-General des Affaires Etrangers, with countenance full of intellectual fire, *pensante et instruit;* not one dandy or dunce amongst them. Could one say as much for a diplomatic table of London? In short, I was better pleased with this royal dinner than with anything royal I have ever yet assisted at. "Il faut avoué que votre Roi est le plus grand Roi du monde," said I to my neighbour; "S'il n'est pas, il le doit être," said he.

September 20.—What an odd coincidence. We had last night nearly the whole of the last Provisional Government of the Belgian Revolution, with the addition of Colonel Prozinski, Mr. White, author of *The King's Own*, the two De Brouckers, Henri et Charles, Quételet, the Royal Astronomer, Jullien, the Orator of the Opposition, Sir Robert Adair, our Ambassador, and the dear, charming, La Tour Maubourgs. The evening was amusing. I had also Van Hullan, the accomplished author of an historical tract of the *Trouble Belgique* in 1718; he is the type of the character and national feelings of the Belgian youth, and one among the many illustrations of the beneficial change in the character of a people effected by the removal of oppressive and anti-national institutions.

September 26.—A week of carnival festivities. The Concert d'Harmonie à la Place Royal, by six hundred musicians, consisting of the corps of the army, with an audience of nearly ten thousand persons in front of the beautiful Hotel de Ville,—really one of the most imposing sights I have ever seen. In front was inclosed a space for the Ministers, the Deputies, and the Senate. The windows and balconies belonging to the houses and hotels all round filled with elegantly-dressed women. To the right, in a balcony window, sat the King and Queen and officers of state. The royal party were received by the music of the " Marscillaise," mingled with the "Brabançon." There was no loud enthusiasm, for these people now repose upon their past emotions, and their recollection of their past hard-won liberties is now enjoyed by them in sober satisfaction, and the full consciousness of their happiness suffices them. The beautiful music elicited more applause than any other occurrence of the day. Alas! the rain fell in torrents before it was over, and Bruxelles presented a canopy of umbrellas which had the most extraordinary effect.

September 28.—The races went on yesterday in spite of the rain; rather a laughable business, men and horses stuck in the mud, and one poor horse broke his back, and the jockey, I fear, much hurt. These are happy times when events are greater than the men that are placed at their head. It is something to represent the first state that has thrown off its slavery. The immense masses of opinion now afloat upon the surface of the political society of Belgium forced into collusion by the ferment and kicking against each other. It requires a cool head and a firm hand to wield the sceptre, and Leopold seems to have both, and has a fine career before him. On the king's visit to Verviers, he said to the bourgmestre, "Qu'il protegerait toujours l'industrie." "Sire," replied the burgomaster, "il n'y en est pas besoin ça va bien comme ça." The king laughed much at the *naïveté* of this good fellow," and this is the essence of all the philosophy of commerce—*laissez nous faire*.

October.—Just returned to London, and St. James' Street, after the most delightful tour up the Rhine that ever was made. A day or two for seeing friends, and a few visits, and then—off for wretched Dublin!

Lady Morgan, who had been very kind to Madame Belzoni, as to all classes of foreigners, received from her at this time a curious present.

Madame Belzoni to Lady Morgan.

September 25th, 1833.

DEAR LADY MORGAN,

On my arrival at Jerusalem, 1808, the Temple of Solomon was then under repair, and nearly finished. The Turks, whenever they require any work of importance done, send out an order to arrest such Christian workmen as may be required for the undertaking, paying them with the greatest liberality; so much so, that they frequently return to their homes with a little fortune. Living in the same quarter, I naturally went with them. Among those whom I was acquainted with, were an old man and woman, whose son was employed as Scrivener at the temple, a place of some importance. For his particular privilege and emolument, an old door of cedar was given him; this door had been placed on the same site that tradition reputes that our blessed Saviour used to pass through.

The Turks hold in the greatest veneration all places that are sacred to our Saviour, *excepting the Sepulchre;* considering *Christ* as a spirit, consequently a spirit could not be crucified, and that it was the body of Judas that had been taken into the *Sepulchre*, of course they ridicule the Christians for worshipping there. I am ashamed of this *preamble* about nothing, but the insignificancy of the article required it. The accompanying cross was made out of *that door*, and it received the benediction in the holy *Sepulchre*, under my own sight. Will Lady Morgan accept my *offering of thanks*, poor as it *is*.

S. BELZONI.

PS.—The basket plate was made above the first cataract of the Nile, *Nubia*. Fruit of the *date tree*, *the inside is dissolved, and made into beads.*

The spoon that I bought in grand *Cairo*, 1837, which the grand Turk's people eat their rice with.

Forgive, dear Lady Morgan, the insignificant offerings of a *human heart*. I have often longed to see you—that wish is at last gratified. In 1822, I passed the Simplon, two days after you had passed, and was much mortified at having missed seeing one who had charmed me so often.

Again, we return to the diary:—

December 24.—We returned to Ireland the middle of October, after our most delightful, gratifying, and interesting visit to the Continent, but I had not the heart to resume the thread of my chronicles till this day, and now only because the year is winding up, and I am going away for a time. During my charming June and July in London, I kept a very rough outline of what I was about, and whom I saw (and whom I did *not* see who was worth seeing)! My principal impressions are in my head, for I had no intention of ever writing a journey again till I was urged to do it by all parties and classes in Brussels. On my return to this dreary city, my house full of dirty, idle, loitering workmen, I set to work myself, hurried them through theirs, and got ill, and went to recover with my dear friends at Malahide, whose castle is always open to us. On my return, settled in to write, in spite of some pleasant intentions. We have dined with the Littletons; Mr. Littleton, his lovely wife and daughters. He is in politics honest, frank, and straightforward, but new. I have had various and curious conversations with him, I wish I had written them down.

Contrary to our intentions, we accepted an invitation from Sir Thomas and Lady Chapman, for the sake of my dear girls, who were included. A most joyous and agreeable fortnight. Think of their being *afraid* of asking *me* to their superb castle, lest I should be *ennuyée* with their society, and doing the honours by me as if I were a little queen! Talking with Lady Chapman the other day, on the radical liberalism of her three sons and two nephews (the Tighes), I said, laughingly, "With a Tory father, a Tory uncle, an aristocratic mother, how comes it that all your young men, bred up in absolution, should be such liberals! who converted them?" She smiled, and said, "Why, then, to tell the truth, it was your Ladyship." "I? Why, I have talked so little to them since they grew up." "You have talked enough, and written more than enough to make them what they are!" It is thus we women, the secret tribunal of society, can mine and countermine.

We returned to town on Saturday, 21st, and dined with Mr. Wallace, my old lover, M.P. for Carlow. I sat at dinner between the Provost and the Secretary of State, Mr. Littleton. I attacked the Provost's college wall on one side (as we are struggling to have it down to open narrow Nassau Street), and *other* walls on the other side. I took the opportunity of bringing forward the honest and the clever, who never make their way; I always do this when I get beside the great and influential. I spoke of Dr. Macarthy, the honest and philosophical, and I put a spoke in the wheel of the College of Surgeons, the jobbing, exclusive, monopolising College of Surgeons. When we got upon O'Connell, I said, "Listen to a foolish woman's prophecy. O'Connell is veering towards you, because, just now he is losing hold on the people, and the rent for the time has failed. If you meet him a step he will entangle you, perhaps betray you; at all events, he will make a merit of it in the eyes of his dupes."

MR. LITTLETON. "But do you not think he will be worth having?"

"Yes; if you can catch him and *keep* him, but he has an Irish *physical* talent none of you can cope with, *subtlety*. The eel is a lump of lead compared with O'Connell, he has no one fixed principle; the end, with him, consecrates the means, and *that* end is—O'Connell, the beginning and end of all things." Mr. Littleton was silent, and then asked me if I were pleased with the batch of commissionerships he had given away.

I said "yes, if they are to get nothing." He said, "Nothing but the honour; they are all rich men."

Christmas Eve.—Eating, drinking, flirting, and reading. I must register an odd thought. The Irish destiny is between Bedlam and a jail; but I won't pursue it. So ends my journal of 1833. How much I have felt, suffered, enjoyed, seen, and heard in that year!!

CHAPTER XXIII.

THE BEGUINE—1834.

The diary for 1834 begins early in January.

PORTRAN, *January 5th.*—Here we are with our friend the honourable, uncompromising M.P. for Dublin, George Evans, the butt and victim of all O'Connell's hatred, malice, and calumny, because he will not crawl after him, and resists his repeal. Mrs. Evans is the sister of Sir Henry Parnell, and daughter to the late Irish Chancellor of the Exchequer; she is a first-rate woman, but, perhaps, too ambitious about her husband's parliamentary career. They are both excellent, and I always enjoy my sea-girt dwelling; in spite of the wind howling without, all within is peace, comfort, and good cheer; by-the-bye, à propos to the latter, they possess the first cook in Europe.

KILDARE STREET, *January 9th.*—Came into town to dine at Lord Wellesley's. Had some chat with the Viceroy, the Vice Queen; the Duke of Leinster, and the Littletons were of the party. I was congratulated on the approaching marriage of my dear niece, Sydney, which gives us all great satisfaction.

After this came other dinners and parties, too numerous to specify.

February 14th.—I had a little musical soirée last night. The last time my three girls may, perhaps, ever sing together, for Sydney is to be married next week, and then off to England. Vaccai sang with them; he is a charming composer.

February 17th.—I am so busy with other people's affairs, Miss O'Keefe, Madame Belzoni, Vaccai,—writing my new book, and Sydney's marriage, and letters and felicitations, that I have not a moment to give to journalising. Lord Cloncurry has lent Sydney Lawrence his villa of Maritimo till they go to England.

February 21st.—I am like Lady Teazle, "drawing patterns for ruffles; I shall never have materials to make up," for here are two fine receipts just as I have given up giving dinners! The reason I am up to my eyes in fuss, is that I am so occupied with Sydney's marriage, and my new work on Belgium, of which I can make nothing; the fault is in me, and not in my subject, which is fine. I am living without servants; oh, would that I could live for ever without those impersonations of whiskey, the Irish servants; *ce chapitre là* would take a volume, the whole history of the country is concerned in it,—priests and bad government!

Poor Miss O'Keefe! her father's book has just come in; what feebleness, but what amiable feeling! She quotes my account of him, which I sent to all the papers, to try and get a subscription, but all in vain.

I have had to begin my *Belgium* all over again on a new plan. I have now made up my mind to make a Belgian novel of my materials, instead of a history; my heroine shall be a *Béguine*.

The feebleness of present men and present times is fully illustrated by the fuss and agitation in which Lords and Commons are thrown by discovering men to be rogues whom nobody ever suspected of being honest.

February 28.—Just had a visit from old, queer, Weld Hartstronge—a flirtation of near twenty years' standing; *ma foi*, Time has left him as quizzical as Nature intended him to be! His uncle, Sir Harry Hartstronge, was the Protestant gentleman who knocked the Catholic petition over the bar of the House of Commons some forty years back. This little Parliamentary anecdote would be a *floorer* to Mr. O'Connell's raving for the repeal—such was the Irish House of Commons! Would any one dare to do this in the Imperial Parliament? My friend, Weld Hartstronge, is author of a large portion of those books " that ne'er were read;" but he is a worthy man, a great antiquary, and my walking Encyclopædia.

May 24.—Half an hour back, writing hard at my *Béguine*, the bright sunshine drew me with my watering-pot to the balcony; a thundering knock at the door drove me in—somebody had entered the study. I went down. It was Cuthbert of Altadore.

"I am come," said he, "to tell you—that the news has arrived of—in short—Lafayette is dead!!"

Alas! our last, best tie to France is broken; only aged 76; he would have had some bright years yet before him but for that *one* false step—the restoration of the Bourbons; his death-blow came from that.

May 25.—My dear Francis Crossley arrived from India, *viâ* China; the same friend he ever was—kind, gentle, and devoted. He dines with us to-morrow, and all my own dear family.

June 20.—Malahide Castle; busy all day writing my *Béguine*. Delicious air breathing on me, and beautiful scenery. Just finished a scene—the basse Ville de Bruxelles, the *atélier* of a poor young female artiste. I took the idea from my visit to Fé nie Corr, the young Belgian artist. Rogier, the Minister of the Interior, carried me off one morning to see an old *délabrée* house—pretty much as I have described it —and as we waited for the young struggling *artiste* in her studio, I was struck by its dreariness and picturesque desolation.

My dearest Morgan works with me at this arduous novel—copies and corrects whilst I throw off the proof impressions; but I would rather he walked on the seashore, which now gleams so brightly before me; but he won't. Alas! inertness is his malady.

I have received a letter about the copyright of my ballad of *Kate Kearney*. Somebody wants to publish it afresh. She certainly would be an old woman by this time, if women and heroines had not an escape from old age in immortality.

The Duke of Wellington has been made Chancellor of Oxford. Our Archbishop of Dublin demanded an audience of Lord Wellesley. "I come to demand a troop of horse, my Lord." "For whom?" "For myself." "Oh, I see!"

Sir Charles Morgan was the physician to the Marshalsea, an office which Government had the intention of abolishing at this time. Sir Charles and Lady Morgan naturally expected the compensation usually granted to those who hold a Government appointment believed to be permanent. Their intimacy with persons high in rank and office, was of little practical value to them. As Lady Morgan said herself, they never asked for anything and never received anything.

Mr. Lyttleton, Secretary to the Treasury, wrote to Lady Morgan on the subject.

II. Lyttleton to Lady Morgan.

TREASURY,
December 7, 1834.

MY DEAR LADY MORGAN,

I cannot conceive it possible that the change in the Government can in any manner affect Sir Charles Morgan's claim for compensation for the loss of his office. His having bought it cannot be considered by the Treasury. But his removal will afford the Government an opportunity of making a very economical arrangement in the Medical Department of the

Marshalsea, which will far more than cover any compensation he would expect. His loss, therefore, ought to be liberally considered.

I have not an accurate recollection of the state in which the correspondence with the Treasury on this subject was left to me. When the new Government is organised, I advise Sir Charles to write to Sir W. Gosset to urge dispatch in the settlement of his compensation. The Treasury is slow; is difficult to manage; it is like the hole of a till—it takes in money easily, but requires long fingers to draw it out again.

What do you mean by abusing us miserable servants out of place? When I was in the service of His Majesty, you never asked me for any of the good things from his table. Sir Charles was not considered a candidate for a seat in any of the Commissions, or I should willingly have submitted his claim to the favourable consideration of the Lord-Lieutenant, when a fair opportunity of serving him might have offered.

I never could make out what was meant by the often-repeated charge of the Irish Government forgetting its friends. A Mr. Glasscock, a Tory, was deprived of his office of patentee of first fruits by the Church Act of 1832. Lord Grey, in the House of Lords, promised him the compensation of the first vacant equivalent office. Can you tell me of any other Tory promoted during my short reign? It is possible there might have been one or two Tories in Whig guise who crept into favour, and imposed on the Government. But I believe we were tolerably wary. I admit we did not go far enough in depriving enemies in

power of ill-gotten pelf. We left whips in the hands
of our enemies; and they used them to scourge us
with, knowing we dared not take them from them.

You are very partial, but not unjust to Mrs. Lyttleton, who always makes sunshine wherever she goes.
We are here till Parliament meets, when we shall
hope to renew our acquaintance with you in town.
We are, meantime, all impatience to see your new
work,

    I remain, dear Lady Morgan,
      Very sincerely yours,
        H. LYTTLETON.

Towards the close of 1834, Lady Morgan finished
her Belgian novel called the *Princess, or the Béguine.*
It was published by Mr. Bentley, of New Burlington
Street. She did not gain so much by it as by her former
novels. The sum she received was £350 for the first
edition. It is an admirable novel. Its main intention
was to interest the public in the new kingdom of Belgium, and to give a knowledge of the question and of
the conditions that had led to it. She began the work
as a history; but finding it dull to write, and still more
dull to read, she threw up that design and began it
again as a novel, which was as bright and sparkling as
any of its Irish predecessors. The pictures of English
fashionable life, as it existed at that period, are vivid,
and wonderfully graphic. The characters are all drawn
from the life, and would be easily recognisable by anyone conversant with the men and women of the time;
but though the characters are portraits, the circum-

stances and incidents are fictitious, sketched in to suit the story. The descriptions of the city of Brussels—its antiquities, pictures, historical recollections—are brilliant and masterly, but they interrupt the story. The chief personages of the revolution are historical portraits of great force and spirit. The politics of the time—the state of public feeling—the real condition of things in the kingdom of Brussels—are given with the same enthusiasm and vigour which she had thrown into her Irish stories. She used up some of the materials she had collected for a life of Rubens, and they are worked in with much skill. Those desiring a picturesque guide to Brussels should read *The Béguine;* and it is a novel as entertaining as though it had been written for no other purpose than to adorn the idleness and beguile the *ennui* of *des gens peu amusables*. Lady Morgan always kept to the same type of character for heroines, the heroine being one who has, by the skilful exercise of common sense, risen to a high position in the world,

CHAPTER XXIV.

CHELTENHAM AND LONDON—1835.

AT the beginning of 1835, Sir Charles and Lady Morgan and one of their nieces went to Cheltenham, where they remained some time. The record of her sojourn there is slight; but the following extracts from her diary, and a few letters, indicate the chief events of this period.

January 8.—This place is the grand asylum of mediocrity—the Paradise of old women—the Olympus of old men—the resort of the refuse of all societies: viz., the dull, the old, sickly, or tiresome; and yet it has its aristocracy!

Well, with all this, we have found a few with whom it is pleasant to live, and with them we live a great deal. The dear, old, agreeable, and cordial Corry's—James Corry, once the Coryphœus of the Kilkenny theatricals. They have given up Ireland, like others, and come to live in a pretty cottage here; our other most agreeable, but new acquaintances, the family at

Beaufort House, Sir George and Lady Whitmore, and their most agreeable family, are quite after my own heart. *She,* unique in her way, has lived thirty years in Italy—a divine musician, and full of genius; her son Edmond, a charming little lazzaroni of sixteen, and my *devoué cavalier*—my darling Olivia such a favourite with them all.

January 10.—Moore, talking to Corry on the Whigs having done nothing for him, said of Lord Holland, Lansdowne, and Lord John Russell, "I had no reason to expect it; I live upon equal terms with Lansdowne, and when he is at Bowood I dine there constantly; now there is Macaulay, Lansdowne gave him a place of two or three thousand pounds a year, and never asked him to dinner once. These great men seek people in different ways, and for different purposes. I am quite contented."

And so he is. This is so Irish, and so much an affair of temperament, that there is no arguing about it. Moore is an epitome of genuine Irish character, feeling, fancy, genius, and personal vanity overwhelming all—I know him well.

Last night we had some charming music at the Whitmore's—my little Olivia sang divinely; but the dowagers and their turbans were too much for me.

Lady Charleville has one of the finest minds that ever took a wrong direction. The ingenuity with which she argues on false principles, the eloquence with which she does the honours of error, are curious; but if you *force* her to step out of the track in which her position has placed her, as a great lady, reared in the bosom of high Toryism, she is amazed, bewildered, but admires the new doctrines she fears, and it is thus she listens to and bears with me.

A letter from Sir Henry Hardinge to my husband about the compensation for his office. Nothing definite.

Sir H. Hardinge to Sir C. Morgan.

CASTLE, DUBLIN,
February 10, 1835.

DEAR SIR CHARLES,

I have had some correspondence with the Treasury on your subject, and was in hopes to have induced them to have made a more desirable arrangement. They adhere, however, to that of their predecessors, and when I return to London, which I do this day, you shall hear from me officially; the exact amount of the retiring pension not having been as yet communicated. The division shall be expedited without delay.

I hope Lady Morgan enjoys the fine air of Cheltenham, and that her unrivalled talents are employed in amusing and instructing all classes and ages.

I am going to see Lady Clarke. I beg to offer my best regards to Lady Morgan, and am, my dear Sir Charles,

Yours very truly,
H. HARDINGE.

On leaving Cheltenham, Sir Charles and Lady Morgan proceeded to London, where they were joined by their niece, Josephine. Their first locality was in St. James's Place. Afterwards, they removed to 49, Grosvenor Place, of which she says: "delicious lodgings—just after my own heart; an old house, built a hundred years ago—a balcony, a verandah. I had great difficulty in getting Morgan out of St. James's Place, where I was dying. He considers this delightful site banishment." They entered on their new quarters on the 1st of March, and she already began to contemplate writing a history of Pimlico. The diary continues:—

This pretty district, the principality of his highness the Duke of Westminster, is just the *locale* that suits me, hanging on the verge of the world's bustle, not in it. The district of fashion, with all the advantages of seclusion; a garden before, though a royal one, and space and fresh air everywhere. In short, I am charmingly lodged. Yesterday, Morgan and I dined with Lord and Lady Charleville; left my dear Olivia at home. Lady Charleville growing finer by time,—noble, better and pleasanter. Lord Charleville a fearful monument of vitality, surviving all but its infirmities. His son, Lord Tullamore, a Lord in Waiting, a Tory, a dandy, an exclusive. He talked to me of *the class and order* to which he belonged! I told him the Irish story of the *Baymishes of Cork*, which set them all in fits of laughter, and even the servants were obliged to rush out of the room to hide their faces: so much for the *class* and *order* to which *I* belong.

March 2.—Received, to-day, a most gracious and

grateful letter from Monsieur Northomel (Secretary of State for Belgium), conveying his thanks and those of his friends, for my Belgium novel; and says, all the journals are loud in its praise. Another, from the Minister of the Interior to the same effect. I am so glad they like my little *Béguine.*

Last night I met Moore at Lady Stepney's—looking old and ill—much out of spirits, and, he says, weary of London after a few days' residence. He had come to publish his *History of Ireland,* but Longman and Co. found it was not half bulky enough, so he was sent back to enlarge it. He would not sing. I delivered a message to him from Lady Charleville. "Tell him he must, as an historian, rectify an error in the life of Lord Edward Fitzgerald." He praises Lord Camden (then Viceroy) for giving Lady Louisa Conolly permission to see the dying Lord Edward; and he accuses Lord Clare of cruelty for refusing her permission to do so. The case was the reverse. Lady Louisa threw herself at Lord Camden's feet, and *he* refused her petition. Then she flew, in her despair, to Lord Clare, who said, "I cannot—dare not—give you a written permission, but I will go with you to the prison myself." They went together, at night. When they came to the door of the miserable room, Lord Clare said, "I cannot leave you alone with the prisoner, but I will send away the jailor and leave the door open, and watch before it myself. I shall hear nothing." Moore seemed much annoyed when I told him this. "I have been bored to death," he said, "by friends of Lord Clare, about this, already;"

but I saw the letter—had it in my hand—in which Lord Clare refused Lady Louisa peremptorily. I have already mentioned the anecdote alluded to by Lady Charleville in my book, but people do not read it. It is not worth while writing for such a public. I am amazed how I have made my way. People read with their prejudices, not with their intellects."

Last night, after our dinner at Lady Charleville's we proceeded to Mrs. Skinner's, Portland Place—*ou par example*, Parnassus and Port Royal—the Sorbonne and the Antiquarian society—a quadrille. I was the lioness of the night, *malgré moi!* and there I sat, couched in a sort of a bay window, and there was presented to me all manner of notabilities, and scores of people from all corners of the earth. Amongst others, Mrs. Somerville, the mathematician, all celestial and descended from her solar system, the learned commentator of La Place! and Miss Herschel, member of the Royal Society. Mrs. Somerville struck me to be a simple little woman, middle aged. Had she not been presented to me by name and reputation, I should say one of the respectable twaddling chaperones one meets with at every ball, dressed in a snug mulberry velvet gown and little cap with a red flower. I asked her how she could descend from the stars to mix amongst us? She said she was obliged to go out with her daughter (who was dancing with my niece in the same quadrille). From the glimpse of her last night, I should say there was no imagination, no deep moral philosophy, though a deal of scientific lore and a great deal of *bonhomie*. She had long wished to know me, and

I replied, with great truth, I had long revered her, without presuming to appreciate her! So we agreed to know each other better, and we are to go and see each other. She and Dr. Somerville live at Chertsey. What a woman! compared to the flum-flamree novel trash writers of the present day!

Then up comes Bob Montgomery, the poet—he bows to the ground, a handsome little black man. I asked him if he was Satan Montgomery? and he said he was, so we began to be very facetious, and we laughed as if the devil was in *us*, till he was obliged to make place for Sir Alexander Creighton! physician to the late Emperor of Russia, author of a treatise on *Insanity*, a most playful and agreeable old gentleman; we knocked up a friendship for life, and should have gone on gossiping nonsense, but for Godwin, to whom Sir Alexander resigned his place. Alas, for Godwin! *Caleb Williams* Godwin, with whom I almost began my literary life at a dinner at Sir R. Phillips's, my first publisher! He talked of Curran, Grattan, Hamilton Rowan, whom he had known in Ireland—wit, eloquence, chivalry!—now all dust! Then we got on the subject of his poor son-in-law, Shelley, and his daughter, whom I shall go and see as soon as she comes to town.

Dinner at Mr. Dilke's—sat near Allan Cunningham—immense fun—Willis, the American poet, and other celebrities.

After our pleasant dinner went on to another congress at Portland place, where we met all the arts and sciences, and where we spent the night on the *stairs*, with the grand Turk (I forget his name) and his suite —I had a deal of fun with them, making *Mr. Urquhart*, the Turkish traveller, our *mutual* interpreter. They are coming to see me. Urquhart's *tic* is Russia, and the necessity of combining against her; but he is a clever creature!

Dined yesterday at Mr. Courtney's, M.P., the great epicure,—an exquisite dinner,—but Courtney so occupied with his dishes, he never spoke to his guests. I sat beside one of the greatest wits of the day, Sidney Smith! what a charmer! so natural, so little of a *wit titré*, so *bon enfant*, that the delicacy of his wit appears the natural result of a fine organization, and of a happy mind ready to enjoy and to receive as much pleasure from others as he confers upon those with whom he converses. He comes to see me to-morrow.

Yesterday, had a long visit and sofa conversation with Lucien Bonaparte,—his Italian ideas, no monarchy without an aristocracy. The reason France is all, *à tors et à travers*, is a wish to remove the peerage. He thinks with me, that Cardinal Richelieu was the founder of the revolutionary system. He said it was Richelieu who turned the cold, brave chivalry of France into the *valetaille d'anti chambre* of an effeminate despot. Speaking of the French, he said, "at the outburst of the Revolution of '88, there were a good many people in France with common sense. The Emperor used to say to me that the French were essentially a monarchical people, and we used to deny this; but everything he ever said has come out true since."

April 3.—My journal is gone to the dogs, *je n'en*

peut plus. I am so fussed and fidgetted by my dear charming world, that I cannot write. I forget days and dates. Ouf! Last night at Lady Stepney's—met the Milmans, Lady Charlotte Bury, Mrs. Norton, Rogers, Sidney Smith, and other wits and authors. Amongst others, poor dear Jane Porter; she told me she was taken for me the other night, and talked to *as such* by a party of Americans! She is tall, lank and lean, and lackadaisical, dressed in the deepest black, with rather a battered black gauze hat, and an air of a regular Melpomene. I am the reverse of all this, *et sans vanité*, the best dressed woman wherever I go. Last night I wore a blue satin, trimmed fully with magnificent point lace and stomacher, *à la Sevigné*, light blue velvet hat and feather, with an *aigrette* of sapphires and diamonds! *Voila!* The party at the Murchison's—Lord Jeffreys, the *Edinburgh Review*—Lockhart, of the *Quarterly;* Hallam, *Middle Ages;* Milman, the poet; Mrs. Somerville; &c., &c. Lord Jeffrey came up to me, and we had such a flirtation. When he comes to Ireland, we are to go to Donnybrook Fair together; in short, having cut me down with his tomahawk *as a reviewer*, he smothers me with roses *as a man;* and so he comes to see me. I always say of my enemies before we meet, "Let me at them."

Mrs. Smith, Moore's first love, and the subject of his graceful song,

"I'll ask the Sylph that round thee flies,"

was a friend of Mrs. Hemans, the touching mention of

whose last illness and death will interest the reader both for the poetess and her friend.

Mrs. Smith to Lady Morgan.

UPPER FITZWILLIAM STREET, DUBLIN,
March 24, 1835.

MY DEAR LADY MORGAN,

It was no common pleasure to receive a letter from you, and I beg you to believe that I know how to value such a favour, given in the midst of all your bustle and gaiety.

I heard with pleasure of your triumphs at Cheltenham; but I knew you would not settle there. It is very well for a few weeks; but I see that dear London will get possession of you at last. It is a dismal thought that you are to leave us, and you are really too sceptical as to the number of those who will feel your absence from Dublin a serious loss.

Of course you have heard of Mrs Hemans' illness. She has long been given over. It is three weeks since her physicians owned they had no hopes, and now a few days will rob the world of one who will not be easily matched. She was *past remedy* when Dr. Graves gave her into the hands of Dr. Croker. The latter has, I believe, done all that could be done; but the constitution was gone. Her fortitude of mind and sweetness of temper shine out to the last. She is quite resigned, and will not allow a mournful look or tone at her bedside. Her sister, Mrs. Hughes, is with her, and her brother, Major Brown, and it is a comfort to know that she has every kind of care.

Sad, most sad has been her history! Those who love her, ought to rejoice when she is at peace; a lofty mind, ever soaring above the realities of life, essentially poetical, and *never otherwise;* ardent, sentient, enthusiastic, and all this contained in a frame of the most fragile delicacy. What chance had she here in Dublin, and with an utter disrelish for the kind of society that was attainable? When she was in the county of Wicklow last August, her anxiety to remain there was like the thirst of fever. Poor thing, I wish I had never known her.

Robert has been hunting the whole winter, till he is more like a horse than a man. I am hoarse with praying him to marry and be respectable; but he grows more hardened daily.

If you have heard that we are to have drawing-rooms in the *daytime,* as in London, I am sure you have laughed at the idea of it. Our whole turn out! our equipages, our poverty, alas! need the friendly cloak of night.

Ever sincerely yours,
Maria Smith.

May.—The other night at Lady Clare's; found myself seated by Pozzo di Borgo (the object of thirty years' despotism). He has a pension settled on him by the Tory government, and still paid him by the Whigs—a disgrace to England. All the three daughters of Tom Sheridan have pensions settled on them. Lord Seymour has resigned Lady Seymour's.

Babbage's party last night very pleasant; got into *mon petit coin*—had a minister, a philosopher, a reviewer, a politician, and a dandy, successively *sur la sellette*. Vanderweyer charming, *spirituel* and *observing*. He inspires one with views and opinions similar to his own, and we agree upon most things. I told him I had received a letter from our mutual good friend, Rogier, in the morning, full of cordiality and warm feeling—reminding me of the old happy days of '33.

July 21.—Last days in London.

With a heavy heart, as with a presentiment of the misery that awaited me. Even before leaving London, at seven in the morning, my dearest Morgan looked ill, and complained. At the end of the first stage he was taken ill—this was Barnet, and before we reached the second stage it was an interval of agony to both. He became very faint; I fanned and bathed his face with eau de cologne—it was very hot—and becoming fainter, he fell lifeless into my arms. As we were galloping down hill at the time, the carriage could not stop. At last we drew up at a little pothouse inn, the Black Bull, London Colney, where he was taken out of the carriage helpless, and thrown on a wretched bed.

No medical aid nearer than St. Alban's, four miles off; thither I sent. What an interval! His extremities cold; his hands blue; congestion coming on; I, helpless, hopeless, watching all this!

The arrival of surgeon Lipscomb—his active practice—covering him with hot tiles, mustard, blisters, bleeding him profusely, in a word saved his life—and mine. If there is desolation on earth, and misery in its supreme helplessness, it is the situation in which I was placed. I dare not think of it.

I discovered I was in the neighbourhood of Royal Porters! and making my dreary position known to Colonel and Mrs. White, they came to invite us to the great house; but this was impossible, so they supplied us with fresh flowers, fruit, and wine, and with the delight of my dear husband's hourly recovering under my eyes, I began to think the Black Bull a very liveable, enjoyable place.

I filled the little Sunday parlour with flowers, and heard the whole history of Mrs. Black Bull, the hostess, and of her son, the butcher; and in the evening, when Morgan slept, I took my seat on a bench before the door with "boots" (Sam Edgell) and "mine host," with a pot and a pipe on a round table before us, with such stories of highways and byeways!—a new view to me of humanity and society.

Wayworn travellers stopping and economizing a few halfpence in the matter of refreshment—and the poor weary women—and the pleasure I felt in turning a pint of small beer into a pint of good ale, which was thought so noble on my part—and the joke cracked by Sam, with the natty, returning postilion—for little Sam, a ricketty fellow of two feet and a half high, the Asmodeus of the Black Bull, was evidently the wit *titré* of London Colney! Then the lovely, quiet scene, the pond and the stream, the parson's house; the cattle coming home, and the shower of red sunset showing over all! A gentleman in black passed us twice, and stared, and at last took off his hat. Our landlady said, "'Tis our rector, who sent your ladyship the sal volatile and offers of services."

The great skill and vigilance of Dr. Lipscomb brought back my husband and life to me. In London he might have died for want of that close attention paid him by this country doctor. We have had more opportunity of becoming acquainted lately with this order of medical men. What talent in obscurity! What worth unknown! while charlatanism is fed and flourishes in this world, beyond all talent and all worth.

July 25.—While seated on the stone bench of the Black Bull, the rector approached me with a look of curiosity and doubt, and said he had heard of Sir Charles' illness, and he had come to offer his services to us both. He told me he was a Divine of two pluralities, the rector of London Colney, and something else that I forget, and while we sat gossiping before our cabaret, he said he could scarcely believe that the companion of Sam and of the master of the Black Bull was Lady Morgan of whom he had heard so much, &c. As the dew and darkness were falling, we adjourned to the little sanded floor parlour and a pair of tallow candles, and talked of books and the fashions of the neighbourhood of London Colney. In short, my parson was a parson of gentility, and an agreeable man of the world.

August 1.—DUBLIN.—After an anxious and fatiguing journey, and having been on the point of losing all that was most dear to me, and necessary to the future remnant of my life—my husband, after having witnessed the distress of my sweet Sydney in the dreadful illness and threatened death of her almost bridegroom husband, I have at last reached wretched Dublin, the capital of wretched Ireland. I found our house in a wretched condition, half-painted, half-repaired, and full of dawdling drinking workmen, so we were obliged to take up our abode with my sister and Sir Arthur Clarke. Morgan laid up with a second attack; I, obliged to trudge over, at eight in the morning and remain till two with the workmen, who made a strike and left their employer, all because he employed a man whom they did not like.

August 9.—Tom Moore, the poet, arrived yesterday, so Clarke went to ask him to dinner to-day. Clarke met him in the street going to mass, near the Metropolitan Chapel, and accompanied him; he accepted the invitation, but conditionally—*à l'ordinaire*—if some great person, who he was pretty sure would or had asked him, did not renew his claim. This is his old way of accepting invitations. His old friend—his and mine—Edward Moore, of Cleveland Row, told me a pleasant story of Tom having made *three* of those conditional promises in one day, and got through two of them. Clarke was struck with the earnestness with which he performed all the acts of grace during that picturesque service; nobody, however, knew him, or noticed him. Clarke told the beadle it was the great

Thomas Moore, upon which he went to the organ-loft, and announced in a loud voice—Sir Thomas Moore!

As the great man (who turned out to be old Jockey Hume of the Treasury, whose brother Tom came over with t'other Tom) did not send the invitation expected, Moore dined with us. We were only *en famille* with the addition of Mr. Reynolds Solly. Moore looks very old and bald, but still retains his cock-sparrow air. He was very pleasant; but rather egotistical and shallow, justifying all we ever thought of his little mind and brilliant imagination. He declaimed against the spread of knowledge and the diffusion of cheap literature, as destructive to wit and talent of the highest order; pronounced that the throwing open of high and royal society would leave no play for all those epigrammatic touches and charming literary effusions (in which he by-the-bye excels); above all, he said the unclassical and uneducated people meddling with literature (Gad-a-mercy fellow!), and the *dilettanteisms* of the age were destroying genius. I said, " But if the greater number are to be the happier, the wiser, and the better for this spread of knowledge, the goal of all human effort and labour is obtained?" with many other things that seemed to strike him as new.

After dinner, he sighed and said, " I walked through the streets of Dublin all day, and not a human being knew me. I suppose they will, before the week is over." He exclaimed bitterly against writing-women, even against the beautiful Mrs. Norton. " In short," said he, " a writing-woman is one unsexed;" but suddenly recollecting himself, and pointing at me, said to my sister, "except her," (me) whom, in all his works, he had passed over in silence.

August 12.—In the midst of all my workmen, philosophers from the British Association have made incursions—Babbage, Lardner, Whewell, Sedgwick, and about a dozen other Oxford and Cambridge Fellows—and Wilkie, too; so I throw open the house to them, *tale quale*, to-morrow evening. But I am worn out, miserable about Morgan, and Sydney being away from us all.

August 14.—My *soirée* very fine, learned, scientific, and *tiresome!* Fifty philosophers passed through my little *salon* last night.

My sister, Lady Clarke made a song about the philosophers, which she sang to them with great effect.

FUN AND PHILOSOPHY.

BY LADY CLARKE.

Air, "*All we want is to settle the play.*"

I.

Heigh for ould Ireland! oh would you require a land
Where men by nature are all quite the thing,
Where pure inspiration has taught the whole nation
To fight, love and reason, talk politics, sing;
'Tis Pat's mathematical, chemical, tactical,
　Knowing and practical, fanciful, gay,
　　Fun and philosophy, supping and sophistry,
　　There's nothing in life that is out of his way.

II.

He makes light of optics, and sees through dioptrics,
  He's a dab at projectiles—ne'er misses his man ;
He's complete in attraction, and quick at re-action,
  By the doctrine of chances he squares every plan ;
In hydraulics so frisky, the whole Bay of Biscay,
  If it flowed but with whiskey, he'd stow it away.
    Fun and philosophy, supping and sophistry,
    There's nothing in life that is out of his way.

III.

So to him cross over savant and philosopher,
  Thinking, God help them ! to bother us all ;
But they'll find that for knowledge, 'tis at our own College.
  Themselves must inquire for—beds, dinner or ball ;
There are lectures to tire, and good lodgings to hire,
  To all who require, and have money to pay ;
    While fun and philosophy, supping and sophistry,
    Ladies and lecturing fill up the day.

IV.

Here's our *déjeuner*, put down your shilling, pray,
  See all the curious bastes, *after* their feed ;
Lovely lips, Moore has said, must evermore be fed,
  So this is but suiting the word to the deed ;
Perhaps you'll be thinking that eating and drinking,
  While wisdom sits blinking, is rather too gay ;
    But fun and philosophy, supping and sophistry,
    Are all very sensible things in their way.

V.

So at the Rotundo, we all sorts of fun do,
  Hard hearts and pig-iron we melt in one flame ;
For if love blows the bellows, our tough College Fellows
  Will thaw into rapture at each lovely dame.
There too, sans apology, tea, tarts, tautology,
  Are given with zoology to grave and gay ;
    Thus fun and philosophy, supping and sophistry,
    Send all to England home happy and gay.

Mrs. Smith (Moore's old flame, and the subject of his poem, "I'll ask the sylph that round you flies," came to me on Friday, and said Moore wanted to get up a play for himself, and Calcraft, the manager, said that I ought to bustle about it and go. Then comes the strangest advertisement, viz., " That whoever wished to see the illustrious bard, &c., &c., might do so at the theatre on such an evening!"

August 16.—The theatre was crammed last night. *The Great Unknown*, and *The Gentleman in Search of a Religion*, and—*popularity*, was called forth by the galleries, with "Come out here, little Tom! Show your Irish face, my boy; and don't be ashamed now!" Tom descended from the manager's-box to the stage-box, and there made a speech, and was encored and bravoed.

Sunday, Moore dined in Kildare Street, and spoke in raptures of his reception at the theatre. We had, also, Mr. Coombe, of Edinbro' (the phrenologist).

Wednesday last we lighted on Hayward, translator of *Faust*, in Sackville Street. We asked him to dine with us the day after. Just as we were sitting down, *en tiers*, enter Professor Whewell, of Cambridge, so we seized on him, and we had a rather awkward but pleasant little dinner party. Awkward, because our Irish cook was drunk, our English butler insolent, and the dinner bad.

September 8.—What times! what a country is Ireland! The O'Connell "rint" already accumulated for this year, is thirteen thousand four hundred and fifty pounds—a census of the gullibility of the poor Irish,

and of the incapacity and roguery of the Tory party
and their House of Lords—the true partisans of
O'Connell and the founders of his fame and fortune.

September 9.—So the Lords have rejected even the
moderate amendments of the Church Bill; and wretched
Ireland, or rather the independence of England, and
her efforts for Ireland, are baffled in all their expectations; not a grievance removed, not an abuse abolished,
not a step taken for the improvement of education or
the peace of the country—the "Church Establishment,"
the filthy corporations, the Orange powers, sheriffs,
magistrates, jury, placemen, and even *habitués* of the
Court—all the elements of misrule, are retained in their
primitive force. Ascendancy still flourishing, Catholi-
cism undermining, and the nation prostrate to both!
The turbulence of the Irish is coupled with their
stupid acquiescence in every wrong, and oppression
and intolerance. For six hundred years they have
borne a greater sum of oppression, injustice and wrong
than any other people in the world. Their submission is their ignorance. There is a long and very new
chapter on this to be written—and then—!

Since my return I have been given up to my usual
domestic duties. Morgan begins the day with his
face buried in the newspaper while at breakfast, then
sets in to read and write, if he can, the whole of the
rest of the day, in a close room by a hot fire. I try to
get him out at two o'clock, and then there is a painful
struggle; if I succeed, I can see he is impatient to
come home, and then, after dinner, he reads till bed-
time, and so reads and writes to the end of the

chapter. My most painful efforts to draw him off these destructive habits are met with violent resistance and temper.

A more blameless life was never led; some great occasion would soon rouse him; he is always ready to meet an event with energy, he has no external world; his world is within, and were it not for his fidgetty wife, he would never look out of it. He is inherently shy, timid, proud, anti-social, and neither acts nor writes in reference to society or its opinions, but always to its interests. He does this on a principle in his nature, a love of liberty and of ease in his own person, and desiring the same for his species.

September 18.—We are going to-day to Portran (the Evans') thank God!

Two hard-headed English lawyers, Jos. Evans and Mr. Blackburn, M.P. I was baited by the first for the amusement of the second. Mr. Evans himself always attacks me with some bitterness about my fashionable friends and my aristocratic tastes. They have all got something, these Irish Liberals—one brother a place of one thousand five hundred a-year, the other his election for Dublin, and Blackburn a commission. We, who live with aristocrats, that is people of good taste who happen to bear some rank, have got nothing, asked for nothing, and never can get anything.

Whilst here, Morgan, who is ill and weak, would take no exercise, so my sole object in coming here was disappointed.

October 2.—A charming note from Lord Morpeth,

asking us to dinner, and begging me to bring "one of my harmonious nieces." I know there will be a storm in great George Street at the "harmonious nieces," as their mother does not like to let them from her side. After some debate and a lively resistance, I carried my point (as I usually do). The invitation of a secretary of state cannot be expected every day by *des petites demoiselles*.

October 6.—Dinner at Lord Morpeth's—what a charming host! The absence of all the official *morgue* by which we have so long been oppressed, was delightful. The new officers of the Crown amuse me very much by being the least amusing men possible—iron-bound men, all their muscles rigid, like men who, living out of society, have lost the play and movement of gesture which men of the world exhibit from long practice; but what uncompromising minds and characters! What honest men! How much and how long they have been wanted, and here they are, thank God, after five hundred years of struggle!

October 11.—Just heard of the deaths of Bellini and of Don Telesforo de Trueba—these two fine emanations of talent—extinguished, and oh, the blockheads who go on living and boring for ever! I think it was in the summer of 1833, on our way to Belgium, that Captain Marryatt brought Don Telesforo to us in St. James's Place. He was one of the refugee victims of Ferdinand "the Beloved," whose tyranny deprived Spain of the services of this able and estimable man. On the death of the king he returned, and was elected member of the Chamber of Procuradores and secretary of the Cortes. His literary and conversational talents were of a very distinguished order, but what was perfectly miraculous, was his speaking and writing of English; he wrote his *Sandoval* and other works in English; contributed much to the *Metropolitan*. Such bright glances of mind flash across one in life to light up its ordinary horizon of dulness, and then vanish for ever.

CHAPTER XXV.

LAST RETURN TO KILDARE STREET—1836.

January 1836.—What a melancholy winding-up of the year 1835, and commencement of the year 1836. I went ill to Malahide Castle for Christmas-day—tried to bully a sore throat and head-ache, but finally knocked down and took to my bed, which I only left at the end of eight days, to be wrapped in hot blankets and conveyed to my own bed in Kildare Street. The united skill and hourly attendance of my dear husband and good Doctor O'Grady, shirked old death, and saved me from a delirious fever. How my head worked! what books I wrote! what plans I laid for the good of those I loved! what regrets that I had not settled my worldly affairs as I wished! But did I recant one opinion? Not one! I thought I should die, and yet I repeatedly said to myself, had I the sorry battle of life to fight over again, I should just take my old ground!

January 20.—The Registration Society is going on famously, all the young liberals of the highest rank have joined. They say it is entirely got up by "Lady Morgan's School of young men." The high compliment!

January 30.—I have met with a loss that breaks my heart; I have lost the locket with lord Byron's hair, sent me by Countess Guiccioli, enclosed in a curious reliquary. The small gold chain which I wore round my neck, and from which it hung, broke; I must have dropped it walking down Kildare Street this morning, to warm myself after a cold drive. I am the most unlucky woman in England.

February 1.—The Tories, at last, have placed O'Connell at the head of ascendancy in England; of this, his speech at Birmingham the other day, is a proof. It represents the spirit and opinion of England.

O'Connell is one of the instances of men who have been the offspring of events. From event to event he has climbed. He has grasped his opportunities; where will he end?

February 5.—Read last night Mrs. Lee's *Life of Cuvier*. It gives me no just idea of the man, and still less of his reputation in France—where he was considered a great naturalist and bad philosopher. He was a man of the highest scientific genius and of the highest personal character; but vain, ambitious, tergiversating, serving all the powers that could serve him; equally subservient to Louis XVIII. as to Napoleon; and prouder of his station, honours, and title, than of his immortal scientific reputation.

March 20.—Death of my old friend Sir William Gell. Poor Gell! it seems but yesterday that I saw him walking up Berkeley Square, the mirror of fine men upon town. He had written a *Topography of Troy* as early as 1804. How often we met in my gay days in London, again at his residence at Rome, and a great deal at Naples, at the Margravine of Anspach's, and many other places. He died at Naples, on the 4th February, 1836, worn out by twenty years' gout.

April 1.—Busy to-day with my *Woman and her Master*, making extracts for it.

April 2.—I have been reading Von Raumer's *Letters on England*. Clever, but German; a laborious but inconclusive book—full of brilliant incoherences. The product of a bold mind grappling with strong truths; but not following them to their consequences.

A letter to-day from Lady Cork, announcing the death of her macaw, the original of my article in the *Book of the Boudoir*.

Lady Cork to Lady Morgan.

6, NEW BURLINGTON STREET,
April 3, 1836.

DEAR LADY MORGAN,

Your old friend departed this life a few days ago; he is buried in my garden, and his merits well deserve an epitaph from your pen. He committed but one crime, and only made a bit of an assault on George the Fourth's stocking. That was an offence merely, the *crime* was running away with a piece out of Lady Durlington's leg. I have been ill with the *tic*, but am better now, and just going out of town for the holidays. Your admirer, Lady Hatherton, has just returned from Paris. Are you coming to England—and when? I am more stupid than ever—only pick a little bit of dinner and drink a little drop of tea. I have neither vocals nor wit going on, *chez moi*. Don't forget that I am ninety years old, and was, and am, and shall be to the end,

    Your ever affectionate,
      M. COBB AND OBREBY.

A charming note from Lord Morpeth.

      NUNEHAM,
     April 5th, 1836.

MY DEAR LADY MORGAN,

How am I to thank you enough for your most amiable letter, which has just come to divert the not-unoccupied repose of my holidays?

> "In vain to deserts my retreat is made,
> The *titles* attend me to the silent shade."

And so far, not inappropriately, as I am the guest of the Archbishop of York, and within seven miles of Oxford. But then there is another awful phantom, styled poor laws,

> "Whose gloomy presence saddens all the scene,
> Shades every flower, and darkens every green."

I am showing symptoms of bolting from the stout turnpike, where I ought to travel into pleasant pastures. I am convinced that Dublin has been very gay, though you will not allow it. I am very sorry to miss the occasion of renewing my acquaintance with Mrs. Laurence.

I cannot but be glad that Sir Charles has worked so hard for the lobster and anchovy sauces; I wish that his country might continue to appropriate some still more persevering labour from him. I shall feel the grey towers of Malahide a great and real loss. But we will have a look and luncheon there some morning.

Your most loyal servant,
MORPETH.

April 11.—Working all day and all night; spirits at a low ebb.

April 13.—Another, too, gone! Poor Godwin died on the 7th, at the Exchequer Office, Whitehall Yard, aged eighty-one. I saw the last of him in his den at the Star Chamber, *last year*.

April 18.—I am getting down my old harp, which I had exiled to a lumber-room, and will have it put in order. I will then get up a song or two.

April 24.—Unable to use my eyes, in any way, since the 19th. I write these few lines unknown to Morgan. Indebted all this time to the charity of strangers for the distraction of a little conversation, all other resources bereft me. Lady Beecher has been very kind in coming to me; the once celebrated Miss O'Neil—the "Juliet" of admiring thousands. When she was a poor, obscure young actress, I saw her by chance as Belinda, in "*All in the Wrong*," and afterwards in a suit of armour, dressed as an Amazon, as the heroine in *Timour the Tartar*. I sought her out, and asked her to a party the next evening, and predicted her future triumph. Shortly after I followed her triumphant success in London. She is passing through Dublin on her way to see her old mother. She comes every day to see me while she stays here. The poetry of her own voice remains; it is still Juliet's voice in the balcony; but all else that was poetical in her beauty has gone. She is now a thin, elegant-looking lady; but no beauty, except that she has the indestructible beauty of goodness.

May 20, *London*.—Arrived in London quite safely, and we settled in pleasant lodgings in Stafford Row, Buckingham Gate.

Poor Lady Glengall died on Monday, seventy years of age. She was the daughter of *the celebrated* Mrs. Jeffries (Groves of Blarney) of county Cork. She was the Lady Cahir of my youth.

May 22.—We are charmingly lodged, and in a quarter I like above all others. Yesterday, dined with some of my literary friends at Mr. Dilke's. Kind, gay, and pleasant. After dinner, I got up and danced a *reel* with the *grave editor*, "to my girls playing," and then we walked home, and sauntered till midnight, and by moonlight, under the trees of my pretty Grosvenor Place; how pleased I am with it, what true delight to live with trees!

May 27.—Got a cheerful letter from my beloved Sydney, so up early and at work for *Woman and her Master*.

I have made acquaintance with the Lockharts, he editor of the *Quarterly*, and she Sir W. Scott's daughter; we were mutually charmed with each other, and have sworn an eternal friendship.

Ambition, and vanity, and *social tastes*, have led me much into that chaos of folly and insincerity called the world; but domestic life is my vocation—unfortunately, my high organisation, and my husband's character of mind, our love of art, and all that is best worth knowing, renders *la vie domestique* impossible. Yesterday, I went with Lady Dudley Stuart, and Urquhart (the Turkish traveller) to visit Wilkie, and see his pictures—a charming Flemish painted-like house, Knightsbridge, in a garden, and a pretty, "neat-handed Phillis," opened the door. The great picture was the "Columbus in the Convent," which is to be removed to-day to Somerset House. Fine heads for expression, and a fine conception; but in execution slap-dash—no finish, but good effect at a distance. A picture of the Duke of Wellington, much flattered; Lady Salisbury who was standing before it, remarked, "he is much changed *now*," (the tiresome *Liberals* would change everything.)

Wilkie is simple and enthusiastic—he is the *Teniers* of England—domestic interiors. He told us an amusing story of the Turkish ambassador sending him, on his arrival, a *cake* for his breakfast, *à la Turque*.

CHAPTER XXVI.

FAREWELL TO IRELAND—1837.

THE year 1837 was marked by a handsome recognition of Lady Morgan's literary merits, and by the grant of a pension of three hundred a year. She used to tell the story that one morning, on coming down to breakfast, she found her letters as usual laid beside her plate. Sir Charles, seeing her much occupied with one of them, said impatiently, "Sydney, I wish you would eat your breakfast, and never mind your d—d dundies," (it was his usual alliterative for the tribe of men who came about his wife). She said nothing, but handed him the letter and enclosures, which were as follows. Nothing could be more gracious or more gracefully done. The announcement from Lord Melbourne, the William Lamb of other days, being sent through Lord Morpeth, the friend whose kind regard lasted to the end of Lady Morgan's life, gave it additional value.

Lord Morpeth to Lady Morgan.

GROSVENOR PLACE,
May 8th, 1837.

MY DEAR LADY MORGAN,

I thought the enclosed note came very *à propos* after my agreeable visit to you yesterday. I hope the contents will be acceptable to you, as I am sure they are creditable to Lord Melbourne for offering to your merits, literary and patriotic, the highest scale of acknowledgement which our *material* times permit. I ought to state that Lord Mulgrave has been a joint solicitor to Lord Melbourne, with myself.

Very sincerely yours,
MORPETH.

Enclosed, was the note, as follows:—

Lord Melbourne to Lord Morpeth.

SOUTH STREET,
May 7th, 1837.

MY DEAR MORPETH,

I have settled that Lady Morgan shall have a pension of three hundred, as you wished.

Yours faithfully,
MELBOURNE.

May 8.—The very first intimation I received *of my pension!* Lord Morpeth never alluded to it on his visit the day before.

There is a break in the diary for five or six months. Among Lady Morgan's papers is Lord Melbourne's graceful reply to her letter of acknowledgment. The allusion to the "pressure of suffering" refers to her failing eyesight, which at that period threatened total blindness.

Downing Street,
May 11th, 1837.

My dear Lady Morgan,

I have derived great satisfaction from your letters; I am very glad to find that what has been done is agreeable to your feelings, and I can assure you that I have had much pleasure in doing that which may in some degree alleviate the pressure of the infirmity under which, I very deeply lament to hear that you are suffering. It is also a gratifying reflection that no doubt can exist but that your talents and exertions afford ample grounds for the advice which I have humbly given to His Majesty upon the present occasion.

Believe me, my dear Lady Morgan,
Yours faithfully,
Melbourne.

In the absence of a diary for this summer, the following extracts from a letter may be given:—

"I must tell you I am perfectly enamoured of my present residence, and am determined on writing a

Pimlico; it ought to be a most interesting bit of topography, and I am urged to it by Mr. Lemon, my landlord, who is first clerk in the Rolls Office—a most intelligent and learned man. We are within reach of every one we wish most to see of interest. We had a long and cordial visit from Lord Adolphus Fitzclarence, who has invited us to dine with him, at St. James's Palace; he is very like his royal father, with all the *naïveté* of his mother in her dramatic characters. Lady Aldborough wanted to take Morgan to see a famous mesmerist—a magnetic séance which set him into a rage, as humbug always does. Lady Arthur Lennox was here, also, to recommend me a bit of a house which she thinks will suit me; but the flower of all flowers in my garland of friendship, is Mrs. Dawson Damer. You know she is the adopted child of the Prince and Mrs. Fitzherbert, whose property she has inherited, and *such* property! I spent two hours with her, yesterday, in her house in Tilney Street, *tête-à-tête*—the house, observe, of Mrs. Fitzherbert! What a *causerie!* No one now talks like her; and she is so handsome, so elegant, and genial. She told me that she was at the Duchess of Gloucester's, the other night—a child's ball. The young Queen was there, looking quite a child herself. When her uncle, the Duke of Sussex, was leaving the room, she ran after him and said, 'Won't you give me a kiss before you go?' and then whispered in his ear, 'you have forgotten to wish mamma good night.' What a charming trait; it is a pity to make a queen of this creature, with these warm affections!

Tilney House is full of reminiscences of its celebrated but, I suspect, unhappy late mistress—the true, legal wife of that type of heartless roués, George IV. Mrs. Dawson Damer said she had got up a table expressly for me—it was covered with beautiful relics. In a coffer filled with pledges of love and gallantry from the Prince in the hey-day of his passion—a Pandora's box *without* Hope at the bottom! The most precious were a number of their own portraits, set in all sorts of sizes and costumes, and oh *what costumes!* Toupées, chinons, flottans, tippy-bobby hats, balloon handkerchiefs, and relics of all the atrocious bad taste of succeeding years, from the days of Florizel and Perdita, to the 'fat, fair and *fifty*' of the neglected favourite, a series of disfigurements rendering their personal beauty absurd. The Prince's face was insignificant, through all his ages and disguises, a fair, fat, flashy young gentleman, his mother's snubby features spoiling his pleasant smile; in short, he was the old queen *bleached white!* By-the-bye, the last time I saw him was in a doorway at Lady Cork's which he filled, to the utter annoyance of Lady Cork, who was obliged to open another doorway, contrary to her arrangements. The pictures of the Prince and Mrs. Fitzgerald were all splendidly set in brilliants, with hearts and ciphers, crowned with royal coronets and true lovers' knots. The initials G. P. were never omitted.

There were two lockets of very curious description, minutely small portraits of the Prince and the lady; they were each covered with a *crystal*, and this crystal was a diamond cut in two! They were less than the

size of a halfpenny, set in small brilliants. Each wore
the portrait of the other next their heart—at the depth
of their love.

On the death of George IV., Mrs. Fitzherbert sent
to William IV., to request back some of her pictures,
gems, and letters, left in the late King's hands.

William IV., always the kind and constant friend
of Mrs. Fitzherbert, sent her everything that he could
find in the cabinet of his brother, and a beautiful
picture in oil of Mrs. Fitzherbert; but the diamond-
enshrined miniature was not forthcoming. After some
time, however, she received a letter from the Duke
of Wellington, who wrote to say, having heard that such
a locket had been enquired for, he would be happy to
place it in her hands, as it was in his possession. He
added, that in his quality of the King's executor, he
had gone into his room immediately after his decease,
and perceiving a red cord round his neck, under his
shirt, discovered the locket containing the miniature.

The correspondence of the Prince and Mrs. Fitzherbert, most voluminous, and doubtless full of interesting
political and social incidents, which have escaped history, were burned by Mrs. Fitzherbert's trustees—one
of these was Sir C. Seymour, Mrs. Dawson Damer's
brother; the other was Colonel Gurwood, who was
one of her best and most intimate friends. I think
she added that the Duke of Wellington and Lord
Albemarle were present, and that the room where
this *auto-da-fé* took place, smelled of burnt sealing-wax
for weeks afterwards! Mrs. Fitzherbert had labelled
all the letters she wished to be destroyed—a few, how-

over, escaped—a few in Mrs. Dawson Damer's casket, Mrs. Fitzherbert had ordered to be preserved.

Mrs. Fitzherbert was *never* in love with the Prince, and much of her virtuous resistance may be ascribed to her indifference. The Dowager Lady Jersey was the true object of his passion, or if not the object, at least the disport of his weak mind, and certainly the cause of his infidelity to his mistress and his cruelty to his wife. When that most fashionable of French novels, *Les Liaisons Dangereux*, came out, it became the subject of much fashionable criticism, and one evening, in the circle at Devonshire House, it was disputed whether the character of Madame la Presidente was not an outrage upon probability and female humanity. The late Duke of Devonshire observed, that he thought he knew *one* such woman; but refused to name her. The next moment every one present confessed they had known *one* such woman, also; but refused to denounce their fair friend. Curiosity became vehement, and Lord John Townsend proposed that each person present should write their secret on a slip of paper, and throw the slips into a veiled vase, and he would draw them out slip by slip, and read them for the benefit of the society present, under the solemn seal of silence,—when, to the surprise and amusement of the distinguished society, every little rouleau, as its contents were announced, bore the inscription of 'the Countess of Jersey!' When the anecdote was told to the author, he exclaimed, '*Heureux pays! où l'on ne peut trouver qu'une seule Presidente!*' I saw the last picture of poor Mrs.

Fitzherbert ever taken; it was done on the day of her death, and yet was lovely, though she died in her eightieth year. It was curious (but not an unusual thing) that her face had fallen into its original form; its fine osteology was perfect; the few furrows that time had traced upon its round muscles had disappeared—it presented a fine and firm oval face—the beautiful mouth—a high and rather Roman nose. The simple dress of death (not the most unbecoming she ever wore) added to the solemn beauty of her appearance.

Mrs. Fitzherbert died in the beginning of 1837, and Mrs. Dawson Damer's expressive countenance changed often as she spoke, and tears fell from her eyes as she deposited the relics of her adopted mother in the casket whence she had drawn them. She was still in mourning for her.

We had a very amusing, and to me, very interesting dinner at Lord Adolphus Fitzclarence's, in the *old* St. James's Palace, comprising the Marquis of Belfast, Sir George and Lady Wombwell, the handsome Mr. Stanley (alias Cupid), Josephine, and ourselves,—a round table dinner. Lord Adolphus took me into his boudoir in the evening; we were alone, and he showed me a miniature set in brilliants. 'The king!' I said. 'Yes, my father,' said he, taking another picture out of the casket, 'and,' added he, with emotion, 'this was—my mother.' After a pause, I said, 'It is a great likeness, as I last saw her.' 'Where was that?' 'In Dublin.' 'On the stage?' 'Yes, in the *Country Girl*, the most wondrous representation of life and nature I ever beheld! I saw her, also, when she was on a visit at Sir Jonah Barrington's. She sent to my father to go and visit her, he did so; she called him the most amiable of all her managers.' After a pause, he said, "Sir Charles and you will accompany me to *Chantrey's* to-morrow, to see her beautiful monument, which they have refused to admit into St. Paul's, though Mrs. Woffington's monument is still expected there!' I said I could not express how much I honoured his sincere feelings to the most attentive of mothers, whose fault was, that she loved not wisely, but too well.

We found Chantrey, as frank, simple, and cordial, as when some seventeen years back, we trotted *en groupe* with Moore, Playfair, and Lord John Russell through the streets of Florence, and paused to worship the memory of *Jean de Bologne*, the key note of our conversation whenever we met. Well, the Gordon monument is a beautiful *work of art*, I had almost said of nature; but no time to write more. I have to dress for Lady Charleville's dinner, and here is the carriage, and Morgan roaring like a bull."

In the autumn of 1837, Sir Charles and Lady Morgan carried into effect their intention of leaving Ireland, and taking up their residence permanently in London.

Dublin had long become distasteful to Lady Morgan, for Dublin is, after all, a provincial city, and the society lacked the brightness and freedom of a great capital. Except a separation from her sister and her sister's family, there was not much to regret. Sir

Charles Morgan's desire to settle in London had only been yielded to his wife's wish to live in Dublin; now they were agreed to seek a new home. They first freighted a small vessel with all their household goods, and then came over themselves to England.

The following extracts from Lady Morgan's journals will tell the reader the incidents of the removal and settlement in their new abode:—

> "Oh Ireland, to you
> I have long bid a last and a painful adieu."

You have always slighted, and often persecuted me, yet I worked in your cause, humbly, but earnestly. Catholic Emancipation is carried! It was an indispensable act—of what results, you fickle Irish will prove in the end. To predicate would be presumptuous, even in those who know you best. Creatures of temper and temperament, true Celts, as Cæsar found your race in Gaul, and as I leave you, after a lapse of two thousand years.

I shall meet in England the effects of the glorious Reform, after seven years' experiments; that is the event that opens the free port of constitutional liberty, so long struggled for by the Saxon in England.

We bid our last adieu to Ireland, October 20, 1837, accompanied by my niece Josephine; we proceeded to Leamington, where Mr. and Mrs. Laurence joined us; they left us on the 25th, and José with them; we were very sad after the departure of our young people.

October 28.—Received the intelligence of poor Mr. Laurence's sudden death! My poor Sydney! We left instantly to go to her.

December 23.—Lord Morpeth sent us, with one of his kind notes, two tickets of admission to the body of the House of Lords to see the Queen open Parliament and return thanks to her faithful Commons, &c. I went with Lady Georgina Wortley and my dear Mrs. Dawson Damer. We were placed close to the bar of the House of Commons, being rather late. It is a gorgeous, imposing, but rather theatrical *spectacle*. The young Queen's *aplomb* was truly wonderful; her voice clear and sonorous—whoever "taught the young *girl* to read," did every justice to the development of her vocal organ, and her small person seemed to dilate under the pressure of her conscious greatness; for the Queen of England is, at this moment, certainly the greatest sovereign in the world, because she is the chief of a free people—what charmed me most, however, was her inexpressibly girlish laugh. When the House of Commons rushed in with all their rude, rough, schoolboy boisterousness, Philip Courtnay, and some of my Irish members, were so close to me, that I could not help turning to them and muttering, "My faithful Commons, *why* are you so vulgar?" When the royal *cortège* had moved off, and we paused at the head of the stairs whilst my husband was looking for our carriages, dear Lord Melbourne came up and shook me heartily by the hand, and said he was glad to see me there; Lord Brougham also joined us, and two or three other agreeable men.

Our lodging in Pimlico, 6A, Stafford Row, is opposite a wing of Buckingham Palace, and commands a view of its gardens. What an historical, what a charming site. I shall make myself mistress of it before I have done with it.

I have finally given up all hopes of getting ★ ★ ★ ★ ★ ★ ★ ★ ★ pretty house at Buckingham Gate; after a most capricious negotiation on his part, redeemed, however, by many charming notes and letters from a charming man, which are always worth something. I think I have found the clue of his

"*Letting I dare not wait upon—I would,*"

"like the poor cat in the adage." It happened thus: —I have been in the habit of popping, at all hours, into the house, which I considered all but my own, and the other day I found a fine embroidered pocket-handkerchief on the table and a tiny pair of gloves. I saw at once that the gloves had carried it, and that the handkerchief would never be flung at my feet, and that there was a tenant who was resolved not to quit, and whose lease, perchance, would not be renewable for ever; and so we have given up, and are again on the search for a house.

December 25, 1837.—My birthday. London, 6, Stafford Row, opposite the King of Buckingham's house. I open this new journal at the close of the year 1837, a year to me full of events of good and ill together, to commemorate most gratefully *my partial restoration to sight*, so far as to enable me to write an hour a day without pain or annoyance, and I trust to recommence a work undertaken in the sincere spirit of philanthropy and the inextinguishable desire to do good—*Woman and her Master*. I have this day put aside the long green sheets of paper on which I have been scrawling *Woman and her Master*, which that dear thoughtful Morgan got for me in Dublin.

December 26.—I am really beginning my regeneration and new life as a denizen of London. Everybody congratulating us: old friends are true, new ones all agreeable.

Lady Normandy has most kindly offered to present me at the Queen's first drawing-room.

CHAPTER XXVII.

SETTLEMENT IN LONDON—1838.

THE first entry in the journal for 1838, refers to a work which caused a great scandal and excitement at the time, though now it has fallen into the heap of things forgotten—*The Diary of the Court and Times of George IV.*

6, STAFFORD ROW, PIMLICO.

January 3.—The murder is out! There is the *Diary* in everybody's hands, and since the publication of the *New Atlantis*, by Mrs. Manley, in the reign of Queen Anne—a scandal, a libel on the queen, people, and court of that day; such a book has not been seen, written, nor read.

January 8.—For the last month nothing has been thought of or talked of but the *Diary*, and now Animal Magnetism has taken its place, and all the titled credulity in London have been putting their fatuity to the test of exhibiting themselves under the hands of Baron du Potet. I was busy writing my article on Pimlico, when Lady Arthur Lennox came to know what were my intentions. I told her of my search after a house in the new quarter of Belgrave Square, I wanted one which should be cheap and charming. She advised me to look in a new street containing only two or three houses as yet, built by the great builder Cubitt.

January 9.—I am just returned with Sydney and José from looking at such a charming maisonette in William Street, which will meet our taste, and not exceed our means; no houses opposite, and all looks rather wild and rude (a thing that would be a field if it could), and a low wall round it; but then there is to be a pretty square, and then, no doubt the street will soon be built. The street terminates in Knightsbridge, of which *locale* I had a curious account from Dr. Milman, prebend of Westminster, which he has extracted from the rolls.

At the bottom of William Street, bounding the park, is a little bridge over the great sewer of this quarter, behind which stands the hideous gate of the beautiful Hyde Park. The tops of two poplar trees are all we can see of it. This bridge was the spot where the Knights of St. John of Jerusalem used to assemble on a certain day in October to give convoy to the monks of Westminster Abbey, on their return from their quest for provisions, &c., for the convent, and to conduct them through the perilous jungles of what is *now* Piccadilly, through which they were obliged to pass on their way to the Abbey, according to an ancient tenure. Next to this gate stands the Cannon Brewery, with its eternal smoke. On the other side of the Knightsbridge Gate stands a little hostelric called the 'White Hart,' now a shabby public house; though it was here that the Duke of Buckingham, in James the Second's time, came to sleep the night before his appointed duel with Lord Rochester, because it was out of London.

I saw Mr. Cubitt yesterday, a good, little, complying man; he has yielded to all my suggestions; will knock down walls between the rooms, build balconies, and a terrace, and is to give me a tree to plant in my bit of a garden (four feet by two) though I heard him say to Sir Charles, "She shall have it, but it will not grow in so confined a place."

Mr. Cubitt was quite mistaken, the tree was planted (a plane tree), it grew and throve from the first day, it is now a fine piece of timber, standing higher than the chimneys.

To the diaries again:

January 11.—The fatal and almost pathetic conflagration of the Royal Exchange and its neighbourhood has swallowed up the discussions on all minor subjects. A note from my poor dear Sydney, who was an eye witness of the scene, sets my heart at ease as regards any harm having extended to her. It is one of the great fires that are historical.

Mrs. Lawrence to Lady Morgan.

January 11, 1838.

What a sight I came in for last night, my dear Little Mamma. The burning down of the *Royal Exchange!!* I write you a few lines this morning to put your mind at ease respecting me. Being so close to it, we were, as you may suppose, kept in a state of great excitement and alarm. It was splendidly awful to see the beautiful dome all in a blaze, and tumbling piece by piece into the flames below, and the bells chiming their last in the midst of the fire, and strange to say, the last tune they chimed was at twelve o'clock, and *that* tune was "There is na luck about the House." It quite affected me to hear it, and it had a *choking* effect upon us all, for the bells literally dropped one by one as they were playing the tune. All that now remains of this once great work of Sir Thomas Gresham's, are the pillars! What ages it took to build that which a few hours has consumed! The gentlemen here rendered all the assistance they could, and when they came home at six o'clock this morning, the frost was so hard, that their clothes were literally frozen upon them, and they waited to melt them before they could take them off. We ladies have never been in bed, and have been kept very busy making *hot tea* all the morning for the frozen men who have dropped in. The house has been thronged all the morning with Lloyd's people. I shall be with you to-morrow, dearest; so more anon.

S. L.

January 14.—Colburn, my persecutor, has become my slave and blackamoor! He has written Morgan a letter, offering to suppress the libellous passage about me in the Diary (a funny term for being represented as an ugly monster!). I have refused his offer, and given him a *coup de patte* for lending himself to such nastiness! Here is his letter, and the rough draft of my answer.

Mr. Colburn to Sir C. Morgan.

MY DEAR SIR,

I was very much disconcerted on having pointed out to me a day or two ago, a passage in the diary about Queen Caroline, which refers in a very bad spirit to Lady Morgan. Unfortunately, the work was never properly examined by me, having been hastily published the moment it was finished at press.

On enquiring how it was that the passage came to be overlooked by the reviser, I am told it was thought that the note at the foot of the page was considered as a perfect refutation of the unjust and ill-natured remarks. I need not say that if I had been made aware of them, and had had time to give them proper consideration, I should certainly not have allowed them to appear, and I will now cancel them with great pleasure, if you wish it, being anxious to do everything that is honourable towards Lady Morgan, with whom it gives me great pleasure to be again on the most friendly terms.

With my best compliments and apologies to Lady Morgan and yourself, I beg to remain,

Dear Sir,

Yours very faithfully,

H. COLBURN.

P.S. I had not either the least knowledge that such a person as Lady Holland was alluded to in the book, and few others would have been aware of it, had not Colonel Webster made it public, and acted against my advice, very urgently given, of submitting first to Lord Holland the letter he sent to the *Literary Gazette*.

H. C.

Lady Morgan to Henry Colburn.

STAFFORD ROW,
Tuesday, 16th January, 1838.

DEAR SIR,

I beg to thank you myself for volunteering in a letter to Sir Charles the offer of suppressing a passage in the Diary of Queen Caroline, which you say, "refers in a very bad spirit to Lady Morgan." I never in my life interfered with the printed expression of an opinion relative to myself, personal or literary; of this you are well aware, and whether you repeat through future editions, or suppress in the next, a passage which you say ought never to have appeared, I leave to your own taste, feeling, and discretion. On your confession that "unfortunately the work was never properly examined by you, and was hastily published," &c., I beg to remark, that such conduct in a publisher will be taken by the public as anything but an apology for the consequences, and to remind you that in the course of the many years you published for me, I have repeatedly urged for the interests of literature, and your own, that you should confine your publications to works which should, in a moral as well as in a literary sense, reflect credit on and give consideration to the publisher. Among the many temporary causes which in the present moment have tended to degrade British literature, is the promptitude of publishers to produce such works as the one you have just brought out. You say, that "on inquiring how it was *that the passage came to be overlooked by the reviser, I am told that it was thought that the note at the foot of the page was considered as a perfect refutation of the unjust and ill-natured remarks.*" That note, like all the other apologetical notes in the book, only proves that the author was fully cognisant of the malice and impropriety of the text. In return for the many kind expressions in your letter with respect to myself, I beg to reiterate an advice so often given: in a literary, as well as in a social sense, confine your dealings to honest men and women; when you did so, you were among the first of European publishers.

I am, dear sir,
Yours, &c.,
SYDNEY MORGAN.

CHAPTER XXVIII.

ALBERT GATE—1838.

On the 17th of January, 1838, we, viz., my beloved husband and myself, accompanied by our dear niece, Josephine Clarke, and our trusty servants from Ireland, John and Mary Forman, took possession of our dear, *very dear* house, No. 11, William Street. Belgrave Square is the only place of any note, *i.e.*, of gentility near us. I take great interest in this new and pretty *quartier*; but I must have a new Gate where the Fox and Bull pot-house now stands; there is a rural air over the whole that is pretty; but a gate we must have into the park at the top of William Street, for pretty it will be when it is finished, though I shall regret having houses opposite to me in place of the green swards. We have a branch-Gunter, the confectioner, near us, and I have paid my score to that illustrious house, by giving him a receipt for a *plombière*, which I had from Carême in 1829.

March 5.—Colburn followed up his efforts at reconciliation, by presenting Lady Morgan with a beautiful mirror for her new drawing-room, which was graciously accepted; and the old terms of friendly goodwill were restored, after eight years' interruption.

March 11, William Street.—I see it is quite absurd to attempt keeping a diary here within the sound of workmen and mills; I give it up. I have been so busy, with my good *Woman and her Master,* lying in abeyance—heaps of letters to write—having to receive all day and go out every evening. When I had nothing to write about, then I had time to journalise. Now, when every day would supply a volume, I have not a moment to write a line!

Lady Morgan always got up the history and traditions of whatever place she visited. She wrote some charming papers upon the history of Pimlico, which were published in the *Athenæum.* They excited interest in the neighbourhood, as appears from the following note, selected from many others.

Lady Carlisle to Lady Morgan.

April 26th, 1838.

Lady Carlisle presents her compliments to Lady Morgan, and must tell her how much pleased and gratified she was by the interesting paper she was so obliging as to send her. She thinks the inhabitants of Pimlico ought to give her a vote of thanks for making their situation classic ground by the associations of her mind and genius.

May 14.—My first shaking of the Albert Gate! What a charming *quartier!* what capabilities! I have been talking it over with Cubitt, the *Pontifex maximus* of this new estate. What I want is a Gate, where the old sewer tap now moulders and flanks a ditch of filth and infection; a sort of little rustic bridge should be over it, which would not be without its picturesque effect. Cubitt wants it too, but despairs of getting it. That terrible brewery points its *cannon* against all improvement! even whilst we spoke, a volume of smoke rolled out from its chimney, making its curling way direct for the Duke's windows. "That smoke will serve us yet," I said; "it will ruin the Apsley House picture gallery, if the Cannon Brewery be not removed, the Duke must know of it." "I will buy out the Cannon Brewery," said Cubitt. He is a great little man!

May 29.—Last night we were at Lady Stepney's great rout. I was presented to the Duke of Cambridge all over again, who shook hands and said he remembered me. I had much to do to persuade Miss José to sing for his Royal Highness, and though she sang *pretty bad*, yet he praised her beyond beyond, and said her voice and school were equally fine. I have had a great many people come to call on me. The Queen's coronation is put off till August next; not to cut short the season, she does not go to Ireland. I have just returned from the Queen of *Modistes*, Madame Dévey, getting a hat for Lady Clanricarde's concert. Never were hats worn so *small*, but pretty

and new. Everything is *black*, lace or silk, and all
caps or *fraises* under bonnets, *black*, ditto gloves and
fichus, loose sleeves and large, from shoulder to elbow.
The Queen wore them at the Duchess of Somerset's.

Yesterday we were at Lord Ducie's, where the
Chanoiness Talbot had just arrived per diligence from
the top of the Pyramid, and was the fun of the party.
Every one was in their Devonshire House full dress,
and she in a black frieze gown, leather brogues, and a
green pocket-handkerchief on her head, and *no* gloves
on her naked stout arms. She will not be here long.
Rogers was here all yesterday; he has sent José all his
works as a present.

London looks like the last scene in a pantomime, all
transformed for the Coronation. Every house, from
Hyde Park Corner to the Abbey, cased up with
wooden platforms, canopied balconies. The Duke of
Devonshire's house, and the great houses in Piccadilly,
which have courts before them, have superb boxes
erected as in a theatre, all draped and gilt. The
whole front of the Ordnance, where we are to have
a grand *déjeuner*, is fitted up as an amphitheatre, deco-
rated with the Queen's arms and crown. The streets
all barricaded, and on *the* day, no carriage is to pass
after eight in the morning.

August 26.—Here is a letter which I have just sent
to Lord Duncannon. Another touch at my gate.

Lady Morgan to Lord Duncannon.

11, WILLIAM STREET,
August 26*th*, 1838.

Lady Morgan presents her compliments to Lord Duncannon, presuming upon the kindness with which his Lordship received the petition for the opening of an ancient gate in Hyde Park, Knightsbridge. She takes the liberty of enclosing a plan of the district to which this ingress to Hyde Park would be of such an incalculable advantage, together with an explanatory letter from Mr. Cubitt, the founder of this new capital of the west, who is willing to incur the expense of the alteration. Should the lords of the woods and forests not dismiss that petition (as frivolous and vexatious), the spirit of which is to preserve the health and beauty of thousands of fair pedestrians, now denied the advantages of their neighbourhood by the noxious atmosphere they must pass through to attain it, Lord Duncannon will receive the gratitude of many a fair generation yet unborn, and merit a statue, which, compared with the bronze gentleman in the park, and the wooden one, who *tête-à-têtes* him on the other side of the way, will be as an "hyperion" to two "satyrs."

Lord Duncannon's Answer to Lady Morgan.

OFFICE OF WOODS AND FORESTS,
August 28*th*, 1838.

Lord Duncannon presents his compliments to Lady Morgan, and regrets that he cannot recommend to her

Royal Highness, the Ranger, to comply with the wishes expressed by her ladyship and the other persons in the neighbourhood of Belgrave Square. Buildings are growing up in all directions adjacent to Hyde Park, and there is no doubt that similar applications will be made for a similar accommodation. At present, there are six public entrances into Hyde Park, besides five or six foot gates, and when the contiguity of Hyde Park Corner is considered, in reference to the present application, it would not appear desirable to establish another thoroughfare so near to the former one. Under the circumstances, Lord Duncannon regrets that he is under the necessity of declining to forward the proposal.

Well! we have got our answer; but we are not beaten. Cubitt has actually bid for the Cannon Brewery, and will buy out all the old houses, including the dear old 'White Hart.' We are going to get up a memorial to the Queen, signed by all the respectable inhabitants of Cubittopolis, with the Duke at the head of it. We have got the Duchess of Kent to give her name also.

A letter from General Sir John Burgoyne, whose alarms on the subject of the defences of England have made his name familiar to all. It relates to an article in the *Athenæum* upon one of his reports on railways.

General Sir John Burgoyne to Sir Charles Morgan.

DUBLIN,
October 2nd, 1838.

MY DEAR SIR CHARLES,

I am much obliged to you for sending me the *Athenæum*, but I had been on the look out on each of the last three Saturdays, and at last found the article and read it with much interest. I am particularly pleased with the dissertation on commissions, which is most just, and is a subject on which the world (that is the British imperial world) rejoice to be enlightened; for a pack of interested jobbers have been calling mad dog till they have almost persuaded John Bull out of his senses, that is, out of his commissions. It is something on a par with the London thieves, who made a bold effort to cry down the police, when they were first instituted. Because a commission cannot perform a miracle, such as making Ireland in a moment rich and happy (and a greater miracle than that was never yet achieved), they abuse it; but there are none, I believe, that have been appointed, but have produced at least a great amount of most useful information, that in one way or another has been of the greatest service.

Your remarks on the report in general are very good. I have been arrested by various persons, with—
" *Have you seen a very moderate and sensible article on your Railway Report in the Athenæum, &c.*"

Lord Cloncurry tells me that the Duke of Leinster

is about to agitate for our course of railways; he has read the report attentively, and approves of it much; is about to signify to the government (with others) a hope that some measures in conformity with our recommendations, may be taken. The *Government* can do nothing of this kind without being pressed, and the Duke of Leinster is the best possible man for the purpose. He is a man of strong sense, anxious for the good of Ireland, and works for no *party*. His *personal* interests, I imagine, ought to lead him to favour the Kilkenny and the Great Central Irish, &c., that our plan condemns; therefore, his opinions should carry weight. The journalists ought also to use a little of the pressure from without on the government and on parliament for this object.

Dear Sir Charles, I am just going to Paris, to bring home my wife.

Yours faithfully,
J. F. BURGOYNE.

December 23.—We went last night to a literary *soirée* given by Messrs. Henry Chorley and Henry Reeve, authors and sub-editors. Count Alfred de Vigny was presented to me, and I said all sorts of things *en gracieux* on his "*Cinq Mars;*" he talks well, and is high bred. I joked a little about the present state of literature in France, and its melodramatic character, *du plus beau noir*. He said "Oui, mais croyez moi milady le fonds du caractère Français est la tristesse." I gave a little *soirée* for him, very pleasant. He said, in answer to my observation on the bright, gay literature of the eighteenth century in France, "La jeune France prend pour model Byron, et puis Napoleon." This was too pleasant. The one an Englishman, and the other an Italian. Voltaire called the French, "*les singes tigres.*" It was the *doctrinaires* who upset the throne of Louis Phillippe, and now they are "*les singes Anglais*," and very agreeable monkeys they are.

CHAPTER XXIX.

LONDON LIFE—1839.

THE reader, who has had so many letters from Madame Patterson Bonaparte, may like to see that her husband, King Jerome, in his later time, found himself living on very familiar terms in Lady Morgan's London circle.

Jerome Bonaparte had been, from the beginning, the plague of his family. Thoughtless, idle, vain, extravagant, and inconsiderate, the one idea which his mind was capable of containing, was a supreme conception of his own value, or, as his biographer politely expresses it, "le trait dominant de son caractère etait le sentiment profond de sa dignité personelle." He tried the patience of his august brother as no one, except his wife, Josephine, had ever ventured to do. Being the youngest of the family, he was a spoiled child, and developed into a prodigal son, with an unlimited faculty for spending money, getting into debt and mischief, varied by an occasional duel, the ferocity of which was only equalled by the absurdity. Like other scapegraces, he was sent to sea to get him out of the way, and in the hope that his troublesome wilfulness might take the shape of a genius for adventure and command; but he had no genius except for pleasing himself. Jerome was a caricature of his great brother. He possessed the true Bonapartean imperious will; but it was never exercised except in following his own inclination, in spite of remonstrance. He was the torment of his commanders, and refused to be amenable to discipline. He would neither join his ship, if he chanced to be amusing himself on shore, nor learn his duties as a sailor. At Martinique, he had an attack of yellow fever, which so disgusted him with the service that he expressed a wish to throw it up altogether; this his Admiral refused to allow, and ordered him to rejoin his vessel; but just then, Jerome chanced to be amusing himself on shore at Martinique, where the Governor invited him to dinner, and received him with garrison turned out, under arms, and he refused to obey. Jerome was a *parvenu* to the backbone; and his vulgarity was ingrained. The Admiral, Villaret Joyeuse, exasperated by his stupidity, and fearing that if war broke out between England and France, some mischief might befall Jerome, who, as Napoleon's brother, had an importance quite distinct from himself, ordered him to return to France. Jerome loitered and made excuses till the opportunity of a safe return was gone, and then the Admiral, anxious to be rid of him, gave him permission to go to America.

Jerome went, glad at the prospect of being out of the reach of his Admiral and of his brother. He landed with three companions, whom he called "his suite," at Norfolk, in Virginia, where he gave himself the airs of a Prince in disguise. He went to Washington, and announced to Pichon, the French Consul, that he must supply him with funds and find means to convey him and his suite to France, which, as war was by this time declared, and English vessels were on the watch, outside the bar, for every French ship leaving America, was no easy matter.

At first, there was an affectation of incognito observed; but Jerome, with his vainglorious folly, was quite unable to keep it up, and all the United States were made aware that the brother of the First Consul of France had come among them. They proceeded to offer the homage so dear to Jerome's heart; and he was flattered and fêted to the top of his bent. He proceeded to Baltimore, and was received with enthusiasm. For the first time in his life he was entirely his own master, and he gave himself up to the pleasures of the position. Pichon had not much money to give him, but all Baltimore asked for the honour of giving him unlimited credit. At Baltimore, he met Miss Elizabeth Patterson,—whom all contemporary testimony declares to have been extremely beautiful, agreeable, witty clever, and ambitious. Her father was a rich merchant, well known and respected. All her family belonged to the American aristocracy of the upper ten thousand. In birth, parentage, and education, she was Jerome's equal. In intellect and character, she was much his superior, but Jerome's brother was rising to the ranks of royalty, and carrying his family with him. Jerome fell violently in love with Miss Patterson, and proposed marriage. She accepted an offer which made her the envy of all the women of Baltimore. Jerome was in the zenith of a vulgar success; he was young, lively, and tolerably good looking. Mr. Patterson, the father, in consideration of the connection, overlooked Jerome's want of actual fortune, and gave his consent.

Pichon was frightened out of his senses at what the First Consul would say, and made formal representations, both to Mr. Patterson and the French consul at Baltimore, declaring that he was under the age at which a lawful marriage could be contracted. Jerome feigned to comply; but not the less, on the 25th of December, 1803, he was married to Miss Patterson by Bishop Carrol, the Roman Catholic bishop of Baltimore. The marriage was regular and legal in every particular, and so far as rites and ceremonies could make her so, Miss Patterson became the lawful wife of Jerome Bonaparte,—qualified to share in all the honours of his rising star. Jerome coupled this announcement to Pichon with orders to supply him with funds; and then proceeded on his wedding tour.

They passed a few months in the midst of all the social gaieties and splendours that American society could bestow. On the 18th of May news came that the First Consul had been declared Emperor. Jerome had not yet received his brother's answer to the announcement of his marriage. He had not, however, to wait much longer for it. In June, 1804, the answer came. Napoleon declined to recognise the marriage, taking his stand on a recent French law of February, 1803, which prohibited all French subjects, under the age of twenty-five, to contract marriage without the consent of parents or guardians. Pichon, and all French officials, were ordered to treat Madame Jerome Bonaparte as Jerome's mistress; French vessels were forbidden to afford her a passage to France; and if she attempted to enter France with Jerome, orders were given that she should be arrested and conveyed back to America.

Jerome himself was ordered to return home immediately. A pension was offered to Miss Patterson of sixty thousand francs a year on condition that she never assumed the name of Bonaparte, nor molested Jerome. Napoleon could not, however, alter the law of marriage as recognised by the Catholic church and by the consent of all Christendom. Except the local enactment, which only held good in France, Miss Patterson's marriage with Jerome was as valid as the sacraments of the church could make it. If Jerome could only be firm, the marriage must hold good whether the Emperor recognised it or not; but Jerome could not hold firm to anything but his own inclination. He was, in fact, a man—who could see nothing, feel nothing, care for nothing, except the whim of the moment.

He had had his whim out in marrying Miss Patterson, and now to go back to France and be the Emperor's brother, was the idea that possessed him. He was already beginning to feel his wife a clog and an encumbrance. He embarked with great secrecy on board an American merchantman bound for Portugal, accompanied by his wife and secretary. The vessel arrived quite safely at Lisbon; the French consul refused a passport to Madame Jerome, and wrote to Paris to announce their arrival. Jerome had already pretty well proved that no consideration stood in the way of pleasing himself; without any consideration of his duty as a husband, or the common feelings of humanity for a woman about to become the mother of his child, he abandoned her in a strange country, where she had neither friends nor relatives, and where, if she were not in want of the necessaries of life, it was no thanks to Jerome, who made no arrangement for her support. He left her, a beautiful woman of seventeen, entirely unprotected, and in a condition which rendered her return to her father's house physically impossible; he left her almost immediately on their arrival in Lisbon, professedly with the intention of throwing himself at the feet of the Emperor, and obtaining his pardon and recognition of the marriage, but the whole of his subsequent conduct showed that he had no intention of ever again encumbering himself with her. Jerome found his brother at Turin; he wrote a letter of abject submission, offering to recognise his marriage as absolutely null from the beginning, and his offspring illegitimate, submitting himself absolutely to his brother's pleasure. In return for this submission, Jerome was pardoned. Napoleon married him to a German princess, who was a great deal too good for him, and made him king of Westphalia, where he caricatured royalty until the fall of the empire. His royal wife died in Italy, and Jerome was now an elderly widower travelling in England, and mixing in society with the chance of encountering his first wife in the doorway or on the staircase of a London party.

Jerome Bonaparte to Lady Morgan.

FENTON'S HOTEL,
May 22nd, 1839.

DEAR LADY MORGAN,

I regret very much that I cannot have the pleasure of passing this evening with you; the news of the death of my uncle, Cardinal Fesch, which has just reached here, would render my presence too unseasonable. I shall probably leave here on Friday, for the interior of England, and eventually for Ireland; would you be so kind as to send in the evening of to-morrow the letter you were good enough to offer me for Lady Clarke.

I am most truly yours,
JEROME BONAPARTE.

In the course of the same season, Lady Morgan received a note from Madame Patterson Bonaparte.

Madame Patterson Bonaparte to Lady Morgan.

> PARIS, RUE D'ALGERS, No 4,
> *September* 22*nd*, 1839.

DEAR LADY MORGAN,

You will be less surprised to know of my arrival in Europe than I am to find myself here. I never supposed that I had preserved sufficient energy or moral courage to put into effect my inclination to absent myself from the *République par excellence*. A residence of a few months in the *Etats Unis* would cure the most ferocious Republican of the mania of Republics. We have security neither for our lives nor our persons in America. I have been two months nearly in France, a period of time which has passed very dully; I have found few of those persons whom I knew and saw habitually five years ago. Death, time, and absence have left me scarcely an acquaintance at Paris. If our friends do not die, their sentiments change towards us so much, that really I know not which is most distressing, to hear that they are gone to the other world, or that they have forgotten us in this vale of tears, and have become strangers to us. I have met few persons who possess the stability of friendship that I find in yourself. You are, in this particular, as in most others, *une personne distinguée*. My son is gone from Geneva to Italy, to visit his relatives, and to see after a legacy, which the late Cardinal Fesch, his grand uncle, had the goodness to leave to him. He wanted me to go to Geneva to see him, but I could not attain the courage to extend my long journey farther than Paris. Here I am in solitary existence. In one of his letters he remarked that it had been your intention to write to me; If you have had that goodness, your letter must have reached Baltimore after my departure. I regret this circumstance very much. I have seen Mr. Warder; his regard for me has held out against time and circumstances; he is unchanged in kind feelings; but, poor man, time has dealt hard with his exterior; he looks as if he had begun to exist a century ago.

Madame Benjamin de Constant is an agreeable person; has had the goodness to recollect me. I dined yesterday at her house, *en petit comité*. I have myself grown fat, old, and dull,—all good reasons for people not to think me an intelligent hearer or listener. They mistake, however; I have exactly the talent to appreciate the high powers of all others, without being able to contribute much to the liveliness of conversation myself.

Have you no agreeable work to promise us?

The poor Duchess d'Abrantes, Madame Junot, made a sad end, the natural consequence of her prodigal expenditure. Her pecuniary difficulties, it is said, caused her death. I liked her very much, and I always felt pained at the misery which her want of judgment in the direction of her affairs had brought on her. I believe that her heart and feelings were generous and warm.

I wonder that you did not select Paris in preference to London, for a permanent *séjour*. I should much prefer living at Florence, but there lives there one individual whom I wish not to meet again. Whether persons have been the voluntary or the unreflecting cause of having spoiled a destiny, I would sooner avoid their presence. I know not whether the princess Charlotte, the late daughter of Joseph Bonaparte, was fortunate enough to be personally of your acquaintance. I did not myself know her, but I have heard from those who did, that she possessed some mental superiority, and a great many noble qualities.

I hope that Sir Charles Morgan still recollects me, and preserves for myself the friendship he formerly entertained for me.

Adieu, my dear Lady Morgan,
  Believe me, ever your sincere and
      Affectionate friend,
        E. PATTERSON.

It was during this year that Lady Morgan completed the first portion of her important work, *Woman and her Master*. It was published by Colburn. The sum she received for it does not appear. It is only a first instalment of a very extensive project. The design is nothing less than to demonstrate that in all ages, women, in spite of the systematic depression and subordination in which they have been kept, and in spite of all difficulties, have not only *never* been subordinated, but have, on the contrary, been always the depositories of the vital and leading IDEA of the time; that the spiritual life in women has always been more pure and vigorous than in men;

that women have a more subtle and delicate instinct for whatsoever is "pure, lovely, and of good report," and that, alike among the most degraded savage tribes (those in Australia and New Guinea), as among the Hebrew of old, women were held the oracles, and proved themselves to be of "finer clay" than their so-called "master," man. This doctrine Lady Morgan illustrates by historical examples, which exhibit industry and research. Of course there is much eloquent and special pleading and declamation, but the work is wonderfully clever, and the lady having all the talk to herself, she rides on to the end upon a gently undulating wave of triumph, which, to disturb, would be to break the charm of the book. There is nothing American or strong-minded in *Woman and her Master.* It is a contrast to the *Rights of Woman* tone, in which the question is generally discussed; on the contrary, nothing can be more pretty and persuasive; no man in the world could find in his heart to interrupt the pleasant flow of narrative and assertion by a question, much less by a contradiction. There are some true observations; the work evinces a great deal of laborious and industrious reading, and the style is not so much disfigured by a mixture of languages, as is usually the case. It is evident, from the beginning, that her ladyship is riding her "hobby," which, well bred and well broken, obeys her hand, shows the smoothest action and carries her along like a Pegasus. The work was never completed; her eyesight failed; and, when restored, was still precarious; but she had collected an ample store of materials to finish her task, had her health and eyesight remained in their natural force. Some portions of the second part were left by her almost ready for the press.

We return to the diary, in which there is a brief reference to this book.

June 9, 1840.—The first time I have written in this journal during the year 1840. *En attendant,* I have finished and published the first and second volume of my *Woman and her Master.*

Just read the account of the funeral of Mary, Dowager Countess of Cork and Orrery; she died in harness, full of bitterness and good dinners.

The following note from Mrs. Otway Cave is about the Braye peerage. Lady Braye, as she ultimately became, was one of the closest of Lady Morgan's friends.

Mrs. Otway Cave to Lady Morgan.

Thomas's Hotel,
Wednesday Evening, August 14th.

My dear Lady Morgan,

I am going to be very troublesome, but I am quite sure you will be kind and indulgent. The case is this:— The Lord Chancellor has fixed *to-morrow* afternoon, at half-past three o'clock, to give judgment as to my claim to the Braye Peerage, and it is *my* business to obtain a sufficient number of peers to form the committee; numbers of whom, as you know are gone out of town, and I have a thousand fears, lest we should fail in obtaining the right number, for a female, and an *aged* one like myself, must of course find it a difficult task, without the aid of kind friends. The purport, therefore, of this application, my dear Madam, is to request you would do me the favour to ask any peers, who are friends of yours (and *very* many, I know, are on your list), to be at the House of Lords to-morrow, rather before three o'clock, as *that* is the hour which the Lord Chancellor has fixed to give the final judgment. If you can, without inconvenience, do me this favour, I need not say what an essential service you would render me, and my servant shall call at your house to-morrow morning, at any hour you may kindly appoint, in case you may write any notes for him to convey; and, perhaps, you would be so good as to give him the directions to each. I am quite distressed to give you such trouble, but will not detain you with more of this.

Remaining with best compliments to Sir Charles,
Your much obliged,
SARAH OTWAY CAVE.

PS.—I would have *called* to petition you in person, but my carriage has been in a distant quarter all the day, and I could not leave the house.

I shall hope to call very soon, after the present fatigue is over.

The judgment was given in Mrs. Otwny Cave's favour, and she became Baroness Braye in her own right. Lady Braye died February 21st, 1862. She and her daughter, Lady Beauchamp, were among Lady Morgan's warmest friends.

The next letter will interest readers who knew the fine though undeveloped genius of George Darley.

George Darley to Lady Morgan.

CLARENCE CLUB,
January 23, 1841.

DEAR LADY MORGAN,

I felt very much flattered by your warm praises of *Thomas à Beckett*, and the more so, as its rough nature is opposed to the present refined and polished mode of poetry. Most persons prefer a Paris or a Perseus by Canova, to a Knight-Templar on a tombstone, and looking as if he had been sculptured with a pickaxe, not a chisel. But I suppose you have a heart big enough for both styles, a heart on both sides, while most critics have only the sinister one, or none at all. Your suggestion about "a series of historical dramas," such as *Beckett*, encouraged me in that design, and hence *Ethelstan*. I hope not to have presented this subject in all the mere ruggedness and rust of antiquity, yet to have preserved some of its simple relish and raciness. If my recurrence to such olden times be objected, you will say for me, (as your countryman, proud of the name) that King Ethelstan is, to us living now, a far more poetical personage than the Emperor Napoleon, and that history often teaches us nearer the farther it removes, like "dear home," which is seldom so very dear until it is rather distant. There are a thousand better reasons for loving the antique than the antiquarian one; but you are familiar with them all, and to my distaste for the present style of poetry, I confess myself the bee in the honey-bottle—quite sweet-sick, and although my palate is not altogether assinine and made for thistles, yet it does prefer even the *amari aliquid* to chewing an eternal cud of rose-leaves.

Dear Lady Morgan, excuse the liberty of this long answer to your note; but as I am, in a worse sense than the weird woman, one of the "imperfect speakers," [he had an impediment in his speech] it forces me to spend all my tediousness in writing. Sir Charles will perhaps take the trouble of decyphering these hieroglyphical characters for your convenience.

With best respects to him and your ladyship, I remain what all the world is towards you, and to what I need not say besides,

Yours much favored,
GEORGE DARLEY.

John Poole, the dramatist, and author of *Paul Pry*, had made the acquaintance of Sir Charles and Lady Morgan. From the letters of this singular and farcical genius, the following note may be given:—

John Poole to Lady Morgan.

BRIGHTON, 40 BLACK LION STREET,
March 28, 1841.

DEAR LADY MORGAN,

I wish I could come and see whether you are better. I hope you are. *Are you?* Mr. Herring was here a few days ago—very funny; but I could learn nothing from him distinct about you.

So here I am still, seeing everybody out. None of your acquaintances here, I believe, but Edwin Landseer, who is gone, and Colonel Webster, whom I don't know, so *faites vous en une idée!* The fish are all in the water, because there is nobody here to want them out; the flies stand sulkily waiting to be caught, and nobody to catch them; the goats' occupation's gone—two, with their pretty baby-carts at their tails, are at this moment fast asleep under my window, and likely to remain so till next September—because there are not sufficient *carriage*-children to wake them; the theatre is closed, because, as nobody went to it when the town was full, it would be very stupid indeed of them to expect people to go to it now that the town is empty. The only happy person in the place I believe to be Garcia, who is in the seventh heaven at Sir Charles's notice of him in the Brighton article. *A propos* of theatre—*our tragedy* will be in the *Miscellany* next month. Bentley has had it for a long time under a restriction that he should not publish it till then, I expecting to have finished what I am about for his dear friend that time; but, alas! though every day adds a little bit to the heap, it is *so* little!

When I come to town I hope to find some or all of your charming nieces with you. Has some lucky Irishman caught Miss Josephine yet? Oh, how I do wish I were *two or three* years younger and thirty thousand pounds richer!

That being all, with kind regards to Sir Charles, who, I take it for granted is well,

   Believe me, dear Lady Morgan,
    Your ladyship's, very sincerely,
          JOHN POOLE.

Sir Charles and Lady Morgan this year made another visit to Germany; they went to Kissingen for Lady Morgan's health. She did not keep a journal while in that country; but the following letters to Lady Talbot gave some account of her progress:—

Lady Morgan to Lady Talbot de Malahide.

        BADEN,
      September 30, 1841.

MY DEAR LADY TALBOT,

In the course of our delightful and prosperous tour in this region of plenty and *bonhomie* I have often thought of writing to you; but, strange to say, having come to the very *heart* of Germany, as a retreat from bustle of all sorts, I have been living in a continual fuss and movement, and, except to my family, to tell them I am "alive and kicking," I have never put pen to paper since I left London. I requested Lady Clarke to send you a fragment of my scrawl as a remembrance. I have derived infinite benefit from the waters of Kissingen, and I was delighted with the society I found there, and gratified *up to my bent*, by the manner of our reception everywhere. The kindness of the Esterhazys and several other distinguished

Austrians, was extreme; and that we are not now on our way to Vienna and divers chateaux in Germany and Hungary, is not from the want of invitations. We fell in with many friends of *Madame la Chanoinesse Talbot*, and heard many characteristic anecdotes of her, that I shall reserve for our next meeting. Amongst others, the beautiful Countess Assemay, Count Mulgan (the Russian ambassador), the family of the Von Walthers, charmers, and who spoke of the Chanoinesse with great kindness; but all seem surprised how any one distinguished with the illustrious name of Talbot should accept of a German title! for, in Germany, ancient descent, not title, is the illustration most prized. I suppose Josephine has told you how courteous the amiable Queen of Wurtumberg was to us, and what a pretty royal rural *fête* we assisted at. In short, we left pretty, salutary Kissingen with infinite regret. We made our journey here by a long *detour*, in an open carriage. We stopped at Wurzberg and Heidelberg for a couple of days; and the palace of the first, and the ruined castle of the second, are well worth the fatigue of the whole journey; and oh, such a land of abundance as we passed through! There is nothing I ever saw comparable to the Valley of the Neckar, and the scenery from Heidelberg to Baden. I shall never forgive myself for having lived so long without having visited this paradise. I cannot tell you how it seized on my imagination—such a combination of all that is civilised and romantic, enjoyable and sublime. The Grand Duchess has rendered it delightful to us in a social point of view, by the distinction of her attentions. The day after our arrival she sent (through the Baden minister) to invite us to go to her in the morning, so we went to the *vieux chateaux*, and were presented by *la grande maitresse*, who left us to the enjoyment of a most agreeable and intellectual conversation, with one of the most *spirituelle* and gracious persons imaginable. The next evening we were invited to her concert, and presented to the Prince and Princess Vasa. The Countess Merlin sang, and still charmingly.

Last night we were at the most original entertainment ever given since the days of Charlemagne! by the Princessa Vasa, for it was amongst the ruins of the old castle (Alte Schloss) at the top of that steep rugged mountain, which I need not describe to you. I got very nervous about going, as the descent at night was no joke! We assembled at five in the centre of the ruins, all in grand toilette—the men all *chapeau bas!* The grand spectacle was the sun setting—and the moon rising over such scenes! Here there was a collation—three tables. I was summoned to her Royal Highness, where, by-the-bye, Lord Douglas and myself were the only British. As the night advanced, the rest of the ruins were suddenly illuminated, as if by magic, and we ascended to a Gothic chamber, superbly furnished *en rococo*, where there was a concert, and a ball terminated the whole. The old dungeons rang with the echoes of the most delightful bands of music all night. To-night is the Grand Duke's *fête*, to which we are invited. And now I think I have tired you out, and shall beg of you to give my people a peep of this letter, which will save me going over this ground to them. So God bless you.

With kind respects to Lord Talbot,
Yours,
SYDNEY MORGAN.

In the autumn, Sir Charles and Lady Morgan returned to England by way of the Rhine, Brussels, and Ostend. By the end of September, they were again in William Street. Of their pleasant journey, no literary use was made by Lady Morgan. She spoke, for years to come, with ardour of the beauty of German scenery and the cordiality of German manners; but she had long ago given up the thought of making a book on that country, to range with her *Italy* and *France*. Another race of writers, younger and less scrupulous than herself, had rushed into the field which her genius had first laid open to feminine adventurers.

Even in the lighter sphere of fiction, the public mind had somewhat changed, as Lady Morgan thought, for the worse. The days of sentimental and patriotic novels had passed away,—Ireland had no serious wrongs to redress; and the story, with a purpose graver than the amusement of a passing hour, no longer warned, or even found, a public. In place of laughing and musing over adventures like those of *O'Donnel*, the world was sneering and mangling over the character of *The Dowager*, by Mrs. Gore.

In this once popular novel, Mrs. Gore was supposed

to have sketched with a free and wicked hand that
ancient dame, Mary, Countess of Cork and Orrery,
who had just died, as Lady Morgan said, "full of
bitterness and good dinners." Much scandal thereupon
ensued. Mrs. Gore abstained from making any reply
at the time to those who accused her of traducing
private character in her book; but to Lady Morgan,
personally, she made a clean confession of her offence,
so far as she had been guilty of offence.

Here is her note:—

Mrs. Gore to Lady Morgan.

DEAR LADY MORGAN,
You are very kind to like my new book. Till you
praised it, I was in despair. It *sells*, and I was convinced
of its utter worthlessness; for surely nothing
can equal the degradation of the public taste in such
matters! The subject and title were of Bentley's
choosing; and my part distinctly was to *avoid* hooking
" M.C.O." into the book. In certain *mannerisms*
the *Dowager* may resemble her; but not in essentials.
She was *better* or *worse*. I never heard of her troubling
herself about her opposite neighbours, except so
far as by sending her dog to walk in their gardens,
when under a course of Epsom salts.

I am grieved (*à propos* to being sick) to hear that
you have been so great a sufferer. No person who
writes books has the least claim to a digestion; and I
wonder you should ever have thought of such a thing!

My French books will disappoint you. Paris has been a land of Canaan to me, and the milk and honey will necessarily find their way to my pen, and prevent the possibility of adding shades to the picture. I love them all so well as to see everything *en couleur de rose.*

The English (except you, who are frank and generous, but then you are not English) are not half so good to me; and I therefore permit myself to see them as nature made them and art has spoiled them.

My daughter is going to Brighton in the course of the week, and will throw herself at your feet. I hope she will send me better news of you.

Sincere regards to yourself and Sir Charles, from

Yours faithfully and obliged,

C. F. GORE.

CHAPTER XXX.

ALBERT GATE CONCEDED—1842.

In 1842, the *Book without a Name*, by Sir Charles and Lady Morgan, appeared, published by Colburn. It was a collection of sketches and articles which had been contributed by them from time to time to the *Metropolitan*, *New Monthly*, and the *Athenæum*. It was not then so common to collect fugitive articles as it is now. These articles had obtained a good deal of notice when they originally appeared, and Mr. Colburn found his account in their republication. *The Memoir of the Macaw of a Lady of Quality*, to which reference has been made, will be found in these pages. We resume the diary as it occurs in a letter from Lady Morgan to her niece:—

April 12, 1842.—Talk to me of *your* gardens! I have at this moment, perfuming my rooms, twelve hyacinths, mignionette, sweet briar, and verbenas; follow me that in *your* garden!

My right eye is very weak and painful, causing me

to spare it as much as possible. You have got the *Athey.*, and books to keep you *au courant*. We had Captain Marryatt to dine with us on Saturday, a pleasant, cosy little day, and I bore it very well, although Morgan exclaimed against my *lights*, and wanted to *extinguish* them; but I would rather give up my *rouge* than my lamps, *et c'est de beaucoup dire*.

I can do nothing for your young friend, P——; never encourage young people to suppose they are to throw themselves on their friends; they should be early taught to have no dependence but upon their own exertions. At fourteen, I worked for myself, and disdained living on my fine relations, the Croftons, and if I was left destitute to-morrow, I should begin and write again, as of old. How often have I preached this to you all?

Well, I am working at my *Gate;* the Cannon Brewery is *blown down*, and the Counter intrigue *blown up*. We have got the Duchess of Kent on our side, and that there is a likelihood of our having the Queen, whom we have petitioned. Lord Duncannon is dead against us, but I do not despair, for it will be a great *public* benefit.

April 17.—Hurrah! have got my Gate, just as we got Catholic Emancipation, by worrying for it!

It was said of somebody that he could be eloquent on a broom-stick. Sidney Smith could be lively about the gout, and Horace Smith about everything. A note from each may be given,—the first, for its graceful turn; the second, for its puns and conceit.

Sidney Smith to Lady Morgan.

56, Green Street, Grosvenor Square,
November 14th, 1842.

My dear Madam,
Among incitements so numerous that it would weary you to mention them, there are two obstacles, a late dinner, to which I am engaged, and uncertain health. I had last week an attack of gout, which is receding from me (as a bailiff from the house of an half-pay captain) dissatisfied and terrified by the powers of colchicum; but I swear by that beautiful name we both bear, that I will come if it is possible.

Ever, dear Lady Morgan,
Truly yours,
Sidney Smith.

Horatio Smith to Sir Charles Morgan.

Brambletye House, Brighton,
December 30th, 1842.

My dear Sir Charles,
(Which, of course, includes Lady Morgan, you two being one) the same to you, and many of them (I mean happy returns, &c., &c.) Right glad am I to hear that Lady Morgan has thrown off her coughs and colds.

We are as dull here as you can be in London, with nothing half so good to enliven us as Lady Morgan's *improvement* on Webster's *Cracked Rib.* Your riddles are excellent, and so is your doggrel, which I must leave Eliza to answer. We must borrow Borrow's book, which seems to be the best thing recently published.

As to my Adam Brown, I know nothing about him, except that Colburn seems rather ashamed to bring him out. I don't mean to write any more, being quite worn out; so I resign Adam to his fate without any compunctious visitings of nature. I have had as much success as I deserved, and much more than I expected, and more money too, which was ever my sole inspiration.

Make sugar of paper! then there is a hope that poor authors may make *plums*, and critics become *candied*, and writers of tragedies may be more successful in the *writing mood*, and the worst productions be constantly in the mouths of the public, and all the evils of literature be twined into *bonbons!* I always said and felt that to restore the taste for tragedy, she must be taken from the stilts, and brought down to common life and common language. Everything is a round robin, rudeness, simplicity, perfection, decay, simplicity, rudeness. You *must* have novelty, and after you have reached perfection, you can only innovate by inferiority.

Never mind, it's a very pretty world, and I am perfectly well contented with it, especially now that my wife is better, and my three girls at home, and all of us us *cozy* as possible, trying which can talk the most nonsense, and laugh the loudest at a bad joke.

Our united regards and wishes for lots of happy new years are wafted to you and Lady Morgan from the family amanuensis.

Yours very faithfully,
HORATIO SMITH.

PS.—Should this papyro-saccharine process go on, what capital kisses will be made from Little's poems and sugar of *lead* from my works! You will see in the Magazine a poem of mine which will remind you of the fellow's *recantation* for calling another a swindler. "I called you a swindler, it is true; you're an honest man, I'm a liar."

The diary resumed:—

11, WILLIAM STREET, *January 1st, 1843.*—I enter on my third year's illness, which has interfered with my enjoyment of life, my worldly interests (for I cannot write without pain and palpitation), and all my social pleasures. My dear family are all far away, and I am deprived of my liberty at home and abroad, still, two of the great blessings are left me, the society of my most dear and true friend, my husband, in full health and spirits, and my own consciousness that I never lost an occasion of working or rendering a service during my long life, to the best of my ability; my sight has wonderfully recovered since my other attack.

January 28.—" Charming well again!" and in my pretty drawing-room. An old friend dropped in to-day, and found Morgan and myself sitting over the fire and laughing, *à gorge deployé*, at some nonsense, and he said, "You ought to work it up for the *New Monthly*." And so we will; we are to call it the *Memoirs of Margery Daw*. A hit at a *fadaise*, which has come out lately, about good little fools.

The following notes are from Lady Morgan's letters to her niece:—

February 6th, 1843.—Your uncle has made a very perfect recovery from a very alarming illness, but is still rather more "pale, mild, and interesting" than, in *my* unromanticism, I am desirous to see him! *au reste*, I, too, am beginning to turn the corner of my three years' malady (though even writing such a scrap as this brings on my old heart-beat), and so we have launched once more our old bark the *Darby and Joan*, on the broad seas of society; but with all the caution and *inland* steering of old and shipwrecked mariners. We did our Babbage last Saturday (his first of the season), where were all the *habitués* of the good old times, "your slave, but now your slave no longer," Rogers, gave me a crush of the hand as he passed me in the crowd, and turned his eyes tenderly on me, whilst I averted mine disdainfully; we looked an illustration of *Death and the Lady*, and I had a mind to ask Landseer, who stood near me, to take it for his next subject. Before I drop the *Yellow Poet*, I must tell you that he is the slave and blackmoor of another lady, who is now the receiver of all his pretty speeches, and the idol of his *iced butter parties, que vous connaissez si bien.*

Diary again:

June.—Is it possible that I am again restored to health and sight. My dear Morgan is well and hearty, and Olivia better.

Soirées, operas, concerts, *à discretion*, which we (old fools as we are) enjoy *à l'indiscretion!* Well, so here I am, taking a new lease of life, available for any length of time, with a peppercorn fine, which is about the worth what we give in return. And here, if I open my journal again, it shall be to write something new and pleasant.

My life may be deemed a frivolity for one of my age, but no, it is a philosophy, a profound and just philosophy, founded upon the wisdom of the principle, to *do* and enjoy all the good I *can*, while I submit to the penalty of that mystery called life.

Some of the "young Englanders" have just been here; they might as well have been New Zealanders, for any advance they make in the art of thinking. But they are *good boys*, of the school of Tommy Goodchild, in the *Universal Spelling Book*, and they know it. All little "Jack Horners" in their way,

> "Who put in his thumb,
> And pulled out a plumb,
> And said what a good boy am I!"

Their plumb is a *green*-gage, poor dears! I knew the firstlings of this school of good boys, some thirty years ago. Some of them are now cabinet ministers, and others—nothing; and they are the best off, as the world has not been put in the secret of their inaptitude.

Sidney Smith has been in the Thames Tunnel, and sent me his experiences:—

Sidney Smith to Lady Morgan.

56, GREEN STREET, GROSVENOR LANE,
June 5, 1843.

I had fully intended, my dear madam, to have been of your party to-night; but I went to the Thames Tunnel, and have destroyed myself by walking under the river, and descending and ascending one hundred and twenty steps; there was a suffocating heat and a want of ventilation for which I was not prepared. I am astonished the Thames submits to the insult; one day or another it will come down upon the subaqueous intruders with all the force of a basin of water flung from the seventh story of a house in Edinburgh.

Yours, my dear madam,
Very sincerely,
SIDNEY SMITH.

P.S.—Mrs. Sidney (ill with the influenza) desires me to say that she depends upon Sir C. Morgan and you for Thursday; I beg you will keep away from the Tunnel in the interim.

June 30*th.*—One of the most wretched days of my life—bad letter from Ireland.

"Yet love hopes on, when reason would despair."

My dear, dear Olivia; *my* hereafter in this world—gentle, spiritual, intellectual, full of the finest affections—unselfish beyond all comparison! My beloved Morgan said to me, as I wept over Dr. Carmichael's letter—" Oh, Sydney, if you grieve thus for a *niece*, whom you never see much of, what is to become of you if *I* were to go?" This dreadful idea consoled me. How strange—my present loss appeared less; my beloved husband took me off to Richmond, and I came back in better spirits, and again full of hope—and Morgan beside me.

In Richmond Park we sat under an old tree, within view of the Mount where Henry VIII. stood when a cannon announced to him the decapitation of Anne Boleyn.

CHAPTER XXXI.

DEATH OF SIR CHARLES MORGAN—1843.

The sorrow felt by Lady Morgan for the death of her niece, was soon to be merged in a deeper grief. The suggestion thrown out by Sir Charles to moderate her grief about her niece was suddenly realised. That expedition to Richmond was the very last they had together. They had seldom been separated during their long married life; but the final separation came when least expected. Lady Morgan had often complained of Sir Charles Morgan's disinclination to take exercise, and of his love of remaining all day at home, engrossed in reading and writing, never feeling the need of fresh air. It would seem that this was connected with his state of health, though she did not then suspect it. He was ill only a fortnight; he had an attack of heart-disease, sank into a state of stupor and died before those round him had begun to fear danger.

It was the second great sorrow of her life. The death of her father, a few months after her marriage, was her first grief; the death of her husband was a far heavier affliction. As years went on, she felt his loss more and more. She had loved him thoroughly; her respect for him was equal to her affection; his influence over her and his wise judgment had greatly contributed to her brilliant success. He had been her best friend, her guide and counsellor in all things, and her constant companion, sharing all her employments and pursuits. He used to correct her writings, and curtail them of the redundancies and extravagances in which she took delight. He had no petty jealousy in his nature—he admired her genius and rejoiced in her success as much at the end of his life as he had done when he first knew her. The love-letters which the reader has seen in the first volume were redeemed; every promise and every profession was fulfilled. It had been a thoroughly happy marriage.

It was not in Lady Morgan's nature to cherish grief; she could not bear to be unhappy; she resolutely put sorrow away from her throughout her life. It is not the noblest way of treating sorrow, nor the most profitable; but it was her nature to refuse to entertain it, and she could not do otherwise. But if she endeavoured to bury her misery out of sight, she did not forget the dead. One who knew her very intimately in the later years of her life, bears testimony to the fresh tenderness with which she, from time to time, spoke of her husband, as though she had lost him but yesterday; but it was never for more than a moment; she always broke off abruptly, saying, "I must not think of that," and turned to something else.

The death of Sir Charles cast a gloom over the whole circle of their friends; he was a man singularly beloved by all who knew him both in public and in private life; he was of a sweet, affectionate, noble nature; he was thoroughly true and honest, and to be depended upon in every relation of life. "He was," says one who knew him well, "a man of a refined and philosophic mind, of varied accomplishments—a scholar and a gentleman in the largest sense of those comprehensive words."

It is long before there is any further entry in Lady Morgan's diary. She was as much crushed down by her great sorrow as she could be crushed by anything. The innumerable letters of sympathy which she received, the public testimonials to the worth and memory of her husband soothed her feelings; but she was in deep and bitter affliction. The first entry in her diary after her widowhood is—

Oh, my husband! I cannot endure this—I was quite unprepared for this. So ends my life.

November, 1843.—Plus ne m'est rien, rien ne m'est plus.

The winter fire kindles alone for me now. The chair, the table, the lamp, the very books and paper-cutter, all *these* are here, this November—gloomy, wretched November!! How I used to long for November—social, home-girt November; now I spend it in wandering through this deserted house. Is it possible? "Ce que je serai dorénavant ne sera plus qu'une demi être!—ne sera plus moi—je m'échappe tous les jours." When I first transcribed that monologue did I ever dream the dreadful dream that it would serve for me!

The next entry in her journal is many months later; but it is given here not to break the thread of the subject:—

April, 1844.—Time applied to grief is a worldly common place—time has its due influence over visible grief, that which is expressed by visible emotions—it softens sighs and dries tears! but *le fond* remains the same! Time gives you back to the exercise of your faculties and your habits; but the loss of that which is, or *was*, part of yourself, remains for ever. This melancholy Sunday morning, April! The first word written in this once gay record of pleasant sensations!

There is a long blank, and then the following entry, headed—

"*A period without date.*"

In the most awful moment of my life, I was not without aid and solace; my sister was with me, my brother-in-law, and my niece Sydney Jones and her husband came to me immediately, and I was removed from my own house to lodgings, whilst all the wretched business that necessarily followed my most miserable loss was arranged. After that, I accompanied my sister to Brighton, where I was received by the dear, kind family of Horace Smith, with affection and sympathy.

My dearest sister being obliged to return to her family in Ireland (she had been with me ever since the death of her own dear child Olivia—Mrs. Savage); Lord and Lady Beauchamp, who were then at Brighton, insisted on my going to them at their delightful seat, so I went, and, removed from all local association, without domestic cares (or joys), surrounded by pleasant distractions and excessive kindness, I recovered my health and *constitutional* cheerfulness much more rapidly than I should otherwise have done. My return to my own lonely house was woeful. The night I arrived, my servant Delahaye attended me at my solitary dinner; I bade him recount to me the *Battle of Waterloo*. He was an old soldier of the 18th, and fought there.

July 28.—Everybody makes a point of having me out, and I am beginning to be familiarised with my terrible loss. I go in and out of drawing-rooms, and "sit at good men's tables," and submit to the influence of the *laughing-gas of society*. I was told, only the other day, " I was *so* brilliant at somebody's dinner;" all this is very contemptible, but it is inevitable.

I *could* read now, if I had sight—once, and *so lately*, I never missed my eyes! One thing cheers me—my beloved sister comes to me soon, and will meet under my roof her beloved children and *mine*—the *all* that is left me now.

London is the best place in the world for the happy and the unhappy, there is a floating capital of sympathy for every human good or evil; I am nobody, and yet what kindness I am daily receiving!

If I were not incapacitated by a weak sight and a heavy heart, and above all, by the eternal "*qui bono?*" that now impedes every flow of thought, and checks every tendency to action, what amusing memoranda would I not set down from the ceaseless anecdotes dropped by the congress of visitors, foreign and home, that daily fill my little *salon*. Poor, dear, kind Sir Mathew Tierny has just been here; his loss, like my own, is irreparable, and of the same nature.

CHAPTER XXXII.

FIRST YEARS OF WIDOWHOOD.

LADY MORGAN resolutely entered on life again, determined not to be more unhappy than she could possibly help. The sense of her loneliness, her inward sorrow was never entirely absent from her thoughts; but she endeavoured to stifle it, and in some measure succeeded—at least, when she was in society.

July, 1844.—Another gone—poor Campbell! Oh for the day that I first saw him led in by Sir Thomas Lawrence, up the great dining-room of the Priory (Stanmore), in the middle of one of the great Saturday dinners! I was seated between Lord Aberdeen and Manners Sutton—the latter gave Campbell his seat beside me—opposite to us was Lord Erskine, and the Duchess of Gordon. Campbell was awkward, but went on taking his soup as if he was eating a haggis in the Highlands; but when he put his knife in the salt-cellar to help himself to salt, every eyeglass was up, and the *first* poet of the age was voted the vulgarest of men. His *coup de grâce*, however, was in the evening, when he took the *unapproachable* Marquis of Abercorn by the buttonhole that joined his star! Oh, my stars! I thought we should all die of it, knowing the *extreme* fastidiousness of the possessor of the star. Next morning he went about asking every one if they could "take him into town with a wee bit of a portmanteau?" Lady Asgill (the most charming of coquets) gave a place in her carriage to the man who, by a line, could give her immortality.

My kind old friend, Horace Twiss (by-the-bye what a pair of coxcombs he and I were when we first met in the salons of Cork and Charleville), has just sent me, most kindly, his *Life of Eldon*, and with a flattering word of presentation to boot. It is an honest book, for the author believes every word he advances, in form of faith or opinion, and it is the work of a gentleman and a scholar, and of a good artist, too, for he knows his craft. His personal partiality for Eldon, though *apparent*, is never officious. He is above his subject —a narrow-minded, timid, and unenlightened man. Horace Twiss's text is clear and brief, and in the best taste and style.

In the autumn Lady Morgan paid a visit to Boulogne; her account of it to her niece, Mrs. Geale, shows that, although she kept down all manifestations of depression and sorrow, she felt her changed and lonely situation very acutely. It alludes to the precarious state of Lady Clarke's health, which gave fears for another grief in prospect. She says:—

You have long since heard of my melancholy illness—utterly alone, and in a foreign hotel; and I really believe that if Sir Joseph Lafansa had not arrived I should have been at peace by this. What a curious proof of the incoherency of all things—to have lived for my family, and to have died without *one* of its members near! But above all, I missed *the one* who had been so long the comfort and saviour of my life! Still I acknowledge, with gratitude, the most kind and charitable attentions of the humane and kind strangers I have found here—among them, Lady Banks and her sweet, good girls; Lady Dundonald, the Cochranes, Storys, and many others. Lord Wellesley calls often at my door, offers me his carriage, and has ordered his gamekeeper to supply me. Still I am longing to get back to England, and was to have sailed yesterday, only Sir Joseph thought me too weak to run the risk of sea-sickness.

The health of Lady Clarke had been failing for some time, her state was causing deep anxiety. In the following extract from a letter, describing a mesmeric sitting, Lady Morgan shows how she was endeavouring to cheat herself into hope, and to keep the impending sorrow out of sight.

If you could recover your sleep without opiates you would soon be quite well. Mesmerism does this. I am going to Doctor Ashburner's to-day, to witness an exhibition *solely* on your account (for you know my organ of anti-humbugism). I shall be able to tell you more to-morrow on this head.

Monday.—Now, here is a full and true account. "Well, my dear, our party consisted of the Marchioness of Hastings (a very fine woman, and going to be married to Captain Hastings, Henry, her cousin), both the Henrys and Colonel Lumley—*all believers,*— and *two sceptics,* Lady Morgan and the Rev. Charles Darley, who gave themselves great airs. Lord Anglesey was invited, and tried to come, but could not get out of an engagement. We were all vastly clever at dinner, when at the dessert enter a lovely little girl about twelve years old, in cloak and bonnet, which being doffed, she was brought forward as "little Jane," and presented to Lady Hastings (the queen mesmeriser of London). "Little Jane" looked modest, simple, and childish, until Lady Hastings, drawing her closely to her, fixed her fine eyes on hers, and in a few minutes the child fell back as in a swoon. Dr. Ashburner caught her, and then she stood fast asleep at the table, her eyes shut, but looking flushed and fussy, and talking under the influence of any organ on which Lady Hastings pressed her fingers. The first was music, and she sang all sorts of scraps of songs sweetly, but incorrectly! but when Clifford Henry joined her in *My Father's Marble Hall,* she flew into a rage and said, "you put me out of tune." Then came the organ of affection, and she nearly suffocated Lady Hastings with caresses, and threw herself into the Doctor's arms, and ran round the table and poked every one together, and was, upon the whole, so tender that the Rev. Charles Darley and I got alarmed. The next organ touched was self-esteem, acted to the life, and when I said, "Oh,

Jane, you are a little rogue," she flew into a rage with me, and said, "You mean I am a thief, that is very wicked of you," and away she went, and sat in a *niche* under the side-board, in great dudgeon and dignity. As to the organ of *imitation*, it was to the life; she personified Tom Thumb, several London cries, and danced a polka, and so ended act the first.

She was then de-mesmerised, and was again modest and childlike, and said she hoped she had not done anything rude, or sang an improper song; "I hope I shall soon be married." The two sceptics decided it was *acting* equal to Mrs. Jordan's. When the men came up, after dinner, act the second: I assisted to paste black sticking plaster over her eyes, so her seeing was impossible. The Doctor, standing behind her, held his folded hands over her eyes, and Darley and I held a book open to her page after page; she read all, but complained of the small print. Sceptics startled; she sang scraps of songs. She frequently said to me, "that lady is a sceptic."

Act third. Lady Hastings insisted on Clifford Henry being mesmerised, and this was no joke, but a perfect exhibition of poor humanity exposed to an influence over which it had no control, and which subjected it to external impressions which left it but a complicated piece of machinery.

I now tell you all *I saw*, but as to my *faith*, it rests much where my ignorant interests left it some years ago. That the powers of magnetism and electricity are great, and may be beneficially applied in medical practice, I believe there is no doubt, and that they have induced sleep without the previous use of opiates, and by what I saw, muscular power increased to a miraculous extent. The whole of the doctrine is to be found in the *Philosophy of Life*, a work yet destined to give immortality to its author, whose misfortune was to have lived in advance of his age. To *this truth* all my convictions subscribe; and now, dear Olivia, I have done for you and your amusement what I would not do for myself. God help you, my dear Olivia, and be of good heart, all will go well."

The next entry in the journal is a sad one. The sorrow she had feared had fallen upon her.

Sunday, April 27.—The re-opening of my *Doomsday Book*, after a struggle of nearly two years; submitting to the grave law of necessity by which all known things are governed, I have endeavoured to make head against that prostrating melancholy which poisons and embitters life, but does not destroy it, and to live in that world I could not leave by any voluntary act (for mine is not a suicidal temperament). Now I am again crushed by the *last* of the two greatest calamities that could befal me in this life. My noble-minded and affectionate sister, my first friend and earliest companion, with whom I had struggled through a precarious youth. My beloved Olivia is no more! I open this page in my *Doomsday Book* to note this; but I cannot go on, three of the dearest and the best in *two* years; it is *too* terrible.

April 29.—All is now over in Dublin, and the

mourners are returned to their homes, *with time to weep*. Oh! I *cannot weep*, and have none to weep with, for I am alone. All my old friends and new acquaintances have been to my door to offer their sympathy, but I am beyond the reach, *the reach of solace now*, I almost think this last blow has struck most home.

So I reel on! the world is my gin or opium, I take it for a few hours per diem, excitement, intoxication, absence! I return to my desolate home, "and awaken to all the horrors of sobriety." My impressionableness of spirits, my debility of body, my sight dim from nervousness, my heart palpitating at the least movement; and yet I am accounted the "agreeable rattle of the great ladies' coterie," and I talk *pas mal* to many clever men all day. This is surely mechanism, for it is done without effort on the voluntary system, and yet, when alone, books, pictures, flowers, everything has the touch of death on it, and that *park* so near me, of which my beloved Morgan used to say, "It is ours more than the queen's, we use it daily and enjoy it nightly!"—that park that I worked so hard to get an entrance into, I never walk in, it seems to me covered with black crape.

CHAPTER XXXIII.

RETIRED FROM WORK.

In the year 1846 Colburn brought out a cheap edition of the *Wild Irish Girl*. Lady Morgan sent a copy of this new edition of her first work to Mr. Macaulay, who at once wrote to thank her.

T. B. Macaulay to Lady Morgan.

ALBANY,
August 15th, 1846.

DEAR LADY MORGAN,

I have received a copy of the *Wild Irish Girl*, of which the value is increased by a line which tells me that the author has been kind enough to think of me. I shall always value the book for its own sake, and for the sake of the giver.

Believe me,
Dear Lady Morgan,
Your faithful servant,
T. B. MACAULAY.

We return to the diary:—

November 4.—I am thankful to say that all my roamings are over for this year, and that I am safe at home in dear William Street, in sight of all that is best. I got so ill at Worthing I was obliged to leave the Duchess and her family party which, by-the-bye, like most family parties (except it is one's own), was dull. There was one member of this party with whom I got on well, and who talks soundly upon all high *class subjects*, but he talks like a ghost, only when spoken to; and as no one ventured to draw him out but myself, I had him all to myself. He appears cold and self-reliant, stands apart from all contact with his species. Apparently he was never in love, and his family (who know him best) say never will marry. When I left this ducal *ménage* and its aristocratic *morgue*, I started off for my dearest Sydney's pretty little parsonage at Gelderton, in Suffolk, rather a different scene to be sure; but its sunny and cheerful atmosphere made everything bright and happy, and it was not till my return to town with a severe *attack of rheumatism*, that I found out their cottage was damp and low, and I *suspect* disagrees with them, but they will not allow it. I was obliged to send to my good friend Dr. Latham, and have his advice and prescriptions, which set me up again, and enabled me to go to Serge Hill, Herts, to my dear old Solley's, where I was shown off to divers Hertfordshire magnates, and made to trot out and show my paces in the old style.

December 14.—I dare not trust myself to chronicle my feelings as to passing years more! To forget is my philosophy, to hope would be my insanity, to endure (and that I *can*) is my system; but it is only a system, from which the dreary impulses of my state and condition revolt but too often. Still I am grateful for the good I yet enjoy—to be so is my religion.

Nothing is left me to love; but, also, nothing to fear.

December 25.—I am endeavouring to make head against the sad associations of this month, and to give evidence of my cheerful philosophy if not of my happiness. And so I end this old year quietly, somewhat anxiously, but with increasing social popularity.

January, 1847.—Another year! I cannot say I hailed it with a welcome or with a hope; but I endeavour to *cheer it in,* and gave a dinner for my most dear husband's family and friends, a large musical party in the evening—all the neighbours I could collect.

All my servants laid up with influenza.

I sent these rhymes, with a winter bouquet, to a friend:—

> Spring flowers,
> With spring showers,
> Like Love's promise,
> Pass, fleet away.
>
> While winter weaves
> His ivy leaves,
> For deathless wreaths
> For friendship's day.

August.—Death of the O'Connor Don. Another

gone! my esteemed and tried friend, one of the honestest and best men Ireland ever had to boast of. It is but the other day since he was at one of my *soirées*, talking of old times. He was the lineal descendant of the supreme kings of Ireland. I saw the old crown of Irish gold at a jeweller's, in Dublin, when I was a little girl.

Lady Charleville, one of the very few old friends left to Lady Morgan, was growing very old and infirm, but she still retained the same warmth of regard for her as ever. Lady Charleville had also met with much sorrow, which she bore in a different way to Lady Morgan—she did not put it away from her.

Lady Charleville to Lady Morgan.

March 8, 1847.

I am very very sorry to be deprived so long of any enjoyment from your society, which I always cared for and valued when there seemed to be more of the same stamp current than in our latter days! Is it that as age advances we think complacently on those scenes we passed under the blaze of a meridian day with capabilities now blunted, and which neither can impart or receive pleasure with the same gusto as heretofore? Be that as it may, my dear Lady Morgan, I shall always rejoice in seeing you again, and be most anxious for the recovered health of Mr. and Mrs. Jones.

Yours affectionately,

C. M. CHARLEVILLE.

April 15.—I look into my old journals and find that my first lesson in *salad making* was given me by Lord Chancellor Manners—about the time my novel *O'Donnel* appeared. The day after getting my book, when he discovered its emancipating tendency, he ordered it to be burnt in the servants' hall, and then said to Lady Manners, (who told it to my sister) "Jenny, I wish I had not given her the secret of my salad." Ever after, he only *bowed* to me when we met at court, never spoke to me. Jenny was my old crony, friend and confidant up to that moment; but *O'Donnel* lost me my charming friend. She had been educated in a Catholic convent, was the child of Catholic parents, her mother born in low life, and she only became a Protestant on becoming a peeress. Her brother, Lord Glengall, was converted before.

A note from Sir William Napier, the great historian, though a trifle, is a trifle full of grace and character.

Sir W. Napier to Lady Morgan.

SCINDE HOUSE, CLAPHAM,
October 20, 1849.

Let me jump over all propriety—it is the only thing I can now jump over, but early practice and long, has kept me vigorous in that particular—let me jump over it, the tiresome obstacle, and address you at once as dear Lady Morgan.

What can I offer in excuse, what say for myself that

I accept your promise of a visit by letter, instead of paying my homage in person? Rudeness I am guilty of "*Mais avec des circonstances extenuantes.*" I am seventy-two—that is no defence; but I am also like the prince in the Arabian tale of the coloured fishes, half flesh half marble, and I can scarcely move across a room; to get in and out of a carriage is almost as bad for me as it was for the genie to get in and out of the vessel sealed by Solomon, not that Solomon ever put his seal on me. I am, however, wise enough to be delighted at the prospect of seeing Lady Morgan, and if she will allow me to say Thursday, as soon after two o'clock as she likes, luncheon will be ready, and an humble admirer at her commands, meanwhile he remains, Her devoted admirer,

W. NAPIER.

December 12.—What a *villegiatura* I have made for the last three months—a honeymoon spent with Lady Laura and Mr. Grattan, at their pretty villa at Hampton Court, then for a fortnight at Lady Webster's, Roehampton, and, *en passant*, I paid a visit at the Grove, and found all the family at home except its illustrious chief. Then to Dover with my poor Jones for his health; but the place disagreed with me after a fortnight, and so I left them and went to the Deepdene, Mr. Hope's—all *en grand seigneur*, and *most* of all the master. It is much to say that the wealthiest man in England is also the highest bred, the fine gentlemanism of good society when it was *best*, with great natural kindness. The party gay and charming.

Then from Deepdene I went to Llanover Court, Monmouthshire (Sir Benjamin Hall's, now Lord Llanover's); staid there a week, and departed from it with my dear Mrs. Murray, for a visit to her mother's, Baroness Braye, at Malvern, and so on to the Duchess of Cleveland's, Yorkshire; a fine party, who moved and breathed by the *Lodge Peerage*, and then back to town, where my dear niece and her husband was waiting to receive me, the first time for years that I was welcomed with cordial affection in my own lonely dwelling.

December 22.—I am actually off for Brighton! on a visit to my kind old friend Lady Webster, I little thought I could visit this sad place again. All my old friends have come about me. The dear, warmhearted and *clever* Horace Smith; the Duke of Devonshire reproached me for not having called on him on my first arrival, and sent me an invitation to dine, immediately he heard I was here. Alas, we first met, a few days before he came of age, at the Priory, Stanmore.

January 12, 1848.—Went to Elliot Warburton's marriage with my friend Miss Groves—a marriage made, I do believe, on my *little balcony*. All the muses assisted at this literary nuptials—Monckton Milnes, Hayward, Eothen Kinglake,—I was the only *she* muse there. I offered two unfinished MSS. to any lady who might adopt them for the nonce, to qualify them for being present.

Dined yesterday with Milner Gibson; amongst the agreeables were Lord Dudley Stuart, that amiable *roué*, Sir Henry Mildmay, and the most illustrious Mr. Punch; *yes, really* and literally, *Punch* ; Douglas Jerrold—a very remarkable-looking man—diminutive, plain, and evidently a valetudinarian; his manners simple, mild and gentleman-like. We chatted across the table, and agreed about the *national defences* and the *national timidity* having brought on the coming invasion. He said he would lower the prices of house-rent at Brighton, if I would return there! I said I would; and lo! there is an admirable and humorous paper on "Brighton panic," in the *Punch* of this day.

February 12.—I have been very ill indeed for a month, and my poor Sydney has been in much sorrow; and I have been more miserable than I ever thought I should be again. After my three great calamities I did not suppose time *could* have another in store for me; but I have been threatened with the loss of all I have left me.

November 25.—The death of Lord Melbourne is one of the *triste* incidents of this *triste* month. How many passages of my own life are recalled by his death! How long I knew him, how much I owed him, what joyous days and nights I have passed in his charming society, from my girlhood to this moment! I called to inquire for him before I left town in October; he sent his valet down to request I would come up. He was sitting in his back drawing-room, amidst books and papers, *en robe de chambre ;* he was quite himself, pleasant and chatty, and asked me what was the little packet I had in my hands. I said, invites for a little *soirée* the next evening, and I had not the courage to ask him. "Why not?" said he, passing his hand over his head in his old way; "I should like it much." "You don't mean that, Lord Melbourne," said I. "Yes I do, and if I feel up to it when the time comes, you will see me;" but when it came, he did not come, and sent me a verbal message. He was looking ill, and I did not *think* of asking him. Alas! I never saw him again!

CHAPTER XXXIV.

THE LEAVES FALLING.

The diary of the year 1849 begins thus:—

My first entry this year is to record a loss. Another old friend is gone,—Sir Robert Wilson. Sir Robert Wilson was born in 1777. He entered the army very early. He was much employed on diplomatic missions of delicacy and importance. In 1812, he was associated with Sir Raoul Liston on a mission to the Emperor Alexander, to prevail on him to make peace with Turkey, and *not* to enter into any negociations with Napoleon. He had seen a great deal of service; but the action with which his name will be for ever associated in the memory of Englishmen is the generous and gallant assistance he lent to effect the escape of Count Lavallette, generously perilling both his personal liberty and his position in life. It was an act of pure generosity, for he had never even seen the Count. It was in January, 1816. Lavallette had been condemned to be guillotined, and all the attempts to soften the stupid and callous heart of Louis XVIII. had failed. Lavallette's heroic wife had effected her husband's escape from the walls of the Conciergerie, and he had been concealed in Paris; but the police were on his track, and he must soon have been discovered if Sir Robert Wilson and two of his friends had not given their services to aid his escape over the frontier into Belgium. Sir Robert Wilson conveyed him in his own carriage in the uniform of a British officer, as far as Mons.

The escape was entirely successful; but on Sir Robert's return to Paris the police, seeing his coach covered with mud, as though from a long journey, set their spies upon his servant, and contrived to extract from him that his master had been to Mons with an officer of the guards who could not speak a word of English. They bribed him to carry the correspondence of Sir Robert to the prefect of police (for he was trusted by his master to carry his letters). The servant betrayed his trust, and the first letter they got hold of was a long despatch to Earl Grey, containing full details of the escape. Sir Robert and his two friends were immediately apprehended; but eventually they did not fall victims to their generosity. Sir Robert, when young, had been a very handsome man, with a fine commanding presence.

A letter from Madame Bonaparte, chronicling the changes that even dull times never fail to bring, and, accordingly, her experience of republics.

Madame Patterson Bonaparte to Lady Morgan.

BALTIMORE,
March 14, 1849.

MY DEAR LADY MORGAN,

I was most agreeably surprised by your letter of the 17th February. I had heard and believed that you were living in Dublin. You may be quite convinced that I consider it a *bonne fortune pour moi* that you inhabit London. To enjoy again your agreeable society will be my tardy compensation for the long, weary, unintellectual years inflicted on me in this my dull native country, to which I have never owed advantages, pleasures or happiness. I owe nothing to my country; no one expects me to be grateful for the evil chance of having been born here. I shall emancipate myself, *par la grâce de Dieu*, about the middle of July next; and I will either write to you before I leave New York or immediately after my arrival at Liverpool. I had given up all correspondence with my friends in Europe, during my vegetation in this Baltimore. What could I write about, except the fluctuations in the security and consequent prices of American Stocks. There is nothing here worth attention or interest, save the money market. Society, conversation, friendship, belong to older countries, and are not yet cultivated in any part of the United States which I have visited. You ought to thank your stars for your European birth; you may believe me when I assure you that it is only distance from republics which lends enchantment to

the view of them. I hope that about the middle of
next July I shall begin to put the Atlantic between
the advantages and honours of democracy and myself.
France, *je l'espère dans son interêt* is in a state of transition, and will not let her brilliant society be put under an extinguisher *nommée la République*. The Emperor hurled me back on what I most hated on earth
—my Baltimore obscurity; even that shock could not
divest me of the admiration I felt for his genius and
glory. I have ever been an imperial Bonapartiste
quand même, and I do feel enchanted at the homage
paid by six millions of voices, to his memory in voting
an imperial President; *le prestige du nom* has, therefore, elected the Prince, who has my best wishes, my
most ardent hopes for an empire. I never could endure universal suffrage until it elected the nephew of
an emperor for the chief of a republic; and I shall be
charmed with *universal* suffrage *once* more if it insists
upon their President of France becoming a monarch.
I am disinterested personally. It is not my desire
ever to return to France.

My dear Lady Morgan, do you know that having
been cheated out of the fortune which I ought to have
inherited from my late rich and unjust parent, I have
only ten thousand dollars, or two thousand pounds
English, which conveniently I can disburse annually.
You talk of my "*princely* income," which convinces
me that you are ignorant of the paucity of my means.
I have all my life had poverty to contend with, pecuniary difficulties to torture and mortify me; and but
for my industry, and energy, and my determination to

conquer at least a decent sufficiency to live on in Europe, I might have remained as poor as you saw me in the year 1816.

I shall have much to tell you. Lamartine, and Chateaubriand are giving their memoirs to the public. The first *de son vivant*. I am now reading *Les Mémoires d'outre tombe*. I have no doubt that your memoirs would be infinitely better, more piquant, and more natural. When I knew Lamartine he was chargé-d'affaires from Charles X. Florence was then a charming place; I met him every night at parties. How little did I foresee that he was to become a poetical republican, and that dear Florence was to be *travestie en République! ni l'un ni l'autre, ne gagnera par le troc.* Hoping that England may remain steady and faithful to monarchical principles, that at least some refined society may be left in the world, I shall, *Dieu permettant*, have the satisfaction of seeing you in the course of next summer.

I am, as ever,
My dear Lady Morgan,
Your affectionate and obliged friend,
E. PATTERSON.

May.—The death of my husband's and my own dear old friend, Horace Smith, has not the least shocked me, being long expected. He was my blessed Morgan's intimate friend—an intimacy founded on the singleness of their character, their pure and honest lives, and the similarity of their political and social opinions and habits. Gay, tender, kind, hospitable, and intellectual. I have known him since the first day of my marriage.

Death of Lord Jeffrey. Jeffrey gone! Oh, for the last, gay, classic evening he spent with us at our *Taudis*, in Grosvenor Place! How many bright and brilliant women who were with us that evening are gone now!

December 30.—Confined to my room; my maid reading to me *Shirley*, by the author of *Jane Eyre*. It is high-flown, and the talent factitious. Great force of style, great feebleness of action, incoherent in its working out; but original in its thinking.

CHAPTER XXXV.

LADY MORGAN AND CARDINAL WISEMAN.

In the early part of 1850 there was rather a lively discussion about abolishing the office of Lord Lieutenant of Ireland. It excited more vehemence and party spirit than the question was intrinsically worth. English people were inclined to think, that one real queen was enough for the United Kingdom and the colonies besides; but the Irish clung tenaciously to having a viceroy of their own to preside over the festivities of the Castle, and to give a "court circle" to their capital, and they saw in the reported measure, only one insult more from England. Lady Morgan was appealed to by persons on both sides of the question for her opinion. Her political judgment was considered good; and her experience of the old vice-regal times had given her a knowledge which made her opinion worth listening to. She wrote one or two "letters" on the subject, which are not to be found now. The question fell into speedy abeyance; and the Lord Lieutenant is still "to the fore." Lady

Morgan's opinion was to abolish the office. This note from Mr. Hallam refers to one of her articles.

Mr. Hallam to Lady Morgan.

April 14, Friday Morning.

DEAR LADY MORGAN,

Yours is a sharp pen, and I hope it will never be directed against me, of which, indeed, I have no fears whatever. What you say of old viceroys is, I fear, true enough. Yet, in those times it was impossible to dispense with them—the necessity ought now to be at an end; though I am not master enough of the state of Ireland to *pronounce absolutely* against their continuance. But you can make any case a good one with wit or raillery.

Truly yours,
H. HALLAM.

The following pleasant note from Douglas Jerrold refers to a *coup de patte* in *Punch*, where Lady Morgan took her share of life's game of give and take. Jerrold's note would be a compensation for a much more disagreeable dispensation. The only thing Lady Morgan could *not* forgive, was neglect!

PUTNEY,
June 9.

DEAR LADY MORGAN,

I was very sorry that I had promised my friend—and all the world's friend—Mr. Paxton, to dine with him at a dinner where he presides to-day; and so I further miss the opportunity of personally avowing to you my opinion of that smallest of the small, and dullest of the dull onslaughts upon your party. I had not read it until I received yours; and I think *Punch* does not often make such a blunder, for which he owes you penitential reparation; but when he *does* blunder, he does it with a courageous stupidity. The editor is one of the best hearted of men, and will, I know, be annoyed when brought face to face with the absurdity.

    Believe me, dear Lady Morgan,
     Your old and early reader,
     And therefore most truly yours,
       DOUGLAS JERROLD.

Another note from Douglas Jerrold.

Douglas Jerrold to Lady Morgan.

    WEST LODGE, PUTNEY,
      December 20.

DEAR LADY MORGAN,
 The devil—the devil take him—brings me your hospitable summons for last night—here in the wilderness this morning! Next time, pray *do* remember—PUTNEY! Gibbon's Putney—Fairfax's Putney—Cromwell's Putney—the Marchioness of Shrewsbury's Putney (where she held her horse whilst Buckingham

made her a widow)—Putney, with a hundred other
pleasant associations,—and the Putney of its humblest
inhabitant, but
Yours faithfully,
DOUGLAS JERROLD.

This year was also enlivened by a controversy between Lady Morgan and Cardinal Wiseman. Let any one who knew Lady Morgan imagine if she did not enjoy a pen-to-pen encounter with a great churchman on a statement made in her long-ago work on Italy! 1850 was, as the reader may or may not recollect, the date of the Papal Aggression; when England, for the first time since the Reformation, was adorned by a Cardinal. Public feeling ran high, and any *pièce de circonstance* was sure of meeting with readers. Lady Morgan, in her work on Italy, had said, concerning that relic of ancient upholstery, so carefully preserved in the Vatican—the Chair of St. Peter—"that the sacrilegious curiosity of the French broke through all obstacles to their seeing the chair of St. Peter. They actually removed its superb casket, and discovered the relic. Upon its mouldering and dusty surface were traced carvings, which bore the appearance of letters. The chair was quickly brought into a better light, the dust and cobwebs removed, and the inscription (for inscription it was) faithfully copied. The writing is in Arabic characters, and is the well-known confession of the Mahometan faith: "*There is but one God, and Mahomet is his Prophet.*" It is supposed that this chair had been, among the spoils of the Crusaders, offered to the Church at a time when a taste for antiquarian lore and the deciphering of inscriptions was not yet in fashion. This story has since been hushed up, the chair replaced, and none but the unhallowed remember the fact, and none but the audacious repeat it. Yet such there are even at Rome."

This statement Dr. Wiseman had contradicted in a pamphlet written about 1833, and it might for ever have remained in the limbo assigned to pamphlets which reach their regulation term of a nine day's life, if he had not been made a cardinal, and the bran new light from his title shone into the literary corners of "dusty death."

Whether Lady Morgan had ever before seen or heard of the pamphlet in question is doubtful. She says herself, "I know not what rank your Eminence then held in that Church, of which you are now so brilliant an illustration, on your way to the '*all-hail hereafter*.' It is a singular fact that I never saw this able attack of your Eminence on my work until *lately;* and so the thunders of the Vatican rolled over me innoxious. I heard, indeed, that a very learned diatribe had been written against my description of St. Peter's chair; but I carelessly dismissed the subject with the observation of a French wit—

'*Que les gens d'esprit sont bêtes.*'"

At any rate, the present occasion was too appropriate to resist; an Irishman could as soon have refrained from hitting a head at Donnybrook Fair, as Lady

Morgan have abstained from a tilt with a Roman Catholic Church dignitary who had attacked a work of hers, no matter how many years before. She wrote, accordingly, a very lively *brochure* in her best style, entitled *Letter to Cardinal Wiseman, in answer to his remarks on Lady Morgan's statements regarding St. Peter's Chair*. It had a great success, both because it was amusing and because it was well-timed; and it had a run of criticisms in all the newspapers and journals of the day;—*il faisait le frais* of *Punch*, both in prose, and verse, and illustration, for several weeks; and it was to Lady Morgan a return of the *beaux jours* of her literary celebrity.

December 25.—Christmas day—my birthday; another and another still succeeds.

December 27.—Lots of notes and notices of my Letter to Cardinal Wiseman! It has had the run of all the newspapers. *La petite vielle femme vit encore.*

Lady Morgan, from age and weakness, was unable to be present on the 1st of May, 1851, at the opening of the Crystal palace in Hyde Park. But she paid a visit to that wonderful edifice early in June, and described the scene in a letter to her niece, under date of June 26.

I am leading a very gay life, for I think with so solitary a home as mine is, social excitement is almost necessary for me. I am, thank goodness, in better health than I have been for a long time. I will turn to *mon livre des bénéfices* and give you the cream of the day as it passed me, leaving the skim milk in oblivion.

First, Lady Beauchamp's grand majority rout (where I only staid half an hour) the heat and crowd was too much for me; but I had a "word and a blow," with fifty of my particular friends—old Rogers in the thick of the fight. *Next on my list,* on the 24th a dinner at Wentworth Dilke's; dinner excellent; company, the Earls of Carlisle and Granville, and all Her Majesty's commissioners for the Exhibition, and many other eminent persons—a charming dinner. I must tell you of my visit to the Crystal Palace the other morning, where I have permission to go early, as I cannot encounter the crowd. It is impossible to convey an idea of the beauty of this miraculous building, *as I saw it,* in the bright sunshine and freshness of the morning, all silent and solitary! The fountains, flowers, statues and gold and silver draperies, and heaps of jewels, sparkling in the sun—a scene of magic, that one dreams of, but never till now was created. Whilst I was lost in wonder and admiration, and fixed in silent adoration of a beautiful statue, I heard a slight movement of feet, and sweet voices approaching me,—when lo! the whole royal party issued from an adjoining compartment; the Queen leaning on the arm of the King of the Belgians, in animated conversation,—Prince Albert, looking both pleased and proud of this great and noble work. The children, with their governess, and the whole charming procession, preceded by our friend, Wentworth Dilke, *chapeau bas!* I never saw so happy a party—certainly, *la Reine est la plus grande Reine du monde,* as my dear Madame de Sevigné said of *Le Roi,* when he asked her to dance. The whole scene was a fairy tale in the Arabian Nights, and had for me a charm that I cannot explain; for there was before me, IN THAT MOMENT, all that was greatest and best, *visible and invisible*, and the sublime sun shining down his rays on this beautiful creation of man!

On my return from this palace of the genii, a charming Bohemian lady, Madame Noel, took me to a *matinée*, given for the benefit of the distressed Hungarians, for which I had passed tickets and subscribed; but it was a hot crowd with cold draughts. Fanny Kemble recited the divine Allegro and il Penseroso. It went to my very soul, where every line was impressed half a century back; but I returned tired and weary. Alas! I feel

"I am wearing away to the land of the leal."

Still my spirits keep me afloat, and I am good for—

"A few gay soarings yet."

Poor Rogers! I sat an hour with him the other day; he is the ghost of his former ghost; he talked with compassion of Moore's state, who is now bed ridden, and has lost his memory,—remembers nothing but some of his own early songs, which he sings as he lies, and which is heartrending to hear by those who are around him.

Moore lingered on a few months longer, and then passed away. Before this event happened, a catastrophe which still retains its fascination for the public—the burning of the Amazon—robbed Lady Morgan of a younger friend. This terrible disaster is the topic of the next letter.

Mrs Gore to Lady Morgan.

HAMBLE CLIFF, SOUTHAMPTON,
January 9.

MY DEAR LADY MORGAN,

I do not often bore you with letters, because I know it troubles you to read and answer them; but I cannot resist my inclination to write and ask you a question or two about poor Eliot Warburton, who, I remember was a friend of yours. I am happy to say I never even saw him; or a double pang would be added to my grief for the poor Amazon. I had watched all her experimental cruises, with much interest, and saluted her as she passed my lawn in triumphant beauty this day week! On the evening we received the news of h.. disaster, I sent off an express, nine miles, to get a second ed'' of the *Times* for the names of the passengers, and till my messenger was gone, solaced myself by reading *Darien*. I had just reached the chapter (at one in the morning) of which the motto is from Shelley,

> The thirsty fire crept round his manly limbs,
> His resolute eyes were scorched to blindness soon,
> His death-pang rent my heart!

when the groom returned with the sad list containing poor Eliot Warburton's fated name!

I cannot tell you how deeply I was shocked. What I want you to tell me is, whether he has left a wife and children (as well as talented brothers), and whether there was any *occasion* for him to cross the sea?

which is, at this moment, looking as bright and beautiful under my windows as in one of Stanfield's pictures, and as if incapable of mischief. My house has been full of juvenile visitors for the Christmas holidays. My son and daughter hunt three days a week—the latter you may infer to be well and happy, for she is often ten hours a day in the saddle, which is the home her soul delights in. I am afraid you are not as much delighted as myself that one is no longer obliged to travel so far as Persia to witness a perfect despotism—the best of all possible governments; the only one where one's head feels quite safe on its shoulders,—till the day on which it is struck off. How I should like to see the press in England equally gagged: *The Times* sent to the Stone-Jug, and little Hayward to Cayenne! I am expecting Mr. Roebuck here to day, and feel it necessary to let my Toryism explode before he arrives. I am also much rejoiced to see the mouldy old Whig cabinet crumbling away like a stale cake. It has done so little to advance the cause of civilisation, that I am fain to believe we should be better off under the most stringent of conservatisms, provided they do not employ Dizzy, who is a radical at heart. I am very much disappointed in his memoirs of Lord George. I expected the book would amuse one by a world of absurdities; instead of which, it is as full of common sense and dulness as his best friends could wish.

A propos of friends, have you seen anything of Mr. Hope? Baillie Cochrane was here lately, who told me he had paid him a visit in the new house; that Mrs. Hope did the honours in the most ladylike manner, and was covered to the chin in crape for Lady Beresford. She spoke very pretty broken English, and has quite *forgotten* she was ever a French woman. The little daughter will be one of the richest heiresses in England, and I dare say we shall live to see her marry a duke.

Do not take the trouble of answering me yourself; let one of your servants be your amanuensis, I have no doubt they all write quite as well as our Hampshire squires. My children are out with the Hambledon hounds, or they would place themselves at your feet, as well, dear Lady Morgan,

Yours sincerely,
C. F. Gore.

CHAPTER XXXVI.

DEATH OF MOORE.

The diary resumes with the notice of Moore's death:

February 28.—On coming down, an hour back, to the drawing-room, *The Times* was lying on my writing-desk; I lighted on the death of the poet Moore. It has struck me home; I did not think I should ever shed tears again; but I have. The funeral attended only by strangers, to the neighbouring churchyard! Surely they will do something to honour his memory in Ireland! I will write on the subject to Saunders' *News Letter* and other papers.

March.—I have written to Mr. M'Garel, sending my contribution to the fund for the benefit of the school of poor Irish children; and I took the opportunity of suggesting that some monumental testimony to Moore, Ireland's greatest poet, should be raised in St. Patrick's cathedral, Dublin; and that no occasion for proposing it could be more aptly made than the celebration of the festival of St. Patrick.

The question of raising a monument to Moore in Dublin was at once taken up, and Lady Morgan was involved in correspondence on the choice of site and other particulars.

Lady Morgan to Mr. Mulvany.

WILLIAM STREET,
March 27.

Lady Morgan presents her compliments to Mr. Mulvany, and, in answer to his flattering note, begs to say, that any project for honouring the memory of their illustrious countryman Moore, cannot fail to interest her feelings or her pride, both as a personal friend and as an Irish woman. With respect to Mr. Mulvany's allusion to Lady Morgan's suggestion of a monumental tablet in St. Patrick's Cathedral (the Westminster Abbey of Ireland) it was only incidentally made in a note to one of the best patrons of the benevolent St. Patrick's School Society in London. For the rest, Lady Morgan presumes to say, that in the choice of a site, and the selection of a monumental testimonial, climate and money are necessary subjects of consideration; to "consult the genius of the place in all," is an old maxim of taste, and to have *some* regard to *financial* means, is an indispensable restraint upon national enthusiasm in Ireland. Lady Morgan has *lived to see* so many "*emerald crowns*," national monuments, tributary cenotaphs, and other such offerings decreed to national merit by Irish gratitude through vocal acclamation and on paper, which "no storied urn or ani-muted bust," ever afterwards realised, that she now ventures to suggest the necessity of first consulting the funds collected for a consummation so devoutly to be wished, before any decision is made as to the quality of the testimonial. Lady Morgan humbly gives her opinion, as Mr. Mulvany asked it, and will be happy to contribute her very limited influence to the promotion of that object, admirable in itself, and doubly consecrated as being decided under the classical roof of *Charlemont House*, where all that was ever done "*wisest and best*," was debated and carried into effect by that illustrious Irishman under whose banner Ireland was first led forth against a foreign invader, and taught to resist domestic despotism, the father of the always patriotic nobleman who is about to honour the meeting by his presence.

This letter received a lively response. It was copied into all the Dublin papers; and a meeting was called at Charlemont House. It was suggested that the site of the proposed statue should be Leinster Lawn, facing Merrion Square.

Lady Morgan also wrote to Mrs. Moore:

Lady Morgan to Mrs. Moore.

WILLIAM STREET, ALBERT GATE,
May 27, 1852.

MY DEAR MRS. MOORE,

In looking over some letters the other day, of the year '46, I found a note of dear Mr. Moore's, which I have copied and sent you, knowing how useful and precious *even the most trifling* memorandum becomes, when collecting materials for the life of an illustrious person. I do not like to part with the *autograph*; though, if I had strength or sight, I am sure I should find many of his little notes written in "Auld Lang Syne," when he lived in the same gay circle in Dublin, and afterwards met in England, France and Italy. He was a good deal with us in Florence.

I assure you, my dear Mrs. Moore, I rejoice to hear, *and from yourself*, that you are so well circumstanced, in a worldly point of view; and the *Memoirs*, edited by Lord John Russell, will, I am sure, prove a *mine*. And should business, connected with that most interesting publication, bring you to town, I shall be delighted to see you, in any way *most desirable to you*. My house is small, but I can offer you a tidy little bedroom, though rather *loftily* situated.

Mr. Rogers called here yesterday, but I was unluckily out. The last time I saw him, though very *helpless*, he was in good force and spirits, and *narrated* with his *usual precision* and accuracy.

I am, my dear Mrs. Moore,
Most truly yours,
SYDNEY MORGAN.

October 1.—Returned to town from my country excursions. I had just come off my journey and was lying stretched on the sofa in the drawing-room, very dead and shattered, when I heard a voice, sharp and Yankee, bullying my maid in the hall, for a free admittance; having, said the owner, come from America, to see me, and was going back the next day. He told me that he was cousin to the American minister, whom he familiarly called "Tom." I never was so bored in my life. My face was dirty, my clothes dusty, my voice husky; I was sulky as a bear; and no doubt I shall see myself, *en longue et en large*, some of these fine days in some American journal, under the head of " An Hour at Lady Morgan's."

My house is greatly improved—looks beautiful in its fresh green paint, but I am more inclined to my inclined plane, a sofa at home, than to gaieties; I am so completely "used up," or, as Madame de Sévigné says—*Je suis affamée pour le silence*—for I am made to talk my life away at these charming country houses.

October 5.—Dined at Lady Talbot de Malahide's; met there the Rajah of Courg, an amiable barbarian, or rather a specimen of the early creation. He played on the fiddle, and gave us " Rule Britannia," to show his allegiance to England.

November 3.—I have missed my beautiful Irish seal with my Irish harp on it; I am astonished and do not know what to think. I have had it thirty years. It has been taken off my bunch of seals, which lies on my Pompadour.

November 4.—My whole nervous system has been upset, by the discovery that I have had a FELON living in my house for the last three weeks. Dr. Ferguson made the discovery. He came to tell me, last night, too late to stir in the business—and such a night as I passed! Locked up; my maid and myself, and had a bell at my window ready to ring it. The felon was my servant, McDonald. An accident revealed to him that measures were being taken to get rid of him. He gave my maid to understand as much, and suddenly took himself off without further trouble. Revelations have come to light which prove that he belonged to a party or gang who get into gentlemen's houses by false characters, to which they affix seals, stolen like mine. I dismiss this disagreeable subject with this remark, that it is impossible to describe the dangers and annoyances to which single women are exposed.

November 18.— The Duke's funeral.—A melodramatic exhibition in the very worst style, in which there was but one noble feature,—the peace, order, and respect, as well as the respectability of the people. We saw the procession from the windows of the Vice Chancellor's house, next door to Apsley House. We had a most sumptuous entertainment afterwards—not the display of "funeral baked meats," but a very *recherché* repast. All London was eating and carousing, and the whole thing was in the spirit of an Irish wake. I hope we shall have no more heroes to bury for a thousand years.

In the last days of November I was struck by the most serious illness I have ever had, but I have been carried through by skill, care, and affection. Dr. Ferguson attended me daily for nearly a month. He has been the successor to poor Dr. Chambers, to my gratitude and confidence. Both are noble specimens of the noblest profession.

August, 1853.—Went to Bognor for my *villegiatura;* a most disagreeable place.

Fiction has nothing more pathetic than that great melodramatic tragedy now performing on the shores of Ireland,—*The Celtic Exodus*. The Jews left a foreign country—a "house of bondage;" but the Celtic exodus is the departure of the Irish emigrants from the land of their love—their inheritance—and their traditions—of their passions and their prejudices; with all the details of wild grief and heart-rending incidents—their ignorance of the strangers they are going to seek—their tenderness for the objects they are leaving behind. Their departure exceeds in deep pathos all the poetical tragedy that has ever been presented on the stage, or national novelists have ever depicted in their volumes.

Left Bognor. Returned to London in September. A long night of blindness and suffering, from the first week in September to the month of March following, when the dawn of light, health, and comfort once more broke upon me.

CHAPTER XXXVII.

FALL OF THE LEAVES.

THE entries in the journal and the letters grow scantier as we proceed. Lady Morgan's life had few changes or vicissitudes; friend after friend departed; but she steadily refused to mourn.

The first entry is:—

'Poor Charles Kemble! I knew the whole dynasty of the Kembles, from King John downwards; Charles was the last and best of the whole stock—beautiful, graceful, gallant, and a very fine gentleman; such he was when I first knew him.

July.—Silvio Pellico is dead.

During our delightful residence on the Lake of Como, the Villa Fontana was frequented by some of the most illustrious men in Lombardy. Confalonieri, Count Porro, Count Pecchio, and the charming women of their family. Silvio Pellico was the delight of all; he was then all poetry. Many a moonlight night he passed with us in a gondola on the lake, while Pecchio sang to his guitar and the others joined in one of their sweet *canzone*. He was a great favourite with my dear Morgan.

The poor Pellico on his deliverance from prison entered into the *travaux forcés* of the old, bigoted Marchesa Barolo. His great merits, his glowing imagination were gone; the most elegant of poets, the most free-thinking of philosophers, became a melancholy monk, and earned shrift by the utter prostration of his intellect.

September 2.—Moore Park. A sort of hospital for odds and ends. Since I arrived here, a month this day, I have been charmed with everything, *en gros et en détail*. I have an obituary already. Abbott Lawrence, my most kind and hospitable host is gone. Poor old Colburn gone too—my brilliant advertiser and publisher of thirty years! one who could not take his tea without a stratagem. He was a strange *mélange* of meanness and munificence in his dealings. There was a desperate vengeance that had more of the jealousy of love than the resentment of business in his attempt to destroy my fame and fortune when I went to Messrs. Saunders and Otley with my second *France*. We had a last quarrel about the cheap edition of my novels two months ago. I read of his death in the papers. I wish that we had *parted friends*.

Another death!—General Pepe is dead at Turin, at the age of seventy-two—one of the noblest men in the contemporary history of modern Italy.

I am getting up memorials for a history of Moore

Park and its many associations. Sir William Temple, Swift, Stella, &c. Shall I ever get it finished?

November.—In the beginning of September I went to Llanover on a visit to Sir Benjamin and Lady Hall. The gardens there are always in their full beauty in the autumn.

I went thence to Stamford Hall, Leicestershire, to pay one more visit to my dear and venerable friend, the Baroness Braye, and her charming daughter, Catherine, Countess of Beauchamp.

I arrived there very ill, with a severe attack of bronchitis. Nothing could exceed their kindness. I left Stamford Hall and my dear friends with the intention of proceeding to Combermere Abbey.

Lady Braye's last words to me were to intreat that I would keep away as long as I could from the fogs of London. But I found myself so unwell on the railway, that is, my eyes so painful, that I proceeded on to London, and found my house more comfortable and pretty than ever. No high stairs! no long galleries and their draughts! and in short, I was *at home.* And so ends my *villegiatura* of the autumn of 1855.

Lady Morgan remained at William Street for the Christmas holidays, surrounded by attached and admiring friends, and drawing to her pleasant drawing-room all the young men who were just gaining public notice by their talents or adventures. Among the correspondents who held to her most loyally was the Earl of Carlisle, then lord-lieutenant of Ireland. One of his letters runs:—

DUBLIN CASTLE,
January 31, 1856.

MY DEAR LADY MORGAN,

How kindly you have written to me. Malahide was indeed full to me of pleasant, though mixed, memories, and I am sure you will not think the vivid historian of its storied site was omitted from them. It appeared to me a great change from former times, when we rollicked on oysters, and barristers sang treasonable songs. Now, we talked of archæology, and looked at old porcelain. The portrait-gallery has received additions. I thought Dublin smiled very graciously on my levee and drawing-room, and my health has not, as yet, at all repined at my splendid captivity in the Castle, and we are to have Grecian theatricals, and an amateur opera, got up by Lady Downshire, and mainly indebted to Mrs. Geale.

Your imperial city is full of a more serious drama. I am sure you are too good a friend to the humanities of every kind not to be a sincere well-wisher to peace.

Macaulay is not in power at the Castle of Tyrconnel, as you may well guess. Have you good authority for the striking speech you recounted to me of the Duchess to James, after the Boyne?

Now, dear lady, I must leave you, for—the Lord Mayor!

Ever gratefully yours,
CARLISLE.

Lady Morgan, like a true Irish woman, clung to her

family. The relations of Clasagh na Valla, had a peculiar interest for her, not only on account of her own recollections of her visit to Longford House, before she had become famous, but because she thought her relations to the Crofton family creditable to her. She wrote to Sir Malby Crofton, challenging the renewal of her ancient acquaintance, and claiming her kinship —here is her letter.

Lady Morgan to Sir Malby Crofton.

11, WILLIAM STREET,
ALBERT GATE, BELGRAVIA,
March 5, 1856.

MY DEAR SIR MALBY,

Maclean, the publisher of a portrait of mine, showed me lately a list of the subscribers names, among whom the one that most gratified me, was YOURS! *You*, probably, scarcely remember a girl with (what in Irish we call) a Cathath head, and a very nimble foot at crossing a ford and dancing an Irish jig, or taking a game of romps out of "little Malby;" but *she* can never forget days so happy and so careless, and which furnished forth the details of the *Wild Irish Girl*—the progenitress of her own little fame and fortune! Still living on amid all these pleasant impressions, I cannot resist writing you a few lines, not only to recal myself to your memory, but to set at rest all my traditional *shanaos* of the Crofton family. I found my claim on your attention by a fact of which perhaps you are not aware—that I have the distinction of being the grand-daughter of one who had the honour to be a daughter of the house of Crofton! Sydney Crofton Bell, in her time celebrated for her poetical and musical talents, and bearing the Irish cognomen of *Clasagh na Valla*—"the Harp of the Valley"; from this gifted individual has been derived whatever talent has distinguished her descendants for three generations. She threw her Irish mantle over us, and though somewhat the worse for the wear (as Irish mantles generally are!), it has stood us all in good stead. Your own amiable and distinguished grandmother, my dear Lady Crofton, the friend and protectress of my own early life, and one of the noblest creatures I ever knew, always acknowledged the Irish cousinship, of which I am as proud as I am of my relationship with Oliver Goldsmith, though his illustrations were not of such genealogical distinction as the descendants of the *friend* of the Earl of Essex, who founded your family. If you admit the "propinquity of kin," dear Sir Malby, I should be much gratified. Now, tell me, dear Sir Malby, why, in *Burke's Peerage*, they date your baronetage only from 1838? *Time immemorial* your grandfather Malby was always titled. I had heard there was some forfeiture "in the time of the troubles!" Why, too, was the ancient seat of the family called *Longford?* had it not an Irish name? and *what* name? Is the old chapel standing? or the original Crofton apple trees, that were brought over to Ireland in the time of Queen Elizabeth? Well, I will *bother* you no more with my antiquarian questions, but in conclusion only say, that if you or any of your family should come to London, and will try my "tap," at the sign of the *Irish Harp*, you will meet with "cead mille fal-thae" from, dear Sir Malby,

Yours very sincerely,
SYDNEY MORGAN.

Sir Malby Crofton to Lady Morgan.

LONGFORD HOUSE,
BELTRA COLLOONEY,
March 22, 1856.

MY DEAR LADY MORGAN,

Accept my best thanks for your kind letter, to which various engagements have prevented my giving an earlier reply.

Believe me, it is our house which should be proud of a kinswoman who, having fought her way to fame, as you have, is willing to remember her friends of "long ago," even to the romps with "little Malby," who, for his part recollects well, one whose name has been a household word at Longford. You desire a history of the Croftons since you were among us; it would be tedious to any one else; should it prove so to you, you must only confess that you provoked it. To begin with the title. It was discovered, some time after my grandfather's death, by the *Herald at Arms*, that we were descended from the *next brother* of the *first* baronet, and not from the first baronet himself, to whose male *issue* that patent limited the title. This was a great trouble to us at Longford, and a surprise

to the whole family, among whom there never had
been any doubt as to my grandfather's right to the
title; but there was no help for it, and after an effort
to obtain a revival of the original grant, my father had
to put up with a new patent, so that now, although I
am the acknowledged head of a family numbering in
it one baron, and, including Lord Crofton's baronetcy,
three baronets, my title dates later than any of the
others. You are too *Irish* to laugh at this trifle being
deemed a grievance; but here, by the shores of the
Atlantic, where little questions of precedence still at
times arise, it was unpleasant, to say the least, to be
obliged to make way for those who ought, as they used,
to follow us.

My father died six years ago. I myself have *left*
to me three sons and three daughters.

Now for the Longford estates. Longeuth, I believe,
is the Irish for it. When this latter passed into Longford, I am unable to discover; but am disposed to
think that the first Crofton possessor changed the
name—so much for the name. The estate itself is the
same as it was,—very large. Since the troubles of
1668, we have not parted with an acre of it, nor are
we likely to do so. Thanks to the Encumbered
Estate Court, which gave every facility for selling
Irish estates when, from the *condition of the country*
they were *least valuable;* many an ancient family has
been *pressed* out of *home* and *fortune*. One family
(some of the members of which you must have known)
the Percivals, of Temple House, in this county, must,
I fear, transfer to strangers an estate which they ac-

quired by intermarriage with us; but God, who gave us the property (you remember the motto "Dat deus incrementum"), still permits the Croftons of Longford to hold their own. They do little more, however, than hold their own, for the family exchequer has never been full enough to rebuild the house, the scene, dear Lady Morgan, of our romps, which was burned down in my father's time; but though the old house is a ruin, there has grown up beside it, by little and little, a house reasonably large and comfortable. That would be a welcome day to it, and its *inhabitants*, on which you would come and visit us; you would find the chapel as in your youth, and beside it, the home of *Friar* John Crofton "Comitesque flavicomæ," the companion which good-natured people represent to have been a fox—the ill-natured, as a *nymph*, with golden hair.

Time has eaten away the trunks of the Longford pearmain, the original Crofton apple; and it is said, but I don't believe it, that with the decay of the original stocks, the apple has universally degenerated.

If ever I have the opportunity, the "Irish Harp" may rely upon a call; but as I seldom leave home, I will, for this once act, if you will permit me, by deputy. Should my son and his bride be in London in June, as is probable, I promise he shall pay his respects to you, and I trust you may esteem him worthy of the ancient stock. Grateful of your kind recollection of me and mine,

Believe me, dear Lady Morgan,
Very sincerely yours,
M. CROFTON.

Early in February had appeared a volume of Rogers's *Table Talk*, which had set the critics of society at war. The indecency of hurrying into print with anecdotes and sayings which could not fail to offend living persons, even before the hatchments were down, or the table at which the jests had been made, was sold, struck every one. Soon, the voice of protest echoed through the journals. Among those who felt themselves most aggrieved were the daughters and friends of Madame Piozzi. For many weeks, the *Athenæum* contained this sparkling controversy, in which Lady Morgan joined with her usual liveliness. From her private correspondence with the connections of Madame Piozzi on this scandal, the following letters are selected:—

J. H. Gray to Lady Morgan.

BALSOVER CASTLE, CHESTERFIELD,
June 19, 1856.

DEAR MADAM,

I take the liberty of addressing you on the subject of our common correspondence with the editor or author of Rogers's Table Twaddle.

There never was anything more false than that my dear old friend, Viscountess Keith, and her sister, Miss Thrale, and her late sister, Mrs. Meyrick Hoare, refused to be reconciled to their mother. On the contrary, as soon as Mr. and Mrs. Piozzi returned from their wedding tour of four or five years on the Continent, Lady Keith and her two younger sisters, then fine, handsome girls, fresh from school, made a point of soliciting a renewal of intercourse. And Lady Keith has often related to me their first meeting, which was a very curious one, at Mrs. Piozzi's own house, and after that Lady Keith, who had a very handsome establishment, gave Mr. and Mrs. Piozzi many good dinners, and thereby aggravated Piozzi's gout,—Piozzi, of whom Lady Keith always speaks very kindly.

Long after Miss Thrale's marriage with Lord Keith, Mrs. Piozzi died, and Lady Keith went from Tulliallan, in Scotland, to Bath, to attend her death-bed. It is very unfair to bring such stories forward, which are calculated to annoy two excellent old ladies—I say *two*, because there never was any question of reconciliation with the youngest, Mrs. Mostyn, *who lived with her mother* until her marriage, which, by-the-way, was a run-a-way one. Old Rogers ought to have known better than to circulate such false trash; for he was at one time intimate, and was, indeed, an admirer, if not a suitor, to one of the younger Miss Thrales.

I could have given the editor of the Twaddle a much more pleasing anecdote of old Rogers than any of those in his book. About nine years ago, a letter containing bills which I had signed, amounting to upwards of two thousand pounds, was not received by my steward, to whom I had addressed it. It was found, a month after, safe at the bottom of the deadletter box, in the post-office of Glasgow, having been oddly mistaken for a valentine. However, for some weeks I was in great alarm, and I called on Rogers, with whom I had, for some time, been acquainted, to ask his advice, as he also, shortly before, had the misfortune to have bills to a very large amount abstracted from his bank. After very kindly telling me how he thought I ought to proceed under my supposed loss, he went on to say (and here his face became quite beaming with benevolence and satisfaction) that, as soon as *his* loss became known, he received offers of pecuniary aid and credit to any amount, from hosts and hosts of friends, amongst the highest character, station, and rank in England—men from whom he little expected such proofs of disinterested regard. He added, that his opinion of human nature had, from that day, been immeasurably improved. This is, I think, a more pleasant anecdote than any contained in the Table Twaddle, and on that account I beg you to pardon this long letter.

I have the honour to be,
Dear Madam,
Very truly yours,
JOHN HAMILTON GRAY.

Mrs. Mostyn to Lady Morgan.

SILLWOOD LODGE,
Tuesday.

Would that I were near you, dearest Lady Morgan, to accept your agreeable invitation of a chat between four and six: but there is always a reaction in our society at Brighton. After our winter season is ended, we begin again with fresh friends, who stay till Easter; and I have not the moral courage to leave them to an empty house.

The *Athenæum* confirms one's opinion of the editor of Rogers's *Table Talk*. As far as I am concerned, they are all wrong. Being but a child of nine years old on my mother's return to England, I was taken home to Streatham, and brought up an opposition child, living with her and dear Piozzi until I was married, in 1795.

On that occasion the reconciliation took place, and I then saw my three sisters for the first time; my mother must have been about sixty, and she always called them "the ladies."

These are not important events to bring before the public; and Rogers appears to have talked very little of Streatham, considering he lived there so much in my time; but he never *was* a talker. I have many letters, or had, and now possess his proposal of marriage to me at *thirteen*, with my impertinent caricature of him, and old Murphy calling me a saucy girl.

Excuse an abrupt conclusion to this family gossip, dear Lady Morgan, for I have a long dinner table to-day, and my head full of domestic cares.

Very sincerely yours,
Dear Lady Morgan,
C. M. Mostyn.

CHAPTER XXXVIII.

PASSING AWAY.

An interesting notice of Lady Morgan's old house at Drumcondra occurs in a letter from her brother-in-law, Sir Arthur Clarke.

Sir Arthur Clarke to Lady Morgan.

Tuesday,
May 19, 1857.

My dearest Sydney,

José and I have just returned from taking a sketch of Drumcondra House, and inclose some flowers, out of your old garden, which is in great preservation. The house is now the post office, kept by a Mr. Heith, and his wife remembers two ladies some years ago calling to see the house;—one was Lady Morgan, and the other was Lady Clarke. José will send you the sketch when finished, and it will look beautiful. Tell little Syd. I received her letter this morning, and that I will write to her in a day or two.

I overheard two gentlemen in the United Service Club yesterday talking of your *matinée*. One said, he had often seen the Miss Owensons in Enniskillen, that he knew their father intimately, and that he was a handsome man; had the heart of a gentleman, the looks of a gentleman, and the manners of a gentleman; and that he also knew Dr. Burroughs, the author of *The Night before Larry was Stretched*.

Ever yours affectionately,
A. C. CLARKE.

A letter to Lady Morgan from her niece, Mrs. Inwood Jones, gives a description of the inauguration of Moore's statue, about which Lady Morgan was much interested, and which she had been the first to suggest.

Mrs. Inwood Jones to Lady Morgan.

DUBLIN,
October 17, 1857.

DEAREST LADY MORGAN,

Your last letter was so *beautifully* written, that it put me *quite out*, and I could not read it! It is too bad, after devoting the *best part* of my life to deciphering your dear old hieroglyphics, to be at this time of day treated to a common place, plain hand writing, that *any one* can read. Well, let it pass; and now for my news. The inauguration of Moore's statue was a curious sight; and I believe that in no town in Europe could there have been another like it. Conceive a *mob* of, I should think, six thousand persons, collected, *perfectly* well disposed, and, I must say, *far* more *civil* and courteous than an *English* mob, for José and I *passed* through it (being separated from our gentlemen) without the *slightest* annoyance or pressure. We were at last discovered by Papa, who, in his capacity of steward of the committee, marshalled us up, with his long white wand of office, to seats near Lady Charlemont and Lord Carlisle. Conceive all this in the open streets, the gentlemen with their hats off, and the ladies in the most charming of light dresses. The speeches were all spoken from the little circle, of which Lord Carlisle was the centre. Lord Charlemont spoke with feeling and good taste; Lord Carlisle's speech was all poetry and pathos, and was charmingly delivered; his quotations from Moore's beautiful verses were very apposite; and of course he was enthusiastically applauded, for his speech did honour to his *heart* as well as his head, which you know always goes a great way with us in Ireland. But the speaker of the day, out and out *for eloquence* and *extraordinary* oratorical powers (such as I never heard, and could only imagine Grattan's or Curran's to have been) was Mr. O'Hagans's! It was perfectly astounding. Now I understand what is called *Irish eloquence*. The immense flow of *words* of the *best* language, gave one the idea that his *imagination* was *overflowing*. It was extraordinary. I think, with all this, he would have no success in our English house of parliament; and that men would go to sleep on the benches with the word "*bosh*" on their lips, and they would not be altogether wrong.

The Lord Mayor said his *petit mot* with the richest of Irish brogues, and with a simplicity that brought us all down from Moore's pedestal (where the great orators had left us) to the *shop* in *Grafton Street*. He created a deal of merriment amongst the mob, who encouraged him with sundry "Don't be frightened, my boy," and "spake out like a man." When all this was over, and the statue uncovered, I could not help thinking that it was the least inspiring object I ever saw. It is almost *grotesque*, and might be any one else than little Moore. The crowd dispersed in perfect good humour. The tops of houses, the roofs of the Bank and College, and lamp posts, were all crowded with spectators. It was really a *very* curious scene, and I was glad to witness it. And now good bye, dear, for I am quite tired after the Powerscourt *fête* of *fêtes*, from which we did not get home till five o'clock this morning, of which I shall tell you in my next.

S. I. J.

Lady Morgan sustained a great sorrow in the November of this year. Sir Arthur Clarke, her friend and brother, died in Dublin, of bronchitis, after a very short illness. To the last he was active, alert, and genial. He had taken great interest in the progress of the "Odd Volume," and in the preparation for her Memoirs, which he had hoped to assist in arranging. He had been the best and truest of her friends, and the most ardent of her admirers. His death was a great shock to Lady Morgan, and she never ventured

to speak of it. It was a sorrow that seemed to resume
in itself all her other griefs, for he was connected with
the memories of her early Dublin life,—with her father,
with her sister, with her niece, Olivia (so early dead),
with her husband;—and when he was taken away, all
her ties with the past were broken. Her niece, again
a widow, was settled near her; but Lady Morgan's
standing point in life was rapidly crumbling away.
Of all who had begun their career with her, and who
had held friends in common, hardly one remained.

Lady Morgan's life passed on with an even tenor,
she never allowed grief to appear, but when alone she
was subject to great depression of heart. She endeavoured all the more to find pleasure in the comforts and
society that surrounded her, although her new friends
could not invest themselves with the charms of old
times and early associations. There was nothing old
or infirm about Lady Morgan, nor was there any decay
of faculty or dimness of intelligence; her vitality
seemed unquenchable. The preparation of the *Odd
Volume* was an amusement to her. Early in the
year 1858 she had an attack of bronchitis, but she
threw it off. A note from Sir William Napier refers
to this period of sickness:—

Sir William Napier to Lady Morgan.

SCINDE HOUSE,
January 26, 1858.

MY DEAR LADY MORGAN,

Having heard that you were ill, I enquired, not at
your house, but of your friends, and was told that

you had got over the attack. Grieved I am to find from your note that you still suffer. My only excuse, and it is a real one, for not having called upon you, is extreme feebleness; not of vitality, but of limb; I can scarcely get across a room, and pain is constant as well as severe.

Believe me to be with most sincere wishes for your immediate restoration to health, your devoted servant in spirit; in flesh I cannot be any person's servant,— at least I should be a very unprofitable one, being only fit for "Worms, brave Percy!" They, indeed, with respect to me, are like the young Irishman who proposed for a lady of fortune; and being asked what *his* fortune was, answered, that he has no actual one, but had *great expectations*—from the lady.

W. NAPIER.

PS.—As to your "*turning to stone*," if you *ever do*, it will be a pumice stone, covered with magic words.

Later in this year, Lady Morgan had another and more severe attack of bronchitis, which was of longer duration than any of her previous illnesses, and gave rise to serious fears of a fatal termination. But she struggled through it, and recovered, to all appearance, her former health. Nothing could exceed the kindness and attention lavished upon her by her friends, nor the care and skill of Dr. Ferguson and Mr. Hunter. When she recovered sufficiently, she went to Sydenham a short time for change of air, and returned to London as bright as ever.

December 25, 1858, was Lady Morgan's last birthday. She assembled a few of her old friends at dinner, and did the honours with all the *verve* and brilliancy of her brightest days. She told stories and anecdotes with delicate finesse and drollery; and after dinner she sang a comic song, because as she said, being written by a Church dignitary, it could be nothing but good words; so she sang "The Night before Larry was Stretched," in a style that was inimitable. At her age, "many happy returns of the day" could not be looked for; but none of those then with her felt it too sanguine to look forward to at least "*one* cheer more;" but this Christmas-day proved to be the very last.

CHAPTER XXXIX.

THE END.

THE first entry in her diaries for 1859 relates to the *Odd Volume*, which she had prepared for the press with all the enthusiasm of a young author. Her spirits and energy, her power of doing hard work, was undiminished from what it had been in girlhood. After working all the morning, from the moment she awoke to two in the afternoon—her dinner hour—and sending the friend who worked with her, home, completely tired out, Lady Morgan dressed for the day, and seated herself on her small green sofa in the drawing-room, as fresh as a lark, ready to receive visitors, to tell and to hear the newest gossip of the day, and she frequently had a large party in the evening, till she retired at last, declaring "she was dead."

January 1.—This day my *Odd Volume*, probably my last, made its appearance in the world, *l'enfant de ma vieillesse*. I lingered over the idea of writing a preface. Starting up one morning, I called to my maid to give me pen and ink, and dashed it off; and so it went uncorrected, and is not the worst morsel I have written. This *esquisse* has a success more universal and cheerful than ever attended any of my works.

A letter to Lady Combermere shows no signs of failing health or strength.

Lady Morgan to Lady Combermere.

DEAREST LADY,

Be all that constitutes a merry Christmas and happy new year laid at your feet for your gracious acceptance, if you please to accept such "tag rag, and bob tail," the rubbish of times old and monastic. I only wish I could lay myself on a sofa beside you. That charming *commérage* which only you know how to sustain! I will not dwell on the recent melancholy events of this season of sorrow, carried on in the midst of storms and fogs, of mists and misery, with death waylaying the young and beautiful, the loving and loved, the happy and prosperous; but it is wonderful in calamity! Of the many distinguished men who gathered round my supposed death-bed *last year*, three have already gone before me! I am getting so blind I must stop.

Well; my life-wearing task is done—my book, I believe, ready for publication; but why not published I know not, its title is impertinently changed by Bentley. Miss Jewsbury gone to the bosom of her family! *chemin faisant*, to the glories of Combermere Abbey, Mrs. Jones off to hers, and I am (or have been) "left and abandoned by my velvet friends," to a degree unexampled in the history of human vicissitudes. London is a desert,

"Silent, oh Moina, is the roar of thy waters,"

and I am literally left "the last woman," looking out in vain for the last man! At last he turns up! It is the Duke of Wellington, on his way from Strathfieldsay to Windsor; others drop in, and so the sun shines upon me again; and now I await some occurrence to conclude this dull note. Yours, dear Lady Combermere, with my most respectful regards to the Field-Marshal *de cœur et de corps.*

SYDNEY MORGAN.

On the 17th of March, St. Patrick's Day, Lady Morgan had a musical morning party,—all that was best and brightest at that time in London were gathered under her roof. Lady Morgan looked as likely for life as she had done any time for the last six years, and no one anticipated that the breaking-up was so near. One week after this gay celebration of her patron saint's *fête*, Lady Morgan caught cold. At first, it did not seem serious.

This letter, dictated by her, and addressed to Lady Combermere, was the last she wrote:—

Lady Morgan to Lady Combermere.

April 11, 1859.

MY DEAR LADY COMBERMERE,

Your letters are always to me fresher than flowers, without their fading so soon. I am still confined to my bedroom and all the tiresome accompaniments of a sick room. My cough and breathing very troublesome, yet, upon the whole, Dr. Ferguson and Mr. Hunter say I am progressing most wonderfully towards health. As to food and nourishment, I have two *detectives* (yourself and Lady Braye) continually watching me, and I must "move on." Nothing is wanting, but the "*nosebag*," (recommended by Lady Combermere) to fill up the interval of eating and drinking—a most capital idea, which nobody but yourself would think of, and worthy of my adoption. I think Ferguson will be rather surprised at finding me *muzzled* in green satin to-day, "by order of Lady Combermere." So much for self, and now for "that fool the public." Yesterday's report of the resignation of ministers I have not yet heard confirmed; but suppose it is true. Mr. Lowe resigns his pretensions to Kidderminster, and seeks a more admiring constituency.

I am, yours, &c.,
SYDNEY MORGAN.

Although she was now very ill, neither Dr. Ferguson, who had attended her in all her illnesses, nor Mr. Hunter, her ordinary medical attendant, feared a fatal termination: they had seen her recover from more dangerous attacks. But the scene was drawing to a close. On the morning of the 16th of April she seemed rather better; she called for her desk and papers, and began to write a letter on business; but although her mind was lucid and vigorous, her bodily powers were fading away; and on the entrance of her doctor, she reluctantly gave up her pen. Painful attacks of spasmodic breathing came on, and at the end of a fierce struggle for breath, she said to her niece, who was supporting her, "Sydney, is this death?" She saw and spoke to an old friend who came to see her in the afternoon. She then lay still, speaking occasionally, and with increased difficulty, but with gratitude, for the attention shown to her to the last by those she most loved and valued.

She met her end patiently and with perfect simplicity. She died on the evening of the 16th of April, 1859.

She was interred in the Brompton cemetery, where a tomb, executed by Mr. Sherrard Westmacott, has been erected to her memory, by her niece.

CHAPTER XL.

CONCLUSION.

LADY MORGAN'S house was the resort of all who were the best worth knowing in London society, and she had the art of drawing out all the best faculties of those who came to her. She herself had become a name connected with the past—a tradition of times, and manners, and events, which had been historical. Her own conversation was to the last hour brilliant and fascinating as it ever had been, not a shadow had fallen over the sparkling wit and grace of her stories and *bon mots*. The sarcastic severity of tongue, which had made her formidable to friends and foes in early life, softened greatly during the later years of her life. She used to say, that it was only the *young* who were pitiless in their judgment of others, and when she heard any one saying bitter things against another, she would say, " Ah ma chère ne vous chargez pas des haines." At the severest, her sarcasm had been always light and airy—it shared the harmlessness of hard words, in that " it broke no bones,"—it glanced off the object, and did not burn into the feelings or rest upon the memory. Lady Morgan was always a true, steady, and zealous friend to those she cared for, and had a singular faculty for attaching her servants to her; she interested herself in their welfare, and treated them with invariable courtesy and respect; during her illness, their affectionate attentions had been those of attached relatives rather than servants; they had all lived many years in her service. She had the courage to tell her friends the truth when it was needful; she was essentially sincere, though not always consistent, for she never troubled herself to reconcile the opinion she might have expressed one year with that which she held another; she said what she thought and felt at the moment, and left discrepancies to take care of themselves. With all her frank vanity she had shrewd good sense, and she valued herself much more on her *industry* than on her genius, because the one she said "she owed to her organisation, but the other was a virtue of her own rearing."

Perhaps no other woman ever received so much flattery, or had such brilliant and tangible success; both as a woman and an author, she seems to have had a larger portion of the good things of this life than generally falls to the lot of the daughters of Eve. Her prosperity was almost unclouded during her long life. The death of her husband, her sister, and her favourite niece, within a short period of each other, was her share of affliction, and she felt it deeply.

She was not afraid of death; but she disliked the idea of dying very much. Often when looking round her pretty room, she would say, "I shall be very sorry to leave all these things, and the friends who have been so kind to me—the world has been a good world to me."

Lady Morgan was not a woman to be judged by ordinary rules. She was the last type of a class long passed away; she belonged to another time and mode of thought altogether; she was like the French women of the old *régime* to whom society was the only condition in which they could exist, who would go to a ball or a hunting party when in the last stage of mortal sickness; who would insist on being attired in full dress on the day of their death, and who would not die except surrounded by their circle and doing the honours of a *salon* to the last. Oddly enough, clergymen were very fond of her society, and she used to tell, with great fun a whimsical incident, *à propos* to this. She had written a note to a dignitary of the Church, a very old friend, addressing him as her "dear father confessor," saying, to pique his curiosity, "come to me—I want to have a talk with you." He was from home and the note went to his curate, who took it *au serieux*, thinking his rector could only be sent for professionally. He went to her house, and gravely said "that as his rector was out of town, he came to see her ladyship, and if she had any thing upon her mind, he would be happy to give her his best advice." Of course he was soon disabused of his mistake; but the drollest part of the story was the indignation of her maid, who, when she was told what had passed, drew herself up and said with scorn, "As if your ladyship had wished to confess, you would open your mind to a *curate!*"

Lady Morgan kept her faculty of enjoyment to the last; she had as much pleasure in her books, music, and society, as in her youth. She loved the young, and was always charming with them. She said that, "living with the young kept her young."

END OF VOL. II.

INDEX.

A.

Abercorn, Marchioness, kindness of, 5.
Abercorn, Marchioness and Marquis, sympathy of, with Lady Morgan, 14.
Aberdeen, Countess, death of, 9.
Aberdeen, Marquis of, 17, 20, 22.
Accomplishments of women of rank, 18.
Advertisement, Colburn's, 327.
Albert Gate, concession of, 469, 470.
Amazon, burning of the, 513, 514.
Amethysts, presentation of, 79.
Anecdotes, 283, 285, 288, 299, 300, 311, 336, 337, 338.
Anglesey, Marquis of, 274, 290, 313, 315, 325, 339, 340.
Arch Duke Regnier, 23.
Ashburner's, Dr., mesmeric experiments at, 486.
Association, Catholic, 273, 275.
Atkinson, Joseph, 331.

B.

Ballad Singers, 232.
Balbo, Count de, 22.
Baron's Court, Sir Charles and Lady Morgan leave, 22, 23.
Bartolini, sculptor, 119.
Beecher, Lady, Miss O'Neile, 415.
Beef Steak Club, 252.
Beggars, 240.
Begaine, 383.
Belfast, Lord, 105.
Belgium, 374, 376, 383.
Bellini, 361, 367; death of, 408.
Belzoni, Madame, 370.
Bingley, William, animal biographer, 30.
Black Bull, the, 401.
Blindness, attack of, on Lady Morgan, 399, 422; partial restoration to sight, 423.

Bologna, 115.
Bonaparte, Madame Patterson, 12, 48, 61, 106.
Bonaparte, Jerome, 9, 10, 447—453.
Bonaparte, Louis, 129.
Bonaparte, Lucien, 365.
Book of the Boudoir, 233; bitter review of, in Blackwood, 283.
Book without a Name, 402.
Bores and Prosers, 124.
Borghese, Paulina, princess, 122, 130; death of, 221.
Bravo peerage, the, 458, 459.
Bride of Lammermoor, the, 102.
British Association, 403.
Burgoyne, General, 445.
Burroughs, Dr., author of The Night before Larry was Stretched, 338.
Byron, Lord, 91, 102, 105, 116, 117, 147, 198.

C.

Camac, brave Colonel, 112.
Campbell, Lady Guy, 347.
Campbell, Thomas, 360; his awkwardness at table, and voted vulgarest of men, 484; death of, 444.
Canning, death of, 246.
Cannon Brewery, 470.
Capponi, Marquis, 118.
Capponi Palace, 118.
Captain Marryatt, 470.
Cardinal Fesche, 129, 137.
Cardinal Gonsalvi, 131.
Carriage, Lady Morgan's first, 284.
Cardinal Wiseman, controversy between, and Lady Morgan, 509.
Carolino, Queen, 187, 188.
Cashel Cathedral, 336.
Catholic Association, 267.
Celtic Exodus, 323.
Charlemonts, the, 130, 137.
Charleville, Lady, 68, 391, 394; infirmity of, 414.

Charwomen, Irish, 235.
Chateaubriand, 504.
Cheltenham, 290.
Childe Harold, 21.
Cholera, 331.
Cinq Mars, 445.
Clanricarde, Lord and Lady, 291.
Clark, Lady, jeu d'esprit on the article in *Quarterly*, 52.
Cleveland, Duchess of, 268.
Cloncurry, Lord, 195, 298, 349.
Cobbett, 267.
Cockburn, General, 299.
Colburn, 30, 51, 52, 53, 72, 78, 79, 143, 145, 152, 435, 440; proposal from for work on Germany, 155; death of, 525.
Colburn and the second work on France, 304—309.
Como, Lake of, 90; festival of the saint of the, 107.
Constant, Madame Benjamin de, 455.
Coombe, the phrenologist, 206.
Confalonieri, Count and Countess of, 93, 95.
Cork, Lady, 237.
Coronation of Queen Victoria, 440, 441.
Gorr, Fanny, Belgian artist, 394.
Count Lavallette, escape of from prison, 501.
Countess of Cork and Orrery, 458; observation on death of, by Mrs. Gorr, 467.
Countess Merlin, 465.
Crawley in *Florence Macarthy*, 75; J. W. Croker, 26.
Crofton, Sir Malby, 528, 529; account of family by, 531, 532.
Croker, John Wilson, 57, 76, 229.
Crossley, Francis, 352.
Crowds, Italian, 157.
Cubitt, 433, 440, 443.
Curran, Counsellor, 282.
Curran Miss, 120.
Cuvier, Life of, by Mrs. Lee, 412.

D.

D'Albany, Countess, 111, 110, 122.
Davy, Sir Humphrey, and Lady, 115.
Dawson, Mrs. Damer, 422.
Deaths of Mrs. Tighe, Cooper, Walker, Kirwin, noticed, 22.
Delahaye, servant to Lady Morgan, recounts the battle of Waterloo, 412.
Dixon, death of, 222.
Deputation of Weavers, 245.

Descriptions, Lady Morgan's, 94.
D'Houchin, 222.
Diary, 1825, 214-219; 1826, 229-233; 1827, 235 253; 1829, 254-270; 1829, 271-246; 1830, 206-317; 1831, 318-324; 1832, 833-352; 1833, 353-380; 1834, 381-389; 1835, 390-411; 1836, 411-418; 1837, 419-432; 1838, 433-446; 1840, 458; 1842, 469-472; 1843, 473-480; 1844, 481-488; 1845, 489-490; 1846, 491-493; 1847, 493-497; 1848, 497-499; 1849, 500-505; 1850, 511; 1852, 520-522; 1853, 522-523; 1854, 524-525; 1855, 526; 1859, 544-545.
Dilke, 343, 394, 416, 417, 512.
D'Israeli, 360, 364, 365.
Devonshire, Duke of, 38.
Devonshire, Duchess of, 124, 128, 169.
Don Juan, 104, 105.
Douglas Jerrold, 507, 508.
Dowry, Miss Owenson's, &c.
Dramatic Scenes and Sketches, 302, 353, 354.
Duc de Berri's murder, 132.
Dufour, 143.
Duke of Wellington, 546.

E.

Edgeworth, Miss, 141.
Emancipation, Catholic, 275; dissolution of the Association, 275.
Embroidery, 532.
Esther Kinglake, 497.
Eternal City, first view of, 122.
Excavations, 160, 161.

F.

Fesche, Cardinal, 129, 454.
Fitsclarence, Lord Adolphus, 421-425.
Fitzherbert, Mrs., 421, 425; death of, 401.
Florence, hotels at, 116.
Florence Macarthy, 74, 110; price of, 74; fifth edition of, 105; translation of, 119; pavers of amethysts presented to Lady Morgan, by Colburn, as a tribute of admiration, 79.
Fontana, Villa, 97.
France, book on, 61; price offered for, 51; price agreed on, 53; publication of, 56; account of, 56, 57; second edition of, 73, 302.

INDEX. 555

France, first visit to, 89; second visit to, 283.
Fun and Philosophy, song by Lady Clarke, 404.

G.

Cabanis, 266, 267.
Garcia, notice of, by Sir Charles Morgan, 482.
Gell, Sir William, death of, 413.
General Pepe, death of, 525.
Genlis, Madame de, 41, 224, 229, 247.
Genoa, 112; streets of, 113.
George IV., diary of the Court and Times of, 431, 435.
Gifford, 241.
Glengall, Lady, death of, 416.
Godwin, 394; death of, 415.
Gonsalvi, Cardinal, 120.
Gore, Colonel, 7.
Gore, Mrs., 344.
Grace O'Malley, 330.
Guiccioli, Countess, 345, 412.

H.

Hamilton, Lord Archibald, 215.
Harlstronge, Weld, 382.
Hayward, 446.
Heart of Mid Lothian, 106.
Heidelberg, castle and scenery of, 464.
Hemans, Mrs., 322, 350, 397.
Holy Week, 127.
Hood, Thomas, 343.
Horace Smith, 471.
Hortense, son of, 120, 122.
Hospitality in Italy, 95.
House of Lords, debate, 304.

I.

Italian ladies, 123.
Italy, proposal for work on, 76; journey in, 89.
Italy, publication of, 143, 144; price paid for, 146; second edition of, 142.

J.

Jeffrey, Lord, death of, 505.
Jenner, Dr., 25.
Johnson, Judge, 209.
Juan, Don, 103, 109.

K.

Kemble, Fanny, recitation of *Allegro* and *Il Penseroso* by, 513.
Kemble, Charles, death of, 521.

Kildare Street, Sir Charles and Lady Morgan settle in, 23; library in, 23; description of house in, 24, 30.
Kissingen, departure from, 464.
Knightsbridge, 432.

L.

Lady Morgan, her kindness to refugees, 148; attack of blindness on, 432; failing eyesight of, 457, 469; early self-dependence of, 470; illness of, 478; recovery of, 479; affliction of for Sir C.'s death, 480; reception of at Brighton by Horace Smith, 481; visit to Lord and Lady Beauchamp, 482; visit to Boulogne, 485; melancholy at, 488; deep affliction of, 490; attack of rheumatism on, 492; excursions of to Hampton Court and to Dover, 496; to Llanover Court, Malvern, and Brighton, 497; dines at Milner Gibson's, 497; illness of, 498; visit of to Crystal Palace, 512; return to town, 520; visited by a Yankee, 521; discovery of a felon in the house of, 521; visit of to Bognor, 522; return from, 523; relationship of with Oliver Goldsmith, 529; attack of bronchitis, 543; last birthday, 544; comic song sung by, 543; party at, 546; troublesome breathing of, 547; increased illness and death of, 548; funeral of, 548.
Lady Beauchamp, 460.
Lady Beresford, 518.
Lady Brays, 458; death of, 459; advice of to Lady Morgan, 528.
Lady Talbot de Malahide entertains Lady Morgan, 521.
Lady Talbot, 403.
Lafayette, General, 48, 86; death of, 383.
Lamartine, 501.
Lamb, Lady Caroline, 161, 245; death of, 254.
Landseer, Edwin, 402.
Lattan Jack, 298, 300.
Laval, Duc de, anecdote of, 300.
Laurence, Sir Thomas, 123.
Laurence, Mr., death of, 427.
Leamington, 345.
Lefanu, Mrs., 19.
Lefanu, Joseph, 212.
Legend of Montrose, 106.
Leinster, Duke of, 351.
Leitrim, Lady, 152.

LETTERS:—
Lady Morgan to Mrs. Lefanu, 4, 6, 15, 19.
Lady Morgan to Lady Stanley, 8, 22.
Lady Morgan to Sir Arthur Clarke, 11 (PS. by Sir Charles Morgan, 16).
Sir Arthur Clarke to Lady Morgan, 27.
Dr. Jenner to Sir Charles Morgan, 25.
William Bingley to Sir Charles Morgan, 30.
Lady Cahir to Lady Morgan, 33.
Duke of Devonshire to Lady Morgan, 38.
Madame de Genlis to Lady Morgan, 41.
Madame Patterson Bonaparte to Lady Morgan, 42, 43, 63, 65, 80, 108, 140, 221, 454, 502.
Lafayette to Lady Morgan, 48.
Mr. Colburn to Lady Morgan, 52, 145.
Mr. Colburn to Sir Charles Morgan, 435.
Mrs. Lefanu to Lady Morgan, 60.
Lady Charleville to Lady Morgan, 79, 104, 130, 185, 249, 272, 293, 424.
Lady Morgan to Lady Clarke, 84, 93, 95, 113, 123, 128, 181.
Thomas Moore to Sir Charles Morgan, 90, 112, 130, 312.
Countess of Albany to Lady Morgan, 111.
Lady Morgan to Mrs. Featherstone, 132.
Hamilton, Rowan, to Sir Charles Morgan, 150.
Lord Erskine to Lady Morgan, 156.
Lord Darnley to Lady Morgan, 158.
Sir Charles Molyneux to Sir Charles Morgan, 161.
Duchess of Devonshire to Lady Morgan, 159, 169.
Hon. William Ponsonby to Lady Caroline Lamb, 161.
General Cockburn to Lady Morgan, 161.
Lady Caroline Lamb and Hon. William Ponsonby to Lady Morgan, 161.
J. Rock to Sir Charles Morgan, 172.
Lady Caroline Lamb to Lady Morgan, 174, 178, 193, 202-213, 216.

LETTERS, continued:—
Joseph Hume to Sir Charles Morgan, 180.
Marquis Wellesley to Lady Morgan, 182.
Lord Cloncurry to Sir Charles Morgan, 196.
Lord Byron's parting letter to Lady Caroline Lamb, 214.
Captain Webster to Lady Morgan, 220.
Sir Charles Morgan to Lady Morgan, 227.
H. Rowan to Lady Morgan, 232.
Dan. O'Connell to Sir Charles Morgan, 244.
Mrs. Hawtre to Lady Morgan, 245.
W. Lamb to Lady Morgan, 242.
Dr. Goddard to W. Lamb, 249.
Hon. W. Ponsonby to Lady Morgan, 252.
Dr. Goddard to Lady Morgan, 256.
Lady Morgan to Lord Aylmer, 258.
Thos. Campbell, to Lady Morgan, 260, 322.
James Devlin to Lady Morgan, 270.
Mrs. Hemans to Lady Morgan, 272, 323, 350.
Lady Morgan to the Marquis of Anglesey, 276, 339, 353.
Marquis of Anglesey to Lady Morgan, 277, 273, 315, 323, 352.
R. Sheil to Sir Charles Morgan, 280.
R. Sheil to Lady Morgan, 323.
Thos. Wallace to Lady Morgan, 295.
T. Moore to Lady Morgan, 310, 342.
Lady Morgan to T. Moore, 314.
Lady Cork to Lady Morgan, 320, 413.
Countess Guiccioli to Lady Morgan, 345.
M. Prosper Merrimé to Lady Morgan, 355.
Madame Belzoni to Lady Morgan, 374.
H. Lyttleton to Lady Morgan, 381.
Sir H. Hardinge to Sir C. Morgan, 390.
Mrs. Smith to Lady Morgan, 397.
Lord Morpeth to Lady Morgan, 414, 419.
Lord Melbourne to Lord Morpeth, 419.
Lord Melbourne to Lady Morgan, 420.
Mrs. Lawrence to Lady Morgan, 431.
Lady Morgan to Mr. Colburn, 436.

LETTERS continued:—
Lady Carlisle to Lady Morgan, 432.
Lady Morgan to Lord Duncannon, 442.
Lord Duncannon to Lady Morgan, 442.
General Sir John Burgoyne to Sir Charles Morgan, 444.
Jerome Bonaparte to Lady Morgan, 453.
Mrs. Otway Cave to Lady Morgan, 458.
George Darley to Lady Morgan, 460.
John Poole to Lady Morgan, 461.
Lady Morgan to Talbot de Malahide, 464.
Mrs. Gore to Lady Morgan, 467; 514.
Sidney Smith to Lady Morgan, 471, 476.
Horatio Smith to Sir C. Morgan, 471.
T. B. Macaulay to Lady Morgan, 481.
Sir W. Napier to Lady Morgan, 495, 541.
Mr. Hallam to Lady Morgan, 507.
Douglas Jerrold to Lady Morgan, 507, 508.
Lady Morgan to Mr. Mulvany, 512.
Lady Morgan to Mrs. Moore, 513.
Earl of Carlisle to Lady Morgan, 527.
Lady Morgan to Sir Malby Crofton, 529.
Sir Malby Crofton to Lady Morgan, 530.
J. H. Gray, to Lady Morgan, 533.
Mrs. Mostyn to Lady Morgan, 535.
Mrs. Inwood Jones to Lady Morgan, 535.
Lady Morgan to Lady Combermere, 545, 546.
Life of Lord Eldon, sent to Lady Morgan, 438.
Literary journalism, 142.
Liver, curious experiments on, by Jenner, 24.
Lock, Mrs., 199.
Locket, with Lord Byron's hair, 212.
Lockhart, 412.
Lombardy, iron crown of, 95.
London, visit to, en route for Italy, 72.
Lord Lieutenant's right to make knights impugned, 172.
Lord Byron and Lady Caroline Lamb, 198—213.
Lord Wellesley, his politeness to Lady Morgan, 436.

Leontine Fay, Mademoiselle, 302.
Lucan, 223, 228.
Luttrell, 211.
Lyons, seat of Lord Cloncurry, 397.
Lyons, 342.

M.

Manor of Lady of Quality, 328; 330.
Madame Mère, 129.
Madder, the, 337.
Magazine, *New Monthly*, 309.
Malahide Castle, 334, 383, 411.
Married life, first year of, 1—4.
Marriage, literary, attended by Lady Morgan, 437.
Marryatt, Captain, 366.
Marshalsea, 223.
Maturin, Rev. C. R., 153—158; anecdote of, 154; death of, 155.
Mazeppa, 104, 105.
Melbourne, Lord, 420; death of, 428; conversation with Lady Morgan, 499.
Memoir of a Lady of Quality, the, 469.
Mesmerism, experiments in, 437.
Metropolitan, 402.
Microscope, hydro-oxygen, 362.
Milan, 102.
Molly, 232.
Montgomery, Satan, 194.
Monza, Cathedral of, 95.
Moore, Thomas, 86, 87, 103, 117; diary of, 118, 301, 311, 312, 313, 320, 321, 389, 394, 403; death of, 117; monument to, mooted by Lady Morgan, 513; proposed site for, 519; inauguration of, 538—540.
Morgan, Sir C. and Lady leave Ireland, 427.
Morgan, Sir Charles, sketch of, 2; appointed physician to the Marshalsea, 23; *Physiology of Life*, 23; assists Lady Morgan, 24; advocate of Catholic Emancipation, 271; contributes to work on France, 53; illness of, 401.
Mostyn, 112.

N.

Naples, 136.
Nell Gwynne, 329.
New Monthly Magazine, 469; connexion of Sir Charles and Lady Morgan with, 187—195.
Northumberland, Duchess of, 285, 295, 296.
Normandy, Lady, 430.

O.

O'Briens and O'Flahertics, 274, 283—335.
O'Connell, 286, 291, 312.
O'Connor Don, the, death of, 472.
Odd Volume, the, 541; publication of, 544.
O'Donnel, first mention of, 10, 11; published by Colburn, 26; paid for copyright of, 30; account of, 36, 37; review of, in *Quarterly*, 37; dedication of, to the Duke of Devonshire, 38; referred to, 406; prejudice against, by Lord Chancellor Manners, 422.
O'Gorman Mahon, 313.
O'Hagan, speech of, at inauguration of Moore's statue, 529.
O'Haggerty, 332.
O'Keefe, Miss, 381.
O'Neil, Miss, marriage of, 154.
Owenson, Mr., death of, 12.
Owenson, Olivia, partial restoration of to health, 478; bad news concerning, 427; return of to Ireland, 462; death of, 489.
Oxmantown, Lord, 337; engaged in constructing powerful telescope, 337.

P.

Paganini, 337.
Palao, Count de Porrio's, 93.
Pallavicchi, Marchese, 113.
Pamela, 347.
Parma, opera box, 113.
Parsons, Sir L., 337.
Pasta, Madame, 360—362, 366.
Patterson, Madame, her opinion of America, 507.
Pension to Lady Morgan, 419.
Pimlico, 391, 421, 431; history of, 446.
Piozzi, Mrs., 113.
Ploughboys first in Ireland, 286.
Plunkett, Lord, 358.
Present of books for *Salvator Rosa*, 161.
Prices of Lady Morgan's Works:— *O'Donnel*, 36; *France*, 51, 53; *Florence Macarthy*, 74; *Life and Times of Salvator Rosa*, 52.
Prince Regent, 131—133, 134.
Prince Pucklau Muskau, 260, 266; his book, 333, 336.
Princess, the, or *Béguine*, 386.
Politics, 405.
Pompeii, 136.

Poole, John, author of *Paul Pry*, 451.
Porter, Jane, 336.
Protestant Petition, 224.

Q.

Quarterly's review of *O'Donnel*, 37; of *France*, 57; jeu d'esprit on, 58; *O'Briens and O'Flahertics*, 287.
Queen, the, and Duke of Sussex, 421; first parliament of, 429.
Quintin Dick, 183, 336.

R.

Refugees, Italian and Spanish, 147.
Regent, Prince, 131—135.
Revolution, French, (1830) 301.
Richmond Park, visit to, by Sir Charles and Lady Morgan, 477.
Richmond, Duchess of, 369.
Rivals, the, note on, by Mrs. Lefanu, 61.
Roebuck, Mr., 515.
Rogers, recognition of Lady Morgan by, 474, 513; his *Table Talk*, air of critics on, 528.
Rogues, 363.
Rome, 126, 187.
Rowan, Archibald, Hamilton, 149—156, 331.
Ross, Colonel, 223.
Rosse, Earl of, 337.
Russian Ambassador, the, 464.
Royal Exchange, conflagration of, 433, 434.

S.

Salvator Rosa, Life and Times of, 158; pictures of, 157, 160, 162—171, 183, 189; second edition of, 213.
Saunders and Otley, 207.
Seanlan, original of *Colleginns*, 288.
School of young men, Lady Morgan's, 412.
Sempire, Countess, 112.
Shangana, 295.
Shee, Irish hero, type of, 32.
Sheil, 267, 274.
Sidney Smith, 326; attack of gout on, 475, 476; illness of Mrs., 476.
Silvio Pellico, death of, 524.
Sir Charles Morgan, perfect recovery from serious illness, 474; death of, 478.
Sir Mathew Tierny, 133, 463.
Sir Robert Wilson, death of, 500; generous act of, towards Count Lavallette, 501.
Smith, Mrs., Moore's first love, 397, 406.

INDEX.   559

Smith, Horace, death of, 504.
Soirée, Association, 404.
Somerville, Mrs., 393; Dr., 394.
Song, by Lady Clarke, 404.
Society in great houses, 10; fashionable, 17; in Paris, 1816, 41; America, 81.
Staël, Madame de, 67.
Staff officer, novel of, 331.
St. Alban's, Duke of, 238; Duchess of, 238, 369.
Stanley, Mr., 326, 351, 352.
Stanley, Lady, last notice of, 79.
St. Peter's Chair, controversy concerning, 509.
St. Peter's, 137.

T.

Taglioni, 362.
Tales of the Hall, 104, 105.
Telesforo de Trueva, death of, 409.
The Collegians, novel of, 283.
Tilney House, Mrs. Fitzherbert's, 422, 426.
Tilney Long, Miss, 20.
Trivulgi, Marchesa, 107; palace of, 107.

V.

Valpergua, Madame, 92; palace, 92.
Vasa, Prince and Princess, original entertainment by, 465.

Villette, Madame de, 66.
Vigny, de, Count Alfred, 417.
Visit to Germany, by Sir Charles and Lady Morgan, 462.
Volta, 95.

W.

Wallace, Thomas, renewal of acquaintance, 294; illness of, 331.
Wallachia, Hospodar of, 421.
Warner, Mrs., 233.
Weld, Hartstronge, 383.
Wellington, funeral of Duke of, 522.
Westmeath, Lord and Lady, separation of, 108.
Whateley, Archbishop, 336.
White, Lydia, 227; death of, 235, 236.
Wild Irish Girl, 491; details of furnished by romps with Sir Malby Crofton, 522.
Wilkie, visit to, 419.
William Street, house in, 434, 438.
Willis, American poet, 381.
Women and her Master, 437; design of, 456, 457; never completed, 457; publication of, 458.
Wordsworth and Jeffrey, 324.
Wurtemberg, Queen of, 464.
Wursberg, palace of, 404.
Wyse, Mr., 270.

Y.

Young Englanders, 475.

www.ingramcontent.com/pod-product-compliance
Lightning Source LLC
Chambersburg PA
CBHW031939290426
44108CB00011B/609